GREEN
PLANET
BLUES

FIFTH EDITION

GREEN PLANET BLUES

CRITICAL PERSPECTIVES ON
GLOBAL ENVIRONMENTAL POLITICS

**KEN CONCA AND
GEOFFERY D. DABELKO, EDITORS**

**WESTVIEW
PRESS**

A Member of the Perseus Books Group

Westview Press was founded in 1975 in Boulder, Colorado, by notable publisher and intellectual Fred Praeger. Westview Press continues to publish scholarly titles and high-quality undergraduate- and graduate-level textbooks in core social science disciplines. With books developed, written, and edited with the needs of serious nonfiction readers, professors, and students in mind, Westview Press honors its long history of publishing books that matter.

Copyright © 2015 by Westview Press
Published by Westview Press,
A Member of the Perseus Books Group

Find us on the World Wide Web at www.westviewpress.com.

Every effort has been made to secure required permissions for all text, images, maps, and other art reprinted in this volume.

Westview Press books are available at special discounts for bulk purchases in the United States by corporations, institutions, and other organizations. For more information, please contact the Special Markets Department at the Perseus Books Group, 2300 Chestnut Street, Suite 200, Philadelphia, PA 19103, or call (800) 810-4145, ext. 5000, or e-mail special.markets@perseusbooks.com.

Library of Congress Cataloging-in-Publication Data

Green planet blues : critical perspectives on global environmental politics / Ken Conca and Geoff Dabelko, Editors.—Fifth edition.
    pages cm
  Includes bibliographical references and index.
  ISBN 978-0-8133-4952-7 (pbk.)—ISBN 978-0-8133-4953-4 (e-book) 1. Environmental policy—Political aspects. 2. Sustainable development. 3. Green movement. I. Conca, Ken. II. Dabelko, Geoffrey D.
  HC79.E5G6916 2015
  363.7—dc23
                                                                            2014008378

10 9 8 7 6 5 4 3 2 1

CONTENTS

PART TWO
ECOLOGY AND THE STRUCTURE
OF THE INTERNATIONAL SYSTEM   87

PART THREE
INSTITUTIONS OF GLOBAL
ENVIRONMENTAL GOVERNANCE   131

PART FOUR
THE SUSTAINABILITY DEBATE   177

PART FIVE
FROM ECOLOGICAL CONFLICT TO ENVIRONMENTAL SECURITY? 235

PART SIX
ECOLOGICAL JUSTICE 311

PREFACE

For their help, advice, and support as we prepared this and previous editions, we thank Michael Alberty, Liliana Andonova, Christine Arden, Jon Barnett, Michele Betsill, Steve Catalano, Beth Chalecki, Elizabeth DeSombre, Kelli Fillingim, Grace Fujimoto, Shannon Green, Peter Jacques, Adam Jadhav, Sara Kamins, Audrey Komey, Tim Kovach, Elisabeth Malzahn, Kay Mariea, John M. Meyer, Ronald Mitchell, Alaina Morman, Adil Najam, Kate O'Neill, Rodger Payne, Rodrigo Pinto, Dennis Pirages, Kurt Rakouskas, Armin Rosencranz, Antoinette Smith, Jennifer Swearingen, Carolyn Sobczak, Joe Thwaites, Marietta Urban, Stacy VanDeveer, Toby Wahl, Greg White, and Sarah Wilton. We also acknowledge the help of students, faculty colleagues, and staff at our current institutions, the Global Environmental Politics Program in American University's School of International Service (Conca) and the Environmental Studies Program at Ohio University's Voinovich School of Leadership and Public Affairs (Dabelko). The first edition of this book would never have been possible without the support of the Harrison Program on the Future Global Agenda at the University of Maryland, and we have benefited for many years from Geoff Dabelko's affiliation with the Environmental Change and Security Program of the Woodrow Wilson International Center for Scholars. We are also grateful to several anonymous respondents to the student and faculty surveys we distributed to collect feedback on previous editions.

As with past editions, we have updated the text to take account of several new developments. In this edition we have added new material on climate justice, environmental peacebuilding, globalization, land grabs, corporate environmentalism, climate adaptation, gender, disaster risk, and resilience. Also, in keeping with our use of global environmental summits as a marker for the historical development of problems and politics, we've added material that frames the debate on the future of global environmental politics in the wake of the fractious "Rio+20" global summit of 2012. In making these changes, we have had to part with some essays used in earlier editions—as always, with regret! Readers may wish to consult earlier editions of the book for these still-useful items, as well as to track the evolution of the field over the past few decades (at least as we see it). We have tried to remain true to the book's original goals of discussing crosscutting issues of power and authority, juxtaposing different environmental paradigms, and presenting a diversity of voices. In addition, we include discussion questions in the introduction to each of the book's parts, which we hope will stimulate critical thought, conversation, and learning.

Because some of the selections presented in this volume are excerpts from longer works, a brief explanation of our editing philosophy is in order. In those cases where space limitations precluded reprinting an entire essay, our goal has been to edit in such a way as to emphasize the underlying ideas and concepts. In many cases, this has meant leaving out complex elaborations, trenchant asides, or supporting examples. We have preserved the original notes corresponding to the material reproduced here but left out notes corresponding to passages of text not included. For one essay containing a large number of in-line citations in the original (Lélé's "Sustainable Development: A Critical Review"), we have preserved the factual citations but removed several of the more general references to enhance readability and conserve space. Readers seeking further background, greater detail, or additional references should consult the original material.

INTRODUCTION: FROM STOCKHOLM TO SUSTAINABILITY?

KEN CONCA AND GEOFFREY D. DABELKO

Think globally, act locally. Spaceship Earth. The common heritage of humanity. The global commons. Pollution does not respect national borders. The Earth is one, but the world is not. We have not inherited the Earth from our parents; we have borrowed it from our children. The Anthropocene.

Each of these well-known phrases invokes similar themes: the interconnectedness of the global environment; the close ties between environmental quality and human well-being; and the common fate that these realities impose upon all of the planet's occupants, present and future. We live, as we have for some time, in an era of global environmental politics.

Pollution, ecosystem destruction, and natural resource depletion are not new problems. Many regions and localities were grappling with these issues long before the industrial revolution or even the emergence of the modern system of nation-states. And just as environmental problems have a long-standing history, so do the political struggles that inevitably accompany those problems. For example, severe shortages of wood led to conservation efforts in Babylonia during the time of Hammurabi.[1] Measures to protect wetlands in recognition of their importance as sources of fish, game, and fuel have been traced to the sixth century AD in the Huang-Huai-Hai Plain of northeastern China.[2] And air-quality crises in London during the early stages of the industrial revolution led to the formation of smoke-abatement societies advocating legislative action.[3] One can easily imagine the political controversies that must have engulfed each of these episodes, given that these measures protecting environmental

1

quality or altering access to natural resources would have offended powerful interests and created new winners and losers in society.

Today, the dramas of environmental politics are often played out on a global stage. It is generally agreed that human transformation of the environment is a global-scale problem.[4] In some cases, the system under stress is globally interconnected in a physical sense, as is true of the Earth's climate, the oceans, or the atmosphere's protective ozone layer. In other cases, accumulated local events produce consequences of global significance, as in the depletion of the world's fisheries or the reduction of the planet's biological diversity.

It makes sense, then, to recognize global environmental *problems*. But what do we mean when we speak of global environmental *politics*? To answer this question, consider what people see when they look at a forest. Some see a stock of timber to be exploited for economic gain. Others see a complex ecological system that holds the soil in place, stabilizes the local water cycle, moderates the local climate, and fosters biological diversity. Still others see the forest as a home for people and other living things, a site to engage in cultural practices, or perhaps an ancestral burial ground. Finally, some see the forest as a powerful cultural symbol on broader scales: the forest is a dynamic living system that reflects the potential harmony between humanity and nature and provides a link between the past and the future. Playing out the differences in these visions of the forest—whether that means trying to reconcile them, seeking a delicate balance among them, or fighting to make one preeminent—is the stuff of politics, by any definition of the term.

We live in a world that is at once fragmented by the political division into sovereign states and reassembled by pervasive flows of people, goods, money, ideas, images, and technology across borders. In such a world, conflicting visions of the forest take on international significance. Some see in the forest an important source of international economic power, giving those who control it influence in international markets and a reliable source of foreign exchange. Others see it as a powerful symbol of global interdependence: the forest reflects the global consequences of local acts in that its destruction may alter the global climate or deplete the global stock of biological diversity. Still others see a very different sort of international symbol: the forest represents national sovereignty in that it confirms a nation's right to do as it sees fit with the resources within its territory—a concept that the United Nations has affirmed as "permanent sovereignty" over natural resources.[5] From the affluent vantage point of a classroom in Europe or America, such rights may seem luxuries that a crowded planet cannot afford. But people who feel their sovereign rights immediately threatened are not likely to agree—particularly if those rights were won in a struggle for independence that forged their very nation.

Often these competing visions reflect different interests held by individuals, groups, and perhaps even entire nations. They are also a product, however, of the structures that govern world politics. The institution of national sovereignty, the division of labor in the capitalist world economy, the rise of transnational networks of environmentalists, the predominance of powerful beliefs about the links between consumption and "progress"—all of these underlying features of contemporary world politics shape what people see when they look at the forest.

Competing visions, values, and interests often lead to conflict. Actors disagree about the nature of the problem, the effectiveness or fairness of proposed solutions, and the appropriate location of responsibility. Thus, studying global environmental politics means understanding the conflicts of interest that surround environmental issues—but also asking how interests, values, and visions related to the environment are shaped.

The study of global environmental politics also involves the search for cooperative solutions to ecological dilemmas. The idea that global environmental problems require "international cooperation" is widely accepted, but the appropriate scope and content of such cooperation are hotly contested. Does international cooperation mean formal, treaty-based agreements among governments? Does it mean a broader "global bargain" between rich and poor nations, linking a number of issues in a single package? Or does it refer to a still broader process of global dialogue not limited to governments, in which different societies move toward a global convergence of values? Does an increasingly global network of environmental organizations represent an effective new form of international cooperation, or is it simply one more way in which the strong impose their will upon the weak? Is the goal of international cooperation to create an increasingly dense web of transnational linkages, one that binds nations to a common future and a common commitment to environmental protection? Or should we instead begin delinking an ever more tightly coupled, "globalizing" world system, so that various localities and regions have more flexibility to pursue responses appropriate to their unique circumstances?

Finally, an important dimension of the study of global environmental politics involves connecting the patterns of international conflict and cooperation over the environment to some of the larger changes under way in world politics. If studying the structure of world politics gives us insight into the character of global environmental problems, the reverse is also true: environmental problems and (sometimes) responses are part of the engine that is changing the shape of the world system. It is no surprise that as the world tumbled into the twenty-first century, environmental problems started to emerge as a critical theme in the study of international relations and world politics. At a time when much conventional wisdom in international relations is being challenged, studying the politics of the global environment may also give us greater insight into the emerging patterns of world politics as a whole.

From Stockholm to Rio, to Johannesburg, Back to Rio—and Beyond

A series of global summit meetings—the 1972 UN Conference on the Human Environment, held in Stockholm, Sweden; the 1992 UN Conference on Environment and Development, held in Rio de Janeiro, Brazil (known popularly as the Earth Summit); the 2002 World Summit on Sustainable Development, held in Johannesburg, South Africa; and the 2012 UN Conference on Sustainable Development, or "Rio+20" meeting, held in Rio de Janeiro—provide useful benchmarks for the evolution of global environmental politics.[6] The contrasts among these four events reflect many underlying changes in the world during the intervening four decades.

One important shift concerned the international political context. The first global environmental summit, in Stockholm, occurred in the shadow of the Cold War. The governments of Eastern Europe and the Soviet Union boycotted the conference after a dispute over the representation of a then-divided Germany. Two decades later, the Rio Earth Summit took place in the relatively optimistic afterglow of the end of the Cold War, amid a general sense of new opportunities for global cooperation. A decade later in Johannesburg, much of that optimism had faded in the face of globalization controversies; increasingly muscular American unilateralism; the gritty reality of enduring global political, economic, and cultural conflicts; and the shocking events of September 11, 2001. Most recently, the Rio+20 summit of 2012 came in the wake of a global financial crisis; the continued emergence of new powers such as India, Brazil, and China on the world stage; and domestic political fragmentation across Europe and North America. Each of the global summits was stamped with the imprint of its context—whether the Cold War–induced boycott of the Soviet bloc at Stockholm, the ambitious optimism of Rio 1992, or the reluctance of the leading powers to make new commitments at Rio 2012 even as the emerging powers worked to reshape the focus of what any such commitments should be.

A second clear change from Stockholm 1972 to Rio 2012 was the emergence of global public awareness and concern. The Stockholm conference took place in the wake of the first Earth Day (1970) and at a time of rising popular concern in the United States and Europe about environmental problems, particularly air and water pollution. Many of the participants at Stockholm—particularly those from the global North—framed environmental problems as the by-products of an affluent, industrialized lifestyle. The implication was that the poorer regions of the world did not suffer as much from environmental problems as did the wealthy, nor (it was said) did they exhibit the same level of concern about such problems. By the time of the first Rio conference in 1992, however, the notion that there is both a "pollution of affluence" *and* a "pollution of poverty" had gained much broader acceptance. As the environmental causes of poverty became clearer, what many of those suffering from poverty have presumably known all along became more generally understood: environmental concerns were not the exclusive property of affluent people or industrialized countries, hence Rio's linkage between environment and development. By the time of the Johannesburg summit, known in United Nations circles as "Rio+10," development issues had become central to the discussion—so much so that some environmental advocates felt the environmental agenda was being largely ignored and referred to the event ruefully as "Rio minus ten." Most recently, at Rio+20, the deemphasis of environmental criteria caused the head of Greenpeace International to famously tweet "longest suicide note in history" in reference to the summit outcomes document.

A third important trend over these decades has been the tremendous growth in the scientific understanding of environmental problems. Stockholm focused attention principally on relatively narrowly defined problems of air and water pollution, whereas Rio embraced a far broader and more complex agenda. This shift reflected, in part, a changing scientific paradigm—one that views the Earth as a single integrated system with complex links among the large-scale ecological systems of land, oceans, atmosphere, and biosphere.[7] The discussion at Rio, especially *Agenda 21*, a lengthy and ambitious blueprint for sustainable development in the twenty-first century, also reflected scientists' greater capacity to measure, monitor, and model complex processes of environmental change.[8] Yet the growth of scientific knowledge is never immune to political context; as delegates gathered in Johannesburg just one year after the destruction of the World Trade Center on September 11, 2001, the continued commitment of governments to open information flows and exchange of environmental data could not be taken for granted in light of fears about "environmental terrorism." And one of the pitched political battles at the 2012 Rio summit concerned whether a set of "sustainable development goals" should be defined primarily by issue experts (the preference of many governments of the North) or by political actors (favored by many in the South, and the ultimate decision of the conference).

Governments and other actors gathering to discuss global environmental problems underwent notable changes themselves in the decades since the Stockholm conference. Almost none of the governments gathered in Stockholm had any form of national environmental bureaucracy; two decades later in Rio, virtually all did. In many cases, these agencies enabled governments to take advantage of the growth of environmental knowledge to analyze more effectively the causes and consequences of environmental problems. In some cases, the agencies had evolved into advocates for various environmental protection programs, producing more complex internal debates within national delegations. Today, environmental considerations have also been mainstreamed in the rhetoric and policy guidelines—if not always the actions—of intergovernmental organizations such as the World Bank, the International Monetary Fund, and the World Trade Organization, and in the development assistance or "foreign aid" practices of donor countries.

Nongovernmental organizations, too, have undergone substantial changes. During the Stockholm conference, 134 NGOs, virtually all from the industrialized world, were officially accredited participants. Two decades later, more than 1,400 NGOs were officially participating in the 1992 Rio summit, with about one-third of these groups from the global South—and countless more unofficial participants.[9] Over time, international networking and coalition building among environmental groups have become much more common.[10]

A final measure of the changes since Stockholm 1972 is the growth in the number of international environmental treaties, agreements, and cooperative accords. According to a database compiled by Ronald Mitchell of the University of Oregon, there are more than 1,100 multilateral environmental agreements (three or more parties) in place, and even more bilateral (two-party) accords.[11] Many are relatively narrow in scope: agreements between two neighboring countries on specific environmental problems or regional agreements involving small numbers of countries and narrow agendas. But the list also includes several major international accords adopted since the Stockholm conference, including agreements on ocean pollution, acid rain, preservation of the ozone layer, the international trade in endangered species, the trade in hazardous waste, and environmental protection in Antarctica. The designers of international accords at Rio rolled out global treaties on biological diversity and climate change, tried but failed to get a global treaty on forests, and set in motion the process for a global treaty on desertification. In doing so, they had a much broader set of examples to draw upon than did their predecessors; as a result, they also had at least a crude understanding of what makes various approaches to international environmental cooperation effective.[12] Since Rio 1992, some important new international agreements have been reached, such as the Cartagena Protocol on Biosafety and the Stockholm Convention on Persistent Organic Pollutants. But the pace of agreement formation has slowed considerably, for both global and regional agreements, and the UN Framework Convention on Climate Change has arguably come unraveled with the ineffectualness of the goals and timetables that its parties adopted in the Kyoto Protocol in 1997, the subsequent decision of the United States and Canada to not meet their commitments under the protocol, and the general lack of a clear and effective way forward in climate diplomacy. These developments have cast a pall over the prospects for ambitious multilateral environmental diplomacy going forward.

It is equally important to stress what has not changed in the more than four decades since the 1972 Stockholm conference. Many of the stumbling blocks to effective global response seen at Stockholm were also in full evidence at the subsequent gatherings and remain with us today. These impediments include the tremendous mistrust and suspicion governing relations between North and South in world politics; the tenacious embrace of absolute conceptions of national sovereignty by governments, even as they acknowledge the need for coordinated global responses to problems that do not respect borders; and the tensions between the long-term vision necessary for ecologically sane planning and the short-term concern for economic growth and political stability that preoccupies most governments.

Perhaps the most important continuity is that global environmental change has continued at an alarming rate. Since 1970, global commercial energy consumption, a major source of environmental impacts, has more than doubled, and other global indicators of human impact on the environment—food production, water use, overall economic activity, and population—have increased in roughly similar proportions. To be sure, these very crude indicators of human stress on environmental systems can mask as much as they reveal. They say nothing about how underlying activities actually affect the environment, about who or what may be responsible, or about who suffers the consequences most directly and immediately. But they do indicate the scale of the problem and the enormity of the challenge of reorienting fundamental practices that drive growth, production, consumption, and environmental transformation in the current world system.

This mixed picture of continuity and change raises an obvious question: Compared to where things stood at the Stockholm conference, where do we stand as we look to the future? Many environmental advocates have grown dismayed or even cynical about what they see as an increasingly ritualized—and increasingly ineffectual—process of global environmental summitry. In this view, Rio 1992, which produced multilateral treaties on climate and biodiversity and the ambitious goals embodied in *Agenda 21,* was the "high-water mark" for diplomatic approaches to global environmental rescue. Johannesburg and the most recent Rio summit, in contrast, were noteworthy mainly for demonstrating the lag in implementing these commitments while producing little in the way of tangible products, specific targets and timetables for action, or creative new ideas.

Does the period since Stockholm tell an optimistic story of global society moving to meet the challenges of ecological interdependence, or do those years chronicle an unwillingness or inability to grapple with the root causes of the problem? Perhaps both are true. Growing knowledge and awareness, organizational adjustments, and occasional substantive breakthroughs over the past four decades may reveal important possibilities for change, learning, and effective global cooperation. At the same time, enduring divisions and the far less optimistic tenor of the times (at least when compared to Rio 1992) have served to underscore the depth of the political challenge posed by global environmental problems.

Conflicting Views of the Environmental Problematique

Growing scientific understanding and shared levels of public concern do not automatically translate into a shared understanding of the social causes of environmental problems. One of the first challenges facing students of global environmental politics is to sort out a potentially bewildering debate on the causes of pollution and environmental degradation. Some of this uncertainty lies in the realm of science. The physical, chemical, and biological mechanisms involved in processes such as climate change, desertification, and deforestation are sometimes poorly understood by leading experts, to say nothing of citizens, policymakers, and interest groups. For example, it is only in the last few decades that the global interaction of oceans, atmosphere, land, and biosphere has become a central concern of such disciplines as oceanography, atmospheric science, and terrestrial ecology, causing a growing number of scholars to rethink traditional disciplinary boundaries in these fields. Although knowledge is expanding rapidly on many fronts, scientific uncertainty remains substantial in the face of the complex processes of environmental change.

These aspects of technical complexity are matched by similar controversies, debates, and uncertainties surrounding the social dimensions of environmental change. In explaining why human beings have had such a substantial impact on planetary ecosystems, different analysts invoke factors as diverse as values, technology, culture, ideology, public policy, demographic change, and the social structures of class, race, or gender. Some observers elevate one or a few of these factors to the role of central cause, treating the others as mere symptoms. Others have sought to develop more complex models that stress the interaction of these various forces and processes.

Many see the problem as essentially one of values—in particular, the value that modern societies attach to consumption. In this view, the soaring levels of consumption that track the rise of the consumer society are also surging indicators of environmental harm. Our consumer culture translates wants into needs, stresses material-intensive forms of social gratification, and overwhelms older, more ecologically sustainable traditions that stand in its way. In doing so, the consumer society's exploitation of resources threatens to exhaust, poison, or unalterably disfigure forests, soils, water, and air. We, its members, are responsible for a disproportionate share of the global environmental challenges facing humanity. Meanwhile, as consumerism spreads through increasingly sophisticated advertising, pop culture, and the global media, more and more regions of the planet adopt the aspirations of the consumer society.[13]

Technology is another commonly cited culprit. Barry Commoner, a key figure in raising public awareness about environmental problems in the United States in the 1960s and 1970s through such widely read books as *Making Peace with the Planet* and *The Closing Circle,* invoked the simple example of the production of beer bottles in the United States to illustrate the technological dimension.[14] Writing in the 1970s, Commoner investigated the impact of three factors commonly cited as causes of environmental problems: population growth, rising levels of consumption per capita, and technological change. He pointed out that the number of beer bottles produced in America increased by a dramatic 593 percent from 1950 to 1967, even though the population grew by only 30 percent and beer consumption by only 5 percent per capita. Clearly, a technological change—the replacement of reusable beer kegs and returnable bottles with single-use, throwaway bottles—had led to the bulk of the increase and, hence, to the bulk of the environmental impact in terms of energy use, trash, and so on. Commoner argued that similar technological changes at work across most of the key sectors of modern society were at the heart of the environmental crisis. The surge in popularity of overly large and fuel-inefficient sport-utility vehicles as a means of single-passenger transportation provides a more recent example of this process.

Some observers argue that prevailing technologies and values are best understood as expressions of underlying power dynamics in society. For example, "social ecologists" such as Murray Bookchin—though not necessarily disagreeing with the critique of the consumer society or the cautions about technology's role— have stressed the importance of social inequality. Bookchin, in particular, warned against attributing environmental problems to such vague and impersonal for- mulations as "values," "technology," and "humanity." Such reasoning "serves to deflect our attention from the role society plays in producing ecological break- down."[15] According to Bookchin,

> a mythic "Humanity" is created—irrespective of whether we are talking about op- pressed ethnic minorities, women, Third World people, or people in the First World— in which everyone is brought into complicity with powerful corporate elites in produc- ing environmental dislocations. In this way, the social roots of ecological problems are shrewdly obscured. A new kind of biological "original sin" is created in which a vague group of animals called "Humanity" is turned into a destructive force that threatens the survival of the living world.[16]

According to Bookchin, the key to understanding lies instead in seeing how social inequality feeds environmental degradation and resource overexploitation. In this view, societies constructed upon hierarchies of race, class, and gender are funda- mentally based on exploitation. For that reason, they have an inherent tendency to seek domination over nature rather than a means of living in harmony with it, just as they promote the domination of some people by others.[17]

Vandana Shiva, who has written extensively about forestry issues in postcolo- nial India, provides a model aimed at linking diverse causal forces such as tech- nology, values, and social structure.[18] For Shiva, history is key: technological and demographic changes, hierarchical patterns of social structure, and consumption- oriented values are co-evolutionary products of Indian society's dominant his- torical experience—the political, economic, and social transformations brought about by more than a century of British colonial rule. Thus, in her view, "causes" of environmental degradation in India as diverse as the industrial revolution, the capitalist world economy, and the destructive power of modern science and tech- nology are "the philosophical, technological, and economic components of the same process."[19]

Sorting out this diverse array of claims about social causes of environmental change requires carefully detailed, historical study of the ways in which economic, social, and political institutions in society co-evolve over time.[20] Many of the se- lections in this volume present their own particular understanding of the causes of environmental problems. It will become apparent to the reader that these var- ious causal claims are based on very different understandings of the sources of power, interest, authority, and legitimacy in society. Sorting out such diverse claims does not guarantee that effective policies and institutions will be designed. Actors may agree on the causes of a problem but still disagree on the appropriate responses; they may see their interests affected differently or hold different views about the fairness or effectiveness of a particular response. But grappling with the complex array of causes does seem to be a necessary preliminary step if appropriate responses are to be crafted. Perhaps just as important, examining the diversity of claims about what is happening also helps us to understand the equally diverse beliefs about history, justice, and responsibility that various actors bring to the debate.

Global Environmental Politics: Power, Ideas, and Voices

The material in this book has been selected with three goals in mind. One goal has been to pay particular attention to underlying questions of power, interest, authority, and legitimacy that shape global environmental debates. The challenges of the global environment are often framed as largely technical and administrative tasks of promoting policy coordination among governments. Clearly, rational policies and effective intergovernmental cooperation will be a crucial part of any meaningful response to such challenges. But a narrow focus on governments, treaties, and public policies can blur our understanding of some of the deeper components of the problematique. The environmental problems facing the global community raise deeper questions of governmental authority, of the relationship between the state and society, and of processes of economic and cultural globalization that challenge state sovereignty and the autonomy of local communities.

Second, we have tried to emphasize the *ideas* that have most powerfully shaped the evolving debate over the global environment. By assembling under one cover some of the most influential voices in the debate, we hope to provide a firsthand sense of how ideas have shaped action, while at the same time stressing the obstacles to changing the world through new ideas alone. Thus we examine some of the most powerful paradigms that prevailed at the time of the Stockholm conference in 1972 and the controversies engendered by those views. We also explore the powerful and controversial new paradigms that have emerged, in the years since then, around themes of sustainability, environmental security, and ecological justice. Comparing these sets of ideas over time not only reveals how people's thinking has changed but also highlights enduring themes.

Our third goal has been to present a broad range of voices in what is and must be a *global* debate. This goal might appear to conflict with our previously stated intention of presenting the most powerful and influential ideas: one might be tempted by a sense of urgency to try to narrow the debate to what the most powerful voices consider feasible or desirable. In our view, however, any such narrowing of the debate on the grounds of political expediency would be deeply troubling on moral grounds, given the stakes involved for people, their livelihoods, their health, and all forms of life on the planet. It also strikes us as potentially disastrous—not expedient at all—given the current lack of global consensus on so many fundamental issues. The poor and powerless might lack the ability to shape the ecological future they desire, but they may well have the power to veto proposed "solutions" that ignore their needs and interests. Although universal agreement is a utopia difficult even to imagine, durable responses to global environmental problems can be achieved only through a broad social consensus. Thus we have chosen essays for this book with the intent of including perspectives from the global South as well as the global North, and with voices that are rural as well as urban, female as well as male, and critical of existing institutions as well as broadly comfortable working within them.

The book's organization is meant to serve these goals. We begin in Part One with a discussion of the dominant paradigms and controversies that shaped debate at the time of the Stockholm conference, and in the twenty years between Stockholm and the 1992 Rio Earth Summit. The views and debates that prevailed in that era provide a useful reference point for measuring what has changed since then. Part One focuses in particular on three provocative and influential ideas of that era: first, the notion that there are inherent "limits to growth" on a planet of finite natural resources and limited ecological resilience; second, the claim that where nature is concerned, self-interested individual behavior often adds up to a collective "tragedy of the commons"; and third, the idea that environmental threats should be seen as matters of national and international security.

In Part Two we examine how the structure of the international system shapes the types of problems we face and the types of solutions we can imagine. The discussion focuses on the roles of national sovereignty, transnational capitalism, and the myriad manifestations of "globalization" in shaping political and economic institutions, patterns of environmental harm, and the possibilities for political responses. Part Two also examines environmentalism as a global social movement, investigating whether we might be seeing the emergence of different forms of political authority that challenge these dominant aspects of system structure.

Part Three examines the challenges of international cooperation and institutional reform. Here we take a tour of several of the most important practices of global environmental governance: through international environmental law and multilateral environmental agreements among governments; through the institutionalized practices of international environmental diplomacy; and through more fluid and emergent approaches such as so-called multistakeholder initiatives.

The volume concludes with three powerful and controversial paradigms that have crystallized and given form to the debates in the period since the Stockholm conference: sustainability (Part Four), environmental security (Part Five), and ecological justice (Part Six). For some observers, these three paradigms are complementary and potentially harmonious facets of a single vision for the planet and its people. Others see tensions and contradictions inherent in the simultaneous pursuit of development, security, and justice in world affairs. Convergent or not, they are likely to remain the conceptual building blocks for environmental initiatives of the future.

In compiling this material, we have deliberately avoided organizing the book around a conventional list of environmental "issue areas" (climate change, deforestation, toxics, acid rain, and so on) or generic types of environmental problems (such as transboundary pollution flows or problems of the global commons). To be sure, these are useful ways to organize one's thinking about complex, multidimensional problems. However, by focusing on crosscutting themes of power, authority, and responsibility, we hope this book will provide a useful complement to these other approaches, which are already well represented in the literature.

NOTES

1. John Perlin, *A Forest Journey: The Role of Wood in the Development of Civilization* (Cambridge, MA: Harvard University Press, 1991), p. 46.

2. Zoo Daqing and Zhang Peiyuan, "The Huang-Huai-Hai Plain," in B. L. Turner II, William C. Clark, Robert W. Kates, John F. Richards, Jessica T. Mathews, and William B. Meyer, eds., *The Earth as Transformed by Human Action* (New York: Cambridge University Press, 1990).

3. Peter Brimblecombe, *The Big Smoke: A History of Air Pollution in London Since Medieval Times* (London: Methuen, 1987).

4. United Nations Environment Programme, *Global Environmental Outlook 5,* available at http://www.unep.org/geo/geo5.asp. See also Turner et al., *The Earth as Transformed by Human Action.*

5. This concept was formally codified in UN General Assembly Resolution 1803 of December 14, 1962.

6. For an overview of the Stockholm conference, see Lynton Caldwell, *International Environmental Policy,* 3rd ed. (Durham, NC: Duke University Press, 1996). On Rio, see Peter M. Haas, Marc A. Levy, and Edward A. Parson, "Appraising the Earth Summit: How Should We Judge UNCED's Success?" *Environment* 34, no. 8 (1992): 6–11 and 26–33; Michael Grubb, Matthias Koch, Abby Munson, Francis Sullivan, and Koy Thomson, *The Earth Summit Agreements: A Guide and Assessment* (London: Earthscan Publications, 1993); and Pratap Chatterjee and Matthias Finger, *The Earth Brokers: Power, Politics and World Development* (London: Routledge, 1994). On Johannesburg, see James Gustav Speth, "Perspective on the Johannesburg Summit," *Environment* 45, no. 1 (January/February 2003): 24–29. On the most recent Rio summit of 2012, see Part Four of this volume.

7. For a statement of this new vision, which emerged around the time of the Rio Earth Summit, see US National Academy of Sciences, *One Earth, One Future: Our Changing Global Environment* (Washington, DC: National Academy Press, 1990), especially pp. 15–19.

8. On the growth of scientific knowledge about the environment from Stockholm to Rio, see Mostafa K. Tolba, Osama A. El-Kholy, E. El-Hinnawi, M. W. Holdgate, D. F. Mc-Michael, and R. E. Munn, *The World Environment, 1972–1992: Two Decades of Challenge* (London: Chapman & Hall, 1992), ch. 20.

9. Haas, Levy, and Parson, "Appraising the Earth Summit."

10. On international coalitions and networking, see Margaret Keck and Katherine Sikkink, *Activists Beyond Borders: Advocacy Networks and International Politics* (New York: Cornell University Press, 1998); Sanjeev Khagram, James V. Riker, and Kathryn Sikkink,

eds., *Restructuring World Politics: Transnational Social Movements, Networks and Norms* (Minneapolis: University of Minnesota Press, 2002); and Sanjeev Khagram, *Dams and Development: Transnational Struggles for Water and Power* (Ithaca, NY: Cornell University Press, 2004).

11. See the International Environmental Agreements (IEA) Database, available at http://rmitchel.uoregon.edu/.

12. On the effectiveness of international environmental regimes, see Oran R. Young, ed., *The Effectiveness of International Environmental Regimes* (Cambridge, MA: MIT Press, 1999); Edward L. Miles, Arild Underdal, Steiner Andresen, Jørgen Wettestad, and Jon Birger Skjærseth, *Environmental Regime Effectiveness: Confronting Theory with Evidence* (Cambridge, MA: MIT Press, 2001).

13. See Thomas Princen, Michael Maniates, and Ken Conca, *Confronting Consumption* (Cambridge, MA: MIT Press, 2002); and John de Graaf, David Wann, Thomas H. Naylor, David Horsey, and Vicki Robin, *Affluenza: The All-Consuming Epidemic,* 2nd ed. (San Francisco: Berrett-Koehler Publishers, 2005).

14. Barry Commoner, *The Closing Circle: Nature, Man, and Technology* (New York: Random House, 1971), pp. 148–150. See also Barry Commoner, *Making Peace with the Planet,* 5th ed. (New York: New Press, 1992).

15. Murray Bookchin, *Remaking Society: Pathways to a Green Future* (Boston: South End Press, 1990), p. 9.

16. Ibid., pp. 9–10.

17. This theme is central to much of the literature on ecological justice; see Part Six of the present volume.

18. Vandana Shiva, "People's Ecology: The Chipko Movement," in Saul Mendlovitz and R.B.J. Walker, eds., *Towards a Just World Peace* (London: Butterworths, 1987). See also Vandana Shiva, *Ecology and the Politics of Survival: Conflicts over Natural Resources in India* (Newbury Park, CA: Sage, 1991); and Ramachandra Guha, *The Unquiet Woods: Ecological Change and Peasant Resistance in the Himalayas* (Berkeley: University of California Press, 1989).

19. Shiva, "People's Ecology," p. 262.

20. On the concept of co-evolution, see Richard B. Norgaard, "Sociosystem and Ecosystem Coevolution in the Amazon," *Journal of Environmental Economics and Management* 8 (1981): 238–254.

PART ONE

THE DEBATE BEGINS

THE 1972 UN CONFERENCE ON THE HUMAN ENVIRONMENT, HELD IN STOCKHOLM, was a seminal event in the history of global environmental politics. Many important international agreements had already concluded by the time of the Stockholm conference, including a treaty governing Antarctica (1959), a partial nuclear-test-ban treaty (1963), a treaty governing the exploration and use of outer space (1967), and several international agreements on ocean-related matters such as whaling, the use of marine resources, and pollution. But the Stockholm conference was the first broadly international effort to evaluate and discuss the environment in systematic, comprehensive terms, and it helped establish the trajectory of future efforts—the complex array of diplomatic initiatives and debates, attempts at transnational institution building, and global movements for social change that unfolded during the decades that followed.

Although the Stockholm conference took place more than four decades ago, many of its central debates are still current. Several key questions appear throughout this book: Is global pollution mainly a problem of poverty or a problem of affluence? What is the balance of responsibility between the countries and societies of the North and those of the South in global environmental degradation? Does the institution of national sovereignty help or hinder the effort to construct international responses to environmental problems? An understanding of the dominant ideas and controversies at the Stockholm conference provides an essential historical perspective on the debates and disputes that dominate contemporary global environmental politics.[1]

In this section we introduce some of the ideas that shaped the debate at Stockholm and in the decades that followed, culminating in the 1992 UN Conference on Environment and Development (UNCED) in Rio de Janeiro. We pay particular attention to three powerful and controversial claims from that era: the idea that there are inherent "limits to growth" facing the international economy, the world's population, and global consumption; the idea that self-interested individual behavior toward the environment adds up to a collective "tragedy of the commons"; and the claim that the environmental crisis contains the potential to catalyze international conflict and therefore represents a threat to national and international security.

Thinking about each of these ideas has evolved considerably in the years since the Stockholm conference. But they are not just of historical interest. Quite the contrary: they have strongly influenced the nature of scientific and social-scientific inquiry since that time, with many analysts and activists working to either prove or disprove the existence of limits to growth, a tragedy of the commons, or environmentally induced conflict. These ideas also have shaped the political strategies pursued by governments, corporations, environmentalists, and other actors seeking to promote or hinder various forms of international environmental cooperation.

For the industrialized countries of the North, the Stockholm conference was a response to mounting public anxiety over the environmental consequences of industrial society. By the early 1970s, concerns over problems as diverse as air and water pollution, wilderness preservation, toxic chemicals, urban congestion, nuclear radiation, and rising prices for natural-resource commodities began to fuse into the notion that the world was rapidly approaching natural limits to growth in human activity. The best-selling book *The Limits to Growth* did much to galvanize public fears. Using a technique known as systems modeling, the authors tried to predict the consequences of unlimited growth in human numbers and consumption. As the passage presented in Chapter 1 indicates, they concluded that the convergence of several trends—accelerating industrialization, rapid population growth, widespread malnutrition, depletion of nonrenewable resources, and a deteriorating environment—was moving the world rapidly toward overall limits on global growth. To avoid a potentially catastrophic collapse of the world's economic and social systems, it would be necessary to implement planned restraints on growth in population and in resource consumption.

Critics of *The Limits to Growth* argued that the book overstated the urgency of the problem, overlooked the possibility of substituting less-scarce inputs, and underestimated the possibility for technological solutions.[2] The book's central claims were highly controversial, and most Northern governments were reluctant to fully embrace its findings. But the fears articulated in *The Limits to Growth* found widespread popular support in industrial societies, where they converged with the arguments of a growing coalition of environmental organizations and activists.

Not surprisingly, the idea of limits to growth was received quite differently in the global South. Among the less-industrialized countries, the idea of such limits evoked intellectual skepticism and outright suspicion. These sentiments were expressed eloquently in a 1972 essay by João Augusto de Araujo Castro (Chapter 2), the Brazilian ambassador to the United States and an influential voice in North-South diplomacy. It should be stressed that the South has never been monolithic in its views on problems of development and the environment. But as Castro made clear, many in the South linked the North's environmental concerns to the broader pattern of North-South relations. There was widespread agreement among "Third World" governments at the Stockholm conference that the North was responsible for the environmental crisis; that the North, having reaped the fruits of industrialization, now sought to close the door on the South; that the environmental problems of poverty differed fundamentally from those of affluence; and that solutions crafted with the North's problems in mind would be ineffective, or worse, if imposed on the South.

The South's unity at Stockholm made it clear that a global response to environmental problems would require linking the environmental debate to the development concerns of the South and to a broader dialogue about the political and economic "rules of the game" in the international system. The message was clear: if such connections were not drawn, the South would not participate.

Just as the idea of limits to growth dominated the debate over the consequences of environmental problems, the debate over causes crystallized around the powerful and controversial idea of the "tragedy of the commons." This view was popularized by biologist Garrett Hardin in a famous essay in the influential journal *Science* in 1968, which we excerpt in Chapter 3. According to Hardin, the "tragedy" occurred when self-interested actors enjoyed open access to, or unlimited use of, natural resources or environmental systems. Because consumers could benefit fully from additional exploitation while bearing only a small part of the "costs" of that exploitation (for example, environmental degradation), the overwhelming tendency would be greater exploitation of the resource. Each actor would pursue this logical individual behavior until the result for the system as a whole was destruction or degradation of the resource in question. Individual logic would produce collective disaster—hence the notion of tragedy. Using the example of overgrazing on the town commons of medieval England (hence the tragedy of the *commons*), Hardin suggested that the same combination of self-interest and open access was at the root of current problems of pollution and overpopulation. The solutions offered by Hardin were either to replace open access with enforceable private property rights, so that individual users would reap the full costs as well as the full benefits of their actions, and thus have an incentive to conserve; or to impose governmental restrictions on access, thereby limiting overuse.

Hardin's model came to be enormously influential in shaping thinking about global environmental problems, particularly for such so-called global commons as the oceans and atmosphere, which do not fall under the domain of any single government. One reason for its influence is the model's simple elegance: the tragedy of the commons combines a recognizable human motive (self-interest) with a recognizable set of social rules (those allowing open access to natural resources and the environment) to produce a result that most would recognize as undesirable (rapid depletion or destruction of the resource in question).

Along with limits to growth and the tragedy of the commons, a third powerful and controversial idea that emerged during this period was the suggestion that environmental degradation and resource scarcity constituted threats not only to human well-being but also to national and international security. Many works of this era cited the potential for violent conflict around these issues. For some, this was a clear message that national-security priorities had to be realigned to deal with these new realities—with defense budgets and policies shifted away from traditional notions of war-fighting and attuned to the idea of "threats without enemies." Chapter 4 presents an excerpt from a 1977 report of the Worldwatch Institute in which its founder, Lester Brown, stresses the need to "redefine security" in these terms. Not all shared Brown's optimism that security could be thusly redefined. Indeed, another identifiable trend of thought during this period was the notion that increasingly authoritarian governance would be needed to keep environmental harm from overwhelming society.[3]

To many observers during the 1960s and 1970s, limits to growth, the tragedy of the commons, and environmental (in)security formed a bleak combination. They also proved to be difficult ideas around which to catalyze international cooperation, given the controversies surrounding them and the strong implications they seemed to have for economic and political business as usual. Yet none of these ideas has gone unchallenged. Hardin's model of the tragedy of the commons, for example, is, at heart, just a metaphor: the English commons is invoked as a simplified representation of the complex social rules, customs, goals, and behavioral incentives that shape how people interact with the environment, individually and collectively. Whether such a "tragedy" actually lies at the center of global environmental problems depends on whether this abstraction is in fact an accurate representation of human behavior and social institutions. Critics have pointed out that Hardin misread the actual history of the English commons from which he drew his metaphor. Historical reconstruction has shown that access to the town commons was never unrestrained but, rather, was governed by a complex set of community-based rules that ensured sustainable use.[4] The commons system, in this view, was destroyed not by population growth and self-interested individual behavior but by changing political and economic conditions in Britain, which gave powerful actors the ability and incentive to privatize the commons and to overwhelm community-based systems of property rights. Thus, rather than representing a tragedy, the endurance of the commons system, in some cases for several hundred years, shows that there may be possibilities other than the stark choice Hardin poses between purely private property and purely open access.

Scholars have also produced a large body of empirical evidence challenging the inevitability of Hardin's tragedy.[5] A wide range of contemporary natural-resource and environmental systems—often referred to as "common-pool resources"—are in theory subject to the "tragedy," including fisheries, wildlife populations, surface water, groundwater, rangelands, and forests. Much of this work has found that whether a "tragedy" of overconsumption in fact ensues depends on the type of social rules governing these natural resources or environmental systems. The enforceable private property rights Hardin advocated are just one such set of rules, and not necessarily the most appropriate for all situations. Elinor Ostrom's influential book *Governing the Commons,* published in 1990, provided both theory and evidence that self-organizing, sustainable management of shared resources is possible under certain conditions.[6] For her work, Ostrom won the 2009 Nobel Prize in economics (despite being a political scientist!). Given the large variation in common-pool resources, their patterns of use, and their users, researchers agree that no single institutional design or set of rules will work in all common-pool resource situations. Nevertheless, we can identify a set of general principles that seem to increase the prospects for sustainable resource use. Chapter 5 presents an excerpt from an essay by Ostrom and her colleague Xavier Basurto that summarizes several of the most important insights from this work.

This analysis is of critical importance in the effort to craft international responses to environmental problems. If Hardin's tragedy does apply to the global commons, it will be exceedingly difficult to craft effective international responses to global environmental problems. Both of Hardin's preferred solutions—privatizing the commons or subjecting it to the control of a powerful central authority—are infeasible in the current international system. However, if Ostrom and others are correct that systems of collective management developed by the resource users themselves can be effective on the local or regional level, then it may also be possible to design such systems to operate on the international level.[7] Indeed, one can view treaty negotiations among countries as just such an effort. If so, there could still be a tragic outcome for the commons, but it would result from our lack of skill and effectiveness in designing fair and efficient international responses, not from the ironclad logic of nature implied by Hardin.

While scholars were busy trying to find an escape route from Hardin's tragedy, the political world sought to bridge the North-South split over limits to growth. Here, the key bridging element was the concept of sustainability, which we discuss in detail in Part Five. In 1983, the UN General Assembly authorized a World Commission on Environment and Development (WCED), which reported its findings in the seminal report *Our Common Future* in 1987. The WCED argued that there were sustainable paths of economic growth that could simultaneously address the South's poverty concerns while putting the planet on a more ecologically sustainable footing.

The combination of greater optimism about rule-governed environmental cooperation, the political bridge offered by the idea of sustainability, and the end of the Cold War created positive momentum for cooperation in global environmental politics, culminating in the 1992 Earth Summit in Rio de Janeiro. Today, Rio 1992 is often looked upon nostalgically as the "high-water mark" for efforts to promote international environmental cooperation. There is some truth to this perspective, but it should not be overstated. At the time, Rio was viewed in very different ways by different stakeholders and generated as much controversy as it did cooperation. In Chapter 6 we present a collection of short statements offered at the time by a range of participants and observers, highlighting the enduring controversies around matters of civil society participation, the efficacy of global environmental governance, the power of ideas such as sustainability, and the conference's likely legacy. These rival interpretations should be kept in mind when assessing the efficacy of subsequent events such as the "Rio+20" summit (see Part Four).

Throughout this era, the enduring contentiousness of environmental politics was seen not only at the Rio summit but also "on the ground." Consider the controversies surrounding deforestation, which raged in settings as diverse as the Pacific Northwest of the United States and the Brazilian Amazon. The autobiography of Brazilian activist Chico Mendes (Chapter 7) reminds us that environmentalism around the world has historically drawn most of its energy from the grassroots. Despite the growing internationalization of environmental politics, domestic political struggles remain the most important pathway to change. Mendes was a labor activist and environmentalist working in the western Amazon state of Acre. He led a movement for the preservation of the Amazon forest and the livelihood of its occupants. Mendes advocated a brand of environmentalism that struggled as much against the oppression of people as against the destruction of nature. Mendes was killed in 1988, assassinated by a local landowner and his son in response to Mendes's efforts to organize rural workers in the region. The powerful vision he expressed, which made him an important political leader of the forest peoples' movement in Brazil, also made him in death a martyr and an international symbol.[8]

The experiences of indigenous peoples during this period reflected the enduring contentiousness of environmental issues in specific places all around the world. Chapter 8 presents two letters published in 1989—two years after the publication of *Our Common Future* and three years prior to the Rio summit—by the Coordinating Body for the Indigenous Peoples' Organizations of the Amazon Basin (COICA). COICA argued that the future of the Amazon basin and the fate of its indigenous occupants are inherently linked. The rampant quest for modernization, colonization, territorial occupation, and economic development of the Amazon basin was damaging natural ecosystems and destroying indigenous communities.

COICA addressed the first of its protest letters to the multilateral development banks. Although the destruction was being driven by the policies of governments of the Amazon basin countries, which largely excluded indigenous communities from decision-making about the region, much of the project activity was being funded by external sources, including multinational corporations and multilateral development agencies such as the World Bank. Its second letter is addressed to the international environmental movement, which is also taken to task for its lack of attention to indigenous concerns. While acknowledging the efforts of environmentalists and the potential for common cause between the environmental and indigenous peoples' movements, the letter points out that governments, international organizations, and Northern environmental groups have struck bargains that leave out the people most directly and immediately affected. As COICA noted, decisions about the fate of the Amazon forest and its people, whether made at the national or the international level, were excluding those most directly affected.

Despite their critics, and despite changes in our understanding since the Stockholm and Rio conferences, the concepts of limits to growth, the tragedy of the commons, and environmental (in)security remain powerfully influential in global environmental politics. The dispute about growth limits has reemerged in current debates over the prospects for sustainability (see Part Four). Similarly, those skeptical about the prospects for effective international cooperation invoke the logic of self-interested behavior and the commons-like features of global environmental systems—just as Hardin did more than forty years ago. And the increasingly widespread fear that environmental degradation threatens national and international security raises for some the specter of violent conflict, geopolitical maneuvering, and authoritarian responses, even as others see environmental problems offering transformative "peacebuilding" potential (see Part Five). The evolution of global environmental politics cannot be understood without examining the history of these ideas; weighing their claims carefully and critically is as important today as it was in the Stockholm-to-Rio era.

Thinking Critically

1. How well have the essays by Meadows, Castro, and Hardin, which were all written between 1968 and 1972, withstood the test of time? Do they still provide an adequate framework for understanding and addressing global environmental problems? What aspects of their essays seem anachronistic? What aspects ring true today? Imagine what a dialogue among these thinkers would be like if they were to meet today and discuss the durability of one another's claims.

2. Contrast Castro's claims about the environment and development with the views of the World Commission on Environment and Development (WCED) and the essays on sustainability in Part Four. Do either the advocates or the critics of the sustainability paradigm frame the problem in the same way as Castro?

3. Does the work of Ostrom and her colleagues invalidate Hardin's central claims about the tragedy of the commons? In other words, can Hardin still be right about the larger problem even if he misread the history of the English commons, and even if exceptions to his pessimistic scenario can be found today? What do you think Hardin would say to his critics? Construct Hardin's argument as a series of logical propositions: If Basurto and Ostrom are correct, which of Hardin's specific claims or assumptions are most challenged, and how?

4. Can we imagine effective rules governing common-pool resources on a larger scale—for example, the global atmosphere or the world's oceans? What are the limits of scale for these forms of governance, and at what scale are these limits likely to be encountered?

5. Contrast Hardin's arguments about the need for strong command-and-control governance with the essays on ecological justice in Part Six. Is the concentration of power in the hands of the state part of the problem or part of the solution? In an era in which many governments face profound skepticism and frequent crises of authority, are people likely to look to the state for solutions to environmental problems?

NOTES

1. For an overview of events leading up to and including the Stockholm conference, see Lynton Caldwell, *International Environmental Policy,* 3rd ed. (Durham, NC: Duke University Press, 1996).

2. Several of these criticisms are summarized in W. D. Nordhaus, "World Dynamics: Measurement Without Data," *Economic Journal* 83, no. 332 (December 1973): 1156–1183. See also Julian Simon and Herman Kahn, *The Resourceful Earth* (Oxford: Basil Blackwell, 1984).

3. An example is William Ophuls, *Ecology and the Politics of Scarcity* (San Francisco: W. H. Freeman, 1977).

4. See Susan Jane Buck Cox, "No Tragedy on the Commons," *Environmental Ethics* 7 (Spring 1985): 49–61.

5. Much of this research is summarized in Nives Dolšak and Elinor Ostrom, *The Commons in the New Millennium: Challenges and Adaptation* (Cambridge, MA: MIT Press, 2003).

6. See Elinor Ostrom, *Governing the Commons: The Evolution of Institutions for Collective Action* (London: Cambridge University Press, 1990).

7. See Robert O. Keohane and Elinor Ostrom, eds., *Local Commons and Global Interdependence* (London: Sage, 1995).

8. On the international pressures surrounding deforestation in the Amazon, see Susanna Hecht and Alexander Cockburn, *The Fate of the Forest: Developers, Destroyers, and Defenders of the Amazon* (New York: HarperCollins, 1990).

1

THE LIMITS TO GROWTH

DONELLA H. MEADOWS, DENNIS L. MEADOWS, JØRGEN
RANDERS, AND WILLIAM W. BEHRENS III*

Problems and Models

Every person approaches his problems . . . with the help of models. A model is simply an ordered set of assumptions about a complex system. It is an attempt to understand some aspect of the infinitely varied world by selecting from perceptions and past experience a set of general observations applicable to the problem at hand. . . .

Decisionmakers at every level unconsciously use mental models to choose among policies that will shape our future world. These mental models are, of necessity, very simple when compared with the reality from which they are abstracted. The human brain, remarkable as it is, can only keep track of a limited number of the complicated, simultaneous interactions that determine the nature of the real world.

We, too, have used a model. Ours is a formal, written model of the world.[1] It constitutes a preliminary attempt to improve our mental models of long-term, global problems by combining the large amount of information that is already in human minds and in written records with the new information-processing tools that mankind's increasing knowledge has produced—the scientific method, systems analysis, and the modern computer.

*Excerpted from Donella H. Meadows, Dennis L. Meadows, Jørgen Randers, and William W. Behrens III, *The Limits to Growth* (Washington, DC: Potomac Associates, 1972). The text is currently available in its third edition, Meadows et al., *The Limits to Growth—the 30-Year Update* (White River Junction, VT: Chelsea Green Publishing Co., 2004). Reprinted with permission.

Our world model was built specifically to investigate five major trends of global concern—accelerating industrialization, rapid population growth, widespread malnutrition, depletion of nonrenewable resources, and a deteriorating environment. These trends are all interconnected in many ways, and their development is measured in decades or centuries, rather than in months or years. With the model we are seeking to understand the causes of these trends, their interrelationships, and their implications as much as one hundred years in the future.

The model we have constructed is, like every other model, imperfect, oversimplified, and unfinished. We are well aware of its shortcomings, but we believe that it is the most useful model now available for dealing with problems far out on the space-time graph. To our knowledge it is the only formal model in existence that is truly global in scope, that has a time horizon longer than thirty years, and that includes important variables such as population, food production, and pollution, not as independent entities, but as dynamically interacting elements, as they are in the real world. . . .

In spite of the preliminary state of our work, we believe it is important to publish the model and our findings now. Decisions are being made every day, in every part of the world, that will affect the physical, economic, and social conditions of the world system for decades to come. These decisions cannot wait for perfect models and total understanding. They will be made on the basis of some model, mental or written, in any case. . . .

Our conclusions are:

1. If the present growth trends in world population, industrialization, pollution, food production, and resource depletion continue unchanged, the limits to growth on this planet will be reached sometime within the next one hundred years. The most probable result will be a rather sudden and uncontrollable decline in both population and industrial capacity.
2. It is possible to alter these growth trends and to establish a condition of ecological and economic stability that is sustainable far into the future. The state of global equilibrium could be designed so that the basic material needs of each person on earth are satisfied and each person has an equal opportunity to realize his individual human potential.
3. If the world's people decide to strive for this second outcome rather than the first, the sooner they begin working to attain it, the greater will be their chances of success.

These conclusions are so far-reaching and raise so many questions for further study that we are quite frankly overwhelmed by the enormity of the job that must be done. We hope that this book will serve to interest other people . . . to raise the space and time horizons of their concerns and to join us in understanding and preparing for a period of great transition—the transition from growth to global equilibrium. . . .

A Finite World

We have mentioned many difficult trade-offs . . . in the production of food, in the consumption of resources, and in the generation and clean-up of pollution. By now it should be clear that all of these trade-offs arise from one simple fact—the earth is finite. The closer any human activity comes to the limit of the earth's ability to support that activity, the more apparent and unresolvable the trade-offs become. When there is plenty of unused arable land, there can be more people and also more food per person. When all the land is already used, the trade-off between more people or more food per person becomes a choice between absolutes.

In general, modern society has not learned to recognize and deal with these trade-offs. The apparent goal of the present world system is to produce more people with more (food, material goods, clean air, and water) for each person. . . . We have noted that if society continues to strive for that goal, it will eventually reach one of many earthly limitations. . . . It is not possible to foretell exactly which limitation will occur first or what the consequences will be, because there are many conceivable, unpredictable human responses to such a situation. It is possible, however, to investigate what conditions and what changes in the world system might lead society to collision with or accommodation to the limits to growth in a finite world. . . .

Technology and the Limits to Growth

Although the history of human effort contains numerous incidents of mankind's failure to live within physical limits, it is success in overcoming limits that forms the cultural tradition of many dominant people in today's world. Over the past three hundred years, mankind has compiled an impressive record of pushing back the apparent limits to population and economic growth by a series of spectacular technological advances. Since the recent history of a large part of human society has been so continuously successful, it is quite natural that many people expect technological breakthroughs to go on raising physical ceilings indefinitely. These people speak about the future with resounding technological optimism. . . . The hopes of the technological optimists center on the ability of technology to remove or extend the limits to growth of population and capital. We have shown that in the world model the application of technology to apparent problems of resource depletion or pollution or food shortage has no impact on the essential problem, which is exponential growth in a finite and complex system. Our attempts to use even the most optimistic estimates of the benefits of technology in the model did not prevent the ultimate decline of population and industry, and in fact did not in any case postpone the collapse beyond the year 2200. . . .

Applying technology to the natural pressures that the environment exerts against any growth process has been so successful in the past that a whole culture has evolved around the principle of fighting against limits rather than learning to live with them. . . . But the relationship between the earth's limits and man's activities is changing. The exponential growth curves are adding millions of people and billions of tons of pollutants to the ecosystem each year. Even the ocean, which once appeared virtually inexhaustible, is losing species after species of its commercially useful animals. . . .

There may be much disagreement with the statement that population and capital growth must stop soon. But virtually no one will argue that material growth on this planet can go on forever. . . . Man can still choose his limits and stop when he pleases by weakening some of the strong pressures that cause capital and population growth, or by instituting counterpressures, or both. Such counterpressures will probably not be entirely pleasant. They will certainly involve profound changes in the social and economic structures that have been deeply impressed into human culture by centuries of growth. The alternative is to wait until the price of technology becomes more than society can pay, or until the side effects of technology suppress growth themselves, or until problems arise that have no technical solutions. At any of those points the choice of limits will be gone. Growth will be stopped by pressures that are not of human choosing, and that, as the world model suggests, may be very much worse than those which society might choose for itself.

. . . Technological optimism is the most common and the most dangerous reaction to our findings from the world model. Technology can relieve the symptoms of a problem without affecting the underlying causes. Faith in technology as the ultimate solution to all problems can thus divert our attention from the most fundamental problem—the problem of growth in a finite system—and prevent us from taking effective action to solve it. . . .

The Transition from Growth to Global Equilibrium

We can say very little at this point about the practical, day-by-day steps that might be taken to reach a desirable, sustainable state of global equilibrium. Neither the world model nor our own thoughts have been developed in sufficient detail to understand all the implications of the transition from growth to equilibrium. Before any part of the world's society embarks deliberately on such a transition, there must be much more discussion, more extensive analysis, and many new ideas contributed by many different people. . . .

Although we underline the need for more study and discussion of these difficult questions, we end on a note of urgency. We hope that intensive study and debate will proceed simultaneously with an ongoing program of action. The details are not yet specified, but the general direction for action is obvious. Enough is known already to analyze many proposed policies in terms of their tendencies to promote or to regulate growth.[2] . . . Efforts are weak at the moment, but they could be strengthened very quickly if the goal of equilibrium were recognized as desirable and important by any sizable part of human society. . . .

Taking no action to solve these problems is equivalent to taking strong action. Every day of continued exponential growth brings the world system closer to the ultimate limits to that growth. A decision to do nothing is a decision to increase the risk of collapse. We cannot say with certainty how much longer mankind can postpone initiating deliberate control of his growth before he will have lost the chance for control. We suspect on the basis of present knowledge of the physical constraints of the planet that the growth phase cannot continue for another one hundred years. Again, because of the delays in the system, if the global society waits until those constraints are unmistakably apparent, it will have waited too long.

If there is cause for deep concern, there is also cause for hope. Deliberately limiting growth would be difficult, but not impossible. The way to proceed is clear, and the necessary steps, although they are new ones for human society, are well within human capabilities. Man possesses, for a small moment in his history, the most powerful combination of knowledge, tools, and resources the world has ever known. He has all that is physically necessary to create a totally new form of human society—one that would be built to last for generations. The two missing ingredients are a realistic, long-term goal that can guide mankind to the equilibrium society and the human will to achieve that goal. Without such a goal and a commitment to it, short-term concerns will generate the exponential growth that drives the world system toward the limits of the earth and ultimate collapse. With that goal and that commitment mankind would be ready now to begin a controlled, orderly transition from growth to global equilibrium.

NOTES

1. The prototype model on which we have based our work was designed by Professor Jay W. Forrester of the Massachusetts Institute of Technology. A description of that model has been published in his book *World Dynamics* (Cambridge, Mass: Wright-Allen Press, 1971).

2. See, for example, "Fellow Americans Keep Out!" *Forbes,* June 15, 1971, p. 22, and *The Ecologist,* January 1972.

ENVIRONMENT AND DEVELOPMENT: THE CASE OF THE DEVELOPING COUNTRIES

João Augusto de Araujo Castro[*]

Introduction

Interest in the field of ecology, which is centered in the developed countries, has recently increased due to the sudden discovery of a possible imbalance between man and earth. Resulting from the population explosion and the misuse of existing and newly developed technologies, this potential imbalance could bring about an environmental crisis menacing the future of mankind. In several countries the emergence of an interest in ecological problems has not been confined to the realm of the scientific community. It has aroused public concern which has expressed itself, although sometimes vaguely, in such initiatives as Earth Week, celebrated in the United States in April 1970, and the mushrooming of a specialized literature.

As would be expected, the methods envisaged to resolve on a world basis the so-called environmental crisis were inspired by the realities of a fraction of that very same world: the family of the developed countries. Furthermore, the bulk of the solutions in hand, mainly of a technical nature, seek primarily to make healthier the consequences of the Industrial Revolution without necessarily providing a tool for a further distribution of its benefits among states.

*Kay, David A., and Eugene B. Skolnikoff, eds., *World Eco-Crisis: International Organizations in Response.* © 1972 by the Board of Regents of the University of Wisconsin System. Reprinted by permission of The University of Wisconsin Press.

This study seeks to introduce some neglected aspects of the interests of developing countries into discussions about a world ecological policy. The working hypothesis is that the implementation of any worldwide environmental policy based on the realities of the developed countries tends to perpetuate the existing gap in socioeconomic development between developed and developing countries and so promote the freezing of the present international order. . . .

Developed Countries

Although there does not yet exist a systematic body of doctrine, the new ecological policy of the developed countries contains several elements that have already stimulated important developments in academic thought, as indicated by the growing literature on the matter, and attitudes of governments and private sectors in these countries, mainly in their relations with the developing countries.

A short historical digression may help in analyzing the rationale of this ecological policy. As a localized phenomenon in the countries of the Northern Hemisphere, the Industrial Revolution of the eighteenth century was not brought about by one single factor. It was not, for instance, the result of inventions or the coming into operation of new machines. As in the case of other major movements in history, it was the result of the interplay of many factors, some obscure in themselves, whose combined effort laid down the foundations of a new industrial system. Growing organically, cell by cell, new patterns of industrial organization were soon translated into the establishment of a new international order. Around the group of countries enjoying the benefits of the Industrial Revolution, there existed an increasing family of countries, trying, mostly unsuccessfully, to modernize their own means of production.

This new international order and the relatively uneven distribution of political power among states, based on the use and monopoly of advanced technologies, may be considered one of the most enduring effects of the Industrial Revolution. And since then, as a normal corollary of the new order, the technologically advanced countries have been endeavoring to maintain their political and economic position in the world while the technologically less endowed countries have been seeking to alter, through development, this global status quo.

This permanent struggle between the two groups of countries persists in the present days and it is unlikely that it will cease in the near future. For this to happen one would have to assume a perfectly homogeneous world community whose conflicts would have been eliminated through a perfect satisfaction, on a homogeneous basis, of all human needs. This condition is most likely to be found only in the realms of utopia. . . .

According to a helpful image taken from academic and governmental sources in the developed countries our planet could be visualized as a "spaceship earth," where life could only be sustained, nay simply possible, through maintenance of a delicate equilibrium between the needs of the passengers and the ability of the craft to respond to those needs. Undisturbed until recently, this equilibrium would now be menaced by an excess of population and the consequences of the use of both previously existing and newly developed technologies. Elaborating the same image, "spaceship earth" would be divided into two classes of passengers, the first coincident with the technologically advanced countries and the second representative of the technologically less endowed countries, which would necessarily have to trade off positions with a view to maintaining the equilibrium of the vessel. . . .

In order to maintain the equilibrium of the vessel the problems created by population explosion and the use of both previously existing and new technologies should, in the view of developed countries, now be dealt with globally, irrespective of the unequal distribution, on a world scale, of the benefits and related destructive effects on the environment engendered by the Industrial Revolution. Germane to such a global ecological policy is the need for world planning for development which, to be successful, might purposely aim at freezing the present relative positions of the two classes inside the vessel.

Provided that the first class already enjoys low average rates of population growth and is unlikely to opt for a slower rate of industrial growth for the sole purpose of guaranteeing a purer atmosphere or cleaner water, the new ecology-saving policy would be more successful if applied in the areas where the environmental crisis has not yet appeared, even in its least acute forms. Actually, these areas would mainly comprise the territory of the second class. Thus: the second class should be taught to employ the most effective and expeditious birth control methods and to follow an orderly pollution-reducing process of industrialization. In the case of industrialization, the mainstream of socioeconomic development, the lesson must be even harsher: The second class must organize production in accordance with environment-saving techniques already tested by the first class or be doomed to socioeconomic stagnation. . . .

Nowadays some ecologists do not hesitate to say that the developing countries can never hope to achieve the consumption patterns of the developed countries. Some seemingly appalling calculations are offered as proof of this. To raise the living standards of the world's existing population to American levels the annual production of iron would have to increase 75 times, that of copper 100 times, that of lead 200 times, and that of tin 250 times. Were a country such as India to make use of fertilizers at the per capita level of the Netherlands, it would consume one-half of the world's total output of fertilizers. Clearly, the parity of the developing countries with the developed ones is no longer compatible with the existing stocks of natural resources. Again, according to those wise men, the increasing expectations in developing countries, which are sometimes associated with something approaching a revolution, are nothing more than expectations of elites and therefore must be curbed. Most of the population of these countries, it is claimed, do not have an ambition to reach Western standards and do not even know that "such a thing as development is on the agenda."

Now, the alleged exhaustion of natural resources is accompanied, in general, by forecasts of the fateful coming of formidable ecological hecatombs. The continuing progress of developed countries would require an economic lebensraum in the Southern Hemisphere. In the name of the survival of mankind developing countries should continue in a state of underdevelopment because if the evils of industrialization were to reach them, life on the planet would be placed in jeopardy. . . .

Very few reasonable people underwrite these fanciful ideas. Yet, it cannot be denied that the environment in developed countries is threatened and that it should be preserved. The difficulty in dealing with environmental problems nowadays is that they have become a myth. . . . From an uttermost neglect of ecological problems public opinion in the United States has swung to an outright "geolatry." The environment has been rediscovered and Mother Earth now has a week dedicated to her in the calendar. Schoolchildren crusade to clean up the streets; college students organize huge demonstrations; uncivilized industries that dump their wastes in the air, in the water, or on the ground are denounced as public enemies.

. . . The simplistic concepts that ecology is disturbed because there are "too many people" or because they "consume too much" must be discarded as nothing more than fallacies. There is abundant evidence that the earth is capable of supporting a considerably greater population at much higher levels of consumption. The simple fact that in half a century mankind found it possible to wage four major wars, with a terrible waste of wealth, is a clear indication that we are not after all so short of resources although we may be short of common sense. . . .

Environmental problems not only pose a new and compelling argument for disarmament and peace but also call attention to the question of efficiency in the organization of production. It is widely known, but seldom remembered when the availability of natural resources is discussed, that in developed countries billions of dollars are spent every year to purchase so-called farm surpluses. Millions of tons of agricultural products have been regularly stored or destroyed to keep prices up in the world markets. . . . These figures and these facts evidently do not agree with the superficial statements which have been made about the irreparable strain being put on natural resources.

Pollution of the air and water and related damages to the environment are loosely attributed, in general, to faulty technologies, but few have bothered to assess objectively the exact proportions of the problem. According to experts at the Organisation for Economic Co-operation and Development (OECD) safeguarding the environment in the United States would require annual expenditures of . . . less than 2 percent of the American GNP [Gross National Product]. Clearly, there is no real cause for most of the fuzzy agitation about the environment. Put in their proper perspective, environmental problems are little more than a question of the reexamination of national priorities. . . .

When discussing the environment some ecologists and other wise men, as often happens in many other instances, try haphazardly to superimpose peculiar situations prevailing in developed countries onto the realities of the developing countries. . . . If the peculiarities of developing countries are taken into account, it will not be difficult to recognize that, in broad terms, they are still at a pre-pollution stage or, in other words, have not yet been given the chance to become polluted. . . . The 24 countries of Latin America, the least underdeveloped region in the developing world, have less than one-tenth of the total number of motor vehicles in the United States. Only a few ecologists and other wise men would say that Latin Americans should rather have fewer cars and cleaner air.

There is a pollution of affluence and a pollution of poverty. It is imperative to distinguish between the two lest some pollution be prevented at the cost of much economic development. Were it not for the dangers arising from the confusion between the two kinds of pollution, there would be no need for calling attention to the precarious housing conditions, poor health, and low sanitary standards not to mention starvation in developing countries. The linear transposition of ecological problems of the developed countries to the context of the developing ones disregards the existence of such distressing social conditions. Wherever these conditions prevail, the assertion that income means less pollution is nonsense. It is obvious, or should be, that the so-called pollution of poverty can only be corrected through higher incomes, or more precisely, through economic development.

The most sensible ecologists are of the opinion that the pollution levels can be attributed not so much to population or affluence as to modern technologies. In the United States the economy would have grown enough, in the absence of technological change, to give the increased population about the same per capita amounts of goods and services today as in 1946. The ecological crisis has resulted mainly from the sweeping progress in technologies. Modern technologies have multiplied the impact of growth on the environment and, consequently, generated most of the existing pollution. Those who haphazardly transpose developed countries' situations to the milieu of an underdeveloped country repeatedly warn the latter against the dangers of modern technologies and rapid industrialization. "Don't let happen to your cities what happened to New York; keep your beautiful landscapes." It is ironic that developed countries, which create and sell modern technologies, should caution developing countries against utilizing them. Is this done to justify the secondhand technologies that sometimes accompany foreign direct investments?

Developing Countries

A somewhat apathetic attitude on the part of the developing countries regarding the environmental issue does not imply negation of the relevance of the matter and the need for true international cooperation to solve the problem it poses for the survival of mankind. This apathetic attitude, however, clearly is derived from the developing countries' socioeconomic experience which differs, to a large extent, from that of the developed countries. Consequently, one has to bear in mind that, not having enjoyed the opportunity to experience their own Industrial Revolution, the developing countries have not been stimulated to think about the environmental crisis as posed in the present days. The phenomenon of urbanization in the Southern Hemisphere, even in the countries experiencing a considerable degree of progress, may raise questions about poor living standards in some areas but has not thus far led to industrial congestion.

As indicated in the elements of the ecological policy of the developed countries, the equilibrium of "spaceship earth" would depend on the enforcement of measures bearing on population and on the use of the previously existing and new technologies chiefly in the second class of the vessel or, in other words, in the territory of the developing countries. Even if applied to their full extent, those measures would not result at some foreseeable date in a single-class carrying vessel, preferably closer to the first steerage. This ecological policy, which aims primarily at the equilibrium of the vessel, could better succeed if the relative positions of the classes were maintained, for the emergence of one single class would presuppose a considerable change in the living standards of the first class, something that may not be attained in the light of present global socioeconomic realities. . . .

On the question of the preservation of the environment the passengers' survival would call for the enforcement of a drastic decision, globally applied, to maintain a "green area reserve" which would have to coincide mainly with the territories of the developing countries. This step would safeguard, against complete exhaustion, the natural elements (soil, atmosphere, and water) still available on the planet just to provide some sort of counteraction to the spoilage of the same natural elements used up in the countries where the benefits of the Industrial Revolution were massively concentrated.

Besides the ethical question raised by this policy, as expressed in the ostensive imbalance between responsibility for the damage and obligation for repair, the developing countries, in abiding by its prescriptions, would make a commitment to conservatism rather than to conservation. Furthermore, the possibility of a widespread application of developed countries' ecological policy, theoretically conceived to secure the equilibrium of "spaceship earth," may risk transforming the Southern Hemisphere countries into the last healthy weekend areas for the inhabitants of a planet already saturated with the environment created by the Industrial Revolution. As a token of compensation the Southern Hemisphere countries could claim to have resurrected, and adequately preserved, the environmental milieu for the living and the survival of Rousseau's "happy savage." In expressing their concern over the environmental crisis the developing countries cannot accept, without further refinement, the ecological policy devised by the developed countries whose socioeconomic structure was deeply influenced by the unique phenomenon of the Industrial Revolution.

The first step toward the refinement of that policy may be the rejection of the principle that the ecology issue, taken on a global basis, can be dealt with exclusively through a technical approach, as suggested by the developed countries. Given the implications for the international order, including the freezing of the status quo, any environment-saving policy must necessarily be imbued with a solid and well-informed political approach. This would provide an opportunity for the developing countries, by preserving their national identities, to join safely in the effort of the international community to preserve the equilibrium of "spaceship earth."

As a normal corollary of the political approach, ecological policy should not depart from the broader framework of socioeconomic development. In this regard a second step of refinement would require a corresponding universal commitment to development if the task of preserving the environment is to be shared by the world community. . . .

Evidently, no country wants any pollution at all. But each country must evolve its own development plans, exploit its own resources as it thinks suitable, and define its own environmental standards. The idea of having such priorities and standards imposed on individual countries or groups of countries, on either a multilateral or a bilateral basis, is very hard to accept.

That is why it is disturbing to see the International Bank for Reconstruction and Development (IBRD) set up its own ecological policy. Repercussions on the environment, defined according to IBRD ecologists, have become an important factor in determining whether financial assistance by that institution should be granted for an industrial project in developing countries. It seems reasonable that the preservation of the environment should not exclude the preservation of national sovereignty. Ecological policies should rather be inserted into the framework of national development.

It is perhaps time for the developing countries to present their own views on the framing of an environmental policy in spite of the fact that the developed countries have not yet ended their own controversial debate or furnished definite and convincing data on the issue. In adopting a position the developing countries recognize the existence of environmental problems in the world and the possibility of finding solutions through both national efforts and international cooperation.

The first point to be touched on concerns the question of national sovereignty. In this regard any ecological policy, globally applied, must not be an instrument to suppress wholly or in part the legitimate right of any country to decide about its own affairs. In reality this point would simply seek to guarantee on an operational level the full exercise of the principle of juridical equality of states as expressed, for instance, in the Charter of the United Nations. . . . Sovereignty, in this context, should not be taken as an excuse for isolationism and consequently for escapism in relation to international efforts geared to solving environmental problems. For the developing countries it is crucial to consider, in the light of their own interests, nationally defined, the whole range of alternative solutions devised or implemented in the developed countries. Naturally, it is assumed that all countries can act responsibly and that none is going to deliberately favor policies that may endanger the equilibrium of "spaceship earth."

Closely linked to the problem of sovereignty, the question of national priorities calls for an understanding of the distinction between the developmental characteristics of developed and developing countries. As has been previously pointed out in this article, while the ecological issue came to the forefront of public concern as a by-product of postindustrial stages of development, it is not yet strikingly apparent in the majority of the developing countries. And different realities, of course, should be differently treated or, at least, given the fittest solutions.

In the developing countries the major concern is an urgent need to accelerate socioeconomic development, and a meaningful ecological policy must not hamper the attainment of that goal in the most expeditious way. . . . In this context the developing countries, while rejecting the implementation of any ecological policy which bears in itself elements of socioeconomic stagnation, could only share a common responsibility for the preservation of the environment if it was accompanied and paralleled by a corresponding common responsibility for development. . . .

Conclusion

This study has probed very briefly some aspects of an ecological policy in the light of the interests of the developing countries. . . . Emphasis has been laid on the undesirability of transposing, uncritically, into the realities of the developing countries the solutions already envisaged by the developed countries to eliminate or reduce the so-called environmental crisis to the extent that those solutions may embody elements of socioeconomic stagnation. . . . Finally, a preliminary and broad picture of a position of the developing countries has stressed the relation between preservation of environment and the urgent need to speed up socioeconomic development and the desirability of a common world effort to tackle both these aspects simultaneously. This common effort, however, should not preclude or trespass on national interest as a departing point for the setting up of concepts and operational guidelines of an ecological policy for the developing countries.

In conclusion, a discussion of any meaningful ecological policy for both developed and developing countries . . . would better reflect a broad socioeconomic concern, as tentatively suggested in this article, rather than confine itself to a strictly scientific approach. Man's conceptual environment, and nothing else, will certainly prevail in shaping the future of mankind, for the preservation of the environment presupposes a human being to live in it and a human mind to conceive a better life for man on this planet. From the point of view of man—and we have no other standpoint—Man, Pascal's "roseau pensant," is still more relevant than Nature.

3

THE TRAGEDY OF THE COMMONS

GARRETT HARDIN*

Tragedy of Freedom in a Commons

. . . The tragedy of the commons develops in this way. Picture a pasture open to all. It is to be expected that each herdsman will try to keep as many cattle as possible on the commons. Such an arrangement may work reasonably satisfactorily for centuries because tribal wars, poaching, and disease keep the numbers of both man and beast well below the carrying capacity of the land. Finally, however, comes the day of reckoning, that is, the day when the long-desired goal of social stability becomes a reality. At this point, the inherent logic of the commons remorselessly generates tragedy.

As a rational being, each herdsman seeks to maximize his gain. Explicitly or implicitly, more or less consciously, he asks, "What is the utility to me of adding one more animal to my herd?" This utility has one negative and one positive component.

1. The positive component is a function of the increment of one animal. Since the herdsman receives all the proceeds from the sale of the additional animal, the positive utility is nearly +1.
2. The negative component is a function of the additional overgrazing created by one more animal. Since, however, the effects of overgrazing are shared by all the herdsmen, the negative utility for any particular decisionmaking herdsman is only a fraction of -1.

---

*Excerpted from Garrett Hardin, "The Tragedy of the Commons," *Science* 162 (December 13, 1968): 1243–1248. Reprinted with permission.

Adding together the component partial utilities, the rational herdsman concludes that the only sensible course for him to pursue is to add another animal to his herd. And another; and another. . . . But this is the conclusion reached by each and every rational herdsman sharing a commons. Therein is the tragedy. Each man is locked into a system that compels him to increase his herd without limit—in a world that is limited. Ruin is the destination toward which all men rush, each pursuing his own best interest in a society that believes in the freedom of the commons. Freedom in a commons brings ruin to all.

Some would say that this is a platitude. Would that it were! In a sense, it was learned thousands of years ago, but natural selection favors the forces of psychological denial.[1] The individual benefits as an individual from his ability to deny the truth even though society as a whole, of which he is a part, suffers. Education can counteract the natural tendency to do the wrong thing, but the inexorable succession of generations requires that the basis for this knowledge be constantly refreshed. . . .

In an approximate way, the logic of the commons has been understood for a long time, perhaps since the discovery of agriculture or the invention of private property in real estate. But it is understood mostly only in special cases which are not sufficiently generalized. Even at this late date, cattlemen leasing national land on the western ranges demonstrate no more than an ambivalent understanding, in constantly pressuring federal authorities to increase the head count to the point where overgrazing produces erosion and weed dominance. Likewise, the oceans of the world continue to suffer from the survival of the philosophy of the commons. Maritime nations still respond automatically to the shibboleth of the "freedom of the seas." Professing to believe in the "inexhaustible resources of the oceans," they bring species after species of fish and whales closer to extinction.[2]

The National Parks present another instance of the working out of the tragedy of the commons. At present, they are open to all, without limit. The parks themselves are limited in extent—there is only one Yosemite Valley—whereas the population seems to grow without limit. The values that visitors seek in the parks are steadily eroded. Plainly, we must soon cease to treat the parks as commons or they will be of no value to anyone.

What shall we do? We have several options. We might sell them off as private property. We might keep them as public property, but allocate the right to enter them. The allocation might be on the basis of wealth, by the use of an auction system. It might be on the basis of merit, as defined by some agreed-upon standards. It might be by lottery. Or it might be on a first-come, first-served basis, administered to long queues. These, I think, are all the reasonable possibilities. They are all objectionable. But we must choose—or acquiesce in the destruction of the commons that we call our National Parks.

Pollution

In a reverse way, the tragedy of the commons reappears in problems of pollution. Here it is not a question of taking something out of the commons, but of putting something in—sewage, or chemical, radioactive, and heat wastes into water; noxious and dangerous fumes into the air; and distracting and unpleasant advertising signs into the line of sight. The calculations of utility are much the same as before. The rational man finds that his share of the cost of the wastes he discharges into the commons is less than the cost of purifying his wastes before releasing them. Since this is true for everyone, we are locked into a system of "fouling our own nest," so long as we behave only as independent, rational, free-enterprisers.

The tragedy of the commons as a food basket is averted by private property, or something formally like it. But the air and waters surrounding us cannot readily be fenced, and so the tragedy of the commons as a cesspool must be prevented by different means, by coercive laws or taxing devices that make it cheaper for the polluter to treat his pollutants than to discharge them untreated. We have not progressed as far with the solution of this problem as we have with the first. Indeed, our particular concept of private property, which deters us from exhausting the positive resources of the earth, favors pollution. The owner of a factory on the bank of a stream—whose property extends to the middle of the stream—often has difficulty seeing why it is not his natural right to muddy the waters flowing past his door. The law, always behind the times, requires elaborate stitching and fitting to adapt it to this newly perceived aspect of the commons.

The pollution problem is a consequence of population. It did not much matter how a lonely American frontiersman disposed of his waste. "Flowing water purifies itself every 10 miles," my grandfather used to say, and the myth was near enough to the truth when he was a boy, for there were not too many people. But as population became denser, the natural chemical and biological recycling processes became overloaded, calling for a redefinition of property rights.

How to Legislate Temperance?

Analysis of the pollution problem as a function of population density uncovers a not generally recognized principle of morality, namely: the morality of an act is a function of the state of the system at the time it is performed.[3] Using the commons as a cesspool does not harm the general public under frontier conditions, because there is no public; the same behavior in a metropolis is unbearable. A hundred and fifty years ago a plainsman could kill an American bison, cut out only the tongue for his dinner, and discard the rest of the animal. He was not in any important sense being wasteful. Today, with only a few thousand bison left, we would be appalled at such behavior. . . .

That morality is system-sensitive escaped the attention of most codifiers of ethics in the past. "Thou shalt not . . . " is the form of traditional ethical directives which make no allowance for particular circumstances. The laws of our society follow the pattern of ancient ethics, and therefore are poorly suited to governing a complex, crowded, changeable world. Our epicyclic solution is to augment statutory law with administrative law. Since it is practically impossible to spell out all the conditions under which it is safe to burn trash in the backyard or to run an automobile without smog control, by law we delegate the details to bureaus. The result is administrative law, which is rightly feared for an ancient reason—Quis custodiet ipsos custodes?—"Who shall watch the watchers themselves?" John Adams said that we must have "a government of laws and not men." Bureau administrators, trying to evaluate the morality of acts in the total system, are singularly liable to corruption, producing a government by men, not laws.

Prohibition is easy to legislate (though not necessarily to enforce); but how do we legislate temperance? Experience indicates that it can be accomplished best through the mediation of administrative law. We limit possibilities unnecessarily if we suppose that the sentiment of Quis custodiet denies us the use of administrative law. We should rather retain the phrase as a perpetual reminder of fearful dangers we cannot avoid. The great challenge facing us now is to invent the corrective feedbacks that are needed to keep custodians honest. We must find ways to legitimate the needed authority of both the custodians and the corrective feedbacks.

Freedom to Breed Is Intolerable

The tragedy of the commons is involved in population problems in another way. In a world governed solely by the principle of "dog eat dog"—if indeed there ever was such a world—how many children a family had would not be a matter of public concern. Parents who bred too exuberantly would leave fewer descendants, not more, because they would be unable to care adequately for their children. David Lack and others have found that such a negative feedback demonstrably controls the fecundity of birds.[4] But men are not birds, and have not acted like them for millenniums, at least.

If each human family were dependent only on its own resources; if the children of improvident parents starved to death; if, thus, overbreeding brought its own "punishment" to the germ line—then there would be no public interest in controlling the breeding of families. But our society is deeply committed to the welfare state,[5] and hence is confronted with another aspect of the tragedy of the commons.

In a welfare state, how shall we deal with the family, the religion, the race, or the class (or indeed any distinguishable and cohesive group) that adopts overbreeding as a policy to secure its own aggrandizement?[6] To couple the concept of freedom to breed with the belief that everyone born has an equal right to the commons is to lock the world into a tragic course of action. . . .

Conscience Is Self-Eliminating

It is a mistake to think that we can control the breeding of mankind in the long run by an appeal to conscience. . . .

People vary. Confronted with appeals to limit breeding, some people will undoubtedly respond to the plea more than others. Those who have more children will produce a larger fraction of the next generation than those with more susceptible consciences. The difference will be accentuated, generation by generation. . . . The argument has here been stated in the context of the population problem, but it applies equally well to any instance in which society appeals to an individual exploiting a commons to restrain himself for the general good—by means of his conscience. To make such an appeal is to set up a selective system that works toward the elimination of conscience from the race.

Pathogenic Effects of Conscience

. . . To conjure up a conscience in others is tempting to anyone who wishes to extend his control beyond the legal limits. Leaders at the highest level succumb to this temptation. Has any President during the past generation failed to call on labor unions to moderate voluntarily their demands for higher wages, or to steel companies to honor voluntary guidelines on prices? I can recall none. The rhetoric used on such occasions is designed to produce feelings of guilt in noncooperators.

For centuries it was assumed without proof that guilt was a valuable, perhaps even an indispensable, ingredient of the civilized life. Now, in this post-Freudian world, we doubt it.

Paul Goodman speaks from the modern point of view when he says: "No good has ever come from feeling guilty, neither intelligence, policy, nor compassion. The guilty do not pay attention to the object but only to themselves, and not even to their own interests, which might make sense, but to their anxieties."[7]

One does not have to be a professional psychiatrist to see the consequences of anxiety. We in the Western world are just emerging from a dreadful two-centuries-long Dark Ages of Eros that was sustained partly by prohibition laws, but perhaps more effectively by the anxiety-generating mechanisms of education. . . .

Since proof is difficult, we may even concede that the results of anxiety may sometimes, from certain points of view, be desirable. The larger question we should ask is whether, as a matter of policy, we should ever encourage the use of a technique the tendency (if not the intention) of which is psychologically pathogenic. We hear much talk these days of responsible parenthood; the coupled words are incorporated into the titles of some organizations devoted to birth control. Some people have proposed massive propaganda campaigns to instill responsibility into the nation's (or the world's) breeders. But what is the meaning of the word *responsibility* in this context? Is it not merely a synonym for the word *conscience*? When we use the word *responsibility* in the absence of substantial sanctions are we not trying to browbeat a free man in a commons into acting against his own interest? *Responsibility* is a verbal counterfeit for a substantial quid pro quo. It is an attempt to get something for nothing.

If the word *responsibility* is to be used at all, I suggest that it be in the sense Charles Frankel uses it.[8] "Responsibility," says this philosopher, "is the product of definite social arrangements." Notice that Frankel calls for social arrangements— not propaganda.

Mutual Coercion Mutually Agreed Upon

The social arrangements that produce responsibility are arrangements that create coercion, of some sort. Consider bank-robbing. The man who takes money from a bank acts as if the bank were a commons. How do we prevent such action? Certainly not by trying to control his behavior solely by a verbal appeal to his sense of responsibility. Rather than rely on propaganda we follow Frankel's lead and insist that a bank is not a commons; we seek the definite social arrangements that will keep it from becoming a commons. That we thereby infringe on the freedom of would-be robbers we neither deny nor regret.

The morality of bank-robbing is particularly easy to understand because we accept complete prohibition of this activity. We are willing to say "Thou shalt not rob banks," without providing for exceptions. But temperance also can be created by coercion. Taxing is a good coercive device. To keep downtown shoppers temperate in their use of parking space we introduce parking meters for short periods, and traffic fines for longer ones. We need not actually forbid a citizen to park as long as he wants to; we need merely make it increasingly expensive for him to do so. Not prohibition, but carefully biased options are what we offer him. A Madison Avenue man might call this persuasion; I prefer the greater candor of the word *coercion*.

Coercion is a dirty word to most liberals now, but it need not forever be so. As with the four-letter words, its dirtiness can be cleansed away by exposure to the light, by saying it over and over without apology or embarrassment. To many, the word *coercion* implies arbitrary decisions of distant and irresponsible bureaucrats; but this is not a necessary part of its meaning. The only kind of coercion I recommend is mutual coercion, mutually agreed upon by the majority of the people affected.

To say that we mutually agree to coercion is not to say that we are required to enjoy it, or even to pretend we enjoy it. Who enjoys taxes? We all grumble about them. But we accept compulsory taxes because we recognize that voluntary taxes would favor the conscienceless. We institute and (grumblingly) support taxes and other coercive devices to escape the horror of the commons.

An alternative to the commons need not be perfectly just to be preferable. . . . The alternative of the commons is too horrifying to contemplate. Injustice is preferable to total ruin.

It is one of the peculiarities of the warfare between reform and the status quo that it is thoughtlessly governed by a double standard. Whenever a reform measure is proposed it is often defeated when its opponents triumphantly discover a flaw in it. As Kingsley Davis has pointed out,[9] worshippers of the status quo sometimes imply that no reform is possible without unanimous agreement, an implication contrary to historical fact. As nearly as I can make out, automatic rejection of proposed reforms is based on one of two unconscious assumptions: (i) that the status quo is perfect; or (ii) that the choice we face is between reform and no action; if the proposed reform is imperfect, we presumably should take no action at all, while we wait for a perfect proposal.

But we can never do nothing. That which we have done for thousands of years is also action. It also produces evils. Once we are aware that the status quo is action, we can then compare its discoverable advantages and disadvantages with the predicted advantages and disadvantages of the proposed reform, discounting as best we can for our lack of experience. On the basis of such a comparison, we can make a rational decision which will not involve the unworkable assumption that only perfect systems are tolerable.

Recognition of Necessity

Perhaps the simplest summary of this analysis of man's population problems is this: the commons, if justifiable at all, is justifiable only under conditions of low-population density. As the human population has increased, the commons has had to be abandoned in one aspect after another.

First we abandoned the commons in food gathering, enclosing farmland and restricting pastures and hunting and fishing areas. These restrictions are still not complete throughout the world.

Somewhat later we saw that the commons as a place for waste disposal would also have to be abandoned. Restrictions on the disposal of domestic sewage are widely accepted in the Western world; we are still struggling to close the commons to pollution by automobiles, factories, insecticide sprayers, fertilizing operations, and atomic energy installations.

In a still more embryonic state is our recognition of the evils of the commons in matters of pleasure. There is almost no restriction on the propagation of sound waves in the public medium. The shopping public is assaulted with mindless music, without its consent. Our government is paying out billions of dollars to create supersonic transport which will disturb 50,000 people for every one person who is whisked from coast to coast 3 hours faster. Advertisers muddy the airwaves of radio and television and pollute the view of travelers. We are a long way from outlawing the commons in matters of pleasure. Is this because our Puritan inheritance makes us view pleasure as something of a sin, and pain (that is, the pollution of advertising) as the sign of virtue?

Every new enclosure of the commons involves the infringement of somebody's personal liberty. Infringements made in the distant past are accepted because no contemporary complains of a loss. It is the newly proposed infringements that we vigorously oppose; cries of "rights" and "freedom" fill the air. But what does "freedom" mean? When men mutually agreed to pass laws against robbing, mankind became more free, not less so. Individuals locked into the logic of the commons are free only to bring on universal ruin; once they see the necessity of mutual coercion, they become free to pursue other goals. I believe it was Hegel who said, "Freedom is the recognition of necessity."

The most important aspect of necessity that we must now recognize is the necessity of abandoning the commons in breeding. No technical solution can rescue us from the misery of overpopulation. Freedom to breed will bring ruin to all. At the moment, to avoid hard decisions many of us are tempted to propagandize for conscience and responsible parenthood. The temptation must be resisted, because an appeal to independently acting consciences selects for life disappearance of all conscience in the long run, and an increase in anxiety in the short.

The only way we can preserve and nurture other and more precious freedoms is by relinquishing the freedom to breed, and that very soon. "Freedom is the recognition of necessity"—and it is the role of education to reveal to all the necessity of abandoning the freedom to breed. Only so, can we put an end to this aspect of the tragedy of the commons.

NOTES

1. G. Hardin, ed., *Population, Evolution, and Birth Control* (Freeman, San Francisco, 1964), p. 56.

2. S. McVay, *Scientific American* 216 (No. 8), 13 (1966).

3. J. Fletcher, *Situation Ethics* (Westminster, Philadelphia, 1966).

4. D. Lack, *The Natural Regulation of Animal Numbers* (Clarendon Press, Oxford, 1954).

5. H. Girvetz, *From Wealth to Welfare* (Stanford Univ. Press, Stanford, Calif., 1950).

6. G. Hardin, *Perspec. Biol. Med.* 6, 366 (1963).

7. P. Goodman, *New York Rev. Books* 10(8), 22 (23 May 1968).

8. C. Frankel, *The Case for Modern Man* (Harper, New York, 1955), p. 203.

9. J. D. Rolansky, *Genetics and the Future of Man* (Appleton-Century-Crofts, New York, 1966), p. 177.

4

REDEFINING NATIONAL SECURITY

Lester R. Brown*

Introduction[†]

The term "national security" has become a commonplace expression, a concept regularly appealed to. It is used to justify the maintenance of armies, the development of new weapons systems, and the manufacture of armaments. A fourth of all the federal taxes in the United States and at least an equivalent amount in the Soviet Union are levied in its name.[1]

The concern for the security of a nation is undoubtedly as old as the nation state itself, but since World War II the concept of "national security" has acquired an overwhelmingly military character. Commonly veiled in secrecy, considerations of military threats have become so dominant that other threats to the security of nations have often been ignored. Accumulating evidence indicates that new threats are emerging, threats with which military forces cannot cope.

The notion that countries everywhere should be prepared to defend themselves at all times from any conceivable external threat is a relatively modern one. As recently as 1939, for example, the United States had a defense budget of only $1.3 billion. Prior to World War II, countries mobilized troops in times of war instead of relying on a large permanent military establishment.[2]

The policy of continual preparedness has led to the militarization of the world economy, with military expenditures now accounting for 6 percent of the global product. Worldwide, the military claims of national budgets exceed health-service

*Excerpted from Lester R. Brown, *Redefining National Security,* Worldwatch Institute, Worldwatch Paper 14, October 1977. Reprinted with permission.

[†]I am indebted to my colleague Frank Record for his assistance with the research for this paper.

appropriations. Most countries spend more on "national security" than they do on educating their youth. The development of new, "more effective" weapons systems now engages fully a quarter of the world's scientific talent.[3]

World military expenditures in 1976 reached an estimated $350 billion, a sum that exceeds the income of the poorest one-half of humanity. At the current rate of weapons procurement, two days of world expenditures on arms equal the annual budget of the United Nations and its specialized agencies. Thirty million men and women in their prime productive years are under arms today.[4]

. . . .

The overwhelmingly military approach to national security is based on the assumption that the principal threat to security comes from other nations. But the threats to security may now arise less from the relationship of nation to nation and more from the relationship of man to nature. Dwindling reserves of oil and the deterioration of the earth's biological systems now threaten the security of nations everywhere.

National security cannot be maintained unless national economies can be sustained, but, unfortunately, the health of many economies cannot be sustained for much longer without major adjustments. All advanced industrial economies are fueled primarily by oil, a resource that is being depleted. While military strategists have worried about the access of industrial economies to Middle Eastern oil, another more serious threat, the eventual exhaustion of the world's oil supplies, has been moving to the fore. If massive alternative sources of energy are not in place when the projected downturn in world oil production comes some 15 years hence, crippling economic disruptions will result.

While the oil supply is threatened by depletion, the productivity of the earth's principal biological systems—fisheries, forests, grasslands, and croplands—is threatened by excessive human claims. These biological systems provide all food and all the raw materials for industry except minerals and petrochemicals. In fishery after fishery, the catch now exceeds the long-term sustainable yield. The cutting of trees exceeds the regenerative capacity of forests almost everywhere. Grasslands are deteriorating on every continent as livestock populations increase along with human population. Croplands too are being damaged by erosion as population pressures mount. Failure to arrest this deterioration of biological systems threatens not only the security of individual nations but the survival of civilization as we know it.

The deterioration of the earth's biological systems is not a peripheral issue of concern only to environmentalists. The global economy depends on these biological systems. Anything that threatens their viability threatens the global economy. Any deterioration in these systems represents a deterioration in the human prospect.

As the [1970s] progress these new threats are becoming more visible. During the decade, food shortages have led to temporary rises in death rates in at least a dozen countries. Indeed, the lives lost to the increase in hunger may exceed the combat casualties in all the international conflicts of the past two decades.

Global food insecurity and the associated instability in food prices have become a common source of political instability. The centuries-old dynasty in Ethiopia came to an end in 1974 not because a foreign power invaded and prevailed but because ecological deterioration precipitated a food crisis and famine. In the summer of 1976 the Polish Government was badly shaken by riots when it sought to raise food prices closer to the world level. In 1977, the riots that followed official attempts to raise food prices in Egypt came closer to toppling the government of President Anwar Sadat than has Israeli military power.[5]

The need for countries to confront these threats and to address them cooperatively suggests that the military's role in securing a nation's well-being and survival is relatively less important than it once was. At the same time, protecting and securing the future of a nation by strengthening international cooperation, developing alternative energy sources, and producing adequate food supplies are escalating in importance.

. . . .

Conclusions

The military threat to national security is only one of many that governments must now address. The numerous new threats derive directly or indirectly from the rapidly changing relationship between humanity and the earth's natural systems and resources. The unfolding stresses in this relationship initially manifest themselves as ecological stresses and resource scarcities. Later they translate into economic stresses—inflation, unemployment, capital scarcity, and monetary instability. Ultimately, these economic stresses convert into social unrest and political instability.

National defense establishments are useless against these new threats. Neither bloated military budgets nor highly sophisticated weapons systems can halt the deforestation or solve the firewood crisis now affecting so many Third World countries. Blocking external aggression may be a relatively simple matter compared with arresting the deterioration of local ecological systems.

The new threats to national security are extraordinarily complex. Ecologists understand that the deteriorating relationship between four billion humans and the earth's biological systems cannot continue. But few political leaders have yet to grasp the social significance of this unsustainable situation.

Analyzing and understanding the nature and scale of these new threats to national security will challenge the information-gathering and analytical skills of governments. Unfortunately, the decision-making apparatus in most governments is not organized to balance threats of a traditional military nature with those of ecological and economic origins. Many political leaders perceive the new threats to security dimly, if at all. Intelligence agencies are organized to alert political leaders to potential military threats, but there is no counterpart network for warning of the collapse of a biological system. Military strategists understand the nature of military threats. Energy analysts understand the need to shift from oil to alternative energy sources, and ecologists understand the need to arrest ecological deterioration. But few individuals are trained or able to weigh and evaluate such a diversity of threats and then to translate such an assessment into the allocation of public resources that provides the greatest national security.

If military threats are considered in isolation, military strength of adversaries or potential adversaries can be measured in terms of the number of men under arms, the number and effectiveness of tanks, planes, and other military equipment, and (where the superpowers are concerned) the number of nuclear warheads and delivery missiles. Given the desire to be somewhat stronger than one's opponents, those fashioning the military budget can argue precisely and convincingly for a heavy commitment of public resources to the manufacture of weapons.

Nonmilitary threats to a nation's security are much less clearly defined than military ones. They are often the result of cumulative processes that ultimately lead to the collapse of biological systems or to the depletion of a country's oil reserves. These processes in themselves are seldom given much thought until they pass a critical threshold and disaster strikes. Thus, it is easier in the government councils of developing countries to justify expenditures for the latest model jet fighters than for family planning to arrest the population growth that leads to food scarcity. Likewise, in industrial societies vast expenditures on long-range missiles are easier to obtain than the investments in energy conservation needed to buy time to develop alternative energy sources.

The purpose of national security deliberations should not be to maximize military strength but to maximize national security. If this latter approach were used, public resources would be distributed more widely among the many threats to national security—both the traditional military one and the newer, less precisely measured ones.

The purpose of this paper is not to argue for specific military budget cuts. Rather it is to suggest that profound new threats to the security of nations are arising and that these need to be fully considered along with the traditional ones. Only then can national security be optimized. The time for discarding long-standing and outmoded assumptions held by the governments of the superpowers is long overdue. The U.S.-Soviet relationship has changed markedly over the years, becoming less belligerent and more cooperative than it once was. During the current decade the Soviets have come to rely heavily on the United States for food, and Western banks and corporations have developed enough confidence in Soviet integrity to extend to the Soviet Union several billion dollars' worth of loans and credits.[46] But military expenditures in the two countries do not reflect this new relationship.

Lags in reordering budgetary allocations to confront the new threats to national security are glaring. In 1977, global research expenditures on arms research are six times those for energy research, but all nations might be far more secure if this ratio were reversed. Even though a 3-percent annual population growth rate in a Third World country (which translates into a 19-fold increase in a century) can destroy a country's ecological system and social structure more effectively than a foreign adversary ever could, expenditures on population education and family planning are often negligible or nonexistent. Countries will expend large sums on tanks and planes to defend their territorial sovereignty but nothing to conserve the soil on which their livelihoods depend.

A scarcity of vital resources such as oil or grain could lead to intense competition among countries for supplies, a competition that could easily escalate into military conflict. Competition between Iceland and Great Britain over the North Atlantic cod fisheries, between India and Bangladesh over the waters of the Ganges, and between Mexican and U.S. workers for jobs in the United States all manifest the new threats to national economic security posed by scarcity.

The continuing focus of governments on military threats to security may not only exclude attention to the newer threats, but may also make the effective address of the latter more difficult. The heavy military emphasis on national security can absorb budgetary resources, management skills, and scientific talent that should be devoted to the new nonmilitary threats. Given the enormous investment required to shift the global economy from oil to alternative energy sources, one might well ask whether the world could afford the sustained large-scale use of military might of the sort deployed in World Wars I and II. Indeed, the absurdity of the traditional view is pointed out by science-fiction writer Isaac Asimov: "Even a nonnuclear war cannot be fought because it is too energy-rich a phenomenon." We cannot afford such extravagance, contends Asimov, "and are going to have to use all our energy to stay alive" with none "to spare for warfare."[47] In effect, there simply may not be enough fuel to operate both tanks and tractors. At some point governments will be forced either to realign priorities in a manner responsive to the new threats or to watch their national security deteriorate.

The scientific talent required to make the energy transition and to prevent the destruction of biological systems is enormous. The all-out mobilization that circumstances call for entails, among other things, shifting part of that one-fourth of the world's scientific talent now employed in the military sector to the energy sector. At a time when oil reserves are being depleted, developing new energy systems may be more essential to a nation's survival than new weapons systems.

Apart from the heavy claim on public resources, the continuing exorbitant investment in armaments contributes to a psychological climate of suspicion and mistrust that makes the cooperative international address of new threats to the security of nations next to impossible. Conversely, a reduction in military expenditures by major powers would likely lead to a more cooperative attitude among national governments.

In a world that is not only ecologically interdependent but economically and politically interdependent as well, the concept of "national" security is no longer adequate. Individual countries must respond to global crises because national governments are still the principal decision-makers, but many threats to security require a coordinated international response. The times call for efforts to secure the global systems on which nations depend. If the global climatic system is inadvertently altered by human activity, all countries will be affected. If the international monetary system is not secure, all national economies will suffer. If countries do not cooperate and preserve oceanic fisheries, food prices everywhere will rise. But political leaders have yet to realize that national security is meaningless without global security.

In some situations, countries could be drawn together into a variety of cooperative efforts to cope with shared problems. The Soviet need for assured access to U.S. grain, for example, has led to a five-year U.S.-Soviet grain agreement, and to strengthened economic ties between the two superpowers. Similarly, Middle Eastern oil-exporting countries have turned to Western banks for assistance in the management of their vast financial reserves.

In the late twentieth century the key to national security is sustainability. If the biological underpinnings of the global economic system cannot be secured, then the long-term economic outlook is grim indeed. If new energy sources and systems are not in place as the oil wells begin to go dry, then severe economic disruptions are inevitable.

Perhaps the best contemporary definition of national security is one by Franklin P. Huddle, director of the U.S. Congressional study, *Science, Technology and American Diplomacy*. In *Science,* Huddle writes that "National security requires a stable economy with assured supplies of materials for industry. In this sense, frugality and conservation of materials are essential to our national security. Security means more than safety from hostile attack; it includes the preservation of a system of civilization."[48]

A forceful argument can now be made that considerations of security are meaningful only when the global threats to security are taken into account. Neither individual security nor national security can be sensibly considered in isolation. In effect, the traditional military concept of "national security" is growing ever less adequate as nonmilitary threats grow more formidable.

NOTES

1. *Mid-Session Review of the 1978 Budget* (Washington, D.C.: Office of Management and Budget, July 1, 1977).

2. Allan L. Damon, "Lots of Defense, How Much Security?" *Washington Star,* March 2, 1975.

3. Ruth Leger Sivard, *World Military and Social Expenditures 1974* (Leesburg, Virginia: WMSE Publications, 1974).

4. Ruth Leger Sivard, *World Military and Social Expenditures 1977* (Leesburg, Virginia: WMSE Publications, 1977).

5. Jack Shepherd, *The Politics of Starvation* (Washington, D.C.: Carnegie Endowment for International Peace, 1975); Flora Lewis, "A Feeling of Crisis Is Rising in Poland," *New York*

Times, September 19, 1976; "Egypt Suspends Price Increases as Riots Worsen," *New York Times,* January 20, 1977.

46. "Russia Won't Meet 5-Year Growth Goal, CIA Says; Tough Problems Seen in 1980s," *Wall Street Journal,* August 18, 1976.

47. "Dr. Asimov: The Future Is No Fun," *Washington Star,* April 27, 1975.

48. Franklin P. Huddle, "The Evolving National Policy for Materials," *Science,* February 20, 1976.

5

BEYOND THE TRAGEDY
OF THE COMMONS

Xavier Basurto and Elinor Ostrom[*]

[Editors' note: The article from which this excerpt is drawn contains case studies of three small-scale fisheries in the Gulf of California, Mexico, as well as the conceptual material presented here. Readers seeking case-related examples or insights are encouraged to consult the original work.]

Introduction

In this paper, we intend to demonstrate the feasibility and challenge of moving beyond "The Tragedy of the Commons" that Garrett Hardin presented in 1968. Hardin portrayed a set of pastoralists—who are inexorably led to overuse their common pasture—as an allegory for what he thought was typical for common-pool resources (CPRs) not owned privately or by a government. CPRs are normally used by multiple individuals and generate finite quantities of resource units where one person's use subtracts from the quantity of resource units available to others (Ostrom and Ostrom 1977). Most CPRs are sufficiently large that multiple actors can simultaneously use the resource system. Efforts to exclude potential beneficiaries are costly. Examples of CPRs include both natural and human-made systems including: Hardin's grazing lands, groundwater basins, irrigation systems, forests, fisheries, mainframe computers, government and corporate treasuries, and the Internet. Examples of resource units derived from CPRs are fodder, water, timber,

[*]Excerpted from "Beyond the Tragedy of the Commons," *Economia delle fonti di energia e dell' ambiente* no. 1 (2009): 35–60. Reprinted with permission.

computer-processing units, information bits, and budget allocations (Blomquist and Ostrom 1985).

In an effort to move beyond Hardin's classic allegory, it is important that one does not dismiss Hardin's predictions for some CPRs. The major problem of his original analysis was that he presented "the tragedy" as a universal phenomenon. No set of users could overcome the tragedy. Thus, CPR users were trapped needing external interventions to extract them from gross overuse. Hardin's presumption of universality is what one needs to move beyond.

Having said this, many field settings exist where Hardin is correct. Overharvesting frequently occurs when resource users are totally anonymous, do not have a foundation of trust and reciprocity, cannot communicate, and have no established rules. Massive overfishing of ocean fisheries and deforestation in many countries illustrate the destruction of resources that occurs when appropriate institutions have not been designed and implemented (Ostrom 2008a). In an experimental lab, eight subjects presented with a common-pool resource problem overharvest when they do not know who is in their group, no feedback is provided on individual actions, and they cannot communicate. . . . They do worse than game theory predicts and fit the behavior predicted by Hardin.

If the experimental subjects are enabled to sit in a circle talking about the puzzle in a face-to-face group, they usually develop trust and reciprocity. Within a few rounds, they reduce overharvesting substantially and do very well (Ostrom et al. 1992). In traditional, non-cooperative game theory, communication is not supposed to improve the outcomes obtained, but many groups solve the problem of overharvesting after engaging in face-to-face communication (Ostrom 2007a). Further, many smaller groups that use CPRs—inshore fisheries, forests, irrigation systems, and pastures—have developed a diversity of norms and rules that have enabled them to solve problems of overharvesting. A diversity of studies illustrate that it is not impossible to overcome the temptation to overharvest (NRC 1986, 2002; McCay and Acheson 1987; Berkes 1989; Dolšak and Ostrom 2003; Basurto 2005; Ostrom 2005; van Laerhoven and Ostrom 2007; Lansing 2008).

We need to build a theoretical foundation for explaining why some resource users are able to self-organize and govern the use of a resource over time in a sustainable manner and why others fail or never make the effort. To do this, we face core challenges to overcome two scholarly approaches adopted by many scholars that limit the development of a predictive theory that is useful in policy analysis. The first problem was stimulated by Hardin's analysis, and we call it the "panacea analytical trap." It treats all resources as having basic similarities. This trap has often led to a recommendation of a preferred institutional solution as a simplified blueprint. The second challenge is the "my-case-is-unique" analytical trap. This approach challenges the usefulness of building theoretical explanations about the fit between diverse types of institutions and local ecological and social settings. To build theory, it is necessary to move away from both extremes to develop an interdisciplinary diagnostic framework that helps to provide a foundation for further empirical research and learning (Bardhan and Ray 2008; Chopra 2008).

Avoiding the Panacea Analytical Trap

Historically, the cure-alls that have been recommended most frequently promote government ownership (Ophuls 1973; Feeny *et al.* 1996: 195) or privatization (Demsetz 1967; Posner 1977; Simmons *et al.* 1996). Panacea-type solutions can be a by-product of approaches that generate highly abstract models and use simple empirical studies to illustrate general patterns of social phenomena (Bouchaud 2008). For instance, since the important early studies of open-access fisheries by Gordon (1954) and Scott (1955), most theoretical studies by political economists have analyzed simple CPR systems using relatively similar assumptions (Feeny *et al.* 1996; Ruddle 2007; Ruddle and Hickey 2008). In such systems, it is assumed that the resource generates a highly predictable, finite supply of one type of resource unit (one species, for example) in each relevant time period. Resource users are assumed to be homogeneous in terms of their assets, skills, discount rates, and cultural views. Users are also assumed to be short-term, profit-maximizing actors who possess complete information. As a result, this theory universally assumes that anyone can enter the resource and harvest resource units. Users are viewed as able to gain property rights only to what they harvest, which they then sell in an open competitive market. Under this approach, the open-access condition is a given. The users make no effort to change it. Users act independently and do not communicate or coordinate their activities in any way. Textbooks in resource economics, and law and economics, present this conventional theory of a simple CPR as the only theory needed for understanding CPRs more generally (but, for a different approach, see Baland and Platteau 1996; Clark 2006).

This approach emphasizes collecting information on a large number of cases to be able to find the correlation of dependent and independent variables with a statistical degree of significance. This can come at the cost of being able to develop in-depth knowledge of each of the cases under study. Homogenization assumptions about the cases under consideration are often necessary to conduct quantitative analyses. In the process, the analyst risks losing track of the importance of context and history and faces challenges to be able to effectively convey the sense of complexity and diversity that exists in the empirical world. The basic theory discussed above was applied to all CPRs regardless of the capacity of resource users to communicate and coordinate their activities until the work of the National Academy of Sciences' Panel on Common Property (NRC 1986) strongly challenged this approach. The growing evidence from many qualitative studies of CPRs conducted in the field called for a serious rethinking of the theoretical foundations for the analysis of CPRs (Berkes 1986, 1989; Berkes *et al.* 1989; Bromley *et al.* 1992; McCay and Acheson 1987).

Avoiding the "My-Case-Is-Unique" Analytical Trap

The rich case-study literature has played a prominent role in illustrating the wide diversity of settings in which appropriators dependent on CPRs have organized themselves to achieve much higher outcomes than is predicted by the conventional theory (Cordell 1989; Wade 1994; Ruddle and Johannes 1985; Sengupta 1991). In being able to tap into the rich case-study literature, however, we also need to move beyond the argument that each resource system, and the people that use it, is unique. At one level, that assertion is true. All humans are unique, and all human organizations are unique as well as the ecological systems to which they relate. The problem comes from assuming that there are no commonalities across cases that can be the foundation for theoretical analysis, explanations, and diagnosis. Ecologists have long dealt with complex systems that at one level are unique (e.g., individual species), but are also able to move outward to larger systems (e.g., populations or ecosystems) and find commonalities among many different species and their behaviors. Medical diagnosis of illness and potential remedies is feasible even though each individual is unique.

Often, the scholarly treatment of social phenomena as unique is the by-product of training scholars in a research strategy that focuses first on understanding the complexity of social phenomena. Qualitative-oriented scholars, such as ethnographers and historians, are usually associated with this approach. Students of this tradition are often interested in understanding how different elements fit together to constitute a case. They examine many parts and attempt to construct a representation from the interconnections among the aspects of each case. In order to be able to do so, it is necessary to acquire in-depth knowledge about the instances under study. Researchers have developed appropriate data-gathering methods and analytical tools to do so. As a result, these scholars are able to uncover complex relationships between causal conditions and outcomes, showing the role that history, context or conjunctural causation can play in social phenomena. Often, the goal of this research approach is to describe how different aspects constitute the case as a whole, which may then be compared and contrasted with other cases. Given, however, the depth of data that scholars amass about each aspect of their case, qualitative scholars frequently work with one or a few cases at a time. Because of their familiarity with the complexity and in-depth understanding of the particularities of the instances that characterize certain phenomena, qualitative scholars tend to avoid making generalizations about their findings. In fact, generalizing statements about social phenomena is usually not the goal of qualitative research. Sometimes it is precisely the rarity of certain social phenomena, characterized by only one, two, or a handful of instances, that might attract a scholar's attention and curiosity to them in the first place (Ragin 2000, 2008).

The sole focus on such an intensive research tradition can also make it difficult to move beyond a conventional theory of CPRs and toward a more diagnostic approach to CPR management. . . . We agree that to build a diagnostic theory, it is important to better incorporate contextual factors into policy analyses. We also need to avoid falling into the presumption that all individual settings are so different from one another that all we can do is describe the intricate detail of particular settings. . . .

Toward a Diagnostic Theory of Common-Pool Resources

So, how can we start moving toward a diagnostic theory of common-pool resources? In the following sections, we provide an overview for how analysts can go about building a diagnostic theory to address two interrelated theoretical puzzles: (1) How do resource users self-organize or create the conditions for institutional change to overcome collective-action dilemmas? and (2) What are the conditions that enhance the sustainability of resources and the robustness of institutions over time?

A Multitier Diagnostic Framework

As a first point of departure, we draw on the multitier framework presented in a recent article in the *Proceedings of the National Academy of Sciences* on "A Diagnostic Approach for Going beyond Panaceas" (Ostrom 2007b). . . . In building a diagnostic CPR theory, scholars need to be aware of the extremely large potential set of variables that might be relevant for their studies. A promising way is to build a conceptual, ontological framework that organizes the relationships among the many variables, posits how they are causally related across scales and among themselves, where these variables are embedded within a system, and how those systems are linked to even larger systems. An ontological system is able to address the infinite regress problem, where a linguistic construction such as a concept is composed of sub-concepts, which are in turn composed of sub-concepts, and further sub-concepts.

The framework starts with a first tier of variables that scholars studying CPRs can use in studying any particular focal system, ranging in scale from a small inshore fishery to the global commons (Figure 5.1). A scholar would first identify which Resource System (RS) and its Resource Units (RU) are relevant for answering a particular question. These then become the focal system for analysis. . . .

FIGURE 5.1 **A multitier framework for analyzing a social-ecologocial system.**

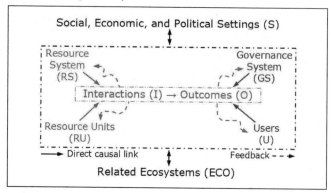

Source: Adapted from Ostrom (2007b: 15183)

To diagnose the causal patterns that affect outcomes such as successful formation of self-organization or its sustainability, one needs to incorporate a set of "second-tier" variables that are contained within the broadest tiers identified in Figure 5.1. The list of second-tier variables in Table 5.1 constitutes an initial effort to help group and classify important variables in a tiered ontology specific to the theoretical puzzles related to CPR problems posited above. It is obviously not "final," even though many scholars across disciplines have contributed to the design of the framework over the years. As we make progress in the development of a tiered ontology, and we gain a better understanding of how concepts are embedded and related with each other, the third, fourth, and fifth tiers of the framework will be further elucidated.

Building ontologies to diagnose policy problems and to design empirical research is a necessary step toward developing better conceptual language and theories. It is important to understand, however, that an analyst does not need to include fifty or more variables when studying CPRs. No one can develop a theory or do empirical research simultaneously that includes all of the second-tier variables (or the many lower-tier variables) that may be important factors affecting particular interactions and outcomes. This is definitely not the intention of this framework. The intention is to enable scholars, officials, and citizens to understand the potential set of variables and their sub-variables that could be causing a problem or creating a benefit. When we have a medical problem, a doctor will ask us a number of initial questions and do some regular measurements. In light of that information, the doctor proceeds down a medical ontology to ask further and more specific questions (or prescribes tests) until a reasonable hypothesis regarding the source of the problem can be found and supported. When we begin

TABLE 5.1 Second-tier variables in framework for analyzing a social-ecological system Resource System (RS)

SOCIAL, ECONOMIC, AND POLITICAL SETTINGS (S)
S1- Economic development. S2- Demographic trends. S3- Political stability. S4- Government resource policies. S5- Market incentives. S6- Media organization.

Resource System (RS)	Governance System (GS)
RS1- Sector (e.g., water, forests, pasture, fish) RS2- Clarity of system boundaries* RS3- Size of resource system* RS4- Human-constructed facilities RS5- Productivity of system RS5a. Indicators of the system* RS6- Equilibrium properties RS7- Predictability of system dynamics* RS8- Storage characteristics RS9- Location	GS1- Government organizations GS2- Non-government organizations GS3- Network structure GS4- Property-rights systems* GS5- Operational rules* GS6- Collective-choice rules* GS7- Constitutional rules* GS8- Monitoring & sanctioning processes*

Resource Units (RU)	Users (U)
RU1- Resource unit mobility* RU2- Growth or replacement rate RU3- Interaction among resource units RU4- Economic value RU5- Size RU6- Distinctive markings RU7- Spatial & temporal distribution	U1- Number of users* U2- Socioeconomic attributes of users U3- History of use U4- Location U5- Leadership/entrepreneurship* U6- Norms/social capital* U7- Knowledge of SES/mental models* U8- Dependence on resource* U9- Technology used*

Interactions (I)	Outcomes (O)
I1- Harvesting levels of diverse users* I2- Information sharing among users I3- Deliberation processes I4- Conflicts among users* I5- Investment activities I6- Lobbying activities	O1- Social performance measures (e.g., efficiency, equity, accountability) O2- Ecological performance measures* (e.g., overharvested, resilience, diversity) O3- Externalities to other SESs

RELATED ECOSYSTEMS (ECO)
ECO1- Climate patterns.   ECO2- Pollution patterns.   ECO3-Flows into and out of focal SES.

Source: Adapted from Ostrom (2007b: 15183)

to think about a particular problem, we need to begin to think about which of the attributes of a particular system are likely to have a major impact on particular patterns of interactions and outcomes. . . .

Toward a Theoretical Integration

The key to further theoretical integration is to understand how a subset of the second-tier variables—and some third-tier variables—listed below and starred in Table 5.1 interact in complex ways in specific settings to affect the basic benefit-cost calculations of a set of users (U) using a resource system (RS). We do not posit that any particular number of second- and third-tier variables discussed here always leads to success or failure in avoiding the tragedy of the commons. Rather, it is the overall combination of these factors that affects how participants judge the benefits and costs of new operational rules.[1] The attributes of resource systems that are potentially relevant include:

- Size of resource system (RS3): The CPR is sufficiently small, given communication and transportation technologies in use, that the users can acquire accurate knowledge about the boundaries and dynamics of the system.
- Productivity of system (RS5): The productivity of the CPR has not been exhausted nor is it so abundant that there is no need to organize.
- Predictability of system dynamics (RS7): The system dynamics are sufficiently predictable that users can estimate what would happen if they continued old rules or changed the rules and strategies in use.
- Indicators of the productivity of the system (RS5a): Reliable and valid indicators of CPR conditions are available at a low cost. The attributes of users that are potentially important include:
- Leadership (U5): Some users of a resource have skills of organizing and local leadership as a result of prior organization for other purposes or learning from neighboring groups.
- Norms/social capital (U6): Users have generally developed trust in one another so as to keep promises and return reciprocity with reciprocity.
- Knowledge of the social-ecological system (U7): Users share knowledge of relevant CPR attributes and how their own actions affect each other.
- Dependence on resource (U8): Users are dependent on the CPR for a major portion of their livelihood.

In analyzing a particular case, a core question is how the above factors affect the potential benefits and costs that users face in continuing present rules and strategies or changing them. One would posit that each user compares the expected net benefits of harvesting, using the old operational rules, with the benefits they expect to achieve using a new set of operational rules. Each user must ask whether their incentive to change is positive or negative.

If [the incentive to change is] negative for all users, no one has an incentive to change and no new rules will be established. If [the incentive is] positive for some users, they then need to estimate three types of costs:

- C1: Up-front costs of time and effort spent devising and agreeing upon new rules;
- C2: The short-term costs of implementing new rules; and
- C3: The long-term costs of monitoring and maintaining a self-governed system over time.

If the sum of these expected costs for each user exceeds the incentive to change, no user will invest the time and resources needed to create new institutions. . . .

Obviously, if one could obtain reliable and valid measures of the perceived benefits and costs of collective action, one would not need to examine how diverse resource systems and user characteristics affect likely organization. Gaining information about specific benefits and costs perceived by users at the time of collective-action decisions is, however, next to impossible. Thus, gaining information about the attributes of the resource system and the users, listed above, is an essential step in increasing our theoretical understanding of why some groups do overcome the challenge of collective action and others do not.

In field settings, everyone is not likely to expect the same costs and benefits from a proposed change. Some may perceive positive benefits after all costs have been taken into account, while others perceive net losses. Consequently, the collective-choice rules (GS6) used to change the day-to-day operational rules related to the resource affect whether an institutional change favored by some and opposed by others will occur. . . .

The collective-choice rule used to change operational rules in field settings varies from reliance on the decisions made by one or a few leaders, to a formal reliance on majority or super-majority vote, to reliance on consensus or near unanimity. If there are substantial differences in the perceived benefits and costs of users, it is possible that [a coalition of] users will impose a new set of rules that strongly favors those in the winning coalition and imposes losses or lower benefits on those in the losing coalition (Thompson *et al.* 1988). If expected benefits from a change in institutional arrangements are not greater than expected costs for many of the relevant participants, however, the costs of enforcing a change in institutions will be much higher than when most participants expect to benefit from a change in rules over time.

. . . This analysis is applicable to a situation where a group starts with an open-access situation and contemplates adopting its first set of rules limiting access. It is also relevant to the continuing consideration of changing operational rules over time.

Diagnostics for the Sustainability of Self-Organization

. . . [L]et us address the question of the sustainability of such self-organized systems. While some self-governed CPR systems are capable of surviving long periods of time, others falter and fail. The particular set of rules used by long-surviving, self-governing systems varies substantially from one another (Schlager 1994; Tang 1994; Ostrom 2005). After working with Schlager and Tang on the development of the CPR database, coding an extensive set of case studies of fishery and irrigation systems around the world (described in Ostrom *et al.* 1994), Ostrom tried to identify specific rules associated with robust systems. She searched a large number of cases to find specific institutions, such as government, private, or communal ownership, that were close to universally successful. After an extensive search and study, no specific set of rules was found to be associated with long-surviving CPR institutions. Instead, she proposed a set of eight design principles (listed in Table 5.2). Most of these principles are present in well-documented, long-lasting systems and are missing in failed systems.[2] Long-term sustainable self-organizations tend to be characterized by the presence of most of these design principles, while fragile institutions tend to be characterized by only some of them, and failed institutions by few (Ostrom 2008b). . . .

Let us be clear, a design principle is not a synonym for a "blueprint." We borrow the use of the term from architecture. When applied to institutional arrangements by design principle, we mean an "element or condition that helps to account for the success of these institutions in sustaining the [common-pool resources] and

TABLE 5.2   Design principles illustrated by long-enduring common-pool resource institutions

1. Clearly Defined Boundaries Individuals or households with rights to withdraw resource units from the common-pool resource, and the boundaries of the common-pool resource itself, are clearly defined.

2. Congruence
    A. The distribution of benefits from appropriation rules is roughly proportionate to the costs imposed by provision rules.
    B. Appropriation rules restricting time, place, technology, and quantity of resource units are related to local conditions.

3. Collective-Choice Arrangements Most individuals affected by operational rules can participate in modifying operational rules.
4. Monitoring Monitors, who actively audit common-pool resource conditions and user behavior, are accountable to the users or are the users themselves.
5. Sanctions Users who violate operational rules are likely to receive graduated sanctions (depending on the seriousness and context of the offense) from other users, from officials accountable to these users, or from both.
6. Conflict-Resolution Mechanisms Users and their officials have rapid access to low-cost, local arenas to resolve conflict among users or between users and officials.
7. Minimal Recognition of Rights to Organize The rights of users to devise their own institutions are not challenged by external governmental authorities.
For common-pool resources that are parts of larger systems: 8. Nested Enterprises Appropriation, provision, monitoring, enforcement, conflict resolution, and governance activities are organized in multiple layers of nested enterprises.

Source: Adapted from E. Ostrom (1990: 90)

gaining the compliance of generation after generation of appropriators to the rules in use" (Ostrom 1990: 90). The design principles work to enhance participants' shared understanding of the structure of the resource and its users and of the benefits and costs involved in following a set of agreed-upon rules. . . .

. . . Nested enterprises are particularly important for those CPRs that are part of larger systems, like coastal fisheries, where appropriation, provision, monitoring, enforcement, conflict resolution, and governance activities are organized in multiple institutional layers (Young 2002). . . . The importance of building appropriate nested enterprises for the sustainability of self-organization cannot be understated. In larger resources with many participants, nested enterprises that range in size from small to large enable participants to solve diverse problems involving different scale economies. In base institutions that are quite small, face-to-face communication can be utilized for solving many of the day-to-day problems in smaller groups. By nesting each level of organization in a larger level, externalities from one group to another can be addressed in larger organizational settings that have a legitimate role to play in relationship to the smaller entities.

Many variables in Table 5.1 that affect perceived costs and benefits of self-organization are strongly affected by the type of larger setting in which a resource and its users are embedded—particularly the type of resource policies adopted by the larger political regimes (S4). Larger regimes may facilitate local self-organization by providing accurate information about natural resource systems, arenas in which participants can engage in discovery and conflict-resolution processes, and mechanisms to back up local monitoring and sanctioning efforts. Perceived benefits of organizing are greater when users have accurate information about the threats facing a resource.

When the authority to make and enforce their own rules is not recognized, the costs of monitoring and sanctioning those who do not conform to these rules can be very high. The probability of participants adapting more effective rules in macro regimes that facilitate their efforts over time is higher than in regimes that ignore resource problems entirely or, at the other extreme, presume that all decisions about governance and management need to be made by central authorities. If local authorities are not formally recognized by larger regimes, it is very costly—if not impossible—for users to establish an enforceable set of rules. On the other hand, if external authorities impose rules without consulting local participants in their design, local users may engage in a game of "cops and robbers" with outside authorities.

Conclusion

In this paper, we have argued that one way in which we can go beyond Hardin's tragedy of the commons is by building a diagnostic theory of CPR management. We believe that it is fundamental to avoid falling into "panacea" or "my-case-is-unique" analytical traps. A diagnostic theory needs to be able to help us understand the complex interrelationship between social and biophysical factors at different levels of analysis. This understanding will be augmented if the rich detail produced from case studies is used together with theory to find patterned structures among cases.

When rich detail is [used] to argue that theoretical analysis focusing on more general variables is not useful, we will continue to fall into "my-case-is-unique" analytical traps. This does not enable scholars to move away from merely describing a particular case or region. Even worse, without a tested diagnostic theory, policy analysts cannot produce theoretically informed public policy that can form the basis of adaptive governance. We cannot forget, however, that uncovering patterns of commonalities and differences among cases without considering the role of context and history can lead to "panacea" analytical traps, such as those that have prevailed throughout the history of fisheries.

A quick view to such history shows that it is rich with examples of technical fixes like individual transferable quotas (ITQs), marine protected areas (MPAs), and community-based management (CBM). As Degnbol and colleagues (2006: 537) argue:

> each of the fixes may alone, or in combination with other management tools, be perfectly adequate and justified in specific situations where the context and management concerns match the assumptions and properties of these tools. But when they are promoted as universal remedies, they cease to be useful tools and enter the category of technical fixes, diverting attention away from the full range of potential solutions to a particular management problem. Fixes are not likely to adequately represent the complexity of a problem nor are they likely to solve a range of problems simultaneously.

Indeed, further development and testing of a diagnostic theory will not be an easy task. . . .

REFERENCES

Baland J.M., Platteau J.P., 1996, *Halting Degradation of Natural Resources: Is There a Role for Rural Communities?*, Clarendon Press, Oxford.

Bardhan P., Ray I., 2008, *The Contested Commons: Conversations between Economists and Anthropologists*, Blackwell Publishing, Oxford.

Bardhan P., Ray I., 2008, "Economists, anthropologists, and the contested commons," in P. Bardhan, I. Ray (eds), *The Contested Commons: Conversations between Economists and Anthropologists*, Blackwell Publishing, Oxford.

Basurto X., 2005, "How locally designed access and use controls can prevent the tragedy of the commons in a Mexican small-scale fishing community," *Journal of Society and Natural Resources* 18: 643–659.

Berkes F., 1986, "Local-level management and the commons problem: a comparative study of Turkish coastal fisheries," *Marine Policy* 10: 215–229.

Berkes F. (ed), 1989, *Common Property Resources: Ecology and Community-Based Sustainable Development*, Belhaven Press, London.

Berkes F., Feeny D., McCay B.J., Acheson J.M., 1989, "The benefits of the commons," *Nature* 340, no. 6229: 91–93.

Blomquist W., Ostrom E., 1985, "Institutional capacity and the resolution of a commons dilemma," *Policy Studies Review* 5, n. 2: 383–393.

Bouchaud J.P., 2008, "Economics needs a scientific revolution," *Nature* 455, n. 30: 1181.

Bromley D.W., Feeny D., McKean M., Peters P., Gilles J., Oakerson R., Runge C.F., Thomson J. (eds), 1992, *Making the Commons Work: Theory, Practice, and Policy*, ICS Press, San Francisco, CA.

Chopra K., 2008, "Commentary 4: disciplinary perspectives and policy design for common-pool resources," in P. Bardhan, I. Ray (eds), *The Contested Commons: Conversations between Economists and Anthropologists*, Blackwell Publishing, Oxford.

Clark C.C., 2006, *The Worldwide Crisis in Fisheries: Economic Models and Human Behavior*, Cambridge University Press.

Cordell J.C. (ed), 1989, *A Sea of Small Boats*, Cultural Survival, Inc., Cambridge, MA.

Costello C., Gaines S.D., Lynham J., 2008, "Can catch shares prevent fisheries collapse?," *Science* 321: 1678–1681.

Degnbol P., Gislason H., Hanna S., Jentoft S., Raakjær Nielsen J., Sverdrup-Jensen S., Wilson D.C., 2006, "Painting the floor with a hammer: technical fixes in fisheries management," *Marine Policy* 30: 534–543.

Demsetz H., 1967, "Toward a theory of property rights," *American Economic Review* 57: 347–359.

Dolšak N., Ostrom E. (eds), 2003, *The Commons in the New Millennium: Challenges and Adaptations*, MIT Press, Cambridge, MA.

Feeny D., Hanna S.S., McEvoy A.F., 1996, "Questioning the assumptions of the 'tragedy of the commons' model of fisheries," *Land Economics* 72: 187–205.

Felger R.S., Moser M.B., 1985, *People of the Desert and Sea: Ethnobotany of the Seri Indians*, University of Arizona Press, Tucson.

Gordon H.S., 1954, "The economic theory of a common property resource: the fishery," *Journal of Political Economy* 62: 124–142.

Lansing J.S., 2008, *Perfect Order: Recognizing Complexity in Bali*, Princeton University Press, Princeton, NJ.

McCay B.J., Acheson J.M., 1987, *The Question of the Commons: The Culture and Ecology of Communal Resources*, University of Arizona Press, Tucson.

NRC (National Research Council), 1986, *Proceedings of the Conference on Common Property Resource Management*, National Academy Press, Washington, DC.

NRC (National Research Council), 2002, *The Drama of the Commons*, Committee on the Human Dimensions of Global Change, E. Ostrom, T. Dietz, N. Dolšak, P. Stern, S. Stonich, E. Weber (eds), National Academy Press, Washington, DC.

Ophuls W., 1973, "Leviathan or oblivion," in: H.E. Daly (ed), *Toward a Steady State Economy*, Freeman, San Francisco, CA.

Ostrom E., 1990, *Governing the Commons: The Evolution of Institutions for Collective Action*, Cambridge University Press, New York.

Ostrom E., 2005, *Understanding Institutional Diversity*, Princeton University Press, Princeton, NJ.

Ostrom E., 2007a, "Collective action and local development processes," *Sociologica* 3: 1–32.

Ostrom E., 2007b, "A diagnostic approach for going beyond panaceas," *PNAS* 104, n. 39: 15181–15187.

Ostrom E., 2008a, "The challenge of common-pool resources," *Environment* 50, n. 4: 8–20.

Ostrom E. 2008b, "Design principles of robust property-rights institutions: what have we learned," paper presented at the conference on "Land Policies and Property Rights," Lincoln Institute of Land Policy, Cambridge, MA, June 2–3, 2008.

Ostrom E., Gardner R., Walker J., 1994, *Rules, Games, and Common-Pool Resources*, University of Michigan Press, Ann Arbor.

Ostrom E., Walker J., Gardner R., 1992, "Covenants with and without a sword: self-governance is possible," *American Political Science Review* 86, n. 2: 404–417.

Ostrom V., Ostrom E., 1977, "Public goods and public choices," in: E. S. Savas (ed), *Alternatives for Delivering Public Services: Toward Improved Performance*, Westview Press, Boulder, CO. Reprinted in: M. McGinnis (ed), *Polycentricity and Local Public Economies: Readings from the Workshop in Political Theory and Policy Analysis*, University of Michigan Press, Ann Arbor, 1999.

Posner R.A., 1977, *Economic Analysis of Law*, 2nd ed., Little, Brown, Boston, MA.

Ragin C.C., 2000, *Fuzzy-Sets Social Science*, University of Chicago Press, Chicago, IL.

Ragin C.C., 2008, *Redesigning Social Inquiry: Fuzzy Sets and Beyond*, University of Chicago Press, Chicago, IL.

Ruddle K., 2007, "Misconceptions, outright prejudice," Samudra report no. 48, *Samudra: The Triannual Journal of the International Collective in Support of Fishworkers*, International Collective in Support of Fishworkers, Chennai, India.

Ruddle K., Hickey F.R., 2008, "Accounting for the mismanagement of tropical nearshore fisheries," *Environment, Development, and Sustainability* 10: 565–589.

Ruddle K., Johannes R.E. (eds), 1985, *The Traditional Knowledge and Management of Coastal Systems in Asia and the Pacific*, Unesco, Jakarta.

Schlager E., 1994, "Fishers' institutional responses to common-pool resource dilemmas," in: E. Ostrom, R. Gardner, J. Walker (eds), *Rules, Games, and Common-Pool Resources*, University of Michigan Press, Ann Arbor.

Scott A.D., 1955, "The fishery: the objectives of sole ownership," *Journal of Political Economy* 63: 116–124.

Sengupta N., 1991, *Managing Common Property: Irrigation in India and the Philippines*, Sage, New Delhi.

Simmons R.T., Smith Jr. F.L., Georgia P., 1996, *The Tragedy of the Commons Revisited: Politics versus Private Property*, Center for Private Conservation, Washington, DC.

Tang S.Y., 1994, "Institutions and performance in irrigation systems," in: E. Ostrom, R. Gardner, J. Walker (eds), *Rules, Games, and Common-Pool Resources*, University of Michigan Press, Ann Arbor.

Thompson L.L., Mannix E.A., Bazerman M.H., 1988, "Group negotiation: effects of decision rule, agenda, and aspiration," *Journal of Personality and Social Psychology* 54, n. 1: 86–95.

van Laerhoven F., Ostrom E., 2007, "Traditions and trends in the study of the commons," *International Journal of the Commons* 1, n. 1: 3–28.

Wade R., 1994, *Village Republics: Economic Conditions for Collective Action in South India*, ICS Press, San Francisco, CA.

Young O.R., 2002, *The Institutional Dimensions of Environmental Change: Fit, Interplay, and Scale*, MIT Press, Cambridge, MA.

NOTES

1. Researchers who are interested in understanding collective action to overcome CPR dilemmas in the field should try to obtain empirical measures for this set of variables in their efforts to understand why some groups organize and others do not. In some settings, other variables will also be important and some of these will play no role, but given the role of this set of variables in affecting the benefits and costs of collective action, they constitute an important set of variables potentially able to explain collective action successes and failures.

2. Costello *et al.* (2008) have a new analysis of fisheries that does provide strong support for a variety of Individual Transferable Quota (ITQ) systems to be associated with reduced likelihood of the collapse of valuable commercial fisheries, but the specific ways that successful ITQ systems have been designed and implemented vary substantially from each other.

6

THE 1992 EARTH SUMMIT: REFLECTIONS ON AN AMBIGUOUS EVENT

Ken Conca and Geoffrey D. Dabelko

For twelve days in June 1992, nearly ten thousand official delegates from 150 nations converged on Rio de Janeiro, Brazil, for the United Nations Conference on Environment and Development (UNCED). At the same time, thousands of activists, organizers, and concerned citizens of the planet gathered for a parallel Global Forum held on the other side of the city. The entire spectacle, often referred to as the "Earth Summit," was covered by more than eight thousand journalists.

It was clear at the time, and remains the case today, more than twenty years later, that the Rio summit marked an unprecedented flurry of activity in global environmental governance. Governments debated, and in most cases signed, an array of official documents: a set of general principles on environment and development known as the Rio Declaration; a several-hundred-page "action plan" for the twenty-first century known as "Agenda 21"; international treaties on climate and biodiversity; an agreement to work toward an international treaty on desertification; and a nonbinding Statement of Forest Principles. Activist groups also generated declarations. For example, a coalition including Greenpeace International, the Forum of Brazilian NGOs, Friends of the Earth International, and the Third World Network sponsored a "10-point plan to save the Earth Summit," challenging governments to embrace legally binding limits on pollutant emissions, to confront the problem of the North's overconsumption, and to rein in harmful transnational economic practices.[1]

Yet the historical legacy of the event remains contested. Was it a global town meeting or a closed-door reunion of political and economic elites? An important step toward institutionalizing global environmental governance or a failure of will? A watershed for a new era, a triumph of business as usual, or simply an irrelevant distraction? Historians, activists, and others continue to debate its significance.

In this chapter, we have gathered a series of observations made at the time of the meeting itself, from a diverse group of participants, observers, advocates, and critics. Our goal is to give readers a sense of the contestation about the meaning of such an event, even as it is unfolding. These perspectives will help us think through the meaning of other key events—be it the annual Conference of the Parties to an international treaty, an activist gathering such as PowerShift or the World Social Forum, or another summit spectacle such as Rio+20 (see the selections by Halle and Khor in Part Three). We present these quotes as opposing viewpoints not to suggest that these are the only perspectives available but rather to show that the event was interpreted, in real time, in radically different ways.

On the power of UNCED's ideas:

In our opinion, as philosophers, the details of the treaties, and whether they were signed by all the parties to the negotiations, will fade in importance. Of lasting importance will be the monumentality of the event itself and the institutionalization of an idea. In June of 1992, in Rio de Janeiro, virtually all of the world's heads of state met for the first time—ever—not to create or dismantle military alliances, not to discuss currency and banking reform, and not to set up rules of world trade, but to try to agree to care for the planet's biosphere. And the idea that was ratified, however little agreement was achieved on how to implement it, is this: Environment and development are inextricably linked. Human economies are subsystems of natural economies. Hence, genuine economic development—sustainable development—cannot be achieved without safeguarding the environmental infrastructures in which human economies are embedded.[2]

—J. Baird Callicott and Fernando J. R. da Rocha, professors of philosophy (United States and Brazil, respectively)

Even as the Earth Summit opened eyes to the need for new North-South discussions, it perpetuated myths about who is to blame for the problems and what steps to take. . . . By the end of the Earth Summit, many participants and journalists were articulating a simple equation to explain the complex relationship between environment and development: Poverty causes environmental degradation. They portrayed rich countries and wealthy people as environmentalists pressing for curbs on tropical deforestation to combat global climate change. They saw developing countries and poor people as fixated on survival and basic development issues—and if exploitation of natural resources contributed to those goals, so be it. . . . By accepting . . . myths about growth, aid, and the poor, negotiators at the Earth Summit conveniently avoided two of the central barriers to reversing environmental degradation across the planet: the widespread inequalities that characterize natural-resource ownership in much of the world and the environmentally destructive tendencies of large corporations in a deregulated world economy.[3]

> —ROBIN BROAD of American University and JOHN CAVANAGH
> of the Institute for Policy Studies (Washington, DC)

On whether UNCED marked a new era in global environmental politics:

In retrospect, there are two observations that stand out as to what happened in Rio. Firstly, this was not a conference about the environment at all; it concerned the world's economy and how the environment affects it. This in itself is a mammoth step forward as politicians come to understand that the issues do not just concern plants and animals, but life itself. Secondly, this was the first meeting of world leaders since the end of the Cold War. The old East-West agenda is dead, attention is now focused on North and South. Rio not only marked the beginning of a new era but a triumph for that small band of campaigners who set out at Stockholm.[4]

> —RICHARD SANDBROOK, executive director of the
> International Institute for Environment and Development (UK)

The Earth Summit showed that unless one deals with political reality, the most impressive statements, agendas, and manifestos will come to nothing. Unfortunately, it was precisely at the political level that the summit was least successful. Getting agreement, in principle, on protecting the environment, on saving human life, on increasing the share of global prosperity to the poorer peoples of the world is relatively simple. . . . The difficulty lies in achieving action. It is at this stage that one hears the global version of the old workplace argument, it is too expensive, it will cost jobs, the electorate would not stand for it. The message, despite grand speeches, appears to be "business as usual" for many governments and businesses.[5]

> —REG GREEN, International Federation of
> Chemical, Energy, and General Workers' Unions

On UNCED as an exercise in global governance:

Where the Rio Conference took a quantum leap forward . . . was in recognizing that the interactions among sectors, and the intertwined nature of economic, social, and environmental trends warranted a new approach to defining and organizing tasks, both at the national level and internationally. . . . The Rio Conference has called for institutions that can expose policy and programme interactions in the planning stages, in order to anticipate and avoid conflicts that might arise later. It has also sought to open these processes to all affected constituencies and major groups, so as to better "ground-truth" the policies and increase the stake of those who can make them work.[6]

> —LEE A. KIMBALL, senior associate at the
> World Resources Institute (Washington, DC)

The best that can be said for the Earth Summit is that it made visible the vested interests standing in the way of the moral economies which local people, who daily face the consequences of environmental degradation, are seeking to re-establish. The spectacle of the great and the good at UNCED casting about for "solutions" that will keep their power and standards of living intact has confirmed the skepticism of those whose fate and livelihoods were being determined. The demands from many grassroots groups around the world are not for more "management"—a fashionable word at Rio—but for agrarian reform, local control over local resources, and power to veto developments and to run their own affairs. For them, the question is not *how* their environment should be managed—they have the experience of the past as their guide—but *who* will manage it and in *whose* interest.[7]

—The Ecologist (UK)

On the debate between the governments of North and South:

The Earth Summit has brought to a final resolution the age-old debate between economic development and protection of the environment. It used to be fashionable to argue in the developing countries that their priority should be economic development and that, if necessary, the environment should be sacrificed in order to achieve high economic growth. The sentiment was to get rich first and to clean up the environment later. Some leaders of the developing countries even accused the developed countries of using the environment as a weapon to retard their economic progress. Such rhetoric and mindset belong to the past. Today, developing countries understand the need to integrate environment into their development policies. At the same time, developed countries have become increasingly aware of the need to cut down on their wasteful consumption patterns. There is growing understanding between the environment community and the development community. They realise that they must seek mutual accommodation. The new wisdom is that we want economic progress but we also want to live in harmony with nature. To be sure, governments have to make hard choices and there are trade-offs between the two objectives. But, since the Earth Summit, it is no longer possible to talk about development without considering its impact on the environment.[8]

—Tommy Koh, diplomat who chaired the UNCED's
Main Committee (Singapore)

Unlike what the term suggests, the global as it emerged in the discussions and debates around the UN Conference on Environment and Development . . . was not about universalism or about a planetary consciousness. The life of all people, including the poor of the Third World, or the life of the planet, are not at the center of concern in international negotiations on global environmental issues.

The "global" in the dominant discourse is the political space in which a particular dominant local seeks global control, and frees itself of local, national, and international restraints. . . . The seven most powerful countries, the G-7, dictate global affairs, but the interests that guide them remain narrow, local and parochial. . . . The North's slogan at UNCED and the other global negotiation fora seems to be: "What's yours is mine. What's mine is mine."[9]

—VANDANA SHIVA, scholar and activist (India)

On the openness of the UNCED process:

The important, indeed vital, role which NGOs and social movements have to play in international negotiations has been broadened through the UNCED process. UN procedures will never be the same again.[10]

—WANGARI MAATHAI, Greenbelt Movement (Kenya)

[The summit] has attempted to involve otherwise powerless people of society in the process. But by observing the process we now know how undemocratic and untransparent the UN system is. Those of us who have watched the process have said that UNCED has failed. As youth we beg to differ. Multinational corporations, the United States, Japan, the World Bank, the International Monetary Fund have got away with what they always wanted, carving out a better and more comfortable future for themselves.[11]

—WAGAKI MWANGI, International Youth Environment and Development Network, Nairobi (Kenya)

On the effectiveness of NGOs at UNCED:

Through the mass media, UNCED was able to focus attention on the emerging environmental and developmental problems in a manner that was inconceivable even a few years ago. . . . NGOs helped create a "civil society" at the discussions, they managed to keep a check on diplomats from their own and even other countries. They were often better informed and more articulate than government representatives, and better at obtaining and disseminating information than were the journalists themselves. They also engaged themselves in writing and speaking openly and forcefully on the issues involved, and lastly they were also more capable of creating the drama which makes good copy. For all these reasons, the eyes of the world became focused on the event, and therefore on the ideas behind the event.[12]

—TARIQ BANURI, executive director, Sustainable Development Policy Institute (Islamabad, Pakistan)

Quite logically, the UNCED process sought to divide, co-opt, and weaken the green movement, a process for which the movement itself has some responsibility. On the one hand UNCED brought every possible NGO into the system of lobbying governments, while on the other it quietly promoted business to take over the solutions. Non-governmental organizations (NGOs) are now trapped in a farce: they have lent support to governments in return for some small concessions on language and thus legitimized the process of increased industrial development. The impact of the lobbying was minimal, while that of the compromise will be vast, as NGOs have come to legitimize a process that is in essence contrary to what many of them have been fighting for for years.[13]

> —MATTHIAS FINGER, co-author with Pratap Chatterjee of
> *The Earth Brokers: Power, Politics and World Development*

On North-South cooperation among NGOs:

The UNCED process forged new and stronger links between Northern and Southern groups, between development and environmental activists. It would now be difficult for environmentalists to stick to wildlife issues or population, without simultaneously addressing international equity and global power structures. A major step forward has been the increasing involvement of Northern-based environment groups like Greenpeace, WWF, and Friends of the Earth in economic issues such as terms of trade, debt, and aid.[14]

> —MARTIN KHOR, president, Third World Network (Malaysia)

Negotiations between the NGOs at UNCED were certainly not as difficult as the official negotiations, but they were hardly easy, and it requires little imagination to foresee the depth of disputes had they been negotiating real policy and trying to take account of the full range of viewpoints and affected parties (for example by including NGOs from industry or trade unions).[15]

> —MICHAEL GRUBB, MATTHIAS KOCH, ABBY MUNSON,
> FRANCIS SULLIVAN, and KOY THOMSON, scholars and
> co-authors of *The Earth Summit Agreements: A Guide and Assessment*

On UNCED's legacy:

If historians in the 21st century have the fortunate task of explaining how global society was capable of solving the intertwined problems of environment and development, UNCED will undoubtedly figure prominently in their accounts. The conference has laid a foundation with which governments and other social actors will be able to pressure each other to maintain a high level of commitment to environmental protection and development; it established institutions and informal networks that will facilitate the striking of effective agreements; and it added momentum to the building of national capacity in weak governments. Moreover, it endorsed a tightly linked policy agenda that reflects the complex ecological and sociopolitical links among various human activities and between human activities and the environment. As governments are swayed by the array of international pressures that UNCED helped to reinforce, more comprehensive and holistic public policies for sustainable development will follow.[16]

> —scholars PETER M. HAAS, MARC A. LEVY, and EDWARD A. PARSON (US)

The United Nations Conference on Environment and Development, the self-styled Earth Summit, finished where it began. After ten days of press conferences, tree-planting ceremonies and behind-the-scenes wheeling and dealing, the diplomats went home to their various other assignments and the politicians to their next round of international talks. Rio gave way to the Munich conference and the more familiar territory of GATT, G-7 power politics and interest rates. . . . Unwilling to question the desirability of economic growth, the market economy, or the development process itself, UNCED never had a chance of addressing the real problems of "environment and development." Its secretariat provided delegates with materials for a convention on biodiversity but not on free trade; on forests but not on logging; on climate but not on automobiles. Agenda 21—the Summit's "action plan"—featured clauses on "enabling the poor to achieve sustainable livelihoods" but none on enabling the rich to do so; a section on women but none on men. By such deliberate evasion of the central issues which economic expansion poses for human societies, UNCED condemned itself to irrelevance even before the first preparatory meeting got underway.[17]

—The Ecologist

NOTES

1. See Pratap Chatterjee and Matthias Finger, *The Earth Brokers: Power, Politics and World Development* (London: Routledge, 1994), pp. 39–40.

2. J. Baird Callicott and Fernando J. R. da Rocha, eds., *Earth Summit Ethics: Toward a Reconstructive Postmodern Philosophy of Environmental Education* (Albany, NY: SUNY Press, 1996), pp. 3–4.

3. Robin Broad and John Cavanagh, "Beyond the Myths of Rio: A New American Agenda for the Environment," *World Policy Journal,* vol. 10, no. 1 (Spring 1993), pp. 65–72.

4. Richard Sandbrook, "From Stockholm to Rio," in *Earth Summit '92: The United Nations Conference on Environment and Development* (London: Regency Press, 1992), p. 16.

5. Reg Green, "Priorities for the Future," *Earth Summit '92,* p. 35.

6. Lee A. Kimball, "The Institutions Debate," *Earth Summit '92,* p. 38.

7. The Ecologist, *Whose Common Future? Reclaiming the Commons* (Philadelphia: New Society Publishers, 1993), p. 2.

8. Tommy Koh, "Five after Rio and Fifteen Years after Montego Bay: Some Personal Reflections," *Environmental Policy and Law,* vol. 27, no. 4 (1997), p. 242.

9. Vandana Shiva, "The Greening of the Global Reach," in Wolfgang Sachs, ed., *Global Ecology: A New Arena of Political Conflict* (London: Zed Books, 1993), pp. 149–150 and 152.

10. Wangari Maathi, "A Growing Strength," *Earth Summit '92,* p. 37.

11. Wagaki Mwangi as quoted in Chatterjee and Finger, *The Earth Brokers,* p. 167. Original source: *Third World Resurgence,* no. 24/25, 1992, p. 27.

12. Tariq Banuri, "The Landscape of Diplomatic Conflicts," in Sachs, *Global Ecology,* p. 63.

13. Matthias Finger, "Politics of the UNCED Process," in Sachs, *Global Ecology,* p. 36.

14. Martin Khor as quoted in Chatterjee and Finger, *The Earth Brokers,* p. 99. Original source: *Third World Resurgence,* no. 24/25, 1992, p. 4.

15. Michael Grubb, Matthias Koch, Abby Munson, Francis Sullivan, and Koy Thomson, *The Earth Summit Agreements: A Guide and Assessment* (London: Earthscan Publications, 1993), p. 46.

16. Peter M. Haas, Marc A. Levy, and Edward A. Parson, "Appraising the Earth Summit: How Should We Judge UNCED's Success?" *Environment,* vol. 34, no. 8 (October 1992).

17. The Ecologist, *Whose Common Future?,* p. 1.

7

FIGHT FOR THE FOREST

CHICO MENDES (WITH TONY GROSS)*

Building Bridges

We realized that in order to guarantee the future of the Amazon we had to find a way to preserve the forest while at the same time developing the region's economy.

So what were our thoughts originally? We accepted that the Amazon could not be turned into some kind of sanctuary that nobody could touch. On the other hand, we knew it was important to stop the deforestation that is threatening the Amazon and all human life on the planet. We felt our alternative should involve preserving the forest, but it should also include a plan to develop the economy. So we came up with the idea of extractive reserves.

What do we mean by an extractive reserve? We mean the land is under public ownership but the rubber tappers and other workers that live on that land should have the right to live and work there. I say "other workers" because there are not only rubber tappers in the forest. In our area, rubber tappers also harvest Brazil nuts, but in other parts of the Amazon there are people who earn a living solely from harvesting nuts, while there are others who harvest babaçu and jute. . . .

Where did we get the idea of setting up the CNS [National Council of Rubber Tappers]? We discovered there is something called the National Rubber Council which represents the interests of landowners and businessmen but not the interests of the rubber tappers, so we thought, why not create an organization as a counterweight to all that bureaucracy and try to stop the government messing the rubber

*Excerpted from Chico Mendes with Tony Gross, *Fight for the Forest: Chico Mendes in His Own Words* (London: Latin America Bureau, 1989). Reprinted with permission.

tappers about? The First National Congress set up the CNS and elected a provisional executive committee.

The CNS is not meant to be a kind of parallel trade union, replacing the Xapuri Rural Workers' Union, for example. [Editors' note: Xapuri is the town where Mendes lived and worked until his assassination in December 1988. It is located in the western Amazonian state of Acre, near the Brazilian border with Bolivia.] It is just an organization for rubber tappers. The growth of the trade unions was very important for us, but other agricultural workers including day laborers and so on are also members of the same union. Other kinds of agricultural workers have been seen as having particular needs and interests, but not rubber tappers; it's as though we were something that existed only in the past. So one of the reasons for creating the CNS was to recognize the rubber tappers as a particular group of workers fighting for a very important objective—the defense of the Amazon forest. The idea went down very well.

The Indians

We also wanted to seek out the leaders of the Indian peoples in Acre and discuss how to unite our resistance movements, especially since Indians and rubber tappers have been at odds with each other for centuries. In Acre the leaders of the rubber tappers and Indian peoples met and concluded that neither of us was to blame for this. The real culprits were the rubber estate owners, the bankers and all the other powerful interest groups that had exploited us both.

People understood this very quickly, and from the beginning of 1986 the alliance of the peoples of the forest got stronger and stronger. Our links with the Indians have grown even further this year. For example, a meeting of the Tarauacá rubber tappers was attended by 200 Indians and six of them were elected to the Tarauacá Rubber Tappers' Commission. Indians are now beginning to participate in the CNS organizing commissions. In Cruzeiro do Sul about 200 Indians are active in the movement and this year they have even joined in our *empates*. [Editors' note: The term *empate* means "tie" or "standoff" in Portuguese. It refers here to a common tactic of the movement in which local people physically occupy the area threatened by deforesters. The goals are to inhibit the destruction of the forest and to convince the workers involved in deforestation that their interests lie in forest preservation.]

Our proposals are now not just ours alone, they are put forward together by Indians and rubber tappers. Our fight is the fight of all the peoples of the forest.

When the Minister of Agriculture met a joint commission of Indians and rubber tappers in his office, he was really taken aback. "What's going on?" he said. "Indians and rubber tappers have been fighting each other since the last century! Why is it that today you come here together?"

We told him things had changed and this meant the fight to defend the Amazon was stronger. People really took notice of that. . . .

The Landowners Strike Back

We know we face powerful opposition. As well as the landowners and business-men who dominate the Amazon region, we are up against the power of those who voted against land reform in the Constituent Assembly. The voting power of these people in Congress has been a problem for us and has encouraged the growth of the right-wing landowners' movement, the Rural Democratic Union (UDR). The defeat of the land reform proposal was a big victory for the landowners and land speculators. Now, since the establishment of the UDR in Acre, we've got a real fight on our hands. However, we also believe our movement has never been stronger.

You can already see how strong the UDR is in Acre—it's just organized its first cattle auction to raise funds. We know, through people who have been to UDR meetings here, that their aim is to destroy the Xapuri union by striking at the grass-roots organizations of the Xapuri rubber tappers. They think if they can defeat Xapuri they can impose their terms on the whole state and further afield in the Amazon region as well. The Governor of Acre himself told me this. Just to give you an idea, it was after the UDR's official launch here in Acre that the first drops of blood were spilt in Xapuri. . . .

The Government Takes Sides

There was a time when the state government seemed to be paying a lot of attention to environmental problems and to the rubber tappers. But we soon realized it was just putting on a show of defending the environment so the international banks and other international organizations would approve its development projects.

We can't see how the authorities can say they defend the ecological system while at the same time deploying police to protect those who are destroying the forest. That happened, for example, in the case of the Ecuador rubber estate where there were many nut and rubber trees. The Governor was warned several times about what was going on there. In fact, I personally warned him and suggested he go and look at what was happening for himself. I told him he was being very hasty in sending police there. Fifty acres of virgin forest were cut down, but thanks to the pressure, thanks to the hundreds of telegrams sent to the Governor by national and international organizations, we managed to get him to withdraw the police from the area and so saved about 300 hectares of forest.

In the area they destroyed there, the last harvest produced 1,400 cans of Brazil nuts, a good crop. We challenged the owner of the land and the Governor himself to work out the annual income per hectare produced by forest products such as

Brazil nuts and rubber and then compare it with that produced by grazing cattle there. They refused because they knew we could prove the income from one hectare of forest is 20 times greater than when the forest is cleared and given over to cattle.

We quoted decree law 7.511 of 30 July 1986 and regulation 486 of 28 October 1986 which prohibit the cutting down and sale of Brazil nut and rubber trees and the deforestation of hillsides. There were two hillsides in the area being cut down on the Ecuador rubber estate and the law was completely flouted. After the second *empate,* when the rubber tappers managed to stop work going ahead, the local IBDF [Brazilian Forestry Development Institute] representative appeared and without even inspecting what was going on, told the landowner he could go ahead and clear the forest. He gave the landowner a license even though the landowner did not present, as he should have done, a written plan for managing the area.

Another law—I can't remember its number—says you can only clear up to 50 hectares of forest without presenting a forestry management plan. Further on it adds that it's forbidden to cut down any area of forest on hillsides or where there is a concentration of Brazil nut and rubber trees. None of these laws were respected. The Governor himself didn't even consider them and the IBDF certainly didn't.

We do have a good relationship with the Acre Technology Foundation (FUN-TAC) which is a state government agency. They really understand how difficult the lives of rubber tappers are and recognize that deforestation is a problem. But despite the good relationship we've got with FUNTAC, we have no confidence left in the state government. How can we believe a Governor who says he defends the forest, and visits Rio and Japan to talk about defending the forest, but who then orders the police to go and protect the people who are destroying it? He ought to be using the political power that his office gives him. If he used his power in favor of the workers he'd certainly get their support. . . .

The rubber tappers aren't saying that nobody should lay a finger on the Amazon. No. We've got our own proposals for organizing production. The rubber tappers and the Indians have always grown their subsistence crops but they've never threatened the existence of the forest. It's the deforestation carried out by the big landowners to open up pasture for their cattle that is threatening the forest. Often, these people are just speculating with the land. What happens in Xapuri and other parts of the Amazon is that these people cut down 10,000 hectares, turn half of it into pasture for their cattle and let the other half grow wild. They are really just involved in land speculation.

The landowners use all the economic power at their disposal. They bribe the authorities; it's common knowledge that they've bought off the IBDF staff in the Amazon region. They also use the law. They request police protection for the workers hired to cut down the trees, saying it is their land so they can do whatever they like with it. They accuse the rubber tappers of trespassing when we try and stop the deforestation. They turn to the courts for support and protection, claiming the land is private property. But the rubber tappers have been here for centuries!

There has been less pressure from the police in the last two years because we are able to present reasoned arguments to them. When we organize an *empate,* the main argument we use is that the law is being flouted by the landowners and our *empate* is only trying to make sure the law is respected.

The other tactic the landowners use, and it's a very effective one, is to use hired guns to intimidate us. Our movement's leaders, not just myself but quite a few others as well, have been threatened a lot this year. We are all on the death list of the UDR's assassination squads. Here in Xapuri, these squads are led by Darlí and Alvarino Alves da Silva, owners of the Paraná and other ranches round here. They lead a gang of about 30 gunmen—I say 30 because we've counted them as they patrol the town. Things have changed recently because we managed to get an arrest warrant issued in Umuarama, in the state of Paraná, for the two of them. I don't know whether it was the federal police, but somebody tipped them off. Now they're both in hiding and have said they'll only give themselves up when I'm dead.

We are sure this will be the landowners' main tactic from now on. They are going to fight our movement with violence and intimidation. There's no doubt in our minds about that. The level of violence that has been common in the south of the state of Pará is already spreading to Xapuri, to Acre.

8

TWO AGENDAS ON AMAZON DEVELOPMENT

Coordinating Body for the Indigenous Peoples' Organizations of the Amazon Basin (COICA)*

For Bilateral and Multilateral Funders

(This document is addressed to the World Bank, the Inter-American Development Bank, the US Agency International Development, and the European Economic Community.)

We, the Indigenous Peoples, have been an integral part of the Amazon Biosphere for millennia. We have used and cared for the resources of that biosphere with a great deal of respect, because it is our home, and because we know that our survival and that of our future generations depends on it. Our accumulated knowledge about the ecology of our home, our models for living with the peculiarities of the Amazon Biosphere, our reverence and respect for the tropical forest and its other inhabitants, both plant and animal, are the keys to guaranteeing the future of the Amazon Basin, not only for our peoples, but also for all of humanity.

What COICA Wants

1. The most effective defense of the Amazonian Biosphere is the recognition and defense of the territories of the region's Indigenous Peoples and the promotion of their models for living within that Biosphere and for managing its resources in

*Originally published in *Cultural Survival Quarterly* vol. 13 no. 4 (1989): 75–78. Reprinted with permission.

a sustainable way. The international funders of Amazonian development should educate themselves about the Indigenous Peoples' relationship with their environment, and formulate new concepts of Amazonian development together with new criteria for supporting Amazonian development projects which would be compatible with the Indigenous Peoples' principles of respect and care for the world around them, as well as with their concern for the survival and well-being of their future generations.

2. The international funders must recognize the rights of Indigenous Peoples as those are being defined within the Working Group on Indigenous Peoples, established by the UN Human Rights Commission. These rights should form the basis of the institution's policy towards the Indigenous Peoples and their territories who live in those areas where the funder is supporting development work. The funders should consult directly with the organizations of the Indigenous Peoples throughout the process of establishing this policy and should distribute that policy widely among governments and the organizations of Indigenous Peoples.

3. There can be no development projects in indigenous areas without the informed consent of the Indigenous Peoples affected. The funders must make every effort, through field research conducted by personnel of the funding institution, to verify the existence of an indigenous population, or the possible negative impact on an indigenous population, in areas where they are considering the implementation of a project. If either is the case, the funder must openly recognize the existence of this population or the negative impact on them, and then should establish as a condition for further funding the project

- that the government responsible for implementing the project also recognize the existence of the population and/or the negative impact;
- that the affected population be informed of the plans and impact of the plans; and
- that the affected population consent to the implementation of the plans.

These conditions should be monitored by both the funder and the organization which represents the affected population.

4. If the indigenous population has given its informed consent to the implementation of a development project within its territory, the project must be designed in such a way that it respects the territories of the population as they define them, their economy and their social organization, according to the institutional policy as described in Point One. There should be special components of the project which lend support directly to the indigenous population for their own needs and for the development proposals which they may have. The organization which represents the affected population should participate in the design of the project.

5. The international funders should enter into a direct relation of collaboration and mutual respect with the organizations of Indigenous Peoples, through their representatives. This relation should establish the basis for:

- *consultations* on all aspects of projects implemented in areas with an indigenous population or which have an impact on an indigenous population;
- *participation* of representatives of Indigenous Peoples in the planning, implementation, and evaluation of projects;
- *exchange* of information of mutual interest on plans, projects, activities, and needs of both. . . .

Indigenous Peoples' Alternatives for Amazonian Development

An important task of the Coordinating Body is to present to the international community the alternatives which we Indigenous Peoples offer for living with the Amazonian Biosphere, caring for it and developing within it. This is one of our important contributions to a better life for humankind. The following represent, in general terms, our program for the defense of the Amazonian Biosphere.

1. The best defense of the Amazonian Biosphere is the defense of the territories recognized as homeland by Indigenous Peoples, and their promotion of our models for living within that biosphere and for managing its resources. This implies:

- education for the national and international communities regarding the Indigenous Peoples' concept of the unity between people and territory, and regarding our models for managing and caring for our environment.
- work with national governments, environmental organizations, and international institutions which fund Amazon development to develop new concepts and models for occupying and using the Amazon Basin in keeping with our long-term perspective (future generations), our respect for the interdependence between humankind and our environments, and our need to improve the well-being of the entire community; further work with the same institutions to translate these new concepts into concrete programs for developing and caring for the Amazon Basin and its inhabitants.
- work with national governments, environmental organizations, and international funders to reorganize the occupation of supposedly empty Amazonian territories by combining indigenous territories, with forest, wildlife, and extractive reserves in favor of the indigenous and other current inhabitants; by discouraging the "conquest and colonization" of our homeland; and by recuperating those vast areas devastated by state policies of conquest and colonization.
- research on the natural resources and traditional crops used by Indigenous Peoples, on the traditional systems for utilizing and conserving resources, and on models for the extraction of renewable resources.
- evaluation and systematization of the development projects implemented by Indigenous Peoples which attempt to combine the demands of the market with a respect for indigenous principles of development.

2. The defense of the Amazon Biosphere/indigenous territories must go hand in hand with the recognition of and respect for the territorial, political, cultural, economic, and human rights of the Indigenous Peoples. This implies:

- continued participation and support for the UN process for establishing an international instrument recognizing the rights of Indigenous Peoples.
- education for the national and international communities regarding the rights of Indigenous Peoples.
- establishment of mechanisms at both the national and international level for defending the rights of Indigenous Peoples in cases of violations of or conflicts over those rights.

3. The right of self-determination for Indigenous Peoples within their environment/territory is fundamental for guaranteeing the well-being of the indigenous population and of the Amazonian Biosphere. This implies:

- respect for our autonomous forms of community, ethnic, and regional government.
- indigenous control over the economic activities within the indigenous territories, including the extraction of mineral reserves.
- respect for indigenous customary law and the indigenous norms for social control.

4. Concrete Proposals for International Cooperation: For many decades now, most of our peoples have been experimenting with ways to participate in the encroaching market economies of our respective countries while trying to survive as peoples intimately linked to the Amazonian forest. We have done this despite the hostility shown us by the frontier society and despite the fact that, within the context of the market economy, we are desperately poor. For these reasons, we have organized ourselves in new ways and developed and managed a variety of small programs to improve our health, education, and economy. . . . It is these small-scale, locally controlled initiatives which should be the cornerstone of future Amazonian development. . . .

To the Community of Concerned Environmentalists

We, the Indigenous Peoples, have been an integral part of the Amazonian Biosphere for millennia. We use and care for the resources of that biosphere with respect, because it is our home, and because we know that our survival and that of our future generations depend on it. Our accumulated knowledge about the ecology of our forest home, our models for living within the Amazonian Biosphere, our reverence and respect for the tropical forest and its other inhabitants, both plant and animal, are the keys to guaranteeing the future of the Amazon Basin. A guarantee not only for our peoples, but also for all of humanity. Our experience, especially during the past 100 years, has taught us that when politicians and developers take charge of our Amazon, they are capable of destroying it because of their shortsightedness, their ignorance, and their greed.

We are pleased and encouraged to see the interest and concern expressed by the environmentalist community for the future of our homeland. We are gratified by the efforts you have made in your country to educate your peoples about our homeland and the threat it now faces as well as the efforts you have made in South America to defend the Amazonian rain forests and to encourage proper management of their resources. We greatly appreciate and fully support the efforts some of you are making to lobby the US Congress, the World Bank, USAID [US Agency for International Development], and the Inter-American Development Bank on behalf of the Amazonian Biosphere and its inhabitants. We recognize that through these efforts, the community of environmentalists has become an important political actor in determining the future of the Amazon Basin.

We are keenly aware that you share with us a common perception of the dangers which face our homeland. While we may differ about the methods to be used, we do share a fundamental concern for encouraging the long-term conservation and the intelligent use of the Amazonian rain forest. We have the same conservation goals.

Our Concerns

We are concerned that you have left us, the Indigenous Peoples, out of your vision of the Amazonian Biosphere. The focus of concern of the environmental community has typically been the preservation of the tropical forest and its plant and animal inhabitants. You have shown little interest in its human inhabitants who are also part of that biosphere.

We are concerned about the "debt for nature swaps" which put your organizations in a position of negotiating with our governments for the future of our homelands. We know of specific examples of such swaps which have shown the most brazen disregard for the rights of the indigenous inhabitants and which are resulting in the ultimate destruction of the very forests which they were meant to preserve.

We are concerned that you have left us Indigenous Peoples and our organizations out of the political process which is determining the future of our homeland. While we appreciate your efforts on our behalf, we want to make it clear that we never delegated any power of representation to the environmentalist community nor to any individual or organization within that community.

We are concerned about the violence and ecological destruction of our homeland caused by the increasing production and trafficking of cocaine, most of which is consumed here in the US.

What We Want

We want you, the environmental community, to recognize that the most effective defense of the Amazonian Biosphere is the recognition of our ownership rights over our territories and the promotion of our models for living within that biosphere.

We want you, the environmental community, to recognize that we Indigenous Peoples are an important and integral part of the Amazonian Biosphere.

We want you, the environmental community, to recognize and promote our rights as Indigenous Peoples as we have been defining those rights within the UN Working Group for Indigenous Peoples.

We want to represent ourselves and our interests directly in all negotiations concerning the future of our Amazonian homeland.

What We Propose

We propose that you work directly with our organizations on all your programs and campaigns which affect our homelands.

We propose that you swap "debt for indigenous stewardship" which would allow your organizations to help return areas of the Amazonian rain forest to our care and control.

We propose establishing a permanent dialogue with you to develop and implement new models for using the rain forest based on the list of alternatives presented with this document.

We propose joining hands with those members of the worldwide environmentalist community who:

- recognize our historical role as caretakers of the Amazon Basin.
- support our efforts to reclaim and defend our traditional territories.
- accept our organizations as legitimate and equal partners.

We propose reaching out to other Amazonian peoples such as the rubber tappers, the Brazil-nut gatherers, and others whose livelihood depends on the nondestructive extractive activities, many of whom are of indigenous origin.

We propose that you consider allying yourselves with us, the Indigenous Peoples of the Amazon, in defense of our Amazonian homeland.

PART TWO

ECOLOGY AND THE STRUCTURE OF THE INTERNATIONAL SYSTEM

ENVIRONMENTAL PROBLEMS ARE THE RESULT OF A COMPLEX ARRAY OF SOCIAL FORCES, including technology, political and economic institutions, social structures, and people's values. In Part Two of this book, we are particularly interested in the subset of causes that can be attributed to the structure of the international system. Scholars in international relations sometimes use the term *structure* to refer to the international distribution of power among states. For example, during the Cold War that followed World War II, the structure of the system was often said to be bipolar, in the sense that the United States and the Soviet Union wielded the most power in international affairs. Here, however, we use the term *structure* more generally, to refer to the relatively·stable, unchanging characteristics of world politics such as the political division of the world into sovereign states, the capitalist and increasingly tightly coupled global economy, and the modern communications order.[1] These relatively permanent features of the world system give shape and definition to the interactions among governments, international organizations, multinational corporations, nongovernmental organizations (NGOs), citizen-activists, and other agents of world politics.

A few aspects of system structure seem particularly important in shaping the array of global environmental problems and the possibilities for responding to those problems. The first is state sovereignty, which many scholars take to be the central feature of world politics. As the World Commission on Environment and Development famously put it, "The Earth is one, but the world is not."[2] One of the main reasons for this absence of unity is the sovereignty of individual states, which gives them, at least in principle, decision-making autonomy over matters falling within their territorial jurisdiction—even if those decisions have extraterritorial consequences for the planet and its people.

The tensions between ecology and sovereignty are due in part to the fact that the boundaries of states and the boundaries of ecosystems do not perfectly coincide, meaning that individual states cannot effectively manage many of their most serious environmental problems. Many large-scale environmental problems cross national borders; many more are tied to global systems, such as the atmosphere and oceans, which are beyond the control of individual states.

Yet governments have clung tenaciously to the notion that they retain exclusive authority over the activities within their territory, including those activities that affect the global environment. The primacy of state sovereignty was one of the few points on which governments could agree during the contentious 1972 Stockholm conference. This agreement was codified in the conference declaration:

> States have . . . the sovereign right to exploit their own resources pursuant to their own environmental policies, and the responsibility to ensure that activities within their jurisdiction or control do not cause damage to the environment of other states or of areas beyond the limits of their national jurisdiction.[3]

Although this principle refers not only to the sovereign rights of states but also to their responsibilities, it has generally been seen as a reinforcement of the legal principle of sovereignty. In most instances, states have guarded this right emphatically when pressured by the global community—whether the state in question is a tropical rain forest country, such as Brazil; a builder of large dams in sensitive ecosystems, such as China; or a leading emitter of greenhouse gases, such as the United States.

Some observers see global environmental challenges as eroding sovereignty, whereby states are forced to accept restrictions on domestic actions. Others argue that international environmental cooperation is boosting the problem-solving abilities of many states, thereby reaffirming and even strengthening their sovereign authority. Is sovereignty, then, part of the problem or part of the solution? As Ken Conca points out (Chapter 9), sovereignty is more complex than simply the right of nations to do as they please or the authoritative ability of governments to act. Conca argues that sovereignty is indeed being changed by global ecological interdependence, but in many ways at once. Using the example of the Brazilian Amazon, Conca sees Brazilian sovereignty as simultaneously bounded by new international norms, broadened as the state is made the foundation for forest-protection strategies, and rendered more brittle as the enormity of the task and the likelihood of failure put the state's legitimacy at risk. Seen in this light, sovereignty is not a fixed feature of the world system but, rather, a historical social institution that may or may not successfully adapt to global ecological interdependence.

A second crucial feature of system structure is the existence of an increasingly interconnected capitalist world economy. If nature refuses to sit still for governance within national borders, so too does commerce. It has long been apparent that the world's major centers of industrial production and consumption, including the United States, Europe, Japan, and increasingly China, are not "ecologically self-contained."[4] These regions rely upon imports of a wide range of commodities, both as raw materials for production and as food for consumption. As a result, the core industrial regions of the world economy draw upon the "ecological capital" of the places that supply those inputs. The production that takes place in the industrialized world thus casts an ecological shadow far beyond the borders of individual industrialized countries.

To be sure, we have had a world-scale economic system for several centuries now, since at least the dawn of the colonial era. Nevertheless, economic interconnectedness is deepened and broadened dramatically by the increasing mobility of goods, services, money, people, technology, ideas, and symbols—the phenomenon often referred to as globalization. What are the ramifications of globalization for the environment? One is the greater dispersion of both positive and negative re-percussions: negative in the sense of invasive species, cross-border pollutant flows, and transnational criminal networks involved in hazardous waste or endangered species; positive in the sense of new knowledge, new ideas, better policy models, and new initiatives for cross-border environmental cooperation.

Globalization also seems to both lengthen and shorten social and geographic distances. On the one hand, globalization means the growth of genuinely global-scale production chains that snake in and out of nominally sovereign territories. People at any one link along that chain—whether citizens, consumers, workers, activists, or government regulators—are further "distanced" from the other links.[5] Most modern consumers, for example, have almost no knowledge of the environmental impact attached to the products they consume, be it an auto or an apple. On the other hand, the communications revolution forges important new linkages that shorten virtual distances, making some forms of knowledge exchange, cooperation, and coalition building possible on a far broader scale—as when activists work to certify and promote "sustainable" timber or food products.

Economic globalization is marked by several characteristics: trade liberalization and the negotiation of "free trade" areas, the acceleration and enhanced mobility of foreign investment and the linking of capital markets, and the development of global-scale systems of production or "commodity chains" that move back and forth across national borders as they link production and consumption. As the Working Group on Development and Environment in the Americas reports in Chapter 10, these processes have had profound ramifications in the Americas over the past few decades. While conceding that one effect has been a shift toward cleaner production systems, the Working Group also notes harmful environmental impacts including increased reliance on natural resource exports and worsening rates of pollution, as well as sluggish growth rates and worsening poverty. Perhaps the most important dimension of globalization's effects is that it undercuts the state's ability to promulgate regulations in a hyper-competitive trade environment.

The transnational character of modern capitalism also raises important questions of responsibility. Who is responsible for the destruction of tropical rain forests, when the "causes" of that destruction range from the chain saws in the hands of local timber cutters to the global economic system that creates a demand for tropical timber products? Do we blame local people, the transnational banks and corporations that carry economic practices across borders, distant people who may benefit from these activities, remote consumers of those forest products, or the structure of the world capitalist economy as a whole?

Just as state sovereignty imposes a pattern of political authority that does not correspond exactly to the underlying ecological reality, so transnational capitalism imposes patterns of economic activity that do not wholly correspond to the prevailing pattern of political authority. Both features of system structure give environmental problems an inherently transnational dimension, and both greatly complicate the prospects for global cooperation. Yet it is critical to keep in mind that these "structural" properties of the international system are not natural or automatic features of world politics—they are the results of human choice and behavior.

This distinction leads us to the question of how ideas, beliefs, and worldviews give structure to the behavior of various actors in world politics. Obviously, sovereignty and capitalism are two ideas that have had a powerful structuring influence. Some observers have argued that these two ideas are embedded in the more fundamental ethos of "modernity"—a complex set of beliefs that came to dominate European culture in the modern era and subsequently spread to the Americas, Africa, and Asia via colonialism and other manifestations of European power.[6] Some of the principal ideas that make up the modern worldview involve beliefs about the autonomy of the individual, the power of science and technology, the desirability of increased consumption, and the inevitability of progress. Thus, the ideological bedrock of modernity is as central a feature of world politics as the political structure of state sovereignty and the economic structure of global capitalism.[7]

But not all actors embrace the dominant social paradigm. Indeed, many environmentalists argue that environmentalism is a social movement that rejects core features of the dominant paradigm. Is this the case? Does environmentalism transcend the limits of state sovereignty, oppose the unfettered operation of global capitalism, and reject many central tenets of the modern worldview? Is it possible the idea of environmentalism is fostering a new global structure: a network of individuals and groups with an *antisystemic* orientation in the sense that they reject many values and preferences of the dominant social paradigm?[8] Or is environmentalism better understood as a set of ideas that fits comfortably within the confines of a statist, capitalist, modernist world? These questions are hotly debated by environmentalists and their critics, and there may be no single answer: the environmental movement consists of a patchwork of groups with widely differing goals and views, working at levels ranging from local to global. As Parts Four, Five, and Six of this book make clear, the diversity of ideas driving various forms of environmental advocacy can make collaboration among environmentalists as difficult as collaboration among sovereign states.

Nevertheless, the environmental movement has emerged as a force to be reckoned with in international affairs. Environmental NGOs and movement groups change world politics when they engage in domestic political struggles, build transnational networks, and promote large-scale sociocultural change.[9]

Consider the example of Kenyan environmental and antipoverty activist Wangari Maathai. Maathai was a Kenyan academic turned activist turned parliamentarian who, like Chico Mendes (see Part One), became famous around the world for her efforts to protect forests and their people. Kenyan and Brazilian forest politics differ dramatically, and Mendes and Maathai come from very different personal backgrounds. Yet some of the similar themes in their experiences are apparent: the emphasis on people's livelihoods, the centrality of struggle, and the challenges of organizing and mobilizing a sustained movement. In this section we include

Maathai's acceptance speech when she was awarded the Nobel Peace Prize in 2004 (Chapter 11), making her the first African woman to receive the award. Her selection was controversial given her image as an "environmentalist" rather than as a figure central to the annals of war and peace. But her work bridging environmental protection, positive social change, and political transformation foreshadowed the concept of "environmental peacebuilding" (see Part Five). Maathai's experience also points to the significant role of gender dynamics, a theme taken up in Part Six.

Tellingly, even as economic globalization has intensified pressures on many local communities and spawned the sort of activism characteristic of the movements Chico Mendes and Wangari Maathai led, so too has it promoted growing transnational linkages among activists with a common cause. Recognizing that struggles to determine the future of resource use, livelihoods, community, and environmental quality have a transnational dimension, many networks, coalitions, and full-blown social movements have sprung up linking activists across borders.[10] Jethro Pettit describes one such movement around the theme of climate justice (Chapter 12). Writing in 2009, Pettit focuses on the particular context facing the then-emerging movement—including a recalcitrant Bush administration in the United States and uncertainty as to the fate of the Kyoto Protocol, at a time when its 2008–2012 targets and timetable for greenhouse-gas reductions were just coming due. In the years since Pettit wrote his essay, the movement has continued to develop, mounting major protests at the 2009 Copenhagen Conference of the Parties (COP) climate negotiations; conducting a civil society sit-in at the 2011 COP in Durban, South Africa; and spawning a robust movement of youth groups (see youthclimate.org). To be sure, questions remain about the strength and efficacy of such efforts. Pettit not only describes the campaign at a crucial stage in its emergence but also notes several important challenges facing transnational activist networks and coalitions—including splits over "insider" versus "outsider" tactics—that continue to mark its activities to this day.

If a sustained global movement of environmentalism is to exert political power, it will be because movement groups as diverse as the ones seen in these examples can find ways to establish effective and durable international networks to coordinate efforts, exchange information, and pool resources. The barriers to such cooperation are formidable: a lack of resources compared to those of the forces they oppose; the frequent opposition of governments, corporations, and other powerful actors; conflicting viewpoints on goals and means; and unequal power between relatively well-heeled and influential groups from the North and some of the less institutionalized, grassroots groups of both the North and the South. Nor can we assume that international environmentalism automatically produces environmental or social benefits: as the letters from the Coordinating Body for the Indigenous Peoples' Organizations of the Amazon Basin (COICA) in Part One showed, and as the environmental justice essays in Part Six will underscore, there have been troubling cases in which transnational environmental groups have sometimes sought to preserve, say, Latin American rain forests or African wildlife in ways that fail to involve local communities, perhaps even contributing to the continued oppression of such communities.

Despite these obstacles and potential pitfalls, there have been examples of effective international networking among environmentalists, as in the case of the internationally coordinated campaigns to change the environmental practices of the World Bank or to confront unfettered trade liberalization. Moreover, the activities of transnational environmental networks need not be limited to lobbying efforts by well-heeled organizations with access to power. As American academic Ronnie Lipschutz suggests:

> The notion of "civil society" is one with a long history, but it generally refers to those forms of association among individuals that are explicitly not part of the public, state apparatus, the private, household realm or the atomistic market. Civil society is important in global politics in that it is a sector of the state-society complex where social change often begins. This does not mean that global civil society is a unity; it is riven by many divisions, more than one finds in even the international state system. Nonetheless, there are segments of this global civil society that are oriented in ways that specifically promote social and political change.[11]

Whether it makes sense to extend to the global realm the idea of "civil society," which originated with the study of domestic politics in industrial democracies, remains the subject of much debate. But even for skeptics, the idea serves as an important reminder that the state is not the sole or even the primary source of political, social, and cultural change.

Thinking Critically

1. Are the problems confronting the Brazilian state in the Amazon applicable elsewhere? Is the pattern of transformation of Brazilian sovereignty hypothesized in Conca's essay likely to be found on a broader scale? What allows sovereignty to endure in the face of such pressures?
2. Does globalization promote or inhibit international environmental cooperation? Which seems to be growing more quickly—the pressures on countries to solve problems collectively or the loss of control in an increasingly transnationalized world economy?
3. Is Wangari Maathai describing a struggle similar to that experienced by Chico Mendes (Part One)? What are the constants and what are the variables? In other words, what aspects of these movements, their obstacles, and the context in which they operate are likely to be inherent in such struggles? What aspects are likely to be place-specific?

4. What forces push people to mobilize politically? What gives citizen environmental activism its power? What limits its power?

5. Do the cases of citizen action discussed here provide evidence for the emergence of a global civil society? Or do they describe locally grounded political struggles that have little in common beyond occasional, expedient cooperation?

NOTES

1. The term *structure* is also used in this sense in Ken Conca, "Environmental Change and the Deep Structure of World Politics," in Ronnie D. Lipschutz and Ken Conca, eds., *The State and Social Power in Global Environmental Politics* (New York: Columbia University Press, 1993).

2. World Commission on Environment and Development (WCED), *Our Common Future* (New York: Oxford University Press, 1987), p. 27.

3. Quoted in Mostafa K. Tolba, Osama A. El-Kholy, E. El-Hinnawi, M. W. Holdgate, D. F. McMichael, and R. E. Munn, *The World Environment, 1972–1992: Two Decades of Challenge* (London: Chapman & Hall, 1992), p. 808. This principle was reiterated twenty years later at the Earth Summit; see "Rio Declaration on Environment and Development," United Nations Conference on Environment and Development, UN Doc. A/CONF.151/5/Rev. 1 (1992).

4. Jim MacNeill, Pieter Winsemius, and Taizo Yakushiji, *Beyond Interdependence* (New York: Oxford University Press, 1991), p. 58.

5. See Ken Conca, "Consumption and Environment in a Global Economy," *Global Environmental Politics* 1, no. 3 (Summer 2001): 53–71.

6. On the role of colonialism in promoting the spread of European values, see Edward Said, *Culture and Imperialism* (New York: Random House, 1993).

7. This theme is developed in Conca, "Environmental Change and the Deep Structure of World Politics."

8. The term *antisystemic* as used here is derived from G. Arrighi, T. K. Hopkins, and I. Wallerstein, *Antisystemic Movements* (London: Verso, 1989).

9. Paul Wapner, "Politics Beyond the State: Environmental Activism and World Civic Politics," *World Politics* 47 (April 1995): 311–340.

10. See Margaret Keck and Kathryn Sikkink, *Activist Beyond Borders: Advocacy Networks in International Politics* (Ithaca, NY: Cornell University Press, 1998); Sanjeev Khagram, James V. Riker, and Kathryn Sikkink, eds., *Restructuring World Politics: Transnational Social Movements, Networks, and Norms* (Minneapolis: University of Minnesota Press, 2002).

11. Ronnie D. Lipschutz with Judith Mayer, *Global Civil Society and Global Environmental Governance: The Politics of Nature from Place to Planet* (Albany: SUNY Press, 1996), p. 2.

9

RETHINKING THE ECOLOGY-SOVEREIGNTY DEBATE

KEN CONCA[*]

How do mounting international pressures for environmental protection affect state sovereignty? Does it even make sense to speak of sovereignty in a world marked by tight ecological interdependence, massive transboundary pollutant flows, and severe threats to key global environmental services? How will the evolving roles, rules, and understandings that have institutionalized sovereignty adapt to these new ecological realities?

These questions are of particular concern in the South, where the full range of rights and opportunities promised by sovereignty have rarely been realized to the extent enjoyed in the industrialized world. When Third World governments have voiced resistance to the institutionalization of new standards of environmental behavior, they have often done so on the grounds that such rules violate their sovereignty.[1]

In this paper I present a critique of prevailing perspectives on the sovereignty-ecology link. Though the focus is not exclusively on the Third World, the critique illustrates the limited utility of prevailing formulations in a Third World context. I also point the way toward some elements of an alternative conceptualization, and illustrate these propositions with a brief discussion of the case of the Brazilian Amazon.

Two Perspectives on Ecology and Sovereignty

My reading of the ecology-sovereignty literature is that two perspectives dominate the debate. The first argues that we are in fact seeing an erosion or weakening of

*Originally published in *Millennium* vol. 23 no. 3 (701–711). Reprinted with permission.

sovereignty. Environmental concerns are said to be erecting new and effectively global standards for state behavior. These new global standards are said to manifest themselves in several ways: in formal dealings among states (such as the creation of international environmental regimes); in rules of environmental conditionality, attached to the actions of international organizations such as the World Bank;[2] in the evolving norms of a growing body of international environmental law;[3] and in the political pressures brought to bear on governments by increasingly transnational environmental movements, citizens' networks, and non-governmental organizations [NGOs].[4] Such pressures and constraints are unevenly applied and imperfectly enforced, to be sure; but they are beginning, it is claimed, to constrain the autonomy of state action by imposing limits on the menu of policy choices available to states.

This perspective is sometimes, though not inevitably, tied to the view that sovereignty and ecology are inherently at odds. Because ecosystems and environmental processes do not respect state borders, sovereignty itself becomes a key institution of global-scale environmental destruction. It creates a scale for decision-making, adjudication, and authority that does not coincide with fundamental ecological realities, and thus frustrates ecologically responsible management.[5]

These claims about eroding sovereignty can be contrasted with a second identifiable point of view in the literature. Here the claim is that international processes and, in particular, the emergence of multilateral institutions for environmental protection do not inevitably erode state sovereignty and may even strengthen it. By placing states at the center of institutional responses and strengthening their capacity to act collectively, it is argued, the menu of choices available to states is being expanded, not restricted.

For example, Levy, Keohane, and Haas have argued that although environmental regimes may limit the scope of governments to act unilaterally, they also facilitate collective state-based problem solving.[6] The authors draw a distinction between "operational" sovereignty, defined as the legal freedom of the state to act under international law, and "formal" sovereignty, defined in terms of the state's legal supremacy and independence.[7] International environmental institutions constrain operational sovereignty, but formal sovereignty remains largely intact. Implicit in this reasoning is the argument that enhanced problem-solving capabilities more than offset the external limitations on the scope of state authority.

A Critique

These two perspectives inevitably embody normative stances toward the state. In one view, the state is a large part of the problem, whereas in the other it is the foundation for solutions—or, at the very least, a central feature of the terrain on which solutions will have to be built. We can also examine them, however, as claims of what is happening to sovereignty, for better or for worse. Here, although they do make different sets of claims, the two are not necessarily irreconcilable. It is perfectly plausible, for example, that the scope of state autonomy is being nar-rowed (as the first claim would suggest) at the same time that the problem-solving capacity of states is increasing (as the second claim would argue).

However, before concluding that this represents the full range of consequences for sovereignty in an ecologically interdependent world, several observations are in order. The picture sketched above is in fact seriously incomplete, particularly when applied to contemporary international politics in the Third World. I hypothesize that for many Third World states, sovereignty is in fact being transformed as a re-sult of global ecological interdependence, but not in the manner sketched by either of the above claims, or even by the net effect of the two taken together.

I base this hypothesis on two sets of observations. First, both arguments fail to disaggregate what is in fact a complex and highly unevenly distributed set of in-ternational pressures on states to solve environmental problems. Second, both are based on an incomplete characterization of sovereignty itself. They only partially capture what has made sovereignty endure over time, and therefore misrepresent what sovereignty has actually meant for most states.

Let me stress here that the point is not to set up two straw arguments for easy dis-missal. There are important insights in both of these perspectives. But they also ap-pear to miss some potentially important effects on sovereignty, in part because their conceptual approaches to sovereignty limit the range of hypotheses they entertain.

Characterization of Environmental Pressures on the State

One problem is an overly general representation of the types of environmental pres-sure states feel. Clearly, governments do feel mounting pressure to respond to inter-national environmental problems. Cross-national comparisons of public opinion data show consistently high levels of public awareness and concern.[8] While not all peoples, classes, regions, and cultures define the problem in exactly the same terms, widespread concerns about environmental quality cut across simplistic distinctions between rich and poor, North and South, overdeveloped and underdeveloped.[9] The growth of pressures on states can also be seen in the contrast between the 1992 UNCED [UN Conference on Environment and Development] in Rio de Janeiro and the UN Conference on the Human Environment, held two decades earlier in Stockholm. Stockholm was a gathering of 114 nations but was attended by only 2 heads of state; Rio represented an assemblage of more than 150 nations, includ-ing over 100 heads of state. The 134 non-governmental organizations at Stockholm were dwarfed by the 1,400 non-governmental organizations and more than 8,000 journalists from 111 countries who attended the Rio conference.[10]

If it is clear that pressures are mounting, it is also clear that there have been consequences for the range of choices available to states. It has become much more difficult (though by no means impossible) to construct large dams, indiscrimi-nately export toxic wastes, clear-cut forests, traffic in endangered species, or emit unlimited quantities of chemicals that destroy the ozone layer. That governments of both the North and the South so often see these limits (at least when applied to them) as interference in their sovereign right to use natural resources as they see fit indicates a strong perception that the consequences are real.

However, while we may very well be seeing the birth of a generalizable, universal norm of environmental responsibility, the specific pressures on states have thus far followed a much more selective pattern. First, to the extent that a new norm is emerging, it is manifest in a highly segmented set of activities, including the lobbying of scientists, the pressure of public opinion, the calculations of governments, and the targeted political pressures of eco-activists. There is no reason to suppose that these all carry the same implications for sovereignty, or even push in the same general direction.

Second, regardless of their origin, the pressures states are feeling typically flow through multiple channels, including intergovernmental relations, dealings with international organizations [IOs], transnational linkages among environmental groups, and the workings of the media. Can pressures to join state-based international regimes be assumed to affect sovereignty in the same manner as pressures to accept the World Bank's environmental conditions on lending?

Third, current pressures clearly do not touch all states equally. Instead, what we have seen is something akin to assigning ecological pariah status to specific states on specific issues, whether it be Brazil and Indonesia in the case of tropical deforestation, China and India on dam construction, Japan on the trade in endangered species, or the former Soviet Union on reactor safety. Whatever the implications for sovereignty, they are unevenly distributed.

Fourth, and perhaps most important, responding to international environmental pressures can create resources and purchase legitimacy at the same time that it may constrain the menu of policy choices. This is in fact generally acknowledged when the gains for states are directly linked to efforts at environmental management. But these are not the only plausible effects; some of the resources gained or legitimacy purchased may speak to more general questions of the state's legitimacy and capacity to govern.[11]

Conceptions of Sovereignty

A second set of problems involves the specific conceptualization of sovereignty itself that underlies these perspectives. One problem is that both sovereignty and the challenges to it are viewed in essentially functionalist terms. By this reasoning, states exist because they perform key functions better than alternative forms of social organization, and pressures on the state exist because one increasingly important function—environmental protection—is being performed inadequately. The problems with functionalist arguments are well known, and stem from their *post hoc* character: causes are imputed from observed effects.[12] Problems emerge when the function is incorrectly specified—that is, when causal significance is given to an observed effect that is in reality an unintended consequence or less-than-central function. A straightforward example: the notion that international environmental regimes exist because states want to solve environmental problems may in fact be wrong. Regimes may be thrust on states by increasingly powerful non-state actors, or they may serve other fundamental purposes of state, e.g., those having to do with state legitimacy and perceptions of effectiveness. Functionalist interpretations based on each of these widely differing "functions" would lead us to dramatically different conclusions about the implications for sovereignty.

The conceptualization of sovereignty is also excessively general. Sovereignty in historical practice has carried with it the presumption of a complex bundle of rights: equality among states, non-intervention, exclusive territorial jurisdiction, the presumption of state competence, restrictions on binding adjudication without consent, exclusive rights to wield violence, and the embeddedness of international law in the free will of states.[13]

There is no reason to expect that a particular set of international pressures affects these various component norms of sovereignty equally or in parallel fashion. Indeed, to the extent that ecological interdependence highlights tensions among such norms, one would expect just the opposite—that some normative pillars of sovereignty can be strengthened as others are undermined or eroded. Consider transboundary pollutant flows: institutional mechanisms to control them could erode the sovereign right to exclusive territorial jurisdiction, but at the same time strengthen aspects of the principle of non-intervention, if the flows themselves are viewed as unjustified interventions.

Third, the view of sovereignty is largely ahistorical. What rules, practices, or beliefs reproduce sovereignty as an institution? Has this process of reproduction been broadly similar in all entities we regard as states, or is there more than one way to reproduce oneself as a sovereign entity? Are there differences in what sovereignty has meant for states whose organized existence is largely a product of colonialism? Does the territorial basis of the state differ fundamentally in frontier societies or in multi-ethnic ones? Clearly, the answers are unlikely to be uniform across time and for all states. This suggests that we cannot describe in universal terms either the processes rendering states sovereign or the way in which they may be changing as a result of ecological interdependence. Sovereignty as a global institution changes because of what happens to different states over time, at different rates and in different ways.

These weaknesses—functionalist logic, excessive generality, and ahistorical character—are symptoms of more fundamental conceptual problems. One of these is the unresolved tension over whether sovereignty represents, as Robert Jackson has put it, "a norm or a fact." In other words, is sovereignty based on the "fact" of material capabilities that enable organized entities to claim standing as states? Or is it based on the selective extension of recognition as a legitimate state? As Jackson and others have argued, we need to understand sovereignty as at once *both* "fact" *and* "norm."[14]

The perspectives examined here tend instead to fall on one or the other side of this divide. The ecology-erodes-sovereignty view typically frames sovereignty as a formal legal right, de-emphasizing the foundations of the state that make it able to claim domestic authority and international standing. Alternately, the claim of enduring sovereignty in the face of environmental pressures stresses states as problem-solvers (albeit with varying degrees of capability). It thus emphasizes sovereignty as the maintenance of a certain set of capabilities with which to act.

Finally, and perhaps most importantly, sovereignty in both perspectives is essentially conceived as freedom from external constraints on state action and choice. This one-dimensional view overlooks the fact that sovereignty looks inward as well as outward. It finds its basis not only in autonomy relative to external actors, but also in the state's jurisdictional power over civil society. According to Ruth Lapidoth:

> Usually, a distinction is made between the internal and external aspect of sovereignty. The former [internal] means the highest, original—as opposed to derivative—power within a territorial jurisdiction; this power is not subject to the executive, legislative, or judicial jurisdiction of a foreign state or any foreign law other than public international law. The external aspect of sovereignty underlines the independence and equality of states and the fact that they are direct and immediate subjects of international law.[15]

John Ruggie's definition of sovereignty as "the institutionalization of public authority within mutually exclusive jurisdictional domains" also captures this internal dimension.[16]

Historically, the ability to control rules of access to the environment and natural resources—to define who may alter, and to what extent, which specific natural materials, systems, and processes—has been a central component of state authority and legitimacy.[17] Thus the full effects of international environmental pressures on state sovereignty as a collective institution cannot be understood without examining this inward-looking dimension. This is particularly so for much of the South, given the legacy of colonialism and the orientation of so many Third World political economies toward commodity exports.

Like the outward-looking dimension, the state-society dimension of sovereignty represents both fact and norm. It demands not only some minimal level of social recognition of the state's legitimacy, but also a complex bundle of state capabilities. Joel Migdal, for example, disaggregates the notion of state capacity into such varied components as the penetration of civil society, the regulation of social relations, the extraction of resources from civil society, and the use of those resources for defined state purposes.[18] International pressures, whether manifest in state-state, state-IO, or state-NGO interactions, are unlikely to affect these varied capabilities equally. Moreover, state capacity and social legitimacy may be at odds, as appears to be the case when coercive means are used to "protect" ecosystems from local use and encroachment.[19]

Toward an Alternative View of the Sovereignty-Ecology Link

What would an alternative conceptualization look like? Clearly, it will require a multidimensional, less readily operational definition of sovereignty. Sovereignty must be conceived as having both external and internal dimensions; it must be seen as having a basis in both norms of recognition and material capabilities; and both its normative and material bases must be seen as consisting of multifaceted bundles of norms and capabilities, respectively. These complexities should make us humble about drawing general conclusions outside the context of specific cases. A corollary is that there is little to be gained from speaking in general unified terms about sovereignty being "strengthened," "eroded," or "maintained," either with regard to specific states or the institution of state sovereignty as a whole.

The multiple dimensions of sovereignty should not, however, automatically lead us down the path of static 2×3 matrices and reductionist thinking. The focus should be on whether and how *specific* state actions and *specific* aspects of state-society relations create the conditions of authority, legitimacy, and capability necessary for states to make effectively sovereign claims. When the Brazilian government builds a road through the jungle, this must be seen as an act that speaks to each of the dimensions of sovereignty alluded to above: legitimacy as well as capability, international as well as domestic. If the idea of a two-level game is an apt metaphor (and it may not be, for this reason), it is a game in which most of the moves resonate on both boards at once.

An Example: The Brazilian Amazon

Consider the example of the Brazilian Amazon, perhaps the single most widely noted and contentious case to date in the ecology-sovereignty debate.[20] Before the ink had dried on the major agreements signed at the 1992 UNCED Conference in Rio de Janeiro, Brazilian diplomat Marcos Azambuja offered the following analysis:

> Brazilian interests are reinforced in the majority of the documents. At no time did we face opposition to our basic interests. . . . [W]e came out of the negotiations without the slightest scratch to our sovereignty.[21]

As evidence, the ambassador could have pointed to the conference declaration of principles on environment and development. Here the sovereign right of states to "exploit their own resources" is reaffirmed using exactly the same language enshrined in the well-known Principle 21 of the Stockholm Conference 20 years earlier.[22] Or, the ambassador could turn to the specific agreements on climate and biodiversity, which did little to contradict this principle.

The absence of "scratches" on the wall of Brazilian sovereignty was particularly noteworthy with respect to the issue of predominant concern to the Brazilians at the conference: the fate of tropical rain forests, and of the Amazon in particular. Efforts to scratch that wall, by constructing a regime for the preservation (or at least controlled depletion) of the world's remaining rain forests, were soundly defeated. Key points of disagreement included whether to link the regime specifically to an agreement on climate change and whether to cover temperate as well as tropical forests.

But walls have two surfaces, and in the Brazilian case the inside surface has suffered more than a slight scratch. Consider the following testimony of one veteran field researcher in the Amazon:

> Wherever one looks in the Amazonian economy, the state is in retreat: unable to finance tax breaks or build highways without the aid of multilateral banks, unable to include more than one per cent of the rural population in official colonization schemes, unable to control land titling or land conflicts, unable to register or tax the greater part of the Amazonian economy, unable to enforce federal law on more than a sporadic basis.[23]

The irony is that this assessment of the limits of state capabilities comes at a time when the Brazilian state has been placed squarely at the center of most schemes for sustainable development in the region. Clearly, some state actions have been proscribed by international pressures. But, far from prohibiting state action, the net effect of international pressures has been to stimulate a more active, interventionist state role in the region, under the rubric of supporting sustainable development. Far from simply "eroding" sovereignty, these pressures strengthen the presence of the state in the region and in Brazilian society as a whole. They also create opportunities for state actors to pursue long-standing goals having little to do with ecology. In the specifically Brazilian case such goals include the control of remote territories or indigenous peoples, the demarcation and fortification of Brazil's borders, and the reorganization of existing patterns of land tenure.[24]

These extensions of the state are not without cost, however; they can only be realized at substantial risk to state legitimacy, given the enormous complexity of the task of sustainable development and the limited effectiveness of many state actions as sketched in the above quote. Moreover, the risk to state legitimacy may extend beyond the relatively narrow realm of environmental management. Consider the following commentary in the leading Brazilian newsweekly, *Veja,* discussing the highly publicized murder of a group of indigenous people at the Haximu settlement: "The Haximu massacre shows that, in reality, these minorities [indigenous peoples] are protected with the same courage and efficiency that guard the public hospital network and the pensions of the retired."[25] The state's inability to protect the lives and land of indigenous peoples is being linked directly to its other widely perceived inadequacies.

Under such circumstances, it means little to say that Brazilian sovereignty over the Amazon is eroding, strengthening, or maintaining the status quo. Rather, it seems that we are seeing a more complex, dynamic process in which sovereignty is simultaneously being narrowed in scope (by international prohibitions), deepened (by strengthening state capacities and state penetration of civil society), and rendered more brittle (by eroding state legitimacy).

Conclusion

. . . A strong case can be made for both of the perspectives sketched at the outset of this paper. Clearly, the freedom of states to undertake, promote, or tolerate processes of environmental degradation is being limited, and many of the limits emanate from sources external to the state itself. At the same time, there is little doubt that new international institutions have made some governments more effective problem solvers (although we should always be careful about assumptions that the problem to be solved is, from the point of view of state actors, environmental and not political). That both effects could be happening at once is testimony to the multifaceted character of sovereignty.

Whether these represent the full set of effects is another matter. Consider an analogy to the origins of the modern welfare state. States were faced with a new set of challenges (macroeconomic stabilization, creating a social safety net, and so on). In response, states evolved new institutions, some national and some international, and in the process thrust themselves into a whole new set of state-society relationships. The consequences were hardly a lessening of the state's penetration of civil society or a decline in the size and reach of state institutions. At the same time, however, by assuming these new tasks, state legitimacy (both domestic and international) was put substantially at risk. The entire process was of course intensely politicized and political, with both state and non-state actors seeking to turn the new agenda to maximum advantage.

Much the same process may be at work with the challenge of environmental protection. New tasks, for which states are poorly suited and to which they are often opposed, have been thrust upon them by rising social demands. This challenge renders some choices more remote, but it also creates new opportunities, in the form of international resources for state responses and new mandates for state management and regulation. However, because most of the solutions being promulgated have a strongly statist cast, state legitimacy is put at substantial risk. A growing body of evidence suggests that participation, democracy, and legitimate authority are the keys to solving environmental problems. If so, the implications for state legitimacy may ultimately be the greatest consequence, both for sovereignty and for ecology.

NOTES

1. See, for example, the comments of the Malaysian Prime Minister, Mahathir Mohamad, at the 1992 U.N. Conference on Environment and Development (UNCED), in *Environmental*

Policy and Law 22, no. 4 (1992), p. 232, and Somaya Saad, "For Whose Benefit? Redefining Security," *Ecodecisions* (September 1991), pp. 59–60. See also the "Beijing Declaration of 41 Developing Countries," 18–19 June 1991, reprinted in *China Daily* (20 June 1991), p. 4, cited in the introduction to Andrew Hurrell and Benedict Kingsbury, eds., *The International Politics of the Environment* (Oxford, UK: Clarendon Press, 1992), p. 39, note 60.

2. On environmental conditionality, see Andrew Hurrell, "Green Conditionality," Overseas Development Council Policy Paper, March 1993 (Washington, DC: Overseas Development Council, 1993).

3. See Patricia Birnie, "International Environmental Law: Its Adequacy for Present and Future Needs," in Hurrell and Kingsbury, eds., *The International Politics of the Environment*, p. 84, note 1. Birnie refers to what has been described as an emerging, bounded concept of "reasonable sovereignty."

4. On emergent global environmental values carried by transnational networks of activists and advocates, see Margaret Keck and Kathryn Sikkink, "International Issue Networks in the Environment and Human Rights," a paper presented at the 17th Congress of the Latin American Studies Association, Los Angeles, California, 24–27 September 1992. See also Kathryn Sikkink, "Human Rights, Principled Issue-networks, and Sovereignty in Latin America," *International Organization* 47, no. 3 (Summer 1993), pp. 411–441, and Ronnie D. Lipschutz, "Reconstructing World Politics: The Emergence of Global Civil Society," *Millennium: Journal of International Studies* 21, no. 3 (Winter 1992), pp. 389–420.

5. For a discussion of this view, see Hurrell and Kingsbury, "Introduction," in Hurrell and Kingsbury, eds., *International Politics of the Environment*, pp. 6–8. The authors cite the work of Richard Falk and John Dryzek as representative examples.

6. Mark A. Levy, Robert O. Keohane, and Peter M. Haas, "Improving the Effectiveness of International Environmental Institutions," in Haas, Keohane, and Levy, eds., *Institutions for the Earth: Sources of Effective International Environmental Protection* (Cambridge, MA: MIT Press, 1993), especially pp. 415–417.

7. Ibid., p. 416.

8. See Riley E. Dunlap et al., "Of Global Concern: Results of the Health of the Planet Survey," *Environment* 35, no. 9 (November 1993), pp. 6–15 and 33–39.

9. One interesting result of the study by Dunlap and colleagues was the strikingly similar pattern of environmental concerns found in polling data across twenty-four countries of widely differing income levels (see Dunlap et al., "Of Global Concern").

10. These figures are from Peter M. Haas, Marc A. Levy, and Edward A. Parson, "Appraising the Earth Summit: How Should We Judge UNCED's Success?" *Environment* 34, no. 6 (October 1992), pp. 7–11 and 26–33.

11. This observation points to the basically functionalist logic of much of the ecology-sovereignty debate, a theme to which I return below.

12. For a discussion of the limits of functionalist theories, see Robert O. Keohane, *After Hegemony: Cooperation and Discord in the World Political Economy* (Princeton, NJ: Princeton University Press, 1984), pp. 80–83.

13. This list is from Ruth Lapidoth, "Sovereignty in Transition," *Journal of International Affairs* 45, no. 2 (Winter 1992), pp. 325–346.

14. Robert Jackson, *Quasi-States: Sovereignty, International Relations, and the Third World* (Cambridge, UK: Cambridge University Press, 1990), chapter 3.

15. Ibid., p. 327.

16. John G. Ruggie, "Continuity and Transformation in the World Polity: Toward a Neo-realist Synthesis," in Robert O. Keohane, ed., *Neorealism and Its Critics* (New York: Columbia University Press, 1986), p. 143, as cited in J. Samuel Barkin and Bruce Cronin, "The State and the Nation: Changing Norms and the Rules of Sovereignty in International Relations," *International Organization* 48, no. 1 (Winter 1994), pp. 107–130.

17. See Ronnie D. Lipschutz and Judith Mayer, "Not Seeing the Forest for the Trees: Rights, Rules, and the Renegotiation of Resource Management Regimes," in Ronnie D. Lipschutz and Ken Conca, eds., *The State and Social Power in Global Environmental Politics* (New York: Columbia University Press, 1993), pp. 246–273.

18. Joel Migdal, *Strong Societies and Weak States* (Princeton, NJ: Princeton University Press, 1988).

19. For a discussion of this effect in the specific context of wildlife in Kenya and forests in Indonesia, see Nancy Peluso, "Coercing Conservation," in Lipschutz and Conca, eds., *The State and Social Power*, pp. 46–70.

20. I discuss this case in greater detail in Ken Conca, "Environmental Protection, International Norms, and National Sovereignty: The Case of the Brazilian Amazon," in Gene Lyons and Michael Mastanduno, eds., *Beyond Westphalia? National Sovereignty and International Intervention* (Baltimore, MD: Johns Hopkins University Press, 1995).

21. "Summit Documents Safeguard Brazilian Interests," *Daily Report: Latin America,* FBIS-LAT–92–114-S, 12 June 1992, p. 27 (supplement); original source *O Globo,* 11 June 1992, Rio '92 section, p. 1.

22. Principle 2: "States have, in accordance with the Charter of the United Nations and the principles of international law, the sovereign right to exploit their own resources, pursuant to their own environmental and developmental policies, and the responsibility to ensure that activities within their jurisdiction or control do not cause damage to the environment of other States or of areas beyond the limits of national jurisdiction." See "Rio Declaration on Environment and Development," United Nations Conference on Environment and Development, U.N. Document A/CONF.151/5/Rev.1 (1992).

23. David Cleary, "After the Frontier: Problems with Political Economy in the Modern Brazilian Amazon," *Journal of Latin American Studies* 25, part 2 (May 1993), pp. 331–349.

24. These themes are discussed in detail in Conca, "Environmental Protection, International Norms, and National Sovereignty."

25. "Um Grito do Fundo da Selva," *Veja* (August 25, 1993), p. 27. The translation is mine.

GLOBALIZATION AND THE ENVIRONMENT: LESSONS FROM THE AMERICAS

Working Group on Development and Environment in the Americas*

Foreword

Ever since the Earth Summit in Rio de Janeiro in 1992, the concept of sustainable development, the idea that economic development should at the same time ensure environmental protection and social advancement, has gained popularity and credence among scientific and civic groups worldwide. Indeed, in the past decade, many politicians, international organizations and regimes have used explicit reference to sustainable development when negotiating and prescribing political action plans for economic growth and poverty reduction.

However, as a look at globalization processes in the Western Hemisphere in the past 20 years reveals, these references have proved to be mostly rhetorical. Today, the Americas are plagued by growing social injustice and environmental degradation amid sluggish economic growth as a result of a policy strategy for the region that focused predominantly on trade liberalization and open markets.

Far from looking at lessons learned from the past and not even considering alternative economic development models, most national governments in the region, the International Monetary Fund, the World Bank and the Inter-American

---

*Excerpted from *Globalization and the Environment: Lessons Learned from the Americas* (Washington: Heinrich Boll Foundation North America, 2004). Reprinted with permission.

Development Bank continue to seek the political remedy for the policy shortcomings of the past in more, not less market liberalization. The efforts for a Free Trade Area of the Americas (FTAA), the recently negotiated Central American Free Trade Agreement (CAFTA) or a host of future planned additional bilateral and regional free trade agreements in the Western Hemisphere offer conclusive evidence for this myopic political strategy.

While the resistance of many civil society organizations against unfettered economic integration in the region—on environmental and social grounds—has been growing in recent years, political decision-makers have been successful in labeling many of these activists as mere globalization-phobics, anti-globalization protesters that base their critique on incidental evidence rather than hard economic facts and academic scrutiny.

This is one of the reasons why academic research efforts, such as those presented in this publication, are so important in making the case that globalization critique is not only justifiable, but rooted in facts, not fiction. The Heinrich Böll Foundation (committed to supporting sustainable development through its work with 200 partner organizations in more than 60 countries via 23 offices worldwide) is proud to work with the newly formed Working Group on Development and Environment in the Americas in its effort to add empirical-based lessons to the often polarized debates over trade liberalization in the Americas.

Environmental and development economists from seven countries in the Americas undertook detailed analyses of the environmental impacts of reform policies in their various countries. [Editors' note: For the full set of discussion papers and country case studies, see the WGDEA web site, available at http://ase.tufts.edu/gdae/workinggroup.htm.] Their findings, summarized in this policy paper, show that in Latin America the environment has so far not profited from globalization, and the often-held promise that with economic growth regard for environmental protection will inevitably grow, has so far been largely unfulfilled. Rather, the authors show that the burden on the environment in many countries of the Americas continues to increase.

Far from rejecting trade strategies and economic liberalization models outright, these economists warn that governments and policy makers must take on the needs of the environment in the Western Hemisphere directly, as an integral part of regional trade and investment policies and with the flexibility and means for national governments to do so. As such, this policy report adds a scientific and academic voice to a growing choir of voices that hold out a different vision for the Americas.

Our heartfelt thanks goes to members of the Working Group on Development and Environment in the Americas for their valuable work and their success in condensing eight lengthy country studies into this summary policy paper. It is indeed worth the read—and should be required reading for trade negotiators, not only in the Western Hemisphere.

Executive Summary

A comprehensive review of the environmental impacts of trade liberalization and related economic reforms in Latin America suggests that, with some exceptions, free-trade policies have taken a heavy toll on the environment, according to a report by the Working Group on Development and Environment in the Americas. The Working Group, which includes development and environmental economists from the U.S., Mexico, Brazil, Argentina, Chile, Costa Rica, and El Salvador, recommends that far more attention be paid to strengthening environmental institutions, regulations, and enforcement as countries in Latin America negotiate trade agreements.

The report, "Globalization and the Environment: Lessons from the Americas," is the product of a series of studies presented by Working Group members at its first meeting in Brasília March 29–30, 2004, hosted by Brazil's Environment Ministry. The Working Group presented its reviews of the environmental impacts of trade liberalization in the hemisphere, drawing from original research and a growing body of so-called "sustainability assessments"—empirical studies of environmental costs and benefits of the free-market policy reforms that have prevailed in most of the region over the last two decades.

Known in the United States as the Washington Consensus and in Latin America as "neoliberalism," the reforms include a package of economic policies that promote economic development by opening national economies to global market forces. Over the last twenty years, governments throughout Latin America have reduced tariffs and other protectionist measures, eliminated barriers to foreign investment, restored "fiscal discipline" by reducing government spending, and promoted the export sector of the economy.

These policies, which were advocated by the U.S., World Bank and the International Monetary Fund and enthusiastically endorsed by most governments in the hemisphere, have been advanced by trade agreements. The 1994 North American Free Trade Agreement (NAFTA) between the U.S., Canada and Mexico became the template for a range of subsequent regional and bilateral accords, including agreements on the hemisphere-wide Free Trade Area of the Americas (FTAA), Central America Free Trade Agreement (CAFTA), U.S.-Chile Free Trade Agreement, and negotiations toward a pact between the U.S. and Andean nations.

These agreements have raised concerns, in part because the open-market policies they promote have shown poor results. Economic growth in the region was much slower—less than 2 percent—in Latin America and the Caribbean between 1980 and 2000, the period of the reforms, than in previous periods. Chile and Argentina (before its recent crisis) are the exceptions to the rule.

The Working Group found that the environmental record was not much better. U.N. agencies have documented the region's growing problems with air, soil, and water contamination, the result of urbanization and the modernization of agriculture. Working Group studies documented and analyzed the environmental track record in specific countries and sectors:

- **El Salvador** has shifted from an agro-exporter to a labor exporter, with benefits to the rural environment as land pressures eased but with heavy costs in urban areas.
- **Central America** as a region has seen demand grow for some of the agricultural products—bananas, sugar, melons—that impose the heaviest environmental costs.
- **Mexico** has transformed itself from a resource-dependent, closed economy to an export-driven manufacturer, but weak environmental enforcement has allowed rising levels of air pollution and unsustainable resource use.
- **Brazil** has seen rising demand for agro-exports, such as soy, but the expansion threatens fragile lands and ecosystems.
- **Argentina** has benefited from imported technology through liberalization, but the environmental record has been mixed, with some improved practices in industry and agriculture but little institutional capacity to spread such benefits.
- **Chile** has been the only country in the hemisphere to see faster growth rates, but its dependence on natural resource-based exports has increased.

The Working Group's findings, which are summarized in "Globalization and the Environment: Lessons from the Americas" and documented in full in the Brasília papers (available online), include:

- **Pollution rates continue to worsen** because governments have not provided the level of oversight needed to limit environmental damages.
- The region has seen a **gradual shift toward cleaner industrial production,** an expected outgrowth of economic development, yet pollution continues to increase because governments lack the institutional capacity to protect the environment.
- With a comparative advantage in resource-based industries—oil, copper, fishing, agriculture, forestry—**Latin America has grown more dependent on resource-based exports,** putting added pressure on the environment.
- Technological improvements are expected to yield environmental benefits, as foreign firms bring new technology and higher environmental standards. Yet the results are quite mixed. In some cases, foreign firms or technology generated environmental improvements, such as in some large export-oriented firms. Yet other **evidence suggests that foreign firms are no more likely to impose strict environmental standards than domestic companies,** and small and medium-sized enterprises are largely left behind.

- In some cases, trade-led technical change has brought a net worsening of environmental conditions, such as when modern, **chemical-intensive agriculture displaces more sustainable, traditional practices.** This can have potentially irreversible impacts on biodiversity, as studies of Mexican maize and Brazilian soy document.
- **Rural displacement has in some cases reduced pressure on the land, but internal migration has compounded environmental problems associated with unregulated urbanization.** International migration, which has grown dramatically despite the unwillingness of the U.S. government to liberalize labor flows, now assumes a crucial economic role as migrants return wage remittances to family members. For many communities and some countries, these payments are an economic lifeline.

Changing Directions

The Working Group found ample reason to question the prevailing assumptions that trade and investment liberalization will automatically lead to growth and that such growth will naturally lead to environmental improvements. Latin American countries, which have implemented sweeping open-market reforms over the last twenty years, have seen limited benefits from such policies. If trade and foreign investment are going to produce development that is strong and sustainable, governments need to address the environment directly. The report's recommendations include:

- **Strengthen environmental institutions**—Strong environmental legislation, regulation, and enforcement must accompany liberalization. While legislation in the region is generally good, the capacity to enforce it is weak.
- **Build environmental capacity**—Often, open-market reforms impose fiscal constraints on governments, limiting their capacity to finance environmental programs. Developed countries must provide training [on] environmental standards and institutions. Such support should include efforts to improve developing countries' ability to meet international environmental standards so that such requirements do not serve as unfair technical barriers to trade.
- **Reduce resource dependence and promote value-added development**— Latin America must either reduce or upgrade its dependence on resource-based industries, which has increased under open-market reforms. Trade agreements can promote higher value-added development by, for example, reducing tariff escalation on processed goods.
- **Leave governments the capacity to promote sustainable development**— Too often trade agreements constrain government's ability to direct

development in general, and foreign investment in particular, toward desired national ends. Agreements must not proscribe these essential tools for development—performance requirements, technology agreements, etc.

The studies in "Globalization and the Environment: Lessons from the Americas" highlight the social and environmental costs of the present approach. Hopefully they also point to some of the ways in which national policies and international trade agreements can be transformed to better meet societies' goals.

. . . .

Lessons and Recommendations

What lessons can be drawn from these related but disparate studies of the sustainability impacts of economic reforms in Latin America? Based on these experiences, what concrete policy changes are recommended? And what do these cases imply for current trade negotiations?

These questions were the subject of an extensive roundtable discussion among Working Group members in Brasília, as well as subsequent discussions in collectively drafting this chapter. As noted earlier, with the exception of Chile, economic growth rates have been quite low for countries in the region. Slow growth rates, economic crises in many countries, and generally worsening distribution of income in the region have combined to make the social aspects of sustainability worse.

Perhaps the one benefit of slow growth is that the demands of economic activity on the environment, which generally increase with the scale of activity, have grown more slowly than they would have with faster economic growth. Still, rates of pollution continue to worsen.

In addition to scale effects, trade and environment analysts examine two other types of impact. Composition effects relate to the changing composition of economic activity, with increases in some economic sectors and decreases in others creating changing demands on the environment. It is generally assumed that economic development leads in the long run to beneficial composition effects as economies shift more toward services and away from more damaging natural resource sectors and industry. The technique effect refers to changing environmental impact from technological change, for example, the adoption of cleaner, modern industrial equipment. This, too, is generally assumed to improve with economic development.

On average, countries in Latin America and the Caribbean experienced positive composition effects, meaning that the composition of industry shifted toward "cleaner" production. However, pollution in Latin American industry is increasing because nations in the hemisphere lack the proper policies to stem the environmental consequences of trade-led growth in those sectors. In addition, many firms lack the will or ability to adhere to the environmental ramifications of their operations and non-governmental organizations have not always been there to apply appropriate pressure. Of the case studies conducted here, Brazil has actually experienced a general increase in pollution-intensive activity, whereas Mexico follows the general trend.

Reinforcing Resource Dependence

Latin America's comparative advantages include inexpensive labor in some areas and natural resource abundance in general. The trade-led model of development in the region has reinforced these patterns, with significant implications for the environment. Governments now face important challenges to their ability to manage natural resources in the face of the globalization process.

Chile has seen the strongest economic performance and has developed the most diverse trade relations, yet its strong export performance continues to depend on natural resources—copper, agriculture, and fish and other coastal products. All have significant environmental impacts. Brazil and Argentina have seen the most dramatic export growth in agriculture. While Argentina's soy expansion may bring some possible environmental benefits, Brazil is experiencing a soy boom that is imposing high environmental costs. Central America, too, has seen demand increase for the agro-exports that impose the highest costs on the environment.

Some compositional economic shifts have had positive environmental benefits, perhaps in ways unforeseen by trade negotiators. Certainly El Salvador's shift from an agro-exporter to a labor exporter represents one of the more sizable compositional shifts in this report. This is not an isolated phenomenon. Mexico and other countries in Central America and the Caribbean are exporting labor at an increasing rate while growing more dependent on migrants' remittances for foreign exchange. In El Salvador, there have been positive environmental impacts of this shift as land-use pressure has eased, yet there are new environmental costs associated with urban growth. It is noteworthy that trade negotiations continue to focus only on liberalizing the flow of goods, services, and capital, excluding labor. Yet migratory flows continue to rise, as labor markets seek international equilibrium despite Northern trade negotiators' reluctance to address the issue.

Mexico's shift from a resource-based economy—oil and agriculture—to export-oriented manufacturing represents the one case in this report in which development followed its predicted linear evolution toward industry and services. As Gallagher's study notes, this shift has not produced a widespread pollution-haven effect, with U.S. firms shifting their dirtiest production to Mexico. Unfortunately, the shift toward export-oriented manufacturing has not generated the predicted reductions in pollution intensity because Mexico has not put the proper environmental policies in place. In Brazil, liberalization has reinforced a specialization in pollution-intensive exports.

Technical Change a Mixed Blessing

One of the reasons the pollution intensity of industry has not decreased is the disappointing contribution of foreign investment to cleaner technologies. In Mexico, foreign investment has only brought such improvements in industries where new core technologies are required, such as steel. Where so-called end-of-pipe pollution controls are needed, weak Mexican environmental enforcement has allowed both foreign and domestic industrial firms to avoid environmental investments. Notably, the foreign firms show no higher tendency to impose strict environmental standards.

In Argentina, Chudnovsky found some limited evidence that foreign firms place greater emphasis on environmental management practices, but he notes that small and medium-sized enterprises (SMEs) remain unaffected by such changes. As with most countries in the region, SMEs remain the most important in terms of production and employment. Similarly in Brazil, Young found that 41 percent of the export-oriented firms responded that environment played a part in their overall innovation strategies, as opposed to only 18 percent of domestic firms.

Technical change does not always move economic activity toward more sustainable practices. Agriculture is a case in point. While a unique set of circumstances may have allowed Argentina's wholesale adoption of GM [genetically modified] soy production to contribute some net environmental benefits, new technologies for genetic manipulation in agriculture can have direct negative impacts in other areas. To the extent GM soy helps Brazil expand its soy cultivation, this puts added pressure on sensitive lands. The contamination of traditional maize fields in Mexico with imported GM corn from the United States has raised concerns about the new technology's impact on agro-biodiversity.

In general, agriculture is a sector in which less sustainable, intensive agricultural practices tend to displace more sustainable, traditional techniques. As Nadal and Wise note, the net environmental impact of NAFTA on North American corn has been negative, as Mexico's biodiverse, low-input producers see their production supplanted by chemical- and water-intensive U.S. producers. Similar dynamics are at work in Central America. As Murillo and Pomareda point out, export demand is increasing production in those crops that impose the highest environmental costs, such as bananas, melons, intensive hog and poultry production, and sugar cane.

Changing Directions

Given the disappointing track record on sustainable development in Latin America, what policy changes do these studies suggest? Perhaps the most important is also the most obvious: An economic model premised on unmanaged liberalization poses significant perils for countries in the region. It is worth questioning the prevailing assumption that trade and investment liberalization will lead to economic growth, and the related assumption that such growth will naturally lead to environmental improvements. These studies, and the extensive literature on which they are based, suggest that such assumptions are deeply flawed.

Many citizens, and some governments, are now questioning the wisdom of these assumptions and some of the policies that flow from them. In terms of the environment, one of the consistent findings in these studies is that domestic institutions have been inadequate to the task of ensuring that development be as sustainable as possible. The authors found that while environmental legislation is relatively strong, enforcement is weak. Such government failure relates to weak institutional development, one consequence of the tendency of these reforms to weaken government capacity to manage social and economic programs. This affects everything from regulatory capacity to inter-departmental cooperation, from agricultural extension services to institutions to foster innovation. These studies highlight both the costs of such policies and some of the ways in which proactive efforts to protect the environment can further growth and development. Environmental policies can indeed foster growth rather than detract from it.

One of the clear lessons for developing countries is that there is significant risk to signing trade agreements that mandate deep integration without putting in place the domestic institutions to address the environmental consequences of such agreements. Mexico stands as a clear case in which the government was unprepared to address the environmental impacts of liberalized trade and investment. The useful but limited contribution of the North American Commission for Environmental Cooperation, set up by NAFTA's environmental side agreement, suggests that developing countries should demand significant support from their industrialized trading partners to develop such institutional capacity. As Togiero's study of Brazil's capacity to deal with technical barriers to trade shows, trade itself imposes capacity demands on developing countries that industrialized nations should help address.

Finally, these studies suggest that one of the more troublesome aspects of most trade agreements is the extent to which they reduce governments' ability to direct the development process toward sustainability. From the WTO to NAFTA, from the proposed FTAA to CAFTA, trade agreements proscribe some of the tools that have proven most effective in promoting and distributing the gains of development. These same tools—performance requirements on foreign investment, technology agreements, broad social and environmental policies—are critical to making development sustainable. Developing country governments still have a wide range of tools—many unused—in their development toolbox, even under deep-integration agreements. But governments should be wary of agreements that take more of those tools out of their hands.

The studies in this report highlight the social and environmental costs of the present approach. They also point to some of the ways in which national policies and international trade agreements can be transformed to better meet societies' goals.

11

NOBEL LECTURE

WANGARI MAATHAI*

Your Majesties, Your Royal Highnesses, Honorable Members of the Norwegian Nobel Committee, Excellencies, Ladies and Gentlemen:

I stand before you and the world humbled by this recognition and uplifted by the honor of being the 2004 Nobel Peace Laureate.

As the first African woman to receive this prize, I accept it on behalf of the people of Kenya and Africa, and indeed the world. I am especially mindful of women and the girl child. I hope it will encourage them to raise their voices and take more space for leadership. I know the honor also gives a deep sense of pride to our men, both old and young. As a mother, I appreciate the inspiration this brings to the youth and urge them to use it to pursue their dreams.

Although this prize comes to me, it acknowledges the work of countless individuals and groups across the globe. They work quietly and often without recognition to protect the environment, promote democracy, defend human rights and ensure equality between women and men. By so doing, they plant seeds of peace. I know they, too, are proud today. To all who feel represented by this prize I say use it to advance your mission and meet the high expectations the world will place on us.

This honor is also for my family, friends, partners and supporters throughout the world. All of them helped shape the vision and sustain our work, which was often accomplished under hostile conditions. I am also grateful to the people of Kenya—who remained stubbornly hopeful that democracy could be realized and their environment managed sustainably. Because of this support, I am here today to accept this great honor.

---

*Reprinted from Wangari Maathai's Nobel Lecture, December 10, 2004, at the City Hall in Oslo, Norway. © The Nobel Foundation 2004.

I am immensely privileged to join my fellow African Peace laureates, Presidents Nelson Mandela and F.W. de Klerk, Archbishop Desmond Tutu, the late Chief Albert Luthuli, the late Anwar el-Sadat and the UN Secretary General, Kofi Annan.

I know that African people everywhere are encouraged by this news. My fellow Africans, as we embrace this recognition, let us use it to intensify our commitment to our people, to reduce conflicts and poverty and thereby improve their quality of life. Let us embrace democratic governance, protect human rights and protect our environment. I am confident that we shall rise to the occasion. I have always believed that solutions to most of our problems must come from us.

In this year's prize, the Norwegian Nobel Committee has placed the critical issue of environment and its linkage to democracy and peace before the world. For their visionary action, I am profoundly grateful. Recognizing that sustainable development, democracy and peace are indivisible is an idea whose time has come. Our work over the past 30 years has always appreciated and engaged these linkages.

My inspiration partly comes from my childhood experiences and observations of Nature in rural Kenya. It has been influenced and nurtured by the formal education I was privileged to receive in Kenya, the United States and Germany. As I was growing up, I witnessed forests being cleared and replaced by commercial plantations, which destroyed local biodiversity and the capacity of the forests to conserve water.

Excellencies, ladies and gentlemen,

In 1977, when we started the Green Belt Movement, I was partly responding to needs identified by rural women, namely lack of firewood, clean drinking water, balanced diets, shelter and income. [Editors' note: For more information on the Green Belt Movement, see http://www.greenbeltmovement.org/.]

Throughout Africa, women are the primary caretakers, holding significant responsibility for tilling the land and feeding their families. As a result, they are often the first to become aware of environmental damage as resources become scarce and incapable of sustaining their families.

The women we worked with recounted that unlike in the past, they were unable to meet their basic needs. This was due to the degradation of their immediate environment as well as the introduction of commercial farming, which replaced the growing of household food crops. But international trade controlled the price of the exports from these small-scale farmers and a reasonable and just income could not be guaranteed. I came to understand that when the environment is destroyed, plundered or mismanaged, we undermine our quality of life and that of future generations.

Tree planting became a natural choice to address some of the initial basic needs identified by women. Also, tree planting is simple, attainable and guarantees quick, successful results within a reasonable amount [of] time. This sustains interest and commitment.

So, together, we have planted over 30 million trees that provide fuel, food, shelter, and income to support their children's education and household needs. The activity also creates employment and improves soils and watersheds. Through their involvement, women gain some degree of power over their lives, especially their social and economic position and relevance in the family. This work continues.

Initially, the work was difficult because historically our people have been persuaded to believe that because they are poor, they lack not only capital, but also knowledge and skills to address their challenges. Instead they are conditioned to believe that solutions to their problems must come from "outside." Further, women did not realize that meeting their needs depended on their environment being healthy and well managed. They were also unaware that a degraded environment leads to a scramble for scarce resources and may culminate in poverty and even conflict. They were also unaware of the injustices of international economic arrangements.

In order to assist communities to understand these linkages, we developed a citizen education program, during which people identify their problems, the causes and possible solutions. They then make connections between their own personal actions and the problems they witness in the environment and in society. They learn that our world is confronted with a litany of woes: corruption, violence against women and children, disruption and breakdown of families, and disintegration of cultures and communities. They also identify the abuse of drugs and chemical substances, especially among young people. There are also devastating diseases that are defying cures or occurring in epidemic proportions. Of particular concern are HIV/AIDS, malaria and diseases associated with malnutrition.

On the environment front, they are exposed to many human activities that are devastating to the environment and societies. These include widespread destruction of ecosystems, especially through deforestation, climatic instability, and contamination in the soils and waters that all contribute to excruciating poverty.

In the process, the participants discover that they must be part of the solutions. They realize their hidden potential and are empowered to overcome inertia and take action. They come to recognize that they are the primary custodians and beneficiaries of the environment that sustains them.

Entire communities also come to understand that while it is necessary to hold their governments accountable, it is equally important that in their own relationships with each other, they exemplify the leadership values they wish to see in their own leaders, namely justice, integrity and trust.

Although initially the Green Belt Movement's tree planting activities did not address issues of democracy and peace, it soon became clear that responsible governance of the environment was impossible without democratic space. Therefore, the tree became a symbol for the democratic struggle in Kenya. Citizens were mobilized to challenge widespread abuses of power, corruption and environmental mismanagement. In Nairobi's Uhuru Park, at Freedom Corner, and in many parts of the country, trees of peace were planted to demand the release of prisoners of conscience and a peaceful transition to democracy.

Through the Green Belt Movement, thousands of ordinary citizens were mobilized and empowered to take action and effect change. They learned to overcome fear and a sense of helplessness and moved to defend democratic rights.

In time, the tree also became a symbol for peace and conflict resolution, especially during ethnic conflicts in Kenya when the Green Belt Movement used peace trees to reconcile disputing communities. During the ongoing re-writing of the Kenyan constitution, similar trees of peace were planted in many parts of the country to promote a culture of peace. Using trees as a symbol of peace is in keeping with a widespread African tradition. For example, the elders of the Kikuyu carried a staff from the *thigi* tree that, when placed between two disputing sides, caused them to stop fighting and seek reconciliation. Many communities in Africa have these traditions.

Such practices are part of an extensive cultural heritage, which contributes both to the conservation of habitats and to cultures of peace. With the destruction of these cultures and the introduction of new values, local biodiversity is no longer valued or protected and as a result, it is quickly degraded and disappears. For this reason, The Green Belt Movement explores the concept of cultural biodiversity, especially with respect to indigenous seeds and medicinal plants.

As we progressively understood the causes of environmental degradation, we saw the need for good governance. Indeed, the state of any country's environment is a reflection of the kind of governance in place, and without good governance there can be no peace. Many countries, which have poor governance systems, are also likely to have conflicts and poor laws protecting the environment.

In 2002, the courage, resilience, patience and commitment of members of the Green Belt Movement, other civil society organizations, and the Kenyan public culminated in the peaceful transition to a democratic government and laid the foundation for a more stable society.

Excellencies, friends, ladies and gentlemen,

It is 30 years since we started this work. Activities that devastate the environment and societies continue unabated. Today we are faced with a challenge that calls for a shift in our thinking, so that humanity stops threatening its life-support system. We are called to assist the Earth to heal her wounds and in the process heal our own—indeed, to embrace the whole creation in all its diversity, beauty and wonder. This will happen if we see the need to revive our sense of belonging to a larger family of life, with which we have shared our evolutionary process.

In the course of history, there comes a time when humanity is called to shift to a new level of consciousness, to reach a higher moral ground. A time when we have to shed our fear and give hope to each other.

That time is now.

The Norwegian Nobel Committee has challenged the world to broaden the understanding of peace: there can be no peace without equitable development; and there can be no development without sustainable management of the environment in a democratic and peaceful space. This shift is an idea whose time has come.

I call on leaders, especially from Africa, to expand democratic space and build fair and just societies that allow the creativity and energy of their citizens to flourish.

Those of us who have been privileged to receive education, skills, and experiences and even power must be role models for the next generation of leadership. In this regard, I would also like to appeal for the freedom of my fellow laureate Aung San Suu Kyi so that she can continue her work for peace and democracy for the people of Burma and the world at large.

Culture plays a central role in the political, economic and social life of communities. Indeed, culture may be the missing link in the development of Africa. Culture is dynamic and evolves over time, consciously discarding retrogressive traditions, like female genital mutilation (FGM), and embracing aspects that are good and useful.

Africans, especially, should re-discover positive aspects of their culture. In accepting them, they would give themselves a sense of belonging, identity and self-confidence.

Ladies and Gentlemen,

There is also need to galvanize civil society and grassroots movements to catalyze change. I call upon governments to recognize the role of these social movements in building a critical mass of responsible citizens, who help maintain checks and balances in society. On their part, civil society should embrace not only their rights but also their responsibilities.

Further, industry and global institutions must appreciate that ensuring economic justice, equity and ecological integrity are of greater value than profits at any cost.

The extreme global inequities and prevailing consumption patterns continue at the expense of the environment and peaceful co-existence. The choice is ours.

I would like to call on young people to commit themselves to activities that contribute toward achieving their long-term dreams. They have the energy and creativity to shape a sustainable future. To the young people I say, you are a gift to your communities and indeed the world. You are our hope and our future.

The holistic approach to development, as exemplified by the Green Belt Movement, could be embraced and replicated in more parts of Africa and beyond. It is for this reason that I have established the Wangari Maathai Foundation to ensure the continuation and expansion of these activities. Although a lot has been achieved, much remains to be done.

Excellencies, ladies and gentlemen,

As I conclude I reflect on my childhood experience when I would visit a stream next to our home to fetch water for my mother. I would drink water straight from the stream. Playing among the arrowroot leaves I tried in vain to pick up the strands of frogs' eggs, believing they were beads. But every time I put my little fingers under them they would break. Later, I saw thousands of tadpoles: black, energetic and wriggling through the clear water against the background of the brown earth. This is the world I inherited from my parents.

Today, over 50 years later, the stream has dried up, women walk long distances for water, which is not always clean, and children will never know what they have lost. The challenge is to restore the home of the tadpoles and give back to our children a world of beauty and wonder.

Thank you very much.

12

CLIMATE JUSTICE:
A NEW SOCIAL MOVEMENT
FOR ATMOSPHERIC RIGHTS[1]

JETHRO PETTIT[*]

Many of those in the front lines of climate change negotiations are frustrated. The global policy process is moving too slowly in relation to the scale of the problem. Political will is lacking, not only in the North and particularly in the USA, as is well known, but now increasingly in the South as well, in response to the North's foot-dragging, to Organization of Petroleum Exporting Countries (OPEC) pressure, as to perceptions that economic growth will suffer. Civil society coalitions, in the North and the South, are as yet too weak to bring sufficient pressure. "The chances of our getting anywhere near where we need to be with international diplomacy are grim," one policy advocate said. "We need other forces. What might these be and what are the chances of mobilizing them?" This article asks what social movements are emerging as a force for action on climate change, to reinforce the efforts of sympathetic non-governmental organizations (NGOs) and diplomats. Specifically, it asks how such social movements might urge international development actors to move more squarely into the arena from their stance on the sidelines and to recognize climate change as one of the greatest risks to poor people—a force capable of literally "undoing" decades of development. There is also a need to reconcile the sometimes conflicting messages and objectives of civil society coalitions working on the issue in the North and South and to move from protest and criticism to concrete proposals.

[*]Originally published in *IDS Bulletin* vol. 35 no. 3 (July 2004): 102–106. Reprinted with permission.

In the North, civil society has concentrated on climate change more exclusively as an environmental issue, by environmental NGOs and researchers and has focused on scientific and technical solutions such as emissions controls and carbon credits. In the South, however, climate change has emerged primarily as a sustainable development issue, whose solutions are seen as inseparable from larger issues of poverty, trade and globalization. These messages have yet to appear in Northern development discourses and in the policies of international NGOs, though these have begun to address issues of poverty impacts and adaptability (Newell 2000). Climate change is already on the agenda for many marginalized people concerned with protecting their social and economic rights, North and South. From a rapid review of the landscape, they are making links between poverty and climate change in ways that differ from the mainstream international development community. Some social movements are articulating their messages within the theme of anti-globalization, connecting climate change with unjust North/South economic relations. Others build on long-standing traditions of "environmental justice" campaigns, which have been concerned with the hugely disproportionate impact of pollution and ecological degradation on poor communities. Together, these diverse social forces have adopted "climate justice" as a rallying cry.

The climate justice message is that poor people have not been "waiting for the science" on global warming. They have been living with it—and with many other forms of pollution and degradation—for many years, as "social sinks" for the externalization of environmental costs. Articulated in the language of rights, their foremost concern about climate change is with who is responsible for this enormous new threat to their survival. Rather than asking how *we* can mobilize *them* on climate issues, a more important question may be how they can further mobilize and align themselves as a global political force with influence at multiple levels—and perhaps in doing so compel those of us in the poverty industry to take a much stronger stand both on the life-threatening poverty effects of climate change and more importantly, on addressing its primary causes within our own societies and economies.

It is worth listening to these voices and to their differing articulations of climate-poverty links and causes. By and large, the framing of "climate justice" reflects the same social and economic rights perspectives voiced by global movements on debt, trade and globalization. But it is not yet clear that they have been able to mobilize themselves as boldly, or to develop as effective strategies for influencing opinion, or to find sufficient common ground with climate change activists from mainstream environmental organizations. Nonetheless, there are signs of a genuine movement, albeit one with more to offer in the form of protest than constructive alternatives and broader alliances at this stage. Parallel to UN climate negotiation sessions, there have been alternative summits of environmentalists, including climate justice advocates and representing a range of views on the merits of the official proceedings. In India, the 8th Conference of the Parties (COP 8) held in 2002 under the UN Framework Convention on Climate Change(UNFCCC) was accompanied by a Climate Justice Summit attended by hundreds of activists from throughout the country, including farmers, fisherfolk, indigenous people, women, youth and the urban poor (Khastagir 2002). Delhi's rickshaw drivers, banned from the "cars only" city center, came out in force and in defiance of police barricades.[2] The resulting Delhi Climate Justice Declaration cited the unequal impact of climate change on poor people and the exclusion of the poor who are most affected from global processes to address the issue:

> We affirm that climate change is a rights issue—it affects our livelihoods, our health, our children and our natural resources. We will build alliances across states and borders to oppose climate change inducing patterns and advocate for and practice sustainable development. We reject the market based principles that guide the current negotiations to solve the climate crisis: Our World is Not for Sale! (India Climate Justice Forum 2002)

Until the final sentence, this statement is consistent with mainstream development messages on poverty and climate change. Where it diverges is in its reservations about relying upon market solutions, which are seen as having caused the problem in the first place. Elsewhere in the declaration, climate change is recognized (as science and economics also confirm) as originating largely from the activities of industrialized nations and from "unsustainable production and consumption practices . . . primarily in the North but also in the South" (India Climate Justice Forum 2002). The North/South dimension of cause and effect has not been lost on the UN Climate Change Convention itself, which asks the largest per capita emitters of greenhouse gasses (GHG) to take the greatest share of responsibility. The developing countries have largely signed up to Kyoto [Editors' note: "Kyoto" here refers to the 1997 Kyoto Protocol to the UNFCCC, which entered into force in 2005 and which created commitments and timetables for industrialized countries to reduce greenhouse gas emissions. Since the writing of this article, Kyoto's first commitment period of 2008–2012 has ended, and the political debate has shifted increasingly away from implementing Kyoto commitments and toward determining what sort of agreement may come after it.] But for some climate justice advocates, the protocol falls down by absolving the North of its moral and *historical* responsibilities (the latter, when calculated, shift the emissions burden even further north).[3] An exception is the Brazilian proposal, which seeks to link future commitments to historical responsibilities for temperature rises. But Kyoto is still largely perceived by the climate justice movement as a way for the North to buy its way out of altering its unsustainable consumption patterns by trading carbon credits with the South. Some in Delhi "proclaimed that multinational corporations and industrialized nations had hijacked the Kyoto negotiations" (Khastagir 2002: 4).

In the North, where environmental justice has deep roots, social movements have also taken up climate change as a rights issue—but are more supportive of Kyoto, whose neo-conservative opponents are also long-term adversaries of the civil rights and anti-poverty movements. Their messages emerge from long-standing struggles over the adverse and disproportionate impact of toxic waste and pollution on poor and minority communities (cf. Bullard 1996). Climate change has been adopted as a central plank of this movement, reflected for example in the Environmental Justice and Climate Change Initiative (2002), a coalition of dozens of religious and civil rights organizations advocating "the fair treatment of people of all races, tribes and economic groups in the implementation and enforcement of environmental protection laws" (Environmental Justice and Climate Change Initiative 2002). They call attention to a litany of scientific studies linking pollution, health, poverty and race in the USA,[4] and see more disaster on its way with climate change because 80 percent of people of color and indigenous people live in coastal regions (US Census Bureau 1999, cited in EJCCI 2002).

The Climate Justice Summit held in The Hague in 2000, which paralleled COP 6 [Editors' note: The sixth Conference of the Parties to the UNFCCC], was attended by a strong delegation of black, Hispanic and indigenous leaders from the environmental justice movement in North America, who also held their own Forum (Bullard 2000).While there was some skepticism about the official UN proceedings, seen by some as "mired in 'smoke and mirror' technical discussions and sessions dominated by 'emissions brokers' and corporate lobbyists" (Bullard 2000: 2), these groups largely support the Protocol and advocate that it should be signed by the USA. Kyoto had recently become a political football, in which the energy lobby was playing the race card and abusing the language of environmental justice:

> A coal lobby group, Center for Energy and Economic Development (CEED), funded a $40,000 study blasting the Kyoto Protocol. . . . The report entitled "Refusing to Repeat Past Mistakes: How the Kyoto Climate Change Protocol Would Disproportionately Threaten the Economic Well-Being of Blacks and Hispanics in the United States" was trotted out by several minority business and labor organizations . . . none of which have an environmental or environmental justice track record. (Bullard 2000: 3)

The emergence of such industry-sponsored "citizen groups" in opposition to Kyoto, sometimes known as "AstroTurf" organizations, demonstrates how seriously the fossil fuel lobby takes the challenge of winning public opinion and legitimizing its views through the media and contesting the terrain of civil society (Peter Newell, pers. comm. 2004). One strategy being used to counter this has been to create alliances with other sectors of industry that stand to suffer from climate change, such as insurance, tourism and agriculture, in order to challenge the notion that the fossil fuel lobby speaks for all industry (Peter Newell, pers. comm. 2004). Under the Bush administration, the political, social and racial lines around Kyoto have grown sharper within the USA and the climate justice cause has forged new alliances on both the "climate" and "justice" sides of its agenda. Their challenge under Bush, as for the worldwide movement, is to grow sharper teeth that can either break the political impasse or redefine the surrounding terrain. Climate justice needs to evolve from a parallel noise maker into a genuine pincer that cannot be ignored and into a strategic force that can have more direct impact.

Another strategy being attempted is litigation. The Inuit people of Canada and Alaska recently filed a lawsuit against the Bush Administration for posing a climate-related threat to their survival: "By repudiating the Kyoto protocol and refusing to cut US carbon dioxide emissions, which make up 25 percent of the world's total, Washington is violating their human rights"[5] (Power 2003). State governments in the USA are taking similar action against the federal government (ICTA 2003). Litigation in the USA, even where it fails, has a history of being used to the strategic advantage of rights causes over time. According to the International Center for Technology Assessment, "If it takes lawsuit after lawsuit to force the Bush administration to accept its responsibilities and pursue good public policy on this issue, then that's what it will face" (ICTA 2003). In legal terms, it is not just actions, but the failure to act that can be prosecuted as a violation of rights. However, even with this highly symbolic contribution, litigation can be very costly and difficult to access for poorer communities, so there are limits to what can be achieved (Peter Newell, pers. comm. 2004).

While the climate justice movement as a whole is divided in its hopes for Kyoto—at best impatiently supportive and at worst skeptically dismissive—its members resonate clearly on the "justice" side of their message. All of them emphasize the hugely disproportionate effects of climate change on their poverty and marginalization, which they remind us is not a new issue and which they frame in the language of rights. All sound a note of political frustration and even alienation with regard to UNFCCC negotiations, whatever their view of its potential merits. All point to the need to address the underlying causes of climate change, which are seen as rooted in unjust economic relations at all levels and in unsustainable patterns of consumption by the North and by Southern elites. Much of the skepticism with Kyoto comes from a sense that these issues are not on the table, obfuscated by market-led emissions brokering. These are also sticking points for mainstream development actors, who would prefer to talk about poverty impacts and carbon-sinking strategies than social and economic structures. These issues take us away from the "low-hanging fruit" of balancing carbon credits and into the much bigger, more awkward challenges of reengineering the way we live and consume in the North. While more vocal NGOs are taking up these issues in alliance with social movements, the development community as a whole is not engaged in the climate justice agenda, despite its rights-based rhetoric.

On the positive side, it is clear that we have seen only the beginning of the climate justice movement and experience shows that global civil society initiatives can "play an important role in configuring new patterns of global politics," shaping the scope and boundaries of policy debates even where their direct influence may be limited (Newell 2001: 191). Major challenges, nonetheless, lie ahead for this movement. One will be to strengthen its capacities to engage more effectively in policy and negotiation processes—building skills in direct political participation (Gaventa 2001: 286). These and other "lessons for good practice" from diverse experiences of global citizen action (Gaventa 2001: 279–84) suggest that climate justice is only beginning to find a voice that is likely to gain in strength, alliance and sophistication over time. Some would argue that the movement is playing an important "outsider" role in raising the issues and the stakes, so that "insiders" can make headway in policy and negotiations. But there is also doubt as to whether this "outsider-insider" strategy can work at a time when the process itself appears to be unraveling. The climate justice movement may therefore need to shift from protest to proposing alternatives and to reconciling differences with other sectors of climate change activism, as well as finding ways to build common ground with the international development community. Finding a common position on Kyoto would be a positive step. But even then, decisions will need to be made about whether to continue lobbying states to ratify Kyoto, or to tackle the biggest polluters and foot-draggers directly, such as the USA; clearly both are necessary, but which strategy makes strategic sense in the short term? (Peter Newell, pers. comm. 2004).

What can be learned from other global justice campaigns, such as the Jubilee 2000 campaign on debt relief, for example? One lesson is that the campaign had clear proposals and demands, in addition to raising awareness and visible protest. Another is the value of building bridges and strategic alliances, even where there may not be total agreement. At a time when the climate change negotiations are at risk of unraveling altogether, there is a need perhaps for greater unity of purpose and more common proposals. This is difficult at present, given the divide between those in favor of market-based and voluntary programs and those seeking more binding agreements and fundamental changes. The "insider-outsider" approach can only work if there are elements of a common vision and objective, but not if the campaigns are working at cross-purposes or worse, attacking each other. Points of unity and coordinated action are very much needed. Whatever form the agenda takes, the "climate justice" message is likely to gain in strength and credibility over time and will need to be reflected: that climate change must be tackled in an integral way with the problems of poverty and exclusion in the South and overconsumption and fuel dependence in the North. In this sense the development community, too, has a responsibility to find its common ground with the climate justice movement, to seek better understanding of the synergies and implications and to build mutual strategies for action on climate, poverty and social change in the North and South.

REFERENCES

Bullard, R.D., 2000, *Climate Justice and People of Color,* Environmental Justice Resource Centre, Clark Atlanta University, USA, *www.ejrc.cau.edu* (accessed March 2004).

Bullard, R.D., 1996, *Unequal Protection: Environmental Justice and Communities of Color,* San Francisco: Sierra Club Books.

Centers for Disease Control and Prevention, 1996, "Asthma mortality and hospitalization among children and young adults—United States, 1980–93," *Morbidity and Mortality Weekly Report* 45: 350–3.

Environmental Justice and Climate Change Initiative (EJCCI), 2002, *About Us* and *Climate Change and Environmental Justice Fact Sheet, www.ejcc.org* (accessed March 2004).

Gaventa, J., 2001, "Global Citizen Action: Lessons and Challenges," in M. Edwards and J. Gaventa (eds), *Global Citizen Action,* Boulder, Colorado: Lynne Rienner.

India Climate Justice Forum, 2002, *Delhi Climate Justice Declaration,* India Resource Centre, www.indiaresource.org (accessed March 2004).

International Center for Technology Assessment (ICTA), 2003, *States Environmental Groups Challenge Bush on Global Warming,* www.climatelaw.org/media/states.challenge. bush (accessed March 2004).

Khastagir, N., 2002, "The human face of climate change," *Global Policy Forum, www.global policy.org* (accessed March 2004).

NEA Health Information Network, n.d., *Asthma,*www.neahin.org/4c.html.

Newell, P., 2001, "Campaigning for Corporate Change: Global Citizen Action on the Environment," in M. Edwards and J. Gaventa (eds), *Global Citizen Action,* Boulder: Lynne Rienner; London: Earthscan.

Newell, P., 2000, *Climate for Change: Non-State Actors and the Global Politics of the Greenhouse,* Cambridge: Cambridge University Press.

Power, A., 2003, "Inuit to launch human rights case against the Bush Administration," *The Guardian,* UK, 11 December.

Shah, A., 2003, "Climate justice and equity," *Global Issues,* www.globalissues.org (accessed March 2004).

US Census Bureau, 1999, *American Housing Survey,* Washington, D.C.: US Government.

NOTES

1. I would like to thank Mark Kenber and Peter Newell for comments on an earlier draft of this article.

2. "Said one rickshaw wallah: 'the rich people drive around this district of Delhi one person to a car—they are contributing to the pollution. We do not make any pollution yet we are banned from being allowed to work in this district'" (Khastagir 2002: 4).

3. The World Resources Institute calculates that 60 per cent of *annual* carbon dioxide emissions originate in industrialized countries, where only 20 per cent of the world's population lives; *historically* the emissions ratio for industrialized countries shifts to 80 per cent (cited in Shah 2003: 2).

4. In the USA, large numbers of people of color live in areas of sub-standard air quality. They are twice as likely to die in heat-related deaths (Centers for Disease Control and Prevention 1996) and three times as likely to be hospitalized or die from asthma and

respiratory illnesses linked to air pollution (NEA Health Information Network, n.d.), both cited in EJCCI (2002).

5. As the Arctic region warms up and ice and snow diminish, 155,000 Inuit people are facing disaster, as their hunting habitats vanish and the melting of permafrost causes their settlements to collapse. Sheila Watt-Cloutier, chairwoman of the Inuit Circumpolar Conference, says that her people "are already bearing the brunt of climate change—without our snow and ice our way of life goes" (Power 2003).

PART THREE

INSTITUTIONS OF GLOBAL ENVIRONMENTAL GOVERNANCE

EFFECTIVE RESPONSES TO GLOBAL ENVIRONMENTAL PROBLEMS CLEARLY REQUIRE international cooperation. Many environmental problems flow across borders; others, such as climate change, deep-ocean pollution, and destruction of the Earth's stratospheric ozone layer, negate the concept of borders entirely; and still others, such as soil erosion, land degradation, and the depletion of fisheries, may add up to yield global-scale socioeconomic effects despite their physically localized character. To respond effectively to these problems, governments and other actors in international society must cooperate.

But the barriers to such cooperation are substantial. They include uncertainty, mistrust, conflicting interests, different views of causality, complex linkages to other issues, and the myriad problems of coordinating the behavior of large numbers of actors.[1] For some, the challenge of global environmental governance is to fill the "anarchic" space of an ungoverned world system with laws and rules that can change actors' environmentally destructive behavior; for others, it is to reform or transform deeply embedded political-economic practices that already govern the world system: trade, foreign investment, development assistance, multinational corporate activity. With several decades of experience to look back upon, what may we conclude about how successful the international community has been in creating new governance mechanisms that promote sustainability and in reforming existing ones that may undermine it?

Answering these questions requires an understanding of the concept of institutions. Oran Young has defined institutions as "social practices consisting of easily recognized roles coupled with clusters of rules or conventions governing relations among the occupants of these roles."[2] By this definition, stressing roles and rules, institutions are not synonymous with organizations, which are "material entities possessing physical locations (or seats), offices, personnel, equipment, and budgets."[3] Many institutions have a formal organizational base; others, such as language systems or the family, endure informally, being reproduced over time by the beliefs and practices of individuals and groups.

In this section, we examine some of the institutionalized approaches to global environmental governance. In practice, efforts to promote global environmental protection through law have focused on crafting multilateral environmental treaties. Despite the sometimes formidable barriers to cooperation, international agreements of varying scope and effectiveness have been created on a number of important issues, including the international trade in endangered species, international shipments of toxic waste, ocean dumping, the Antarctic environment, whaling, nuclear safety, and the protection of regional seas. One of the most impressive examples of international cooperation is provided by the international agreement on protecting the planet's ozone layer. The successful negotiation of the Montreal Protocol on Substances That Deplete the Ozone Layer in 1987, and its further strengthening in subsequent agreements, signaled what many hoped would be a new era of increased global environmental cooperation. Certainly that enthusiasm carried over into the 1992 Rio Earth Summit, where governments attempted to hammer out agreements that would slow global climate change, protect biological diversity, and reduce land conversion by slowing deforestation and desertification.

But as the international community grappled with more complex and contentious problems than saving the ozone layer—problems involving more actors, greater scientific uncertainty, higher stakes, more deeply entrenched interests, fewer technological alternatives, and higher costs of adjustment—the momentum for forming ambitious new international environmental regimes began to stall in the post-UNCED 1990s. In Chapter 13, Norichika Kanie provides an overview of the pattern of agreement formation in recent decades. Given the tendency of most accords to tackle narrow, issue-specific problems, he characterizes the resulting "multilateral environmental agreement (MEA) system" as fragmented and decentralized. While there may be advantages of flexibility and pragmatism in such a system, most observers would also agree that it brings problems of overlap, redundancy, and poor coordination. Thus, one of the current debates is how to promote better integration and coordination among existing agreements.[4]

Richard Bissell (Chapter 14) summarizes a very different approach to organizing global governance, exemplified by the World Commission on Dams (WCD). The WCD grew out of the controversies surrounding large dam projects; it sought to document the economic, social, and ecological impacts of such projects and to set out rules guiding their selection and implementation in the future. But rather than situate the question of dam-related rules in a sovereign interstate forum such as an international treaty or a UN body, the WCD brought together a group of representative "stakeholders," ranging from environmental and human rights activists to dam-building industrialists and professionals. And rather than beginning with a least-common-denominator foundation on which all actors could agree, as is often done in treaty negotiations, the WCD from the start placed the largest points of controversy surrounding large dams at the heart of its work. Its relative success in hammering out a consensus statement on dams and development has led some to see the WCD as a potentially fruitful model for other thorny international controversies.[5] Questions remain, however: Who exactly is a stakeholder? How broadly participatory can and should such processes be? What constitutes legitimate knowledge? At the end of the day, doesn't the fate of the enterprise rest on the willingness of governments and other powerful actors to embrace the findings? Can such informal processes have real influence?

As the WCD experience shows, not all mechanisms of global environmental governance are formally codified, in the manner of an international treaty or a chartered international organization. Thus, analysis of the institutionalization of global environmental governance must go beyond formal mechanisms to examine broader patterns of activity in the world system. One process that has become deeply institutionalized is that of global summit conferences. Nowhere in the UN Charter does it say that governments should conduct such extravaganzas, and yet in the environmental realm they have become increasingly ritualized, with Stockholm 1972 leading to Rio 1992, which in turn begat Johannesburg 2002 ("Rio+10") and then Rio again in 2012 ("Rio+20"). The issue of climate change has a yearly Conference of Parties (COP) meeting that takes on a similar summit atmosphere. Global summitry is not limited to the environment. The 1990s, which by most measures were the heyday of such activity, saw summits on human rights, population, food, women, children, development, human settlements, and other topics.[6]

Such events are a venue for many forms of politics at once: heads of state and government ministers converge to negotiate the final details of possible agreements, including treaty texts, funding mechanisms, and directives for the UN General Assembly; civil-society organizations gather for the purposes of lobbying, networking, coalition building, public education, and other activities; and media outlets use the occasion to frame stories about the state of the planet. Yet despite theatrical attention-grabbing and predictable regularity, the practice of global environmental conferencing has increasingly been called into question. Chapter 15, by a longtime senior staffer with the International Institute for Sustainable Development, Mark Halle, expresses some of the skepticism that many environmental advocates (and some government officials) have begun to feel. For Halle and such advocates, recent summits have produced little of tangible benefit, failed to create momentum for more effective governance or more robust cooperation, and frankly may not be worth the effort. This view is not universally shared: longtime civil-society activist Martin Khor, of the Global South Centre, argues that Rio+20 should not be so quickly dismissed (Chapter 16). The achievements Khor cites reflect the importance many actors in the South—governments as well as activists—attach to formally maintaining commitments from prior summits. In this view, it was vital to get the United States and other powerful governments "on the record" regarding their commitment to key principles such as "common but differentiated responsibility." Khor also sees value in the conference's commitments to rework the "institutional framework for sustainable development"—replacing the ineffectual UN Commission on Sustainable Development with a higher-level body and resolving to strengthen the UN Environment Programme.

Thinking Critically

1. When it comes to international environmental cooperation, do you think the glass is half empty or half full? Given Kanie's description of the pros and cons of the decentralized approach to international environmental

treaty formation, would it make sense to attempt to deepen and strengthen this approach, or to try something new?

2. Who is a "stakeholder" in global environmental controversies? If you were constituting, say, a World Commission on Climate along the lines of the World Commission on Dams, how would you decide who should have a voice?

3. Is it worth trying to reenergize broadly multilateral North-South bargaining on environment and development? Or do recent global environmental conferences with modest results mark the death of the "global summit" approach to global environmental governance and herald the need for a new approach?

4. In your opinion, how will history judge the world's progress in institutionalizing international environmental cooperation and governance in the period from the Stockholm conference (1972) to the Rio+20 summit (2012)? Imagine that you are a journalist writing about the legacy of this period from the vantage point of someone living in the year 2042. What do you imagine the first paragraph of your story would say?

NOTES

1. A classic work on barriers to cooperation is Mancur Olson, *The Logic of Collective Action: Public Goods and the Theory of Groups* (Cambridge, MA: Harvard University Press, 1965). For a more optimistic perspective on similar questions, see Elinor Ostrom, *Governing the Commons: The Evolution of Institutions for Collective Action* (London: Cambridge University Press, 1990).

2. See Oran Young, *International Cooperation: Building Regimes for Natural Resources and the Environment* (Ithaca, NY: Cornell University Press, 1989), p. 32.

3. Ibid.

4. See United Nations, *Delivering as One: Report of the High-Level Panel on United Nations System-Wide Coherence in the Areas of Development, Humanitarian Assistance and the Environment,* UN doc A/61/583, November 2006.

5. See the symposium "The World Commission on Dams: A Model for Global Environmental Governance?" *Politics and the Life Sciences* 21, no. 1 (March 2002): 37–71; and Navroz K. Dubash, Mairi Dupar, Smitu Kothari, and Tundu Lissu, *A Watershed in Global Governance? An Independent Assessment of the World Commission on Dams* (Washington, DC: World Resources Institute, 2001).

6. For a list of major summits, see the website of the UN Department of Economic and Social Affairs: http://www.un.org/en/development/desa/what-we-do/conferences.html.

13

GOVERNANCE WITH MULTILATERAL ENVIRONMENTAL AGREEMENTS: A HEALTHY OR ILL-EQUIPPED FRAGMENTATION?

NORICHIKA KANIE*

Introduction

This chapter focuses on multilateral environmental agreements (MEAs). Unlike other international policy fields such as trade, labor, or health, where international institutions are streamlined, environmental problem solving is centered around a multiple number of multilateral environmental agreements and their institutions (secretariat and conference of the parties). Although existing environmental institutions such as MEAs and UNEP [the United Nations Environment Programme] have achieved a great deal and reduced the speed with which environmental degradation is proceeding, there still are a number of pressing environmental problems prevailing throughout the world, including air and water pollution, the loss of biological diversity, desertification, and climate change. Furthermore, accelerated globalization has caused cross-border environmental problems to increase. Challenges of environmental governance are huge and still growing. What is necessary to improve the system and make it more effective? Could we head for a more effective environmental governance system based on MEAs on the road ahead, or do we need to change direction towards a more streamlined problem-solving system?

*Originally published in Lydia Swart and Estelle Siegal Perry, eds., *Global Environmental Governance: Perspectives on the Current Debate* (New York: Center for UN Reform Education, 2007). Reprinted with permission.

Questions in the following three areas are considered below:

1. The first set of questions is about the MEA system itself. What is the MEA system? How and why did it come about? Why are there so many independent multilateral agreements in the field of environment and what are the related problems?
2. The second deals with the performance of the MEA system. What are its strengths and weaknesses? Although evaluating the performance of institutions involves many methodological issues which could lead to an interesting academic debate, this chapter will not delve into this.
3. What reforms are required, what are the options? How large is the gap between needed reform and the current political will? What could narrow this gap?

The MEA System: Why are there so many agreements and what are the related problems?

In this chapter, the definition used for a multilateral environmental agreement is "an intergovernmental document intended as legally binding with a primary stated purpose of preventing or managing human impacts on natural resources."[1] Varying methodologies used for counting MEAs have resulted in different numbers, but many researchers and analysts agree that there is a proliferation of MEAs, constituting a key characteristic of the existing environmental governance system. In the International Environmental Agreements (IEA) database, 405 agreements and 152 protocols have been identified, modified by 236 amendments bringing the total to 794 MEAs that came into existence between 1875 and 2005, although many of these are now defunct.[2] The Ecolex project sponsored by UNEP, FAO [the Food and Agriculture Organization], and IUCN [the World Conservation Union] recognizes in total 519 environmental treaties.[3] Other research identifies more than 500 MEAs registered with the UN, including 61 on atmosphere; 155 on biodiversity; 179 on chemicals, hazardous substances, and waste; 46 land conventions; and 197 on water issues.[4]

This apparent disjointed approach to the current form of environmental governance can largely be attributed to two factors. One is the historical development of environmental institutions, and the second is the very nature and complexity of environmental problems.

Historical Development

When the institutionalization of international environmental policy making really began in 1972, the issues focused mainly on the conservation and management of natural resources, both living and nonliving. No one could have predicted, or even imagined at that time, the severity or variety of problems that would arise by the twenty-first century, including such previously unrecognized threats as stratospheric ozone depletion and the trade in hazardous wastes. The manner in which environmental institutions have developed in response to these problems has largely been ad hoc and fragmented. Unlike the postwar financial and commercial regimes, which have been organized around a small number of formal institutions with fairly clearly demarcated norms and rules, environmental governance has evolved incrementally over the last 35 years, and now encompasses a wide array of international institutions, laws, and regimes. Collectively, these institutions serve as a reflection of the muddled hierarchy of real-world issues that compete for global attention. Apart from the multitude of MEAs and a plethora of international organizations, doing the best they can to respond to environmental challenges that range from climate change to persistent organic pollutants, new planning doctrines have emerged concerning critical loads, integrated assessment, and public participation and are being applied to multilateral management efforts. More importantly, environmental issues are now viewed within the framework of sustainable development.

The concept of sustainable development calls for simultaneous and concerted efforts to deal with pollution, economic development, unequal distribution of economic resources, and poverty reduction. It contends that most social ills are nondecomposable, and that environmental degradation cannot be addressed without confronting those human activities that give rise to it. Sustainable development dramatically expanded the international agenda by stressing that these issues need to be simultaneously addressed and that policies should seek to focus on the interactive effects between them. One of the sources of the current debate on environmental governance reform stems from the gap between the historical development of environmental institutions and the new institutional requirements posed by the transition from mere environmental protection to sustainable development. MEAs are, of course, no exception in facing these challenges.

The core of the new sustainable development agenda reflects new thinking among the environmental and the developmental communities about the linkages between key issues on the international agenda.[5] Some critics contend that this new agenda threatens to divert attention from the fundamental goals of fighting poverty, reducing military expenditure, increasing respect for human rights, and promoting democracy. Conversely, though, the broad agenda offers the prospect of strategic linkages between small policy networks in the international environmental and developmental communities which previously lacked sufficient autonomous influence to be able to shape agendas or policies. In this sense, the new agenda of sustainable development provides opportunities as well.

Sustainable development has two core components. The first is *substantive,* as discussed above, stressing the need for an integrative approach to economic development that includes environmental protection along with other goals of growth, social equity, and, according to some advocates, democratization. Accordingly, the MEA system, which has evolved incrementally on a somewhat ad-hoc basis over the last 35 years in a rather narrow-scoped issue-specific manner, is now facing a new challenge that requires adjustments. The second is *procedural*. Sustainable development and Agenda 21 call for a radically broader participation in decision making. [Editors' note: Agenda 21 is the extensive blueprint for implementing sustainable development that was adopted by nations at the 1992 Earth Summit.] Sustainable development is no longer the pure domain of national sovereignty. Agenda 21 calls for multiple stakeholder participation, or "major groups," at multiple levels of international discussions, including NGOs, scientists, business/industry, farmers, workers/trade unions, local authorities, as well as indigenous people, women, and youth and children. The MEA system is also facing these substantive and procedural challenges.

Issue Complexity

One of the major reasons for utilizing the MEA approach to environmental problems arises from the very nature and complexity of the problems. Environmental processes are governed by laws of nature that are not susceptible to conventional bargaining within the domestic or international policy-making processes. Environmental policy makers have to struggle, from the outset, with the issue of "scientific uncertainty" as well as the incompatibilities between the ethical and political ramifications of the precautionary principle. In many ways, the current international legislative environment is not conducive to the development of co-ordinated, or synergistic, approaches to collective environmental—and sustainable development—problem solving. Particular international agreements are often negotiated by way of "specific" regimes that are considered in relative isolation. Each agreement is tackled, more or less, by artificially decomposing the causative complexities involved for the sake of practical "manageability." Agreements are negotiated by specialized ministries, or functional organizations, within forums that are detached from the negotiating arenas of other international agreements. Furthermore, the process of consensus building within the context of noncooperative attitudes, which are characteristic of global multilateral treaty-making, involves a great deal of ad-hoc log rolling. This, all too often, obscures the interconnectedness of the goals to be shared among different issue-specific regimes. The treaty-making process is also extremely time-consuming. It typically takes over a decade to advance from the agenda-setting stage, via a framework agreement, to the negotiation of the first operational protocol for collective action. Even after reaching agreement, ratification of the protocol requires governments to create consensus at the domestic level. In case a government turns out to be unwilling to ratify the protocol—thus politically increasing scientific uncertainty again—there always remains the possibility that the whole negotiation process can unexpectedly be brought back to an earlier stage, causing considerable time delays.

To date, international environmental policy making has generally been segregated on the basis of topic, sector, or territory. The result is the negotiation of treaties that often overlap and conflict with one another. This engenders unnecessary complications at the national level as signatories struggle to meet their reporting obligations under multiple agreements. At the international level, some coordination exists between environmental institutions through mechanisms such as the Interagency Coordination Committee and the Commission for Sustainable Development [UNCSD], but these institutions are far too weak to effectively coordinate MEAs, and to integrate the various dimensions of sustainable development. These mechanisms seem to function more as a *pooling regime* than as an effective *coordination regime.*

And yet there is progress. Describing the difficulty of the endeavor should still not blind us, as analysts, to the fact that amazing accomplishments have been achieved multilaterally over the last 30 years. Most governments created environmental agencies and, since 1992, units responsible for sustainable development. Public expenditures on environmental protection and sustainable development in the advanced industrialized countries now routinely run between 2–3 percent of their GNP. The market for pollution control technology is conservatively estimated at 600 billion dollars per year, and this market did not even exist in 1972. It was created as a result of governments adopting policies in order to achieve environmental protection and sustainable development. As mentioned above, hundreds of MEAs have been adopted. Many of these MEAs have actually been effective at improving the environment by inducing states to change policies in a manner conducive to a cleaner environment. Stratospheric ozone pollution has been reduced. European acid rain is greatly reduced. Oil spills in the oceans are down in number and volume. Considering the pace with which economies have grown in the last 30 years, these should be recognized as considerable accomplishments. But the challenge still remains to do better, and to progress from environmental protection to sustainable development.

It is generally recognized that certain inherent links exist between human activities and the natural environment on which they depend. We know, for example, that there are a number of different gases that all lead to climate change, acid rain, and ozone loss. Similarly, we recognize that the climate, forests, oceans, wetlands, and diverse biosystems are naturally codependent within the global ecosystem. The multilateral approach to these issues still remains fragmented, however, in terms of methods and mechanisms of scientific assessment and the development of consensual knowledge. This is also the case in regard to human capacity building and the art of interfacing domestic, regional, and international policy. At present, it is unlikely that the tendency to simply piggyback new institutions on existing ones will provide a coherent holistic approach to the governance of global sustainable development. The debates on sustainable development and institutional reforms to improve its prospects will surely continue for the foreseeable future. It is now widely recognized and appreciated that the principal characteristic of international issues is their complexity. Yet, traditionally international institutions have been designed according to an organizational logic that addresses problems individually. Sustainable development requires a reorientation of collective understanding and of formal institutions to focus on the key intersecting and interacting elements of complex problems.

How well does the MEA system perform? What are the strengths and weaknesses of the MEA system?

The present international environmental governance system is organized around UNEP, which was established in 1973. But, over the years, many other organizations have acquired environmental responsibilities, including the World Bank, the IPCC [Intergovernmental Panel on Climate Change], the UNCSD, the GEF [Global Environment Facility] and MEA secretariats, as well as numerous non-state actors. Widespread frustration is often expressed about the inflexible and inelastic operation of the current environmental governance system. Those with insufficient information tend to dismiss the ability of this patchwork quilt of governance arrangements to effectively govern, because of the failings of some of its more visible elements. However, to best understand and evaluate the existing system, one must recognize that it consists of a governance system of many interconnected and interactive elements. Nonetheless, one still must acknowledge that environmental treaty-making has often been segregated on the basis of topic, sector, or territory, and the result has sometimes been overlapping and conflicting negotiation processes. It is also the case that the implementation of one treaty can impede on the principle of another. In such cases, conflicting principles should be investigated, analyzed, and revised to achieve a more effective system of environmental governance.

Still, the current environmental governance system also has advantages. Issue-specific regimes have achieved a relatively high level of performance in a wide range of dimensions. As pointed out earlier, the environmental quality of many regional seas has been stabilized, if not improved. We know that depletion of the ozone layer and acid rain in Europe have been reduced. The Convention on International Trade in Endangered Species (CITES) has induced behavioral change by focusing on trade. Scientific understandings of climate change and its solutions have also improved dramatically as a consequence of the performance of UNFCCC [UN Framework Convention on Climate Change] and IPCC. Norms have changed to take into account environmental consideration, as we can tell from the frequent use of the term "sustainable development" in speeches and news articles. Studies on the effectiveness of environmental institutions suggest that these institutions do matter in improving the human environment. In the face of sustained economic growth, these achievements in the last three to four decades are considerable. In addition, research and analysis have shown that the current diffused MEA system has provided at least the following strengths or advantages:

- Current research on institutions has shown that the best institutional design for managing complex problems such as the global environment is a loose, decentralized, and dense network of institutions and actors that are able to relay information and provide *sufficient redundancies* in the performance of functions so that *inactivity of one institution does not jeopardize the entire system.*[6]
- *Multiple forums allow multiple opportunities for multiple actors to hold discussions and to take action.* This increases the visibility of environmental governance and results in norm diffusion.
- A basic principle of the MEA system is to establish one problem-solving rule centered around one MEA. *Specialization* makes it possible to create a tailor-made solution. It is also easier for the public to understand.
- Multiple MEAs and their specific rules of governance *provide civil society with more windows of opportunity for participation in the global debate.*[7] This is actually a very important point in realizing sustainable development in procedural terms.
- A diffused MEA system provides secretariats with *opportunities and flexibility for self-innovation.* It also allows a certain degree of freedom for secretariats to cooperate with agencies dealing with issues other than the environment, where such opportunities exist. Even competition over limited resources often creates positive effects as it encourages the secretariats and other agents to continuously assess their mandates and improve their performances and competencies. Some analysts also see positive effects when host countries of MEA secretariats inject stronger political will in a particular issue (*ownership*).

There are, however, also weaknesses in the current MEA system. In fact, many proponents of environmental governance reform emphasize the shortcomings of the current system, as a coordinated and synergistic approach to solving common problems is lacking. They further argue that inconsistencies in rules and objectives among a large number of MEAs lead to unnecessary duplication. Many analysts have identified the following, greatly interconnected, problems of MEAs.[8]

- As pointed out earlier, it is reported that there are more than 500 MEAs registered with the UN.[9] Many of these are regional in scope or nested within a hierarchical structure of agreements, and a large number are actually defunct, but nonetheless the majority of these operate at the global level. The proliferation of MEAs, with little authority to coordinate activities, leads to *treaty congestion* as well as institutional and policy *incoherence, confusion, and duplication of work. Redundancy leads to inefficiency.* However, the rate with which new conventions have emerged has been decreasing since the late 1990s, which is sometimes described as a result of "negotiation fatigue."[10]

- MEA secretariats tend to develop an institutional interest in expanding their work, which may result in *man-made institutional barriers and may enhance vested interests* over time. In its report entitled "Delivering as One," the Secretary General's High-level Panel on UN System-wide Coherence in the Areas of Development, Humanitarian Assistance, and the Environment also cautioned that fragmentation in environmental governance does not offer an operational framework to address global issues. Illustrating this point, the panel refers to the slight impact more than 20 UN organizations engaged in water and energy issues have been able to make.

- In some cases, MEAs have *conflicting or duplicating agendas.* An often-cited example are the conflicting signals sent by the Montreal Protocol for ozone layer protection and the Kyoto Protocol for climate change: although the former proposes HFCs [hydrofluorocarbons] as an alternative to CFCs [chlorofluorocarbons], the latter considers both gases as greenhouse gases that need to be reduced. Such a conflicting/duplicating agenda is partially due to the nature of multilateral rule-making. Each new negotiation process typically starts with different policy makers and stakeholders who do not have the same institutional and policy-oriented concerns that were present in earlier negotiations on related issues. They often start from scratch and are influenced by their own particular political dynamics. In addition, they tend to end up with ambiguous wording as a result of concessions made in the process of reaching consensus.

- *The proliferation of MEAs increases administrative and institutional costs for member states,* because it leads to an *increased number of meetings, international negotiations, and reporting.* A survey conducted for the aforementioned report "Delivering as One" revealed that the three Rio conventions (climate change, biodiversity, and desertification) have up to 230 meeting days annually. It also points out that adding the figures for seven other major global environmental agreements raises the number to almost 400 days. The increasing administrative and travel *costs are especially burdensome for developing countries, reducing their participation.*

- *The geographically dispersed locations of MEA secretariats may cause MEAs to be reluctant to hold more substantive and frequent coordinating meetings because of travel costs.* To overcome this problem, clustering of MEA secretariats based on issues, themes, functions, or geographical focus have been repeatedly discussed.

- Due to the costs related to attending meetings worldwide, *developing countries tend to be less willing to engage in additional agreements.*

Coordination problems also are apparent in the interaction between science and policy. As environmental policy relies deeply on scientific knowledge, the science-policy interface is key to solving environmental problems. A lot of good scientific information from sources such as the IPCC, the Millennium Ecosystem Assessment, and UNEP's Global Environmental Outlook is available to us. What is lacking is not good information, but a synthesis of the information. In the current situation, multiple sources of information are gathered in multiple ways and relayed to the stakeholders by multiple paths. Such disparate information does not allow for easy integration into the decision-making processes for sustainable development.

Generally speaking, the larger the number of MEAs, the more frequently they need to interact with each other. An MEA frequently influences the development and effectiveness of other MEAs, and in return, it is also influenced by other policy instruments. While the effects of such interlinkages could either be positive (synergistic) or negative (disruptive), recent study has shown that the MEA system creates more synergistic effects of interlinkages than disruptive effects and that "institutional interaction may not primarily be a bad thing that ought to be diminished as much as possible."[11] According to Oberthur and Gehring, institutional interaction led to synergy and improved the institutional effectiveness in more than 60 percent of their sample of 163 cases of institutional interaction in international and European environmental policy.[12] Of course, this does not mean that one can dismiss the 25 percent of cases where disruption does take place. The accumulative impact of disruption is also not clear. Reducing disruptive interlinkages and weaknesses, while enhancing synergistic interlinkages and strengths within the current MEA system, is the way forward towards reform of environmental governance, as discussed in the next section.

What are the reform options?

Over the years, many reform proposals have been circulated.[13] UNEP pursued internal efforts at streamlining its activities and achieving synergies amongst its various projects in its 1990 System Wide Medium Term Environmental Program (SWMTEP). The 1997 Task Force on Environment and Human Settlements, established by UN Secretary-General Kofi Annan, suggested strengthening UNEP by elevating it to a Specialized Agency (and thus entitling it to a fixed and regular budget) and improving its ability to coordinate activities with other specialized agencies, although no clear guidelines were given on how such coordination was to be achieved in the absence of strong political will by member states or the heads of the agencies. This prompted the Task Force to make the recommendation that an "issue management" approach be set up within the UN to address issues that cut across the mandates of specific institutions concerned with environment and sustainable development, such as UNEP and UNDP, and to some extent MEAs.

Subsequently, the High-level Advisory Board on Sustainable Development was discontinued and supplemented by the establishment of the Environment Management Group (EMG), chaired by the Executive Director of UNEP.[14] The EMG was formed to assist in the coordination of activities between UNEP, UNDP, and other UN agencies, funds, and programs and MEA secretariats, and "adopt a problem-solving, results-oriented approach that would enable United Nations bodies and their partners to share information, consult on proposed new initiatives and contribute to a planning framework and develop agreed priorities and their respective roles in the implementation of those priorities in order to achieve a more rational and cost-effective use of their resources."[15] However, to date, its coordination functions are not very effective because: (1) there has been little high-level engagement in its work, (2) [there is a] negative perception of EMG as UNEP's tool to assert control over the work of other agencies, and (3) [there is a] lack of a clear sense of outcomes.[16] A revitalized UNEP has also been supported by UNEP's 1997 Nairobi Declaration on the Role and Mandate of the United Nations Environment Programme.[17]

More far-reaching proposals have called for the creation of a new World Environmental Organization (WEO) or Global Environmental Organization (GEO) which would possibly replace UNEP, and be endowed with stronger and more centralized resources and influence. The proponents calling for the creation of a centralized WEO/GEO assign it many of the responsibilities currently distributed throughout the UN system.[18] It would be responsible for articulating environmental and sustainable development policies for the international community, and have resources to verify compliance and enforce sanctions on those in non-compliance. Such a WEO/GEO might even have the legal authority and staff to advocate for the environment in WTO [World Trade Organization] trade and arbitration panels, or claim authority to adjudicate such disputes on its own. In addition, it would consolidate the vast array of MEAs (or environmental regimes) in one place, supplementing weaknesses of the current system by easing the administrative burden on governments trying to keep up with the vast array of international environmental obligations, as well as bolstering the political influence of environmental officials within their own governments because they would be collectively housed in a centralized environmental embassy. Such a WEO/GEO initially received a favorable reception from Brazil, Germany, Singapore, and South Africa. However, the proposal has met with institutional resistance from institutions that would lose responsibilities, and with disinterest by much of the UN community.

A hybrid version of a WEO/GEO combined with a more streamlined UNEP has also received recent attention to encourage "a new governance approach" based on partially decoupled links amongst formal institutional bodies.[19] Some redistribution of authority would occur, as a WEO/GEO would be established to develop policy, to coordinate the MEAs, and to counterbalance the WTO. The WEO/GEO would work loosely with other international institutions and promote non-state participation, while pursuing possible synergies between MEAs and their institutions. UNEP would continue to coordinate international environmental science management.

Various visionary schemes have also been proposed. The Club of Rome and others have suggested transforming the Trusteeship Council into an Environmental or Sustainable Development body. In 1992, Gus Speth raised the prospect of a massive North-South bargain for sustainable development.[20] Mahbub Ul Haq's proposed focus on human security offers a similar grand systemic focus that would reorganize all institutional efforts.[21]

The preparatory process for the 2002 WSSD [World Summit on Sustainable Development] clearly demonstrated the extent to which many governments were willing to undertake extensive institutional reforms. The WSSD process also reaffirmed the importance of MEAs, and the need to keep them intact from WTO challenges. The February 2002 Cartagena meeting resulted in a decision on International Environmental Governance that made it clear that governments wished to retain UNEP as the center of the governance system, around which other efforts would revolve.[22] This meeting concluded a series of six often wishy-washy preparatory meetings held at the Ministerial Level by the Intergovernmental Group of Ministers.[23] The Cartagena decision suggested that "the process (of institutional reform) should be evolutionary in nature. . . . A prudent approach to institutional change is required, with preference given to making better use of existing structures." Moreover, the Ministers proposed:

- Sustainable development requires better coordination between ministries at the national level.
- The increasing complexity and impact of trends in environmental degradation require an enhanced capacity for scientific assessment and monitoring and for provision of early warnings to governments.
- Environmental policy at all levels should be tied to sustainable development policies.
- NGOs, civil society, and the private sector should be involved more extensively with all areas of decision making within and between governments.
- LDCs [less developed countries] should be treated "on the basis of common but differentiated responsibility."[24]
- Capacity building and technology transfer are vital elements of governance.
- Retain UNEP/Nairobi as a meeting center.
- Strengthen UNEP with regular financing—elevate to UN specialized agency with "predictable" funding.
- The clustering approach of MEAs should be considered.

The Global Ministerial Environment Forum (GMEF) was established to be the cornerstone of the international institutional structure of international governance of the environment and sustainable development. Since its first meeting in 2000, national environmental ministers have met to discuss high-level policy issues,

coinciding with UNEP's Governing Council meetings. Although the GMEF premise remains vague, and its specific architecture remains to be seen, many consider
the GMEF to have the potential to become a more effective forum for high-level
policy interaction amongst environmental ministers [and] non-state actors, and between environmental ministers and ministers from non-environmental sectors.[25] At
the very least, the GMEF needs to clarify its primary mission, its relationships with
the Conference of State Parties of the MEAs, and whether it should have its own
permanent secretariat and where it should meet.

Political analysis of the five years since the Johannesburg Summit and the potential for reform

While ongoing pressures for institutional reform are likely to come from NGOs
and an internationally organized academic network,[26] the political momentum
for multilateral institutional reform for sustainable development is obviously less
evident in the post-Johannesburg period when compared to the early 1990s. The
negotiation on Chapter Ten of the Johannesburg Summit Plan of Implementation on institutions for sustainable development showed that there exists a will
in the international community to discuss sustainable development institutions,
but little political will to actually move forward. In fact, around ten paragraphs in
Chapter Ten had to be deleted at the end of the negotiation in Johannesburg for
lack of agreement. To create a new international governance system supporting
sustainable development would, at minimum, require the agreement of the major
industrialized countries whose economic activities do the most harm to the global
environment and whose financial resources would be needed to overcome the development losses that might otherwise be suffered by the newly emerged manufacturing giants and the states waiting to follow them into the industrial world.

The United States, in particular, has recently tended to impede efforts to
strengthen or deepen multilateral governance in almost all realms. The Bush administration has clearly signaled a retreat from multilateralism, as well as a profound disinterest in multilateral environmental governance and sustainable
development. While domestic groups of academics and NGOs may support sustainable development reforms, the overall administration is uninterested. The
EU [European Union] seems supportive of the idea of sustainable development,
although it has not been able to pass a carbon tax or adopt measures which entail significant economic costs for its member states. G8 Summits have adopted
declarations endorsing sustainable development, although they could be stronger.
The Gleneagles Summit took the important step of inviting some of the leaders
from key developing countries. The collective purpose of the industrialized countries is currently mobilized behind combating terrorism rather than promoting
sustainable development, and there is some degree of institutional fatigue. The
Netherlands and Scandinavia continue to support reforms. Domestic progressive

elements within Canada and Italy may support multilateral institutional reform and sustainable development, but they are too small a coalition to sway the industrialized bloc. Germany and France are strong advocates of institutional reform and the establishment of a World Environmental Organization. Japan remains supportive in principle, but its primary interest in the UN reform agenda is that of the UN Security Council rather than over social and economic institutions.

The developing world remains suspicious of some of the policy goals pursued by the industrialized world, and is adamantly opposed to any reforms that would entail the movement of the headquarters of the principal international environmental institution, now in Nairobi, away from a developing country.

Towards constructive reform

Much progress has been made in the international environmental policy arena since Stockholm. The system remains fragile, however, and requires continuing support to bolster its many policy networks and to maintain the pressure on governments for sustained environmental protection. The current political situation does not seem conducive to far-reaching reform efforts. Indeed, the enemy of the good is the great. Given the strengths and weaknesses of the current environmental governance system centered around MEAs, and of limited political will within the next five years or so, I suggest that some streamlining of the international governance system may be the most politically tractable option for bolstering effectiveness of governance in the environmental and sustainable development arenas. For example, the Kyoto Protocol's first commitment period expires in 2012 and the negotiations on its follow-up will have to be concluded before 2012. The negotiations are likely to focus on climate change but may also provide a rare opportunity to review and streamline environmental governance.

Reform of the international governance structures needs to address the major functions of global governance while providing for the participation of all the principal actors involved at the global level. Financing remains problematic and further research is necessary on the international division of labor in terms of who performs which functions most effectively. For example, international organizations, MEA-related committees, and governments which have ratified MEAs have provided monitoring functions, but informally, this is also a role for scientists and grassroots NGOs. Rule-making, including sponsoring negotiations, is the function that national delegates to negotiation officially play, but NGOs can also participate in the process by providing principled positions (such as the precautionary principle). Business and industry also make rules by providing *de facto* standards.

According to current organizational thinking, decentralized information-rich systems are the best design for addressing highly complex and tightly interwoven problems.[27] Thus, international governance for sustainable development may be best served through a decentralized architecture coordinated by a sophisticated hub that is capable of quickly accessing usable information and transmitting it to the appropriate institutional nodes in the network. As discussed above, redundancy and efficiency turn out to be strengths in such decentralized systems. Redundancy amplifies the political influence of policy networks involved in governance, and also assures that the governance system persists even if one of the nodes suffers political setbacks. Redundancy in funding sources may also compensate for tentative shortfalls in financing from principal funding sources. Similarly, efficiency is a principle that obscures the symbiotic influences between the elements of the network. Decentralized systems do not cede full autonomy to states or markets: rather, they seek to engage states and markets with actors and policy networks that are sensitive to possible abuses of unfettered free markets.

MEAs should be placed in such a decentralized and densely networked system, and reform options for more effective environmental governance should be considered in such a context. The strengths of the MEA system, mostly the same as the very strengths of a decentralized system, should be preserved and further enhanced, while weaknesses should be resolved. When there is not sufficient political momentum for environmental governance reform to fully develop, seeds for reform should be cultivated where relevant so that when the right time arrives, the necessary growth can more easily take place.

The biggest weakness of the current governance system is lack of coordination. UNEP ought to play the central role in coordination, but UNEP's responsibilities have not been matched by adequate resources from the start. It is now widely recognized that UNEP can't perform all its assigned tasks, and some argue that it should rather concentrate on its science function and coordinate scientific activities throughout the UN system.[28] They propose that UNEP should oversee environmental monitoring, and provide the collected information to the international community through a variety of channels. If monitoring activities were clustered across environmental issues, it would be possible to gain economic efficiency and also to accelerate the flow of timely early warning information. In the context of MEAs, most environmental monitoring has taken place at the regional level, and given the current political environment and limited political will, accumulating experience at a smaller scale may facilitate bigger changes when the political environment changes. Some knowledge is also already collected regionally and not globally, as is the case in regard to regional seas. In this sense, institutions such as UNEP's regional offices may serve as a starting point for reform by creating regional hubs for monitoring, collecting, and disseminating environmental information.

At present, UNEP lacks the resources to perform all its governance functions effectively and to pressure states to pursue environmentally sustainable policies. However, it is also true that UNEP has long-standing experience with coordinating loose and decentralized networks around the world. Thus it may be capable of serving a coordinating role to ensure that the multiple elements of MEAs are coordinated, to anticipate any gaps, and to keep members of international policy networks in touch with one another. It could serve as an air-traffic controller for issues on the international environmental agenda, as well as for the multitude of associated ongoing studies and negotiations. The Secretary-General's High-level Panel on UN System Wide Coherence in the Areas of Development, Humanitarian Assistance, and the Environment recommended that "efficiencies and substantive coordination should be pursued by diverse treaty bodies to support effective implementation of major multilateral environmental agreements." It further recommends that "stronger efforts should be made to reduce costs and reporting burdens and to streamline implementation." Rather than serving as a coordinating body of MEAs, UNEP, or a reformed UNEP, it could more effectively serve as an air-traffic controller by sending signals for enhancing synergies and reducing disruption.

Centralization or co-location of MEA secretariats has the potential to reduce overall administrative costs, further increase coordination activities, and possibly increase the number of joint meetings. Increasing the number of simultaneous or concurrent meetings also has the potential to increase participation from developing countries, as mentioned earlier. This is in line with many recommendations on environmental governance reform, including the above-mentioned Secretary-General's High-level Panel on UN System Wide Coherence, as it recommends that "greater coordination at headquarters should promote coherence at the country level, and greater coordination efforts at the country level should promote coherence at the international level."

The coordination of MEAs, or the creation of a sophisticated network hub for the MEA system, could be performed by UNEP if it is upgraded to a specialized agency, or by a reformed EMG or GMEF. But given the current situation regarding environmental and sustainable development issues and the lack of political will to reform, upgrading UNEP and providing it with "real authority as the 'environmental policy pillar' of the UN system, backed by normative and analytical capacity and with broad responsibility to review progress towards improving the global environment,"[29] seems difficult to achieve within the near future, although such a path should be pursued in the long run. As to reforming either EMG or GMEF, its purpose and mandates must first be clarified to make its institutional foundation firmer.

Environmental governance occurs through complex synergies between networks of actors involving various levels of international politics. Current governance arrangements remain a crazy quilt of overlapping activities, about which many governmental, academic, and NGO environmental analysts express misgivings. While the system is probably too complex to grasp easily, it should not be dismissed out of hand because a cursory view makes it appear incoherent. Gus Speth embraces the decentralized system, stressing its potential for innovation.[30] Needless to say, there are weaknesses in the current MEA system which will need to be addressed and unnecessary overlaps should be resolved. In order to identify where and how to reform, I suggest that more attention be paid to clarifying who the key actors are and which governance functions they perform best in addressing particular environmental threats. Only then can the institutional reforms required to create a successful MEA network system in a concrete manner become more apparent.

NOTES

1. Ronald B. Mitchell, *International Environmental Agreements Website,* 2003. Available at http://www.uoregon.edu/~iea/ and described in Ronald B. Mitchell, "International Environmental Agreements: A Survey of Their Features, Formation, and Effects," *Annual Review of Environment and Resources* 28 (November 2003).

2. Mitchell 2003.

3. http://www.ecolex.org/indexen.php.

4. Adil Najam, Mihaela Papa, and Nadaa Taiyab, *Global Environmental Governance: A Reform Agenda* (IISD, 2006); Markus Knigge, Johannes Herweg, and David Huberman, *Geographical Aspects of International Environmental Governance: Illustrating Decentralization* (Berlin: Ecologic, 2005); and Peter Roch and Franz X. Perrez, "International Environmental Governance: The Strive Towards a Comprehensive, Coherent, Effective and Efficient International Environmental Regime," *Colorado Journal of Environmental Law and Policy* 16, no. 1 (2005).

5. Jan Pronk and Mahbub Ul Haq, *Sustainable Development: From Concept to Action,* The Ministry of Development Cooperation (Netherlands), UNDP and UNCED, 1992; Johan Holmberg, ed., *Making Development Sustainable* (Washington, DC: Island Press, 1992); and Joan Nelson and Stephanie J. Eglinton, "Global Goals, Contentious Means," *Policy Essay* No. 10 (Washington, DC: Overseas Development Council, 1995).

6. Vinod K. Aggarwal, *Institutional Designs for a Complex World* (Ithaca, NY: Cornell University Press, 1998); Elinor Ostrom, "Decentralization and Development: The New Panacea," in *Challenges to Democracy: Ideas, Involvement and Institution,* ed. Keith Dowding, James Hughes, and Helen Margetts (London: Palgrave Publishers, 2001), pp. 237–256; Christopher K. Ansell and Steven Weber, "Organizing International Politics," *International Political Science Review* (January 1999); and Peter M. Haas, Norichika Kanie, and Craig N. Murphy, "Conclusion: Institutional Design and Institutional Reform for Sustainable Development," in *Emerging Forces in Environmental Governance,* ed. Norichika Kanie and Peter M. Haas (Tokyo: UNU Press, 2004).

7. Najam et al. 2006.

8. Edith Brown Weiss, "International Environmental Issues and the Emergence of a New World Order," *Georgetown Law Journal* 81, no. 3 (1993): 675–710.

9. Najam et al. 2006; Knigge et al. 2005; and Roch and Perrez 2005.

10. Najam et al. 2006.

11. Sebastian Oberthur and Thomas Gehring, eds., *Institutional Interaction in Global Environmental Governance: Synergy and Conflict among International and EU Policies* (Cambridge, MA: MIT Press, 2006), p. 318.

12. Oberthur and Gehring 2006.

13. For example: Felix Dodds, "Reforming the International Institutions," in *Earth Summit 2002,* ed. Felix Dodds (London: Earthscan, 2000); Steve Charnovitz, "A World Environment

Organization," *Columbia Journal of Environmental Law* 27, no. 2 (2002): 323–362; and Frank Biermann and Steffen Bauer, *A World Environment Organization: Solution or Threat for Effective International Environmental Governance?* (Aldershot, UK: Ashgate, 2005).

14. http://www.unemg.org/.

15. UN General Assembly Document A/53/463, Par. 11.

16. Najam et al. 2006.

17. Dodds 2000; Charnovitz 2002.

18. Daniel Esty, "The Case for a Global Environmental Organization," in *Managing the World Economy*, ed. Peter B. Kenen (Washington, DC: Institute for International Economics, 1994), pp. 287–310; Frank Biermann, "The Emerging Debate on the Need for a World Environment Organization," *Global Environmental Politics* (February 2001): 45–55; and Frank Biermann, "The Case for a World Environment Organization," *Environment* 42, no. 9 (2000): 22–31; German Advisory Council on Global Change (WBGU), *World in Transition 2* (London: Earthscan, 2001).

19. Daniel C. Esty and Maria H. Ivanova, eds., *Global Environmental Governance* (New Haven, CT: Yale School of Forestry & Environmental Studies, 2002); Peter M. Haas, "Pollution," in *Managing Global Issues*, ed. P. J. Simmons and Chantal de Jonge Oudraat (Washington, DC: Carnegie Endowment for International Peace, 2001), pp. 310–353; and Biermann, 2006, identified three types of WEO/GEO in the recent debate.

20. James G. Speth, "A Post-Rio Compact," *Foreign Policy* 88 (Fall 1992).

21. Mahbub Ul Haq, *Reflections on Human Development* (New York: Oxford University Press, 1995).

22. Governing Council of the United Nations Environment Programme, "Global Ministerial Environment Forum," S.S. VII/I. International Environmental Governance (UNEP/GC/21).

23. UNEP/IGM/5/2 and *Earth Negotiations Bulletin* 16, no. 20, IGM-NYC Final Summary, http://www.iisd.ca/linkages/unepgc/iegnyc/.

24. "Common but differentiated responsibility" is agreed as the Principle 7 of the Rio Declaration on Environment and Development (A/CONF.151/26) in 1992.

25. For example, Najam et al. 2006.

26. Biermann 2000, 2001; Esty 1994; Frank Biermann and Udo Simonis, "A World Environment and Development Organization," *SEF Policy Paper* 9 (1998); Geir Ulfstein, "The Proposed GEO and its Relationship to Existing MEAs," paper presented at the International Conference on Synergies and Coordination between Multilateral Environmental Agreements, UNU, 14–16 July 1999. Also see *UNU/IAS Report International Sustainable Development Governance: The Question of Reform: Key Issues and Proposals*, UNU/IAS, August 2002.

27. Aggarwal 1998; Ansell and Weber 1999; Ostrom 2001; and Haas 2004.

28. Haas et al. 2004; see also UNEP Science Initiative http://science.unep.org.

29. The Report of the Secretary-General's High-level Panel "Delivering as One" (A/61/583): 20–21.

30. James G. Speth, "A New Green Regime," *Environment* 44 (7) (2002): 16–25.

14

A PARTICIPATORY APPROACH TO STRATEGIC PLANNING

RICHARD E. BISSELL*

There is a dismal history of international commissions—generally long-winded, obscenely expensive, producing reports with the conclusions decided from the beginning and destined to consume too many trees in publishing a list of platitudes. On occasion, history gets a rude shock. One report that belies such jaundiced prejudices of global observers is the report of the World Commission on Dams (WCD), *Dams and Development: A New Framework for Decision-Making*, released in November 2000.[1] WCD, comprising twelve commissioners, was created in 1998 to review the performance of large dams and make recommendations regarding future water and energy projects.

Consider the words of the commission's chair, Kader Asmal, in the first paragraph of the report: "If politics is the art of the possible, this document is a work of art." Rarely has a commission taken an intransigent international controversy further into politics rather than fulfilling the hopes of the initiators that the commission would find a nonpolitical answer. The commission rejected a purely nonpolitical role, instead opting for the conclusion that politics is inherent in macroscale decisions such as billion-dollar dam projects. The commission determined that it is essential to first establish a fair process, whereby a "rights and risk" approach will put the social and environmental dimensions of dams on a plane with traditional economic and engineering considerations. (A rights and risk approach is a new tool for participatory decisionmaking that recognizes all legitimate rights of stakeholders and requires a complete assessment of risks to provide a full and

*Originally published in *Environment* vol. 43, no. 7, pp. 37–40, September 2001. Reprinted with permission of the Helen Dwight Reid Educational Foundation. Published by Heldref Publications, 1319 Eighteenth St. N.W., Washington, D.C. 20036–1802. © 2001.

fair set of development choices.) In effect, the commission turned upside down the expectations of those who launched this effort—the World Bank and the World Conservation Union (IUCN)—by placing healthy politics at the center of a solution that gives due place to technical criteria that also are essential. [Editors' note: IUCN, the International Union for the Conservation of Nature, was known from 1990 to 2008 as the World Conservation Union and before that as the International Union for the Conservation of Nature and Natural Resources.]

Given the terrible controversies over large dams in the past decade, people can be forgiven for having forgotten the history of water management, power issues, and dams in the twentieth century. In the last 100 years, 45,000 large dams (dams that are more than 15 meters in height) have been built, a record examined with great care by the commission's report. The "boom" in this technology—peaking from the 1930s to the 1950s—was followed by growing caution in the United States and northern Europe in the last two decades. It took many years of experience with dams before people realized that there was no "free lunch" to be had.

The report builds on the progress of recent decades by emphasizing the need for multidisciplinary analysis. In the not-too-distant past, dam construction and management was a preserve for civil engineers. In time, economists began to poach on the engineering preserve, demanding rates of return and other microeconomic standards. In some countries, there has been successful incorporation of people from other disciplines as well—including sociologists, environmentalists, anthropologists, and climatologists—who tended to take a role in dam debates as an assertion of veto rights. Too often the issue on the table was, "Should we build this dam and how high should it be?" rather than "Among the various alternatives, including this dam, how should we achieve the water, energy, development, and environmental goals set by responsible authorities?" There was no uniform standard among countries as these disciplines and questions were adopted.

In the widening gap between national standards, international financial institutions drew crossfire from all sides. The debate took on a particular virulence in the development banks—the one place where all countries met, whether rich or poor—to decide on major infrastructure investments. Developing, maintaining, and removing infrastructure involves enormous resources, and with the payoff occurring over many years, it was natural that developing countries with large hydroelectric potential would look to foreign financiers for the imported component costs—turbines, transmission systems, and engineering skills. Therefore, at one level, the World Bank and the regional development banks were inevitably drawn into the decisionmaking. There were other institutions, however, also stirring the pot. Export credit agencies where turbine manufacturers were located played a part, and bilateral-aid donor agencies often got involved except in rare cases (for example, when the U.S. Agency for International Development removed itself from the capital projects business in the early 1970s by transferring such projects to the World Bank). Finally, the nongovernmental environmental organizations could not resist the opportunity to push their agendas beyond national boundaries and join the debate as well.

The stage was set, therefore, for conflicts such as the Sardar Sarovar controversy in the Narmada Valley of India, a massive project likely to displace several hundred thousand people that ripped apart any semblance of international consensus on dams in the 1990s. The principal external financier of that project, the World Bank, was forced to withdraw in 1993 with the emergence of a profound split among the borrower, the government of India, and the Bank over what kind of conditions could be attached to a loan for construction of the dam. That controversy has been analyzed elsewhere on many occasions, but most importantly, it set the Bank on a course of attempting to clear up its rights and responsibilities with regard to borrowers.[2] The Bank first tried to find agreement on guidelines among its creditors and borrowers, even creating the Inspection Panel in 1994—a three-member, semi-independent body—to monitor and ensure compliance, inter alia, with dam-related policies.[3] Over the first five years of the Inspection Panel's existence, about half of all its project inspections related to the construction of dams in countries ranging from Nepal and India to Brazil, Paraguay, and Argentina.[4]

When it turned out that the effect of the Inspection Panel's presence was unlikely to dampen controversies, senior management of the Bank argued that they needed to either get out of the dam-building business altogether or find a new avenue for reconciliation with all of the stakeholders. Thus it was, in 1997, that the World Bank's Operations Evaluation Division (under the sage leadership of Robert Picciotto) proposed that IUCN host a "dialog" in Gland, Switzerland, bringing together the most outspoken opponents and supporters of dams. The dialog, as it turned out, was sufficiently cordial for the World Bank and IUCN to agree that they should explore the creation of an international commission to review the "development effectiveness" of dams (to be defined by the commission) and to make recommendations for future standards that could be applied globally.

There were skeptics on all sides of this proposal. Bank management had never before gone outside the Bank for policy guidance. Dam opponents had established a public position that *no* large dams were acceptable, limiting the scope for any kind of dialog that might lead to compromise. Dam builders and equipment suppliers had always left discussions with dam opponents to governments and the World Bank, finding the terms of the arguments rather distasteful. Utilities and government ministries of energy doubted the usefulness of dialog in stabilizing the long-term supply of power on which they depended. Despite all these doubts, there was one common element: Because of the ongoing war over each dam project, there was diminishing common ground and therefore less likelihood of persuading the parties of another view. Based on the slim thread of hope of each party that they could achieve more through dialog than confrontation, the planning for a World Commission on Dams went forward. Nevertheless, throughout the next three years, each stakeholder would, on more than one occasion, decide that the potential outcome was not worth the investment of time and political capital and threaten to withdraw. However, in the end, almost none withdrew.

The chair was chosen first: Kader Asmal, minister of water in South Africa, a veteran of the anti-apartheid movement and senior member of the African National Congress Executive Committee, known for bringing consensus out of the most intractable situations. The diverse commission was chosen, including the CEO of a major manufacturer of dam turbines, a leader of a militant protest group against dams in India's Narmada Valley, and a leading academic expert on the social and resettlement issues associated with dams.[5] The commissioners came from all regions of the world and covered most major fields of knowledge relevant to decisions on dams. Parallel to the choice of commissioners was an informal dialog among representatives of some forty to fifty organizations to ensure agreement on the mandate for the commission, the choice of staff and commissioners, the time frame, and the financing of the effort. Each decision had to reflect joint ownership of the commission and a strong sense of shared participation. By the spring of 1998, the commission held its first meeting in Washington, D.C., and began to establish the relationships that would enable them to produce a report by late 2000.[6]

The thirty months of labor that followed included a time-bound mandate and an expectation articulated by the chair that the commission probably would not fulfill 100 percent of its goals. Asmal argued that the commission had a choice: It could labor until it completely met its mandate, which might take decades, or it could use a specific amount of time to solve as much as it could and leave the remainder of the tasks to other bodies. He clearly chose the latter option, saying informally that if the commission could complete 80 percent of the job, it would be an enormous success. Indeed, it was argued that if the commission could establish 80 percent of a consensus, the momentum should be sufficient to carry the multi-stakeholder community towards eventual agreement. By leaving unclear just which issues might remain unsettled at the end of the day, Asmal's formulation served to create more negotiating room during the commission process itself, and he deliberately left all issues on the table throughout the several years of commission deliberations.

The commission went out of its way to create an inclusive process. Meetings were held on all continents, studies were commissioned from experts in any countries with large dams, and contributions were solicited from people and organizations of any orientation. The establishment of a Web site with voluminous information, including drafts of case studies, allowed participation by anyone with Internet access. On several occasions, the process was so open that organizations with established roles in the controversies felt bypassed and had to be persuaded that the openness was not an attempt to sideline them. The WCD experience on transparency and disclosure should be reviewed by anyone establishing a future commission on what can be achieved with current information technologies.

In pursuit of its first mandate—to review the development effectiveness of dams—the commission reviewed more than 1,000 dams to some degree and 125 dams in great detail. It undertook country studies in the two most controversial cases (India and China) and, most importantly, conducted river basin studies in several parts of the world. It also commissioned seventeen thematic reviews that examined the global inventory of 45,000 large dams in the context of specific attributes and policy issues. The thematic reviews involved evaluations of the social, environmental, and economic implications of dam projects, alternatives to dams, and governance and institutional processes. For instance, past plans for building dams included only the dam site and thus did not evaluate the effects of the dam on the rest of the river basin. The WCD staff developed an extensive review of river basins as a planning framework, drawing on the work of a generation of geographers, including the work of Gilbert F. White.[7] WCD proceeded to build a database from which the public could reach conclusions as readily as the commission and staff. The commission drew two lessons from its review of the development effectiveness of the world's large dams. The first lesson was predictable, that dams have brought significant benefits to publics throughout the world, and that a large cost, often unrecognized owing to its diffuse social and environmental impact, was also incurred. The second lesson was that the most successful dams historically shared three characteristics: They reflected a comprehensive approach to integrating social, environmental, and economic dimensions of development; they created greater levels of transparency and certainty for all involved; and they have resulted in increased levels of confidence in the ability of nations and communities to meet their future water and energy needs.

As previously mentioned, WCD accumulated a massive database on large dams in the process of meeting that first mandate. With the termination of the commission, the fate of that database is unclear. The research community needs to ensure its survival and maintenance. [Editors' note: The United Nations Environment Programme subsequently launched a follow-up Dams and Development Project initiative, which has since been discontinued.]

The second mandate of WCD—to develop internationally acceptable criteria, guidelines, and standards, where appropriate, for the planning, design, appraisal, construction, operation, monitoring, and decommissioning of dams, was the main challenge for the commission members. The solution reached by WCD comprised three international norms: international recognition of human rights, the right to development, and the right to a healthy environment. In that context, WCD established seven policy principles for decisionmakers to follow: gain public agreement, conduct a comprehensive options assessment, address existing dams, sustain rivers and livelihoods, recognize entitlements and share benefits, ensure compliance, and share rivers for peace, development, and security.[8] At a minimum, the seven principles would serve as a valuable agenda from which any negotiation over a dam project might begin.

The impact of these seven principles issued unanimously by WCD has already been felt . . . since the report's release in November 2000. [Editors' note: For a more comprehensive assessment of the WCD's impact, see the June 2010 special edition of the journal *Water Alternatives*, "WCD+10: Revisiting the large dam controversy," available at http://www.water-alternatives.org.] Many of the environmental nongovernmental organizations applauded the conclusions; WCD was cited as a legitimizing source by the Narmada Bachao Andolan (NBA)—a grassroots organization in the Narmada Valley of central India—in its press release about the Maheshwar hydroelectric project in India when a foreign financier pulled out.

On the other hand, the World Bank has experienced a major internal debate over the implications of the WCD report. The Bank's board of executive directors is visibly concerned about the "costs of compliance" with the WCD approach and is quite doubtful the Bank can afford the possible increase in design and compliance charges for dam projects. The private sector is reconfiguring its involvement; Asea Brown Boveri, Ltd. (ABB) has sold off its hydro turbine business to focus on other forms of energy-producing capital equipment. In the United States, the reviews of the Snake River dams in Idaho, as well as the Glen Canyon Dam in Arizona, should be conceptually reinforced by the WCD approach because the U.S. Bureau of Reclamation, which is involved in conducting the reviews, closely tracked the commission's process.

At the conceptual level, the WCD report should lead to more integrative, place-based analysis of projects, including alternatives. World Bank staff have already noted the practice in the Asian Development Bank of undertaking analyses of alternatives and impacts of proposed dams further "upstream" in the project design process. The need is not for mere assessment of a dam after deciding on the project but rather the consideration of alternative sources of power, water, and flood control. Indeed, a major contribution of WCD is to expand the contextual understanding for deciding whether to undertake a dam project; in effect, they have said that decisions must involve people from other disciplines besides just engineers and microeconomists. And if those involved in making decisions about whether to begin dam projects are going to include people from other fields, the central questions about rights and risks must be asked earlier in the process. For instance, by arguing that "displacement" is more than just physical loss of land, WCD implicitly endorses the World Bank's proposal to strengthen its policy on involuntary resettlement, an inevitable result of dam or other large infrastructure projects. Such projects also cause "livelihood displacement," because far more people lose their jobs than lose their land as a result of large dams.[9]

The report should also lead to greater focus on accountability for development decisions, a matter of concern to far more than the dam community. The decision-making that goes into building a dam is ultimately a political process as much as a technical issue, and therefore, a political body has to make the decisions about dams. Most environmental issues involve trade-offs between various public interests. The weighing of those trade-offs is not an exact science, and thus, WCD appropriately suggests that a body with political accountability has to make the decisions. Democracies know that to be true, but countries in transition are not sure whether to involve the public in decisions that may have major environmental impacts. WCD is clear: When in doubt, go public.

The commission model is a powerful one: Establish a clear mandate, work for two years, and go out of business. Its exemplar is international strategic planning rather than more international government. It keeps accountability in the appropriate places, locally, nationally, and internationally. It also establishes a means of periodically comparing experience among countries and regions on troubling issues. Finally, this particular commission did an especially outstanding job of keeping the various stakeholders onboard. That may be a function of the personalities rather than the structure, but for whatever reason, it showed that it can and should be done. Other highly contentious global issues could benefit from similar treatment.

NOTES

1. World Commission on Dams (WCD), *Dams and Development: A New Framework for Decision-Making* (London and Sterling, VA: Earthscan, November 2000). This report is available in its entirety at http://www.dams.org.

2. B. Morse and T. R. Berger, *Sardar Sarovar: The Report of the Independent Review* (Ottawa: Resource Futures International, 1992).

3. I. F. I. Shihata, *The World Bank Inspection Panel* (Oxford University Press, published for the World Bank, 1994).

4. A. Umana, ed., *The World Bank Inspection Panel: The First Four Years* (1994–1998) (Washington, DC: World Bank for the Inspection Panel, 1998); and R. E. Bissell, "Recent Practice of the Inspection Panel of the World Bank," *American Journal of International Law* 91, no. 4 (1997): 741–744.

5. The commissioners who signed the report included Kader Asmal (South Africa), Lakshmi Chand Jain (India), Judy Henderson (Australia), Goran Lindahl (Sweden), Thayer Scudder (United States), Joji Carino (Philippines), Donald Blackmore (Australia), Medha Patkar (India), José Goldemberg (Brazil), Deborah Moore (United States), Jan Veltrop (United States), and Achim Steiner (Germany).

6. The author was asked by the World Conservation Union (IUCN) and the World Bank, the two initiators of the commission process, to coordinate the appointment of the chair and commission, to initiate the fundraising, to build consultative mechanisms involving all stakeholders, and after WCD's first meeting, to hand off the management of WCD to the secretariat in Cape Town.

7. G. F. White, "The River as a System: A Geographer's View of Promising Approaches," *Water International* 22, no. 2 (1997): 79–81; G. F. White, "Water Science and Technology: Some Lessons from the 20th Century," *Environment* (January/February 2000): 30–88; and I. Burton, R. W. Kates, and G. F. White, eds., *Selected Writings of Gilbert F. White* (Chicago: University of Chicago Press, 1986).

8. WCD, *Dams and Development*, xxxiv–xxxv.

9. Ibid., 102.

15

LIFE AFTER RIO

Mark Halle[*]

This commentary is the opinion of the author, and does not necessarily represent the considered views of the International Institute for Sustainable Development.

June 23 and the planet continues its slow decline, unimpressed by the sustainable development summit that has just finished in Rio. Yet another UN mega-conference ends in disappointment, the low expectations fully justified. Once again, our governments have failed to demonstrate leadership, have lacked courage to make the compromises necessary to ensure a fairer, more stable world. Once again they have kept their eyes riveted on short-term electoral deadlines and sold out future generations. We have come to a sorry pass.

When, two years ago, the UN decided to hold this conference, there was no particular reason for it except that the twentieth anniversary of the original Earth Summit was looming. There were plenty of general reasons, including the fact that most of the decisions taken in 1992 have been ignored, most of the agreed actions never taken, and the planet has continued to decline. But nothing suggested that the necessary political will could be mustered to take transformative steps, to agree [on] game-changing resolutions, or even to stimulate implementation of the myriad decisions, resolutions and undertakings that were made in Rio in 1992 or in the two decades since.

Instead, we pinned our hopes on the losing prospect that global expectations for Rio, the presence of Heads of State or Government, and the sheer mass of talent concentrated in one place at one time could effect breakthroughs for which our normal political processes have proved inadequate. But if this once worked, it no longer does. Heads of State are perfectly content to make flowery speeches, hobnob with their peers, and head home to face the electorate. Mass is no longer majesty,

*Originally published as "Life after Rio: A commentary by Mark Halle, IISD," by the International Institute for Sustainable Development, *www.iisd.org*, June 2012. Reprinted with permission.

and large conferences, far from generating momentum, have, in the words of one commentator, become "too big to succeed." Global expectations of large UN conferences have, with considerable justification, sunk to very low levels on the back of repeated disappointment.

Things began to go wrong in the preparatory process. Groups of governments camped firmly on their positions; the UN secretariat offered no vision and little mobilizing power and failed to generate the funding needed to put together a proper team. And the host country, Brazil, never gave the sense that this conference was a high political priority. Instead, it looked very much as if it was more a dress rehearsal for the upcoming football World Cup and the Rio Olympic Games.

Despite adding extra negotiating sessions, only about one-seventh of the draft outcome document was agreed before the delegates assembled in Rio. Clearly, there was no way to complete negotiations in time for Heads of State to flourish the pen. So the Brazilians pulled a text from their back pockets and offered it on a "take it or leave it" basis to the stunned delegates. Leaving it would have meant a huge, public failure and, for many countries, an affront to their Brazilian ally. Taking meant giving up aspirations, but not much in reality since the text is free of genuine commitments. Accepting the text and declaring the conference a success was the easy way out, and the one taken.

What's in the Outcome Document?

So what can we conclude from the outcome document, the fruit of tens of thousands of person-hours of effort, the expenditure of tens of millions of dollars, and the repository of so many hopes and aspirations for saving our planet? [Editors' note: The Rio+20 outcome document, *The Future We Want,* is available at http://www.un.org/en/sustainablefuture/.]

Roughly one-third of the text consists of reaffirmation of decisions taken previously. In these reaffirmations, we declare that what we said before is still valid, that these aspirations still exist. By not slipping backwards and by not actually losing ground on these issues, we can to some extent hold the line. Some would say that, in the present global atmosphere of suspicion and mistrust, this is a positive result. If it is, expectations have sunk appallingly low.

Roughly another third of the text spells out considerations that governments should bear in mind in advancing along their development paths. These include the rights of indigenous peoples, the requirements of food security, the special problems of Small Island and landlocked States, and many, many more. While these considerations are no doubt worthy, they do not amount to new visions, new understandings or, sadly, new commitments. They simply spell out our understanding of what good development comprises.

The final third of the outcome document consists of language, mostly familiar but sometimes new, that identifies priorities in a wide array of areas ranging from oceans, cities and food security to water, sustainable consumption, economic development and institutional design. This is the section of the text on which most will focus. It is not that it embodies firm undertakings or calls for action that are targeted, specific and accountable. It is more that it offers hooks on which different stakeholders can hang their hopes. By referring to the specific language in the outcome document, they can claim that their special topic was endorsed by the world's governments in Rio and therefore constitutes a legitimate priority for attention.

The two central themes of the Rio Conference—the green economy and governance reform—fared poorly, in particular the latter. Hopes that the world community would anoint the green economy as the new guiding paradigm of economic development were dashed early on in the preparatory process when much of the developing world expressed severe doubts about it, fearing a resurgence of trade protection, a dominance of rich-country technology, and a commoditization of nature. In the end, the question was whether the notion would even secure a mention in the final text and the fact that it does—that it is offered as an option for countries to consider—is considered a success. It certainly is, considering the alternative.

The real disappointment comes in the failure of the conference to agree on any serious reform of sustainable development governance. If there is a consensus on anything in the international system, it is that the configuration of organizations, conventions and forums dealing with sustainable development is overlapping, inefficient and unresponsive to the fundamental needs. But 60 years of reform ambition have unearthed another immutable rule: that the multilateral system is in essence unreformable. It is possible to add new organizations, forums or processes to the existing maelstrom, but it is impossible to shift what is already there in any fundamental way.

Rio reaffirmed this rule. Efforts to upgrade UNEP [the United Nations Environment Programme] by giving it a higher institutional status failed. The only genuine achievement was to give UNEP universal membership, something that in effect it had already and that is, in any case, a dubious gain. For the rest, UNEP will have to pick apart and analyze the language of the outcome document in the hope of finding something resembling a determination to treat it with more respect.

Nor did the New York end fare much better. The moribund CSD [UN Commission on Sustainable Development] is put out of its misery after 20 years of underperformance; it will be replaced by some form of "high-level forum" whose shape and content is still to be defined. The debate now moves back to the shark pool of the New York UN community for resolution. How it will end up is uncertain, but on past record, it will join the long list of disappointments that the UN community has chalked up over the past decades.

A process was put in place to adopt Sustainable Development Goals by 2015. If successful and if set within a strong accountability framework, these goals might deliver on the specificity that Rio lacked. But this process, too, goes back to New York and will be tossed around on the political currents before sailing into harbor.

So what was good?

It is, of course, short-sighted to see Rio only through the lens of the official process and the conference in which it culminated. The vast majority of the participants did not come for that; certainly, they hoped that by some miracle Rio would prove to be a game-changer, but they came for something else.

Rio and similar events are, like the annual gathering of [Roma] groups in the French Camargue, an important gathering of the tribes, a get-together of the vast and diverse community involved in the search for a better future. Without events like Rio, it is unlikely that they would come together in the same way at any other forum. So what is the value in this assemblage and interaction?

It is, of course, impossible to measure, so anyone can make whatever claim they wish. The networking that goes on is certainly precious; so is the exposure to other ideas, whether from business groups, indigenous peoples, or global think tanks. Rio served as a vast trade fair through which the curious could wander, taking in an exhibit here, a workshop or teach-in there, hearing about experiences often far from their own, and understanding better the issues some stakeholders face. It served as an open university at which you could expose your own ideas and proposals or learn from others. This certainly has some value; indeed, it is undoubtedly the most (and some would say only) valuable thing about the Rio events.

Was it worth it?

In the collective disappointment there were many who felt it was good that we didn't slip back, that we held the line. Many firmly believe that the seeds planted in Rio will bear fruit, that initiatives started here will develop and flourish, and it is certainly true that the value of Rio will only become clear in the next two to three years. Others extolled the energy that was evident everywhere except the official negotiations and came away enriched and inspired by the many encounters and ideas received. Others simply had fun, looking forward to dinners, parties, samba evenings or walks on Rio's wonderful beaches. And it is important not to lapse into jaded cynicism because the world did not take a great leap forward towards sustainable development.

There were, and always are, silver linings, and glittering bits of mica in the general dross. But it is important to step back to secure the necessary breakthroughs. The preparations took up a huge amount of time and engaged a massive expenditure in travel, meetings, side events, exhibits and consultations. That was time and money not spent on alternative approaches. Given that it secured essentially nothing in terms of new engagement for sustainability, the process must be deemed a failure even on its own terms. It is like setting out to build a high-speed rail link between two distant cities and ending up asking people to be satisfied that the station signs received a fresh coat of paint.

Worse still, this failure is not an isolated one. Although it reached a consensus conclusion, what happened in Rio is a mirror of what happened at the climate change summit in Copenhagen [Editors' note: the fifteenth Conference of the Parties to the UN Framework Convention on Climate Change, held in Copenhagen in 2009], and resembles the failure of the last few WTO [World Trade Organization] ministerial meetings. Far from being a sad exception, low expectations and disappointment in global intergovernmental process have become the new norm, at least when success requires consensus on economic policy. We can no longer afford years of straining that ends up giving birth to a mouse.

What can we do to move forward?

If the approach is not working, surely we must change it. So why are we failing and what can we do to fix it? The first observation is that the principal problem lies with national governments, and [in] particular the groupings in which they congregate to negotiate. The rich OECD [Organisation for Economic Co-operation and Development] countries can no longer effectively impose their will on the rest; the G-77 group of developing countries has even more problems in holding to their common positions. Everyone observes the new pride and confidence of the emerging economies—in particular China, Brazil and India—but the groupings to which they belong (BRICS, BASIC) have in common only the fact that they are all, well, emerging. They continue to have vastly different foreign policy interests and do not represent a credible negotiating group. So the old order is fading but the new order has not yet taken its place. We are in abeyance, and this explains much of the negotiation failure.

Further, international negotiation is perceived, especially by the developing countries, as having been long on promise and short on delivery. Nothing in all that we have achieved over the past decades has changed the basic inequity in the international system. That countries like China and Brazil can grow rich is a meager consolation to poor countries like Malawi or Bangladesh. Impatience with the failure to address the equity agenda has been steadily growing and it has now reached the point where it is simply blocking all progress at the international level, whether in UNCTAD, in WTO, in climate change or in Rio. Every issue involving equity in the Rio process was contentious, and none of them was resolved except by draining the language of all genuine content.

If we are to move forward multilaterally, we will have to begin, finally, to address the glaring gaps between rich and poor countries, and the rich and poor within countries. And since we do not seem ready to do that, we must put a stop to the massive waste of money represented by events like the Rio conference. If our governments are not prepared to move towards sustainability, it is better that our voting populations know this. Calling a failure a success—even a guarded success—is to paper over the ever-widening cracks in the system.

So the first conclusion we must reach is that we should call a moratorium on all global multilateral negotiations on the environment and begin to address the thousands of unfulfilled promises and commitments we have made. To do so would be to build a momentum of success that would once again instill hope and belief among our populations. The various meetings, conferences of the parties, etc. should continue to convene, but with the single purpose of addressing the implementation gap and of raising confidence that there is a direct link between promise and fulfillment.

The second conclusion is that our intergovernmental structures are tired, lack vision and courage, and are increasingly left behind by the natural momentum of creativity and innovation in our societies. Worse still, there can no longer be any doubt that they are to all intents and purposes unreformable. Instead of once again launching attempts to streamline the UN system, we should simply assume that coordination, efficiency, accountability, responsible use of scarce funds, good governance and transparent process are now and always will be elusive goals and act accordingly. We should put our money and effort into organizations and processes that are not exclusively government-based.

If we follow these two recommendations, where should we then put our efforts? The good news, and the principal grounds for hope in the future, is that in the face of intergovernmental intransigence and lethargy, the world has not stood still. Instead, it has spawned an explosion of creativity and innovation that is truly impressive.

If national governments have found it difficult to progress, this is not true of sub-national jurisdictions. The movement among states, provinces, megacities and municipalities is taking off with the speed of a rocket, making commitments to the green economy or to climate change action that are truly inspiring. And even national governments, acting regionally, begin to feel that they may make more progress within the region than they can make globally.

The same is true of the private sector. For all the problems still associated with corporate activity, there is more advanced strategic thinking, more deep analysis of problems, more attachment to innovative thinking in the corporate sector than is evident in inter-governmental dialogue.

And, as always, civil society in its diversity and flexibility represents an untapped force which, if harnessed, would wield incredible power. Yet it is extremely difficult to herd the swarm of cats that civil society resembles. They cover the spectrum from multinational centers of intellectual power through to fronts for religions and a wide variety of cranks of all shapes, colors and smells. It is their connection to the ground level, to communities and local interests that gives them their particular strength and value.

So, on the one hand, we have a government-based process that is hopelessly stuck in the mud. On the other we have a mass of energy, creativity and strength that is not only committed to action but raring to go if only we can find the forms and channels to harness it. This, surely, is the creative field of endeavor for the future.

16

THE RIO+20 SUMMIT AND ITS FOLLOW UP

MARTIN KHOR*

The UN Conference on Sustainable Development, more popularly known as Rio+20, to commemorate the 20th anniversary of the 1992 Earth Summit, ended with expressions of deep disappointment from broad sections of members of the media and the environmental NGOs, who saw little new commitments to action in the final text that was adopted by the heads of states and governments and their senior officials.

This was understandable, as much had been expected from the Rio+20 summit, the biggest international gathering of world leaders this year. This is also because the world is facing serious crises in the global environment and economy, thus there were hopes that some decisive actions would be taken, worthy of the 20th anniversary of the original Rio summit, the UN Conference on Environment and Development.

Thus, there was unhappiness and frustration that the hundred heads of state and government who came to Rio de Janeiro were unable or not asked to take decisive actions. There was a sense that the speeches, roundtables and panel discussions at the huge Rio Centro conference center were part of a ceremonial function for the political leaders, while the tough decisions required by the crises were avoided or postponed.

But there are grounds for a more positive assessment of Rio+20. It achieved an agreed outcome, something that is increasingly rare in multilateral high-level meetings. It managed (just) to reaffirm previous understandings thus maintaining the foundations for international cooperation. And it directed the diplomats and officials of all countries to continue negotiating and come up with solutions to

*Originally published in *South Bulletin,* Issue 64, 6 July 2012, pp. 2–7. Reprinted with permission.

important unresolved issues within one to two years—including on sustainable development goals, finance and technology, and a new political forum on sustainable development.

The summit adopted a 53-page document, "The Future We Want." It reaffirmed or recalled what had been agreed to 20 or 10 years ago (at the first Rio Summit that produced the Rio Principles and Agenda 21, and the Johannesburg Summit that marked the 10th anniversary and produced a Plan of Implementation respectively). And it directed that the talks continue in the United Nations (in New York) to strengthen sustainable development and environment institutions, examine how and whether to provide finance and technology to developing countries, and establish new sustainable development goals.

Measured against the urgent tasks needed, there were no breakthroughs. But neither was the summit the failure that many portrayed it to be.

Pre-Summit Negotiations Lowered the Expectations

Those who have been following the negotiations to prepare for the summit had already scaled down expectations, for various reasons. The talks were bogged down by contentious debates on the "green economy," a new concept in the context of multilateral negotiations. There had been little focus on assessing the serious gaps in implementation of the Rio 1992 or Johannesburg [2002] outcomes, including on the commitments to provide finance and technology to developing countries. Only at a late stage was there a discussion on texts on specific environment or development issues, such as food security, water, oceans, poverty, and trade, and on the means of implementation (finance and technology), while a new theme (sustainable development goals) was also proposed at this late stage.

The developed countries seemed to be in little mood for a new boost to international or North-South cooperation, due perhaps to the effects on them of the global financial crisis and insecurity felt by some of them about the rise of potential rivals in the developing world. Even a reaffirmation of past commitments, which is a normal part of UN conferences, became a contentious issue. It was a repeat of UNCTAD [United Nations Conference on Trade and Development] conference XIII in April, when the developing countries had to fight very hard simply to get developed countries to reaffirm the mandate given to UNCTAD in the previous conference in Accra in 2008. And finally, there were just too few negotiating days allocated in the past two years to cover such a wide range of topics embedded in sustainable development.

The impasse in the negotiations continued in the last negotiating session in Rio itself on 13–15 June [2012]. As of the night of 15 June, there were 315 paragraphs in the draft of the outcome, but only 116 of them had been agreed to, with no compromise in sight on many major issues. The Brazilian government, as host country and incoming President of the conference, took over leadership of the negotiations. On 16–18 June, negotiations intensified on the basis of a new draft issued by Brazil. Finally, on 19 June, a final draft produced by Brazil was adopted by the senior officials.

Faced with the prospect of a real breakdown, the officials representing almost 200 countries pulled back from the brink and worked out last-minute compromises in an agreed text just as their political leaders were arriving in Rio. No country or group of countries were satisfied with the text, as some key points wanted by each group were not included. This gave rise to a comment from a senior UN official that everyone was equally unhappy, and thus the outcome was possible. There was above all relief that Rio+20 did not collapse in disarray without an outcome, as happened in some World Trade Organization ministerial meetings (1999, 2003) and in the Copenhagen climate conference (2009). Multilateralism in sustainable development was put to the test and survived to live another day. The outcome document agreed to just about meets the minimum requirements of success, given the deteriorating state of international cooperation and the tough battles that developing countries had to fight in the past year to get their points across. [Editors' note: The Rio+20 outcome document, *The Future We Want*, is available at http://www.un.org/en/sustainablefuture/.] It was often a frustrating and seemingly hopeless task. But in the end, the developing countries prevailed on several issues.

If there is to be reason for some optimism amidst the downbeat atmosphere, it is to be found in the mandate for follow-up actions. At the closing plenary on 22 June night, the Brazilian President, Dilma Rousseff, hailed the outcome document as a historic step for sustainable development. She said it was a "starting point" and not a "threshold or ceiling" for implementing the path to sustainable development that had to be ambitious and should serve as a legacy for future generations. Those were well-chosen words, for the document while not itself containing high action points, is a start in opening the way to potentially important actions.

Common But Differentiated Responsibilities

The biggest battle in the last week of negotiations in Rio was to get developed countries, especially the United States, to renew the original Rio principles on environment and development adopted at the historic 1992 Earth Summit. These include the environmental precautionary principle and polluter pays as well as development and equity principles of the right to development and the common but differentiated responsibilities (CBDR). The CBDR is especially important for developing countries, as it implies that while all countries should take sustainable development actions, the developed countries have to take the leading role in environmental protection, as they contributed the most to environmental problems, and they should also support developing countries with finance and technology in their sustainable development efforts. Some developed countries, especially the

United States, resisted affirming the Rio principles and especially CBDR. For developing countries, the reaffirmation of Rio plus a mention of CBDR was a necessity; without this reaffirmation, the summit would have been a disaster. On almost the last day, the US gave in. The document in Paragraph 15 now reaffirms the 1992 Rio principles, including the principle of "common but differentiated responsibilities" (CBDR).

In a section on climate change, the text (Paragraph 191) also recalls that the UN climate convention (UNFCCC) provides that Parties should protect the climate system "on the basis of equity and common but differentiated responsibilities and respective capabilities." Though this is only a factual reflection of the Convention, it is nevertheless a victory for developing countries since the equity and CBDR principles were notably absent in the decision at the UNFCCC Conference of Parties in December 2011 that mandated negotiations on a new Durban Platform under the Convention on Climate Change. Some developed countries, especially the US, have argued that the absence of the mention of equity and CBDR means that all Parties have to take on similar levels of commitments in a future climate regime, unlike the Kyoto Protocol. Developing countries on the contrary argued that these principles apply since the new regime will be under the Convention. Their position is thus strengthened since Rio+20 "recalled" these two principles in climate protection actions.

Technology and Finance

The Rio+20 outcome was a big letdown on the issues of financial resources for and technology transfer to developing countries. These are the "means of implementation" needed by developing countries to help them implement sustainable development plans, and were very prominent in Agenda 21. The G-77 [Group of 77] and China insisted on reaffirmation of the understanding that developing countries require these means of implementation to meet their obligations, and that developed countries renew their commitments, especially since there are new obligations on developing countries on account of the green economy and sustainable development goals components of the text.

On technology, the G-77 and China proposed a new technology transfer mechanism to promote sustainable development, since there has been little if any real transfers in the past two decades. However, the US and others refused to even reaffirm their commitment to transfer technology to developing countries. They insisted that the word "transfer" be deleted from the title of the technology transfer section, and that the term technology transfer wherever it appears should be accompanied by the words "voluntary" and "on mutually agreed terms and conditions," meaning that technology transfer would be on a commercial basis. The US chief delegate explained that this was to prevent compulsory licensing and imposition of technology transfer requirements by developing countries.

This demand was opposite to the language in Agenda 21 and the 2001 Johannesburg Plan of Action (JPOA) that agreed on pro-active technology transfer principles. After many rounds of intense discussion, the US on the last day agreed to language (in Paragraph 269) that "recalled" the technology text in the 2002 Rio+10 summit in Johannesburg, including technology transfer "particularly to developing countries, on favorable terms, including on concessional and preferential terms, as mutually agreed."

Long negotiations on how to treat the issues of intellectual property [IP] and access by developing countries to environmentally sound technology did not yield any direct results, with the US rejecting even very mild language on a "balanced approach to intellectual property." The only place IP is mentioned in the final text is in Paragraph 269 that recalled "the provisions on technology transfer, finance, access to information and intellectual property rights as agreed in the Johannesburg Plan of Implementation."

On finance for developing countries, the developed countries have watered down their previous commitments, this time refusing to reaffirm the usual terms of providing "new and additional financial resources" for developing countries in the Rio+20 text. This may reflect the budget problems in both the US and Europe, and the decline in development aid in the past year. Instead, there are references in the text to getting funds from a "variety of sources" and "new partnerships," a code for the reduced importance (and quantum) in developed countries' government financing for developing countries. A long paragraph (258) reaffirms the importance of fulfilling the ODA [Official Development Assistance] target of 0.7% of GDP [Gross Domestic Product].

The developed countries also wanted to emphasize South-South cooperation as an alternative source of financing, but did not succeed; instead there is a balanced paragraph on South-South cooperation as solidarity and complement (Paragraph 260).

The G-77 and China had before the Rio meeting proposed that a new sustainable development fund be created, and that at least $30 billion a year be provided in 2013–17, rising to $100 billion a year from 2018. (In Rio 1992, the Secretariat estimated developing countries required $100 billion a year in external funds to implement Agenda 21.) But this was unacceptable to developed countries.

The developing countries were thus very dissatisfied with the retreat in commitments on the means of implementation, and argued that the new Green Economy and Sustainable Development Goals aspects of the outcome would be meaningless without a commitment to finance and technology.

To save the show, it was agreed that there would be a follow-up process in both finance and technology after Rio+20. On finance (Paragraph 255), an intergovernmental process will start under the [UN] General Assembly to assess financing needs, existing frameworks and additional initiatives, to prepare a report towards a Sustainable Development Financing Strategy to mobilize resources for sustainable development. A committee of 30 experts nominated by regional groups will implement this process and conclude its work by 2014.

On technology, developing countries wanted a technology transfer mechanism, or at least a discussion towards that goal. Developed countries would not agree to a direct intergovernmental process. The final text (Paragraph 273) requests UN agencies to identify options for a facilitation mechanism to promote development, transfer and dissemination of environmentally sound technologies by assessing technology needs of developing countries, options to address them and capacity building. The UN Secretary-General is asked to make recommendations on this mechanism to the General Assembly's 67th session.

These are actions to be carried forward, rather than firm commitments, and will hardly convince developing countries that they will get the means (finance and technology) to implement new obligations on environment and sustainable development. Thus, the developed countries have not maintained their level of commitments of 20 or even 10 years ago, whether on sustainable development principles or on finance and technology. Developing countries in effect made significant concessions in accepting the very watered-down language, and this must be seen as their major contribution to an outcome for Rio+20.

Nevertheless, two processes have been put in motion that keep the issue of finance and technology for sustainable development alive, and the follow-up processes for both issues hold the promise of leading to some new strategies and mechanisms.

Sustainable Development Goals

A new item in the Rio+20 outcome with considerable follow-up implication is the decision to formulate sustainable development goals (SDGs). This will be done in the next year through a 30-member working group under the UN General Assembly, nominated by governments through the UN regional groups. The UN Secretary-General is asked to provide initial inputs and the UN agencies' support to the working group, which will submit a report on the goals to the General Assembly next year for its action.

Establishing SDGs was not on the original mandate of Rio+20 topics but entered the process in late 2011 through a proposal of Colombia and a few other countries. It developed increasing support as a concrete "deliverable" for the summit and as a kind of replacement for the controversial Green Economy issue. Although establishing SDGs turned out to be a complex exercise, at least the concept of sustainable development was an accepted and comfortable one, unlike the green economy.

The developing countries during the negotiations fought for several things: to have a good definition of SDGs, to ensure that there is a balanced approach among the three pillars (economic, social, environmental) of sustainable development in the selected goals, that the SDGs be formulated by an inter-governmental process and not "dropped" on the governments by the UN Secretary-General or UN-chosen experts (as in the case of the Millennium Development Goals [MDGs]), and that the SDG process should interact with and not replace the separate process of the UN's post-2015 development agenda after the expiry of the MDGs. They also preferred that no specific SDGs be named in Rio, in order not to pre-empt the approach of having goals balanced from all three pillars.

The developing countries' positions prevailed on all these aspects. In the final text, the SDGs are to be based on Agenda 21 and the Johannesburg Plan of Action, respect the Rio principles, build on commitments already made, and incorporate the three dimensions of sustainable development. They should be coherent with and integrated in the UN development agenda beyond 2015 and should not divert effort from the MDGs. The goals should address priority areas, guided by the outcome document.

Developed countries, especially the European Union (EU), were disappointed that the summit itself did not adopt five specific goals that were mainly environmental in nature, that they put forward as initial and priority SDGs. The developing countries argued there was no time to agree on what the initial goals would be, since economic and social goals also have to be included.

The formulation of the SDGs, and their interface with the post-2015 development agenda, will be one of the most important follow-up actions initiated by the Rio+20 summit.

The Green Economy

The outcome document has a large section on the "green economy." This topic had in fact absorbed most of the time and energy of the summit's preparatory meetings over the last two years. "The green economy in the context of sustainable development and poverty eradication" had been included as one of the two specific themes of the conference (the other being institutional framework for sustainable development). However, it soon became the center of contention and controversy, partly because it was a new subject for multilateral negotiations that could potentially result in new obligations on states, and partly because the subject was being negotiated in the home of "sustainable development" and there was confusion about its interface conceptually and practically with sustainable development.

From the early stages of negotiations, some developed countries, especially the EU, were advocating having an action-oriented and norm-related approach to the Green Economy. The EU proposed that Rio+20 formulate a UN green economy roadmap with several specific goals, targets and deadlines for issues such as water, forests, agriculture and oceans. This was seen as going too far with the concept by many developing countries. They had many concerns, including that the "green economy" concept would replace "sustainable development"; that it may be used to justify trade protectionism against developing-country products and new conditionality for aid and finance; that it would be used to create new markets based on economic valuation of nature's functions, offsets and payment for environment services and thus lead to commodification of nature. There was also concern that there would be a one-size-fits-all approach as well as "green economy" obligations that all countries have to adhere to, without developing counties getting the corresponding means of implementation (finance and technology) from developed countries.

After a long fight lasting over a year, it was finally agreed in the Rio+20 text that the green economy is one of the important tools for achieving sustainable development, providing options but not a rigid set of rules. The green economy policies should be guided by the Rio principles. The text also contains 16 points of what the green economy should be or not be. It should respect national sovereignty, promote inclusive growth, strengthen finance and technology transfer to developing countries, avoid aid and finance conditionalities, not be used for trade protectionism, help close North-South technology gaps, address poverty and inequalities and promote sustainable consumption and production patterns.

The main action points on the green economy are quite mild (Paragraph 66). The UN system and relevant donors are asked to coordinate and provide information on matching interested countries with partners to provide requested support; to provide toolboxes and best practices and good examples in applying green economy policies, methodologies for evaluating policies, and platforms that can contribute.

Institutional Framework for Sustainable Development (IFSD)

The IFSD was one of the two major themes of Rio+20 and the chapter on it could prove to have the most significant results. It is widely recognized that while Rio 1992 was a success, its follow-up mechanisms for implementation were weak. The main body for follow up was the new Commission on Sustainable Development (CSD); it worked well as a convening body for Ministers and senior officials in its initial years, but had lackluster results in recent years. The problem was mainly in design: it meets only two to three weeks in a year and has a small secretariat within the UN department on economic and social affairs, yet it has a large agenda of tasks and issues to fulfill.

Potentially, the most important decision in Rio was to set up a high-level political forum on sustainable development, to replace the CSD. The idea of a Forum had been originally proposed by the G-77 and China, while others, mainly the European countries, proposed transforming the CSD into a new Sustainable Development Council. The final text agreed to establishing the Forum; the text also incorporated some of the ideas proposed for the Council.

According to the text, the high-level forum could have 12 functions, including to provide political leadership and recommendations for sustainable development, provide a platform for regular dialogue and agenda setting, have set the agenda and enable regular dialogue, consider new sustainable development challenges, review progress in implementation and improve coordination in the UN system, have an action-oriented agenda for new and emerging challenges, follow up on implementing all the sustainable development commitments, coordinate within the UN system, [and] promote system-wide coherence and coordination of sustainable development policies.

As the details have not been sorted out, Rio+20 decided to launch an intergovernmental process under the General Assembly to define the forum's format and organizational aspects, aimed at convening the first forum at the General Assembly's 68th session in 2013.

A key issue is the extent to which this forum will only be a series of annual meetings and roundtables (during the time of the annual General Assembly session) or whether it will have a strong structure that addresses the social, economic and environmental dimensions, that meets regularly throughout the year and that is serviced by a strong enough Secretariat.

If the new forum can have a wide agenda, a big enough mandate to act, a dynamic process of discussion and decision making, a strong secretariat and high political backing, then the modest document coming out of the Rio+20 summit can be transformed into a world-changing process and organization.

Rio+20 also agreed that the UN Environment Programme would be strengthened and upgraded, including through establishing universal membership of its governing council and increased, stable and adequate financing, and strengthening its regional presence. It is the only place in the text in which increased and adequate funding is committed. The General Assembly is invited to adopt a resolution on UNEP to this effect.

This decision was a great disappointment to European countries which were strongly advocating that UNEP be transformed into a UN specialized agency. This was also supported by the African Group. However, this proposal was not acceptable to other major developed countries including the US, Japan and Russia, or by many developing countries, each for their own reasons.

Action on Thematic Issues

The document also has a large section (Section V) on action on many thematic issues, including water, oceans, biodiversity, food security and agriculture, energy, transport, health, employment and social protection, cities, disaster risk reduction, poverty eradication and trade. Some of these topics contain proposals and promised actions, most of which are useful as guidelines for countries and institutions to implement. For example, the section on food security and sustainable agriculture reaffirms the right to food, emphasizes rural development and the importance of small farmers and indigenous peoples and their need for secure land tenure and credit, and promotes sustainable agriculture, while stressing the need to address the root causes of food price volatility. It does not however address the key problem of developed countries' agricultural subsidies.

Conclusion

While the Rio+20 Summit fell short of justified expectations that it would be a landmark in addressing the world's current serious crises, it was fortunate that there was even an agreed outcome at all. The present atmosphere of international cooperation has deteriorated recently, as can be seen in the impasse in the WTO's Doha negotiations, the failure of the Copenhagen climate conference, and the uncertainties surrounding the UNCTAD XIII conference. Rio+20 also became a victim of the reduced commitments by developed countries to support the developing countries in their development quest.

Despite some setbacks, the developing countries managed to secure many of their key positions and demands made in the negotiations. It says a lot about the current international situation that a reaffirmation of principles made 10 and 20 years ago is a sign of success.

With the outcome in Rio, the multilateral system in sustainable development lives to fight another day. The mandated actions in the Rio+20 text, on the high-level forum on sustainable development, the finance strategy and technology facilitating mechanism, and the sustainable development goals, point to more and potentially important work in the year ahead at the UN. The success of any conference is ultimately determined on the strength of the follow-up. Rio+20 could remain a disappointment, or could become the start of something significant. In that sense, Rio+20 has not ended, but only started, as the Brazilian President stated at the summit's closure.

PART FOUR

THE SUSTAINABILITY DEBATE

EFFECTIVE RESPONSES TO GLOBAL ENVIRONMENTAL PROBLEMS DEMAND BOTH international cooperation and institutional reform. As previous sections have indicated, these are substantial challenges. The prevailing structures and practices of the international system make attainment of these goals difficult, and they cannot be divorced from the larger political, economic, and cultural struggles that infuse world politics.

It would be a mistake, however, to study global environmental politics solely in terms of international treaties and institutional change. Perspectives on the essence of the global environmental problematique are another key variable, and one that has changed in important ways over time. Few would argue that ideas alone have the power to change history. But there is no doubt that paradigms—bundles of fundamental ideas and beliefs—shape the strategies and goals of actors in important ways. They influence how actors understand their interests, how policies are formulated, how resources are allocated, and which actors and institutions are empowered to make the critical decisions that affect global environmental quality.[1]

One powerful but controversial new paradigm that emerged in the buildup to the 1992 Rio de Janeiro Earth Summit is the idea of sustainability. As previously discussed, one of the central controversies at the 1972 Stockholm conference was the debate over whether economic growth and development are inherently destructive to the environment. This question revealed sharp cleavages between governments of the industrialized North and the developing South, as well as sharp divisions between growth-oriented governments in general and nongovernmental actors concerned about the negative consequences of continually expanding economic activity.

Concepts of sustainability and sustainable development appeal to many people because they hold out the promise of reconciling these divergent views. Sustainable-development approaches are predicated on the premises that poverty and economic stagnation are themselves environmentally destructive, and that some forms of economic organization and activity can reduce environmental impact even as they promote growth and human development. If these premises are true, then it might be possible to design environment-friendly forms of production and exchange that simultaneously facilitate economic development, alleviate the pressures of poverty, and minimize environmental damage. Such forms of production and exchange might be aimed at "development without growth"—that is, improvement in the quality of people's lives without an increase in the aggregate level of economic activity.[2] Or they might be tailored to forms of economic growth that are more acceptable ecologically. Whatever the

179

path advocated, reconciling the tension between ecology and economy is the central goal of sustainable development.

The most frequently cited definition of sustainable development is found in *Our Common Future*—as noted in Part One, the influential 1987 report published by the World Commission on Environment and Development (Chapter 17). In 1983 the United Nations General Assembly charged the commission—also known as the Brundtland Commission, after its chairperson, Norwegian prime minister Gro Harlem Brundtland—with devising a conceptual and practical "global agenda for change."[3] The commission, which included representatives from twenty-two nations on five continents, conducted a series of hearings around the world before preparing its final report and presenting it to the General Assembly in 1987. The report had an enormous influence on the global environmental debate and played a key role in shaping the content and format of the 1992 Rio Earth Summit.

According to the Brundtland Commission, sustainable development is "development that meets the needs of the present without compromising the ability of future generations to meet their own needs."[4] To meet the goal of achieving sustainable development, the commission set forth a policy blueprint based on enhanced international cooperation, substantial changes in national policies, and a reoriented global economy. The report argues that the problem is not economic growth per se but the environmentally destructive character of many current activities and incentives. Economic growth remains vital, in the commission's view, given the substantial impact of poverty on the environment. Thus, the commission combined its recommendations for ecologically sound forms of production and exchange with a call for renewed global economic growth to solve the problems of Third World poverty.

Some observers saw the commission's advocacy of these positions as inherently contradictory. The continued commitment to a basically unreformed global economic system is, in this view, the biggest impediment to true sustainability, rather than a prerequisite for managing environmental problems more effectively. Skeptics such as Larry Lohmann, editorializing in the influential British environmental journal *The Ecologist,* questioned whether the Brundtland Commission had provided an agenda for change at all: "Never underestimate the ability of modern elites to work out ways of coming through a crisis with their power intact."[5]

In Chapter 18, Sharachchandra Lélé provides a different but in some ways equally critical assessment of the concept of sustainable development. A comprehensive review of the burgeoning literature on sustainability leads Lélé to conclude that the concept lacks a clear, widely accepted definition. There are many different conceptions of sustainable development, not all of which endorse the Brundtland Commission's formulation. Lélé argues that because of the many frequently contradictory uses of the term, sustainable development "is in real danger of becoming a cliché . . . a fashionable phrase that everyone pays homage to but nobody cares to define." Lélé accepts the goal of meeting current needs without compromising future generations; his quarrel is with assumptions embedded in mainstream sustainable-development thinking. These include a narrowly technical focus on the problem of poverty while ignoring its fundamentally sociopolitical roots; a neo-classical emphasis on economic growth as an end in itself, rather than a more precise specification of how to meet people's basic needs; and a lack of clarity about exactly what is to be sustained, for whom, and for how long. Lélé also worries that mainstream notions of sustainable development place an undue burden of structural and value adjustment on the South so that current consumption practices in the North may continue. The idea that the challenge lies primarily in the South is more a reflection of the power of some actors and institutions to set the global agenda than an accurate reflection of the true scope of the problem.

Lélé's concerns force us to ask what sustainable societies might look like, and what the pathways for getting there might entail. Some influential actors and institutions prefer the Brundtland Commission's notion of growth-oriented sustainability, emphasizing efficiency in the context of open markets to improve existing systemic structures such as free trade and a modern industrial economy. This perspective takes an optimistic view of the possibilities for "ecological modernization," in which advanced industrial societies are seen as able to make significant environmental progress through reform in production systems, management practices, and market-based incentives, while remaining within the parameters of a globalizing capitalist economy.[6] Reflecting this vision, we present in Chapter 19 a report on the environmental commitments of several leading corporations that have come together under the Corporate Eco Forum, in partnership with a leading conservation organization, The Nature Conservancy. The report makes the case that there is a business argument for sustainability, with the payoffs of greater efficiency of resource use, cost savings, reduced risks, and enhanced corporate reputation.

In contrast to this relatively optimistic scenario, Peter Dauvergne's contribution (Chapter 20) sees a far deeper crisis of global unsustainability rooted in "the consumer society" that is less amenable to technical and managerial solutions. Here, the primary culprit is not the undercapitalized status of the global South but the consumption habits of the smaller but wealthier populations in the North and, through international trade and the diffusion of consumerist lifestyles, the more affluent segments of society in the global South. Consider the state of California in the United States, often held up as the pinnacle of the consumer society. Californians protect their own environment through the implementation of strict conservation laws—while simultaneously continuing their high-throughput lifestyles through international trade and the exploitation of resources from distant lands. A newspaper report documenting these tendencies was called, tellingly, "State of Denial."[7]

The consumer society's ecological shadow raises several questions that challenge mainstream practices in industrial life: Can the Earth survive as a world where more is always assumed to be better? Are technical fixes going to be enough, when influences as varied as Hollywood and the World Bank market this acquisitive logic to developing countries as the proper model for their own development? Or, as one early exploration of the question of consumption put it, quite simply: How much is enough?[8]

Another challenge in developing blueprints for sustainability is the question of scale. The example of California stresses the need to see the whole system, rather than drawing premature conclusions about success or failure from a study of just one component part. In no small measure due to frustration with national governments, the past few decades have seen a burgeoning "sustainable cities" movement.[9] While such movements offer great potential to improve the energy, water, and land-use efficiencies of urban areas, the idea that cities can truly be "sustainable" raises more profound questions. Thomas Elmqvist argues in Chapter 21 that sustainability is often confused with self-sufficiency (a steep challenge if not an outright impossibility for most cities, as the producing and consuming hubs of larger socioeconomic systems), and that the concept must be applied at larger scales if it is to have real meaning. Much the same is true, in his view, of the increasingly important environmental value of *resilience,* or the ability of complex, adaptive systems to respond to significant changes and stresses. An implication of Elmqvist's argument: it is difficult to create either sustainability or resilience in a particular place without assessing and addressing its linkages or "teleconnections" to larger socioeconomic systems.

In conclusion, we might well ask whether the idea of sustainability can break the North-South stalemate on environment and development that emerged at the Stockholm conference, and that remained much in evidence forty years later at the Rio+20 summit. To some extent, it already has; there is no question that the power of the concept—and in particular, its vision of harmonizing environmental quality and economic well-being—has fundamentally altered the global debate. The next and more difficult step is to clarify whether and how that vision can be realized. Whether the debate on sustainability moves to this higher level hinges on our ability to meet several challenges. We must redirect our gaze to encompass the system as a whole and not just the South; we must clarify and reconcile the goals that characterize radically different visions of a sustainable society; and we must broaden our vision to engage the contested issues of power, wealth, and authority that underlie current environmental problems.

Thinking Critically

1. In your judgment, does "sustainable development" represent a powerful synthesis of the twin needs for environmental protection and economic development? Or is it a contradiction in terms? Is sustainability compatible with a wide array of definitions of "development," or does it narrowly limit what development can mean?

2. How do you think the members of the Brundtland Commission would respond to the criticisms voiced by Lélé and Dauvergne? Would they share

the optimism of the Corporate Eco Forum's members about the "business case" for sustainability?

3. Can there be a common framework for sustainability across the diverse societies of the global South? For the North as well as the South? Is a concept such as sustainability universal, or is it inherently contingent on culture?

4. Are you an overconsumer? Is it accurate to say that California, or your community, is in a "state of denial"? Is it fair? How much control do you have over your consumption? What aspects of your life would have to change for you to change from overconsumer to sustainer? What are the barriers to the sort of change that Dauvergne's critique of consumption implies?

5. How can cities seeking resilience and sustainability deal with the scale problem identified by Elmqvist? Does your city's sustainability initiatives offer an answer to that question? If not, what would such a strategy look like?

NOTES

1. For a view stressing the importance of paradigms in shaping global environmental futures, see Dennis C. Pirages, ed., *Building Sustainable Societies: A Blueprint for a Post-Industrial World* (Armonk, NY: M. E. Sharpe, 1996).

2. On the concept of development without growth, see Herman E. Daly and John B. Cobb Jr., *For the Common Good: Redirecting the Economy Toward Community, the Environment, and a Sustainable Future* (Boston: Beacon Press, 1989).

3. World Commission on Environment and Development (WCED), *Our Common Future* (New York: Oxford University Press, 1987), p. ix.

4. WCED, *Our Common Future*, p. 43.

5. Larry Lohmann, "Whose Common Future?" *The Ecologist* 20, no. 3 (May/June 1990). A similar criticism has been made of the "global change" discourse that became increasingly influential in environmental circles beginning in the 1980s. See Frederick H. Buttel, Ann P. Hawkins, and Alison G. Power, "From Limits to Growth to Global Change," *Global Environmental Change* 1 (December 1990): 57–66.

6. On ecological modernization, see Arthur P. J. Mol, "Ecological Modernization and the Global Economy," *Global Environmental Politics* 2, no. 2 (May 2002): 92–115.

7. "State of Denial: A Special Report on the Environment," *Sacramento Bee*, Sunday, April 27, 2003.

8. Alan Durning, *How Much Is Enough? The Consumer Society and the Future of the Earth* (Washington, DC: Worldwatch Institute, 1992).

9. See, for example, Sustainable Cities International (sustainablecities.net) and the Sustainable Cities Collective (http://sustainablecitiescollective.com/).

17

TOWARDS SUSTAINABLE DEVELOPMENT

WORLD COMMISSION ON ENVIRONMENT
AND DEVELOPMENT*

Sustainable development is development that meets the needs of the present without compromising the ability of future generations to meet their own needs. It contains within it two key concepts:

- the concept of "needs," in particular the essential needs of the world's poor, to which overriding priority should be given; and
- the idea of limitations imposed by the state of technology and social organization on the environment's ability to meet present and future needs.

Thus the goals of economic and social development must be defined in terms of sustainability in all countries—developed or developing, market-oriented or centrally planned. . . . Development involves a progressive transformation of economy and society. A development path that is sustainable in a physical sense could theoretically be pursued even in a rigid social and political setting. But physical sustainability cannot be secured unless development policies pay attention to such considerations as changes in access to resources and in the distribution of costs and benefits. . . .

---

*Excerpted from Chapter Two of World Commission on Environment and Development, *Our Common Future* (New York: Oxford University Press, 1987). Reprinted with permission.

The Concept of Sustainable Development

The satisfaction of human needs and aspirations is the major objective of development. The essential needs of vast numbers of people in developing countries—for food, clothing, shelter, jobs—are not being met, and beyond their basic needs these people have legitimate aspirations for an improved quality of life. A world in which poverty and inequity are endemic will always be prone to ecological and other crises. Sustainable development requires meeting the basic needs of all and extending to all the opportunity to satisfy their aspirations for a better life.

Living standards that go beyond the basic minimum are sustainable only if consumption standards everywhere have regard for long-term sustainability. Yet many of us live beyond the world's ecological means, for instance, in our patterns of energy use. Perceived needs are socially and culturally determined, and sustainable development requires the promotion of values that encourage consumption standards that are within the bounds of the ecological possible and to which all can reasonably aspire.

Meeting essential needs depends in part on achieving full growth potential, and sustainable development clearly requires economic growth in places where such needs are not being met. Elsewhere, it can be consistent with economic growth, provided the content of growth reflects the broad principles of sustainability and nonexploitation of others. But growth by itself is not enough. High levels of productive activity and widespread poverty can coexist, and can endanger the environment. Hence sustainable development requires that societies meet human needs both by increasing productive potential and by ensuring equitable opportunities for all.

An expansion in numbers can increase the pressure on resources and slow the rise in living standards in areas where deprivation is widespread. Though the issue is not merely one of population size but of the distribution of resources, sustainable development can only be pursued if demographic developments are in harmony with the changing productive potential of the ecosystem.

A society may in many ways compromise its ability to meet the essential needs of its people in the future—by overexploiting resources, for example. The direction of technological developments may solve some immediate problems but lead to even greater ones. . . . At a minimum, sustainable development must not endanger the natural systems that support life on Earth: the atmosphere, the waters, the soils, and the living beings.

Growth has no set limits in terms of population or resource use beyond which lies ecological disaster. Different limits hold for the use of energy, materials, water, and land. Many of these will manifest themselves in the form of rising costs and diminishing returns, rather than in the form of any sudden loss of a resource base. The accumulation of knowledge and the development of technology can enhance the carrying capacity of the resource base. But ultimate limits there are, and sustainability requires that long before these are reached, the world must ensure equitable access to the constrained resource and reorient technological efforts to relieve the pressure.

Economic growth and development obviously involve changes in the physical ecosystem. Every ecosystem everywhere cannot be preserved intact. . . . In general, renewable resources like forests and fish stocks need not be depleted provided the rate of use is within the limits of regeneration and natural growth. But most renewable resources are part of a complex and interlinked ecosystem, and maximum sustainable yield must be defined after taking into account system-wide effects of exploitation.

As for nonrenewable resources, like fossil fuels and minerals, their use reduces the stock available for future generations. But this does not mean that such resources should not be used. In general the rate of depletion should take into account the criticality of that resource, the availability of technologies for minimizing depletion, and the likelihood of substitutes being available. . . . Sustainable development requires that the rate of depletion of nonrenewable resources should foreclose as few future options as possible.

Development tends to simplify ecosystems and to reduce their diversity of species. . . . The loss of plant and animal species can greatly limit the options of future generations; so sustainable development requires the conservation of plant and animal species.

So-called free goods like air and water are also resources. . . . Sustainable development requires that the adverse impacts on the quality of air, water, and other natural elements are minimized so as to sustain the ecosystem's overall integrity.

In essence, sustainable development is a process of change in which the exploitation of resources, the direction of investments, the orientation of technological development, and institutional change are all in harmony and enhance both current and future potential to meet human needs and aspirations.

Equity and the Common Interest

. . . How are individuals in the real world to be persuaded or made to act in the common interest? The answer lies partly in education, institutional development, and law enforcement. But many problems of resource depletion and environmental stress arise from disparities in economic and political power. An industry may get away with unacceptable levels of air and water pollution because the people who bear the brunt of it are poor and unable to complain effectively. . . .

Ecological interactions do not respect the boundaries of individual ownership and political jurisdiction. . . . Traditional social systems recognized some aspects of this interdependence and enforced community control over agricultural practices and traditional rights relating to water, forests, and land. This enforcement of the "common interest" did not necessarily impede growth and expansion though it may have limited the acceptance and diffusion of technical innovations.

Local interdependence has, if anything, increased because of the technology used in modern agriculture and manufacturing. Yet with this surge of technical progress, the growing "enclosure" of common lands, the erosion of common rights in forests and other resources, and the spread of commerce and production for the market, the responsibilities for decision making are being taken away from both groups and individuals. This shift is still under way in many developing countries.

It is not that there is one set of villains and another of victims. All would be better off if each person took into account the effect of his or her acts upon others. But each is unwilling to assume that others will behave in this socially desirable fashion, and hence all continue to pursue narrow self-interest. Communities or governments can compensate for this isolation through laws, education, taxes, subsidies, and other methods. . . . Most important, effective participation in decisionmaking processes by local communities can help them articulate and effectively enforce their common interest. . . .

The enforcement of common interest often suffers because areas of political jurisdictions and areas of impact do not coincide. . . . No supranational authority exists to resolve such issues, and the common interest can only be articulated through international cooperation.

In the same way, the ability of a government to control its national economy is reduced by growing international economic interactions. . . . If economic power and the benefits of trade were more equally distributed, common interests would be generally recognized. But the gains from trade are unequally distributed, and patterns of trade in, say, sugar affect not merely a local sugar-producing sector, but the economies and ecologies of the many developing countries that depend heavily on this product.

The search for common interest would be less difficult if all development and environment problems had solutions that would leave everyone better off. This is seldom the case, and there are usually winners and losers. Many problems arise from inequalities in access to resources. . . . "Losers" in environment/development conflicts include those who suffer more than their fair share of the health, property, and ecosystem damage costs of pollution.

As a system approaches ecological limits, inequalities sharpen. Thus when a watershed deteriorates, poor farmers suffer more because they cannot afford the same anti-erosion measures as richer farmers. . . . Globally, wealthier nations are better placed financially and technologically to cope with the effects of possible climatic change.

Hence, our inability to promote the common interest in sustainable development is often a product of the relative neglect of economic and social justice within and amongst nations.

Strategic Imperatives

The world must quickly design strategies that will allow nations to move from their present, often destructive, processes of growth and development onto sustainable development paths. . . .

Critical objectives for environment and development policies that follow from the concept of sustainable development include:

- reviving growth;
- changing the quality of growth;
- meeting essential needs for jobs, food, energy, water, and sanitation;
- ensuring a sustainable level of population;
- conserving and enhancing the resource base;
- reorienting technology and managing risk; and
- merging environment and economics in decision making.

Reviving Growth

. . . Development that is sustainable has to address the problem of the large number of people who . . . are unable to satisfy even the most basic of their needs. Poverty reduces people's capacity to use resources in a sustainable manner; it intensifies pressure on the environment. . . . A necessary but not a sufficient condition for the elimination of absolute poverty is a relatively rapid rise in per capita incomes in the Third World. It is therefore essential that the stagnant or declining growth trends of . . . [the 1980s] be reversed.

While attainable growth rates will vary, a certain minimum is needed to have any impact on absolute poverty. It seems unlikely that, taking developing countries as a whole, these objectives can be accomplished with per capita income growth of under 3 percent. . . .

Growth must be revived in developing countries because that is where the links between economic growth, the alleviation of poverty, and environmental conditions operate most directly. Yet developing countries are part of an interdependent world economy; their prospects also depend on the levels and patterns of growth in industrialized nations. The medium-term prospects for industrial countries are for growth of 3–4 percent. . . . Such growth rates could be environmentally sustainable if industrialized nations can continue the recent shifts in the content of their growth towards less material- and energy-intensive activities and the improvement of their efficiency in using materials and energy.

As industrialized nations use less materials and energy, however, they will provide smaller markets for commodities and minerals from the developing nations. Yet if developing nations focus their efforts upon eliminating poverty and satisfying essential human needs, then domestic demand will increase for both agricultural products and manufactured goods and some services. Hence the very logic of sustainable development implies an internal stimulus to Third World growth. . . .

Changing the Quality of Growth

Sustainable development involves more than growth. It requires a change in the content of growth, to make it less material- and energy-intensive and more equitable in its impact. These changes are required in all countries as part of a package of measures to maintain the stock of ecological capital, to improve the distribution of income, and to reduce the degree of vulnerability to economic crises.

The process of economic development must be more soundly based upon the realities of the stock of capital that sustains it. . . . For example, income from forestry operations is conventionally measured in terms of the value of timber and other products extracted, minus the costs of extraction. The costs of regenerating the forest are not taken into account, unless money is actually spent on such work. Thus figuring profits from logging rarely takes full account of the losses in future revenue incurred through degradation of the forest. . . . In all countries, rich or poor, economic development must take full account in its measurements of growth of the improvement or deterioration in the stock of natural resources. . . .

Yet it is not enough to broaden the range of economic variables taken into account. Sustainability requires views of human needs and well-being that incorporate such noneconomic variables as education and health enjoyed for their own sake, clean air and water, and the protection of natural beauty. . . .

Economic and social development can and should be mutually reinforcing. Money spent on education and health can raise human productivity. Economic development can accelerate social development by providing opportunities for underprivileged groups or by spreading education more rapidly.

Meeting Essential Human Needs

The satisfaction of human needs and aspirations is so obviously an objective of productive activity that it may appear redundant to assert its central role in the concept of sustainable development. All too often poverty is such that people cannot satisfy their needs for survival and well-being even if goods and services are available. At the same time, the demands of those not in poverty may have major environmental consequences.

The principal development challenge is to meet the needs and aspirations of an expanding developing world population. The most basic of all needs is for a livelihood: that is, employment. Between 1985 and 2000 the labor force in developing countries will increase by nearly 900 million, and new livelihood opportunities will have to be generated for 60 million persons every year.[1] . . .

More food is required not merely to feed more people but to attack undernourishment. . . . Though the focus at present is necessarily on staple foods, the projections given above also highlight the need for a high rate of growth of protein availability. In Africa, the task is particularly challenging given the recent declining per capita food production and the current constraints on growth. In Asia and Latin America, the required growth rates in calorie and protein consumption seem to be more readily attainable. But increased food production should not be based on ecologically unsound production policies and compromise long-term prospects for food security.

Energy is another essential human need, one that cannot be universally met unless energy consumption patterns change. The most urgent problem is the requirements of poor Third World households, which depend mainly on fuelwood. By the turn of the century, 3 billion people may live in areas where wood is cut faster than it grows or where fuelwood is extremely scarce.[2] Corrective action would both reduce the drudgery of collecting wood over long distances and preserve the ecological base. . . .

The linked basic needs of housing, water supply, sanitation, and health care are also environmentally important. Deficiencies in these areas are often visible manifestations of environmental stress. In the Third World, the failure to meet these key needs is one of the major causes of many communicable diseases such as malaria, gastrointestinal infestations, cholera, and typhoid. . . .

Ensuring a Sustainable Level of Population

The sustainability of development is intimately linked to the dynamics of population growth. The issue, however, is not simply one of global population size. A child born in a country where levels of material and energy use are high places a greater burden on the Earth's resources than a child born in a poorer country. . . .

In industrial countries, the overall rate of population growth is under 1 percent, and several countries have reached or are approaching zero population growth. The total population of the industrialized world could increase from its current 1.2 billion to about 1.4 billion in the year 2025.[3]

The greater part of global population increase will take place in developing countries, where the 1985 population of 3.7 billion may increase to 6.8 billion by 2025.[4] The Third World does not have the option of migration to "new" lands, and the time available for adjustment is much less than industrial countries had. Hence the challenge now is to quickly lower population growth rates, especially in regions such as Africa, where these rates are increasing.

Birth rates declined in industrial countries largely because of economic and social development. Rising levels of income and urbanization and the changing role of women all played important roles. Similar processes are now at work in developing countries. These should be recognized and encouraged. Population policies should be integrated with other economic and social development programs—female education, health care, and the expansion of the livelihood base of the poor. . . .

Developing-country cities are growing much faster than the capacity of authorities to cope. Shortages of housing, water, sanitation, and mass transit are widespread. A growing proportion of city-dwellers live in slums and shanty-towns, many of them exposed to air and water pollution and to industrial and natural hazards. Further deterioration is likely, given that most urban growth will take place in the largest cities. Thus more manageable cities may be the principal gain from slower rates of population growth. . . .

Conserving and Enhancing the Resource Base

. . . Pressure on resources increases when people lack alternatives. Development policies must widen people's options for earning a sustainable livelihood, particularly for resource-poor households and in areas under ecological stress. . . .

The conservation of agricultural resources is an urgent task because in many parts of the world cultivation has already been extended to marginal lands, and fishery and forestry resources have been overexploited. These resources must be conserved and enhanced to meet the needs of growing populations. Land use in agriculture and forestry should be based on a scientific assessment of land capacity, and the annual depletion of topsoil, fish stock, or forest resources must not exceed the rate of regeneration.

The pressures on agricultural land from crop and livestock production can be partly relieved by increasing productivity. But shortsighted, short-term improvements in productivity can create different forms of ecological stress, such as the loss of genetic diversity in standing crops, salinization and alkalization of irrigated lands, nitrate pollution of groundwater, and pesticide residues in food. Ecologically more benign alternatives are available. Future increases in productivity, in both developed and developing countries, should be based on the better-controlled application of water and agrochemicals, as well as on more extensive use of organic manures and nonchemical means of pest control. These alternatives can be promoted only by an agricultural policy based on ecological realities. . . .

The ultimate limits to global development are perhaps determined by the availability of energy resources and by the biosphere's capacity to absorb the by-products of energy use.[5] These energy limits may be approached far sooner than the limits imposed by other material resources. First, there are the supply problems: the depletion of oil reserves, the high cost and environmental impact of coal mining, and the hazards of nuclear technology. Second, there are emission problems, most notably acid pollution and carbon dioxide buildup leading to global warming.

Some of these problems can be met by increased use of renewable energy sources. But the exploitation of renewable sources such as fuelwood and hydropower also entails ecological problems. Hence sustainability requires a clear focus on conserving and efficiently using energy.

Industrialized countries must recognize that their energy consumption is polluting the biosphere and eating into scarce fossil fuel supplies. Recent improvements in energy efficiency and a shift towards less energy-intensive sectors have helped limit consumption. But the process must be accelerated to reduce per capita consumption and encourage a shift to nonpolluting sources and technologies. The simple duplication in the developing world of industrial countries' energy use patterns is neither feasible nor desirable. . . .

The prevention and reduction of air and water pollution will remain a critical task of resource conservation. Air and water quality come under pressure from such activities as fertilizer and pesticide use, urban sewage, fossil fuel burning, the use of certain chemicals, and various other industrial activities. Each of these is expected to increase the pollution load on the biosphere substantially, particularly in developing countries. Cleaning up after the event is an expensive solution. Hence all countries need to anticipate and prevent these pollution problems. . . .

Reorienting Technology and Managing Risk

The fulfillment of all these tasks will require the reorientation of technology—the key link between humans and nature. First, the capacity for technological innovation needs to be greatly enhanced in developing countries. . . . Second, the orientation of technology development must be changed to pay greater attention to environmental factors.

The technologies of industrial countries are not always suited or easily adaptable to the socioeconomic and environmental conditions of developing countries. To compound the problem, the bulk of world research and development addresses few of the pressing issues facing these countries. . . . Not enough is being done to adapt recent innovations in materials technology, energy conservation, information technology, and biotechnology to the needs of developing countries. . . .

In all countries, the processes of generating alternative technologies, upgrading traditional ones, and selecting and adapting imported technologies should be informed by environmental resource concerns. Most technological research by commercial organizations is devoted to product and process innovations that have market value. Technologies are needed that produce "social goods," such as improved air quality or increased product life, or that resolve problems normally outside the cost calculus of individual enterprises, such as the external costs of pollution or waste disposal.

The role of public policy is to ensure, through incentives and disincentives, that commercial organizations find it worthwhile to take fuller account of environmental factors in the technologies they develop. . . .

Merging Environment and Economics in Decision Making

The common theme throughout this strategy for sustainable development is the need to integrate economic and ecological considerations in decision making. They are, after all, integrated in the workings of the real world. This will require a change in attitudes and objectives and in institutional arrangements at every level.

Economic and ecological concerns are not necessarily in opposition. For example, policies that conserve the quality of agricultural land and protect forests improve the long-term prospects for agricultural development. . . . But the compatibility of environmental and economic objectives is often lost in the pursuit of individual or group gains, with little regard for the impacts on others, with a blind faith in science's ability to find solutions, and in ignorance of the distant consequences of today's decisions. Institutional rigidities add to this myopia. . . .

Intersectoral connections create patterns of economic and ecological interdependence rarely reflected in the ways in which policy is made. Sectoral organizations tend to pursue sectoral objectives and to treat their impacts on other sectors as side effects, taken into account only if compelled to do so. . . . Many of the environment and development problems that confront us have their roots in this sectoral fragmentation of responsibility. Sustainable development requires that such fragmentation be overcome.

Sustainability requires the enforcement of wider responsibilities for the impacts of decisions. This requires changes in the legal and institutional frameworks that will enforce the common interest. Some necessary changes in the legal framework start from the proposition that an environment adequate for health and well-being is essential for all human beings—including future generations. . . .

The law alone cannot enforce the common interest. It principally needs community knowledge and support, which entails greater public participation in the decisions that affect the environment. This is best secured by decentralizing the management of resources upon which local communities depend, and giving these communities an effective say over the use of these resources. . . .

Changes are also required in the attitudes and procedures of both public- and private-sector enterprises. Moreover, environmental regulation must move beyond the usual menu of safety regulations, zoning laws, and pollution control enactments; environmental objectives must be built into taxation, prior approval procedures for investment and technology choice, foreign trade incentives, and all components of development policy.

The integration of economic and ecological factors into the law and into decisionmaking systems within countries has to be matched at the international level. The growth in fuel and material use dictates that direct physical linkages between ecosystems of different countries will increase. Economic interactions through trade, finance, investment, and travel will also grow and heighten economic and ecological interdependence. Hence in the future, even more so than now, sustainable development requires the unification of economics and ecology in international relations. . . .

Conclusion

In its broadest sense, the strategy for sustainable development aims to promote harmony among human beings and between humanity and nature. In the specific context of the development and environment crises of the 1980s, which current national and international political and economic institutions have not and perhaps cannot overcome, the pursuit of sustainable development requires:

- a political system that secures effective citizen participation in decision making,
- an economic system that is able to generate surpluses and technical knowledge on a self-reliant and sustained basis,
- a social system that provides for solutions for the tensions arising from disharmonious development,
- a production system that respects the obligation to preserve the ecological base for development,
- a technological system that can search continuously for new solutions,
- an international system that fosters sustainable patterns of trade and finance, and
- an administrative system that is flexible and has the capacity for self-correction.

These requirements are more in the nature of goals that should underlie national and international action on development. What matters is the sincerity with which these goals are pursued and the effectiveness with which departures from them are corrected.

Notes

1. Based on data from World Bank, *World Development Report 1984* (New York: Oxford University Press, 1984).

2. FAO, *Fuelwood Supplies in the Developing Countries,* Forestry Paper No. 42 (Rome: FAO, 1983).

3. Department of International Economic and Social Affairs, *World Population Prospects and Projections as Assessed in 1984* (New York: United Nations, 1986).

4. Ibid.

5. W. Häfele and W. Sassin, "Resources and Endowments, An Outline of Future Energy Systems," in P. W. Hemily and M. N. Ozdas (eds.), *Science and Future Choice* (Oxford: Clarendon Press, 1979).

18

SUSTAINABLE DEVELOPMENT: A CRITICAL REVIEW

Sharachchandra M. Lélé*

Introduction

The last few years have seen a dramatic transformation in the environment-development debate. The question being asked is no longer "Do development and environmental concerns contradict each other?" but "How can sustainable development be achieved?" All of a sudden the phrase Sustainable Development (SD) has become pervasive. . . . It appears to have gained the broad-based support that earlier development concepts such as "ecodevelopment" lacked, and is poised to become the developmental paradigm of the 1990s.

But murmurs of disenchantment are also being heard. "What *is* SD?" is being asked increasingly frequently without, however, clear answers forthcoming. SD is in real danger of becoming a cliché like appropriate technology—a fashionable phrase that everyone pays homage to but nobody cares to define. . . . Agencies such as the World Bank, the Asian Development Bank and the Organisation for Economic Co-operation and Development have been quick to adopt the new rhetoric. The absence of a clear theoretical and analytical framework, however, makes it difficult to determine whether the new policies will indeed foster an environmentally sound and socially meaningful form of development. . . .

*Reprinted from *World Development* 19/6, Sharachchandra M. Lélé, "Sustainable Development: A Critical Review," pp. 607–621, Copyright 1991, with permission from Elsevier.

The persuasive power of SD (and hence the political strength of the SD movement) stems from the underlying claim that new insights into physical and social phenomena force one to concur with the operational conclusions of the SD platform almost regardless of one's fundamental ethical persuasions and priorities. I argue that while these new insights are important, the argument is not inexorable, and that the issues are more complex than is made out to be. Hence . . . many of the policy prescriptions being suggested in the name of SD stem from subjective (rather than consensual) ideas about goals and means, and worse, are often inadequate and even counterproductive. . . .

Interpreting Sustainable Development

The manner in which the phrase "sustainable development" is used and interpreted varies so much that while O'Riordan (1985) called SD a "contradiction in terms," Redclift suggests that it may be just "another development truism" (Redclift, 1987, p. 1). These interpretational problems, though ultimately conceptual, have some semantic roots. Most people use the phrase "sustainable development" interchangeably with "ecologically sustainable or environmentally sound development" (Tolba, 1984a). This interpretation is characterized by: (a) "sustainability" being understood as "ecological sustainability"; and (b) a conceptualization of SD as a process of change that has (ecological) sustainability added to its list of objectives.

In contrast, sustainable development is sometimes interpreted as "sustained growth," "sustained change" or simply "successful" development. Let us examine how these latter interpretations originate and why they are less useful than the former one. . . .

Contradictions and Trivialities

Taken literally, sustainable development would simply mean "development that can be continued—either indefinitely or for the implicit time period of concern." But what is development? Theorists and practitioners have both been grappling with the word and the concept for at least the past four decades. . . . Some equate development with GNP growth, others include any number of socially desirable phenomena in their conceptualization. The point to be noted is that development is *a process of directed change*. Definitions of development thus embody both (a) the objectives of this process, and (b) the means of achieving these objectives.

Unfortunately, a distinction between objectives and means is often not made in the development rhetoric. This has led to "sustainable development" frequently being interpreted as simply a process of change that can be continued forever. . . . This interpretation is either impossible or trivial. When development is taken to be synonymous with growth in material consumption—which it often is even today—SD would be "sustaining the growth in material consumption" (presumably indefinitely). But such an idea contradicts the general recognition that *"ultimate* limits [to usable resources] exist"[1] (WCED, p. 45, emphasis added). At best, it could be argued that growth in the per capita consumption of certain basic goods is necessary in certain regions of the world in the short term. To use "sustainable development" synonymously with "sustain[ing] growth performance" (Idachaba, 1987) or to cite the high rates of growth in agricultural production in South Asia as an example of SD is therefore a misleading usage, or at best a short-term and localized notion that goes against the long-term global perspective of SD.

One could finesse this contradiction by conceptualizing development as simply a process of socioeconomic change. But one cannot carry on a meaningful discussion unless one states what the objectives of such change are and why one should worry about continuing the process of change indefinitely. . . .

Sustainability

. . . The concept of sustainability originated in the context of renewable resources such as forests or fisheries, and has subsequently been adopted as a broad slogan by the environmental movement. Most proponents of sustainability therefore take it to mean "the existence of the ecological conditions necessary to support human life at a specified level of well-being through future generations," what I call *ecological sustainability.* . . .

Since ecological sustainability emphasizes the constraints and opportunities that nature presents to human activities, ecologists and physical scientists frequently dominate its discussion. But what they actually focus on are the ecological conditions for ecological sustainability—the biophysical "laws" or patterns that determine environmental responses to human activities and humans' ability to use the environment. The major contribution of the environment-development debate is, I believe, the realization that in addition to or in conjunction with these ecological conditions, there are social conditions that influence the ecological sustainability or unsustainability of the people-nature interaction. To give a stylized example, one could say that soil erosion undermining the agricultural basis for human society is a case of ecological (un)sustainability. It could be caused by farming on marginal lands without adequate soil conservation measures—the ecological cause. But the phenomenon of marginalization of peasants may have social roots, which would then be the social causes of ecological unsustainability. . . .

The Concept of Sustainable Development: Evolution of Objectives

The term sustainable development came into prominence in 1980, when the International Union for the Conservation of Nature and Natural Resources (IUCN) presented the World Conservation Strategy (WCS) with "the overall aim of achieving sustainable development through the conservation of living resources" (IUCN, 1980). [Editors' note: IUCN, the International Union for the Conservation of Nature, was known from 1990 to 2008 as the World Conservation Union and before that as the International Union for the Conservation of Nature and Natural Resources.] Critics acknowledged that "By identifying Sustainable Development as the basic goal of society, the WCS was able to make a profound contribution toward reconciling the interests of the development community with those of the environmental movement" (Khosla, 1987). They pointed out, however, that the strategy restricted itself to living resources [and] focused primarily on the necessity of maintaining genetic diversity, habits and ecological processes. . . . It was . . . unable to deal adequately with sensitive or controversial issues—those relating to the international economic and political order, war and armament, population and urbanization (Khosla, 1987). . . .

The United Nations Environment Programme (UNEP) was at the forefront of the effort to articulate and popularize the concept. UNEP's concept of SD was said to encompass

1. help for the very poor, because they are left with no options but to destroy their environment;
2. the idea of self-reliant development, within natural resource constraints;
3. the idea of cost-effective development using nontraditional economic criteria;
4. the great issues of health control [sic], appropriate technology, food self-reliance, clean water and shelter for all; and
5. the notion that people-centered initiatives are needed (Tolba, 1984a).

This statement epitomizes the mixing of goals and means, or more precisely, of fundamental objectives and operational ones, that has burdened much of the SD literature. While providing food, water, good health and shelter have traditionally been the fundamental objectives of most development models (including UNEP's), it is not clear whether self-reliance, cost-effectiveness, appropriateness of technology and people-centeredness are additional objectives or the operational requirements for achieving the traditional ones. . . .

In contrast to the aforementioned, the currently popular definition of SD—the one adopted by the World Commission on Environment and Development (WCED)—is quite brief:

> Sustainable development is development that meets the needs of the present without compromising the ability of future generations to meet their own needs (WCED, 1987; p. 43).

The constraint of "not compromising the ability of future generations to meet their needs" is (presumably) considered by the Commission to be equivalent to the requirement of some level of ecological and social sustainability.[2]

While the WCED's statement of the fundamental objectives of SD is brief, the Commission is much more elaborate about (what are essentially) the operational objectives of SD. It states that "the critical objectives which follow from the concept of SD" are:

1. reviving growth;
2. changing the quality of growth;
3. meeting essential needs for jobs, food, energy, water, and sanitation;
4. ensuring a sustainable level of population;
5. conserving and enhancing the resource base;
6. reorienting technology and managing risk;
7. merging environment and economics in decision making; and
8. reorienting international economic relations (WCED, 1987, p. 49).

Most organizations and agencies actively promoting the concept of SD subscribe to some or all of these objectives with, however, the notable addition of a ninth operational goal, viz.,

9. making development more participatory.[3]

This formulation can therefore be said to represent the mainstream of SD thinking. This "mainstream" includes international environmental agencies such as UNEP, IUCN and the World Wildlife Fund (WWF), developmental agencies including the World Bank, the US Agency for International Development, the Canadian and Swedish international development agencies, research and dissemination organizations such as the World Resources Institute, the International Institute for Environment and Development, the Worldwatch Institute (1984–88) and activist organizations and groups such as the Global Tomorrow Coalition. . . .

The Premises of SD

The perception in mainstream SD thinking of the environment-society link is based upon the following premises:

1. *Environmental degradation:*
   - Environmental degradation is already affecting millions in the Third World, and is likely to severely reduce human well-being all across the globe within the next few generations.
   - Environmental degradation is very often caused by poverty, because the poor have no option but to exploit resources for short-term survival.
   - The interlinked nature of most environmental problems is such that environmental degradation ultimately affects everybody, although poorer individuals/nations may suffer more and sooner than richer ones.

2. *Traditional development objectives:*
- These are: providing basic needs and increasing the productivity of all resources (human, natural and economic) in developing countries, and maintaining the standard of living in the developed countries.
- These objectives do not necessarily conflict with the objective of ecological sustainability. In fact, achieving sustainable patterns of resource use is necessary for achieving these objectives permanently.
- It can be shown that, even for individual actors, environmentally sound methods are "profitable" in the long run, and often in the short run too.

3. *Process:*
- The process of development must be participatory to succeed even in the short run.

Given these premises, the need for a process of development that achieves the traditional objectives, results in ecologically sustainable patterns of resource use and is implemented in a participatory manner is obvious.

Most of the SD literature is devoted to showing that this process is also feasible and can be made attractive to the actors involved. SD has become a bundle of neat fixes: technological changes that make industrial production processes less polluting and less resource intensive and yet more productive and profitable, economic policy changes that incorporate environmental considerations and yet achieve greater economic growth, procedural changes that use local nongovernmental organizations (NGOs) so as to ensure grassroots participation, agriculture that is less harmful, less resource intensive and yet more productive and so on. In short, SD is a "metafix" that will unite everybody from the profit-minded industrialist and risk-minimizing subsistence farmer to the equity-seeking social worker, the pollution-concerned or wildlife-loving First Worlder, the growth-maximizing policy maker, the goal-oriented bureaucrat and therefore, the vote-counting politician.

Weaknesses

The major impact of the SD movement is the rejection of the notion that environmental conservation necessarily constrains development or that development necessarily means environmental pollution—certainly not an insignificant gain. Where the SD movement has faltered is in its inability to develop a set of concepts, criteria and policies that are coherent or consistent—both externally (with physical and social reality) and internally (with each other). The mainstream formulation of SD suffers from significant weaknesses in:

- its characterization of the problems of poverty and environmental degradation;

- its conceptualization of the objectives of development, sustainability and participation; and
- the strategy it has adopted in the face of incomplete knowledge and uncertainty.

Poverty and Environmental Degradation: An Incomplete Characterization

The fundamental premise of mainstream SD thinking is the two-way link between poverty and environmental degradation....

In fact, however, even a cursory examination of the vast amount of research that has been done on the links between social and environmental phenomena suggests that both poverty and environmental degradation have deep and complex causes....

To say that mainstream SD thinking has completely ignored [this complexity] would be unfair. But ... inadequate technical know-how and managerial capabilities, common property resource management, and pricing and subsidy policies have been the major themes addressed, and the solutions suggested have been essentially techno-economic ones.... Deeper sociopolitical changes (such as land reform) or changes in cultural values (such as overconsumption in the North) are either ignored or paid lip service....

Conceptual Weaknesses

Removal of poverty (the traditional developmental objective), sustainability and participation are really the three fundamental objectives of the SD paradigm. Unfortunately, the manner in which these objectives are conceptualized and operationalized leaves much to be desired. On the one hand, economic growth is being adopted as a major operational objective that is consistent with both removal of poverty and sustainability. On the other hand, the concepts of sustainability and participation are poorly articulated, making it difficult to determine whether a particular development project actually promotes a particular form of sustainability, or what kind of participation will lead to what kind of social (and consequently, environmental) outcome.

The Role of Economic Growth. By the mid-1970s, it had seemed that the economic growth and trickle-down theory of development had been firmly rejected, and the "basic needs approach" (Streeten, 1979) had taken root in development circles. Yet economic growth continues to feature in today's debate on SD. In fact, "reviving [economic] growth" heads WCED's list of operational objectives quoted earlier. Two arguments are implicit in this adoption of economic growth as an operational objective. The first, a somewhat defensive one, is that there is no fundamental contradiction between economic growth and sustainability, because growth in economic activity may occur simultaneously with either an improvement or a deterioration in environmental quality. Thus, "governments concerned with long-term sustainability need not seek to limit growth in economic output so long as they stabilize aggregate natural resource consumption" (Goodland and Ledec, 1987). But one could turn this argument around and suggest that if economic growth is not correlated with environmental sustainability, there is no reason to have economic growth as an operational objective of SD.[4]

The second argument in favor of economic growth is more positive. The basic premise of SD is that poverty is largely responsible for environmental degradation. Therefore, removal of poverty (i.e., development) is necessary for environmental sustainability. This, it is argued, implies that economic growth is absolutely necessary for SD. The only thing that needs to be done is to "change the quality of [this] growth" (WCED, 1987, pp. 52–54) to ensure that it does not lead to environmental destruction. In drawing such an inference, however, there is the implicit belief that economic growth is necessary (if not sufficient) for the removal of poverty. But was it not the fact that economic growth per se could not ensure the removal of poverty that led to the adoption of the basic needs approach in the 1970s?

Thus, if economic growth by itself leads to neither environmental sustainability nor removal of poverty, it is clearly a "non-objective" for SD. The converse is a possibility worth exploring, viz., whether successful implementation of policies for poverty removal, long-term employment generation, environmental restoration and rural development will lead to growth in GNP, and, more important, to increases in investment, employment and income generation. This seems more than likely in developing countries, but not so certain in developed ones. In any case, economic growth may be the fallout of SD, but not its prime mover.

Sustainability. The World Conservation Strategy was probably the first attempt to carry the concept of sustainability beyond simple renewable resource systems. It suggested three ecological principles for ecological sustainability (see the nomenclature developed above), viz., "maintenance of essential ecological processes and life-support systems, the preservation of genetic diversity, and the sustainable utilization of species and resources" (IUCN, 1980). This definition, though a useful starting point, is clearly recursive as it invokes "sustainability" in resource use without defining it. Many subsequent attempts to discuss the notion are disturbingly muddled. There is a very real danger of the term becoming a meaningless cliché, unless a concerted effort is made to add precision and content to the discussion. . . .

Any discussion of sustainability must first answer the questions "What is to be sustained? For whom? How long?" The value of the concept (like that of SD), however, lies in its ability to generate an operational consensus between groups with fundamentally different answers to these questions, i.e., those concerned either about the survival of future human generations, or about the survival of wildlife, or human health, or the satisfaction of immediate subsistence needs (food, fuel, fodder) with a low degree of risk. It is therefore vital to identify those aspects of sustainability that do actually cater to such diverse interests, and those that involve trade-offs.

Differentiating between ecological and social sustainability could be a first step toward clarifying some of the discussion. Further, in the case of ecological sustainability, a distinction needs to be made between renewable resources, nonrenewable resources and environmental processes that are crucial to human life, as well as to life at large. The few researchers who have begun to explore the idea of ecological sustainability emphasize its multidimensional and complex nature. . . .

In the rush to derive ecological principles of (ecological) sustainability, we cannot afford to lose sight of the social conditions that determine which of these principles are socially acceptable, and to what extent. Sociologists, eco-Marxists and political ecologists are pointing out the crucial role of socioeconomic structures and institutions in the pattern and extent of environmental degradation globally. Neoclassical economists, whose theories have perhaps had the greatest influence in development policy making in the past and who therefore bear the responsibility for its social and environmental failures, however, have been very slow in modifying their theories and prescriptions. The SD movement will have to formulate a clear agenda for research in what is being called "ecological economics" and press for its adoption by the mainstream of economics in order to ensure the possibility of real changes in policy making.

Social sustainability is a more nebulous concept than ecological sustainability. Brown et al. (1987), in a somewhat techno-economic vein, state that sustainability implies "the existence and operation of an infrastructure (transportation and communication), services (health, education, and culture), and government (agreements, laws, and enforcement)." Tisdell (1988) talks about "the sustainability of political and social structures" and Norgaard (1988) argues for cultural sustainability, which includes value and belief systems. Detailed analyses of the concept, however, seem to be nonexistent.[5] Perhaps achieving desired social situations is itself so difficult that discussing their maintainability is not very useful; perhaps goals are even more dynamic in a social context than in an ecological one, so that maintainability is not such an important attribute of social institutions/ structures. There is, however, no contradiction between the social and ecological sustainability; rather, they can complement and inform each other.

Participation. A notable feature of . . . some of the earlier SD literature was the emphasis placed on equity and social justice. . . . Subsequently, however, the mainstream appears to have quietly dropped these terms (suggesting at least a deemphasizing of these objectives), and has instead focused on "local participation."

There are, however, three problems with this shift. First, by using the terms equity, participation and decentralization interchangeably, it is being suggested that participation and decentralization are equivalent, and that they can somehow substitute for equity and social justice. . . .

Second, the manner in which participation is being operationalized shows up the narrow-minded, quick-fix and deceptive approach adopted by the mainstream promoters of SD. . . . Mainstream SD literature blithely assumes and insists that "involvement of local NGOs" in project implementation will ensure project success (Maniates, 1990; he dubs this the "NGOization" of SD).

Third, there is an assumption that participation or at least equity and social justice will necessarily reinforce ecological sustainability. Attempts to test such assumptions rigorously have been rare. But preliminary results seem to suggest that equity in resource access may not lead to sustainable resource use unless new institutions for resource management are carefully built and nurtured. . . . This should not be misconstrued as an argument against the need for equity, but rather as a word of caution against the tendency to believe that social equity automatically ensures environmental sustainability (or vice versa). . . .

Concluding Remarks: Dilemmas and Agendas

The proponents of SD are faced with a dilemma that affects any program of political action and social change: the dilemma between the urge to take strong stands on fundamental concerns and the need to gain wide political acceptance and support. . . . SD is being packaged as the inevitable outcome of objective scientific analysis, virtually an historical necessity, that does not contradict the deep-rooted normative notion of development as economic growth. In other words, SD is an attempt to have one's cake and eat it too.

It may be argued that this is indeed possible, that the things that are wrong and need to be changed are quite obvious, and there are many ways of fixing them without significantly conflicting with either age-old power structures or the modern drive for a higher material standard of living. . . . If, by using the politically correct jargon of economic growth and development and by packaging SD in the manner mentioned above, it were possible to achieve even 50% success in implementing this bundle of "conceptually imprecise" policies, the net reduction achieved in environmental degradation and poverty would be unprecedented.

I believe, however, that (analogous to the arguments in SD) in the long run there is no contradiction between better articulation of the terms, concepts, analytical methods and policy-making principles, and gaining political strength and broad social acceptance—especially at the grassroots. In fact, such clarification and articulation is necessary if SD is to avoid either being dismissed as another development fad or being co-opted by forces opposed to changes in status quo. More specifically, proponents and analysts of SD need to:

A. clearly reject the attempts (and temptation) to focus on economic growth as [a] means to poverty removal and/or environmental sustainability;

B. recognize the internal inconsistencies and inadequacies in the theory and practice of neoclassical economics, particularly as it relates to environmental and distributional issues; in economic analyses, move away from arcane mathematical models toward exploring empirical questions such as limits to the substitution of capital for resources, impacts of different sustainability policies on different economic systems, etc.;

C. accept the existence of structural, technological and cultural causes of poverty and environmental degradation; develop methodologies for estimating relative importance of and interaction between these causes in specific situations; and explore political, institutional and educational solutions to them;

D. understand the multiple dimensions of sustainability, and attempt to develop measures, criteria and principles for them; and

E. explore what patterns and levels of source demand and use would be compatible with different forms or levels of ecological and social sustainability, and with different notions of equity and social justice.

There are, fortunately, some signs that a debate on these lines has now begun.

In a sense, if SD is to be really "sustained" as a development paradigm, two apparently divergent efforts are called for: making SD more precise in its conceptual underpinnings, while allowing more flexibility and diversity of approaches in developing strategies that might lead to a society living in harmony with the environment and with itself.

REFERENCES

Brown, B. J., M. Hanson, D. Liverman, and R. Merideth, Jr., "Global Sustainability: Toward Definition," *Environmental Management,* Vol. 11, No. 6 (1987), pp. 713–719.

Brown, L. R., *Building a Sustainable Society* (New York: W. W. Norton, 1981).

Chambers, R., *Sustainable Livelihoods: An Opportunity for the World Commission on Environment and Development* (Brighton, UK: Institute of Development Studies, University of Sussex, 1986).

Daly, H., *Economics, Ecology, Ethics: Essays Toward a Steady-State Economy* (San Francisco: W. H. Freeman, 1980).

Goodland, R., and G. Ledec, "Neoclassical Economics and Principles of Sustainable Development," *Ecological Modelling,* Vol. 38 (1987), pp. 19–46.

Idachaba, F. S., "Sustainability Issues in Agriculture Development," in T. J. Davis and I. A. Schirmer (Eds.), *Sustainability Issues in Agricultural Development* (Washington, DC: World Bank, 1987), pp. 18–53.

IUCN, *World Conservation Strategy: Living Resource Conservation for Sustainable Development* (Gland, Switzerland: International Union for Conservation of Nature and Natural Resources, United Nations Environment Program and World Wildlife Fund, 1980).

Khosla, A., "Alternative Strategies in Achieving Sustainable Development," in P. Jacobs and D. A. Munro (Eds.), *Conservation with Equity: Strategies for Sustainable Development* (Cambridge, England: International Union for Conservation of Nature and Natural Resources, 1987), pp. 191–208.

Maniates, M., "Organizing for Rural Energy Development: Local Organizations, Improved Cookstoves, and the State in Gujarat, India," Ph.D. thesis (Berkeley: Energy & Resources Group, University of California, 1990).

Norgaard, R. B., "Sustainable Development: A Coevolutionary View," *Futures*, Vol. 20, No. 6 (1988), pp. 606–620.

———, "Three Dilemmas of Environmental Accounting," *Ecological Economics*, Vol. 1, No. 4 (1989), pp. 303–314.

O'Riordan, T., "Future Directions in Environmental Policy," *Journal of Environment and Planning*, Vol. 17 (1985), pp. 1431–1446.

Peskin, H. M., "National Income Accounts and the Environment," *Natural Resources Journal*, Vol. 21 (1981), pp. 511–537.

Redclift, M., *Sustainable Development: Exploring the Contradictions* (New York: Methuen, 1987).

Repetto, R., *World Enough and Time* (New Haven, CT: Yale University Press, 1986a).

Riddell, R., *Ecodevelopment* (New York: St. Martin's Press, 1981).

Sachs, I., *Environment and Development—A New Rationale for Domestic Policy Formulation and International Cooperation Strategies* (Ottawa: Environment Canada and Canadian International Development Agency, 1977).

Streeten, P., "Basic Needs: Premises and Promises," *Journal of Policy Modelling*, Vol. 1 (1979), pp. 136–146.

Tisdell, C., "Sustainable Development: Differing Perspectives of Ecologists and Economists, and Relevance to LDCs," *World Development*, Vol. 16, No. 3 (1988), pp. 373–384.

Tolba, M. K., "The Premises for Building a Sustainable Society. Address to the World Commission on Environment and Development," October 1984 (Nairobi: United Nations Environment Programme, 1984).

World Commission on Environment and Development, *Our Common Future* (New York: Oxford University Press, 1987).

Worldwatch Institute, *State of the World* (New York: Norton, various years).

NOTES

1. More precisely, there are ultimate limits to the stocks of material resources, [to] the flows of energy resources and (in the event of these being circumvented by a major

breakthrough in fission/fusion technologies) to the environment's ability to absorb waste energy and other stresses. The limits-to-growth debate, while not conclusive as to specifics, appears to have effectively shifted the burden of proof about the absence of such fundamental limits onto the diehard "technological optimists" who deny the existence of such limits.

2. Of course, "meeting the needs" is a rather ambiguous phrase that may mean anything in practice. Substituting this phrase with "optimizing economic and other societal benefits" (Goodland and Ledec, 1987) or "managing all assets, natural resources and human resources, as well as financial and physical assets for increasing long-term wealth and well-being" (Repetto, 1986a, p. 15) does not define the objectives of development more precisely, although the importance attached to economic benefits or wealth is rather obvious.

3. It is tempting to conclude that this nine-point formulation of SD is identical with the concept of "ecodevelopment"—the original term coined by Maurice Strong of UNEP for environmentally sound development (see Sachs, 1977, and Riddell, 1981). Certainly the differences are less obvious than the similarities. Nevertheless, some changes are significant—such as the dropping of the emphasis on "local self-reliance" and the renewed emphasis on economic growth.

4. Economists have responded by suggesting that currently used indicators of economic growth (GNP in particular) could be modified so as to somehow "build in" this correlation (e.g., Peskin, 1981). To what extent this is possible and whether it will serve more than a marginal purpose are, however, open questions (Norgaard, 1989).

5. Three other "social" usages of sustainability need to be clarified. Sustainable economy (Daly, 1980) and sustainable society (Brown, 1981) are two of these. The focus there, however, is on the patterns and levels of resource use that might be ecologically sustainable while providing the goods and services necessary to maintain human well-being, and the social reorganization that might be required to make this possible. The third usage is Chambers' definition of "sustainable livelihoods" as "a level of wealth and of stocks and flows of food and cash which provide for physical and social well-being and security against becoming poorer" (Chambers, 1986). This can be thought of as a sophisticated version of "basic needs," in that security or risk-minimization is added to the list of needs. It is therefore relevant to any paradigm of development, rather than to SD in particular.

THE NEW BUSINESS IMPERATIVE: VALUING NATURAL CAPITAL

Corporate Eco Forum and The Nature Conservancy*

Each year, our planet's complex land and water systems—a "natural living infra-structure"—produce an estimated $72 trillion worth of "free" goods and services essential to a well-functioning global economy. Because these benefits aren't bartered and sold in the marketplace, their value is exceedingly hard to monetize on corporate or government financial statements.

As a result, this value has largely been left unaccounted for in business decisions and market transactions. This is starting to change. Top executives at some of the world's biggest companies are awakening to the profound business value of Earth's natural assets—and the business imperative of safeguarding them. Without healthy ecosystems, water and raw materials that were once cheap and abundant can become so costly they erase profits and threaten entire business models. Local communities where companies operate can become unstable, unsafe or otherwise inhospitable. And without natural barriers to protect workers and facilities from increasingly extreme weather patterns and other disasters, even the best-run companies can be hit with catastrophic losses.

Two-thirds of our planet's land and water ecosystems are now significantly degraded due to human activity. Climate change is accelerating the damage. The UN estimates that our collective mismanagement of natural assets is costing the global economy an estimated $6.6 trillion a year—nearly 11 percent of GDP [Gross Domestic Product]—through effects like contamination of water supplies, loss of fertile land to soil erosion and drought, and supply chain disruptions from deforestation and overfishing. At the current trajectory—a conservative scenario

---

*Excerpted from *The New Business Imperative: Valuing Natural Capital*, an e-report of Corporate Eco Forum and The Nature Conservancy, 2012. Reprinted with permission.

unless things change dramatically—these costs could skyrocket to $28 trillion by 2050. No company is immune to the risks from these mounting damages. As naturally produced goods and services are compromised or lost altogether, companies could experience supply chain disruptions, be forced to introduce costly alternatives to traditional inputs or face new regulatory and legal risks. Few will escape pressure from stakeholders (including regulators and investors) to be accountable for their contribution to the problems. In 2012 [the audit, tax and advisory firm] KPMG estimated that if companies had to pay for their own environmental bills, they would lose *41 cents for every $1 in earnings*.

The challenge of reversing these trends should not fall to business alone, but the private sector can no longer afford to wait for governments to act with the speed, scale and vision required. The good news is that companies have the power to leapfrog slow government efforts with their own innovative solutions to ecosystem management. Doing so today will give companies a greater measure of control and competitive advantage.

Taken together, their commitments demonstrate the range of benefits that accrue to companies willing to get out in front of these challenges today—from minimizing risks and cutting costs, to enhancing brand and identifying new opportunities for revenues and growth. Equally important, these commitments point to practical and achievable actions available to companies considering meaningful next steps.

Four Business Benefits

The 24 companies featured in this report are united in the view that immediate leadership to safeguard well-functioning ecosystems is a business imperative, not a matter of philanthropy.

By prioritizing ecosystems in business planning and investments, companies stand to benefit in 4 mutually reinforcing ways:

- Reduce Risks
- Cut Costs
- Enhance Brand
- Fuel Growth

Reduce Risks

Avoid supply chain and operational disruptions caused by scarcities of natural resources.

Reduce threats to business continuity and harm to facilities, workers and communities in places vulnerable to extreme weather, flooding, drought, fires, desertification or resource scarcity.

Stay ahead of impending regulatory changes that could limit product or production choices.

Avoid fines, suspensions, lawsuits or other liabilities due to over-exploitation or contamination of natural systems, and improve relationships with local communities and host governments.

Avoid damage to corporate reputation and brand.

Cut Costs

Discover new ways to slash expenses and increase margins, as reducing ecosystem impacts helps reveal opportunities to boost resource productivity and increase energy efficiency.

Save money by reducing waste and recapturing valuable materials that otherwise could harm ecosystems.

Avoid costly manmade "gray infrastructure" expenses by opting instead for "natural infrastructure" investments in restoration of healthy forests, wetlands, watersheds and coastal ecosystems—often the cheaper and more effective long-term solution.

Explore natural solutions to cut costs on stormwater management, flood mitigation, air quality management, carbon sequestration, water purification and climate-related threats.

Postpone or avoid cost increases due to rising resource scarcities by investing in sustainable sourcing practices.

Enhance Brand and Reputation

Win trust and loyalty from growing ranks of customers that value sustainability leadership.

Differentiate brand from competitors by communicating superior purchasing, operating or investment practices.

Draw and retain top talent, as a growing number of employees value working for a company with a culture and values they share. Attract investors and lenders who increasingly factor companies' environmental performance and exposures into their decisions.

Fuel Revenue Growth

Win sales by meeting customers' growing demands for products and services that do no harm to sensitive ecosystems.

Create new revenue opportunities by innovating solutions that alleviate pressure on the environment or restore healthy ecosystems. Exploit opportunities to educate consumers about high-performance sustainable products to increase demand and create new market segments.

Leverage emerging "natural capital" markets such as water-quality trading, wetland banking and threatened species banking, and natural carbon sequestration.

A Framework for Action

The four business benefits of prioritizing ecosystems within business strategy—(1) cutting costs, (2) reducing risks, (3) enhancing brand and reputation, and (4) growing revenues—are mutually reinforcing and can be achieved through a variety of approaches.

Several practical actions are available to companies considering meaningful next steps to seize opportunities.

1. Assess your company's impacts and dependencies on ecosystems
2. Put a price on nature's value
3. Optimize resource use to minimize environmental degradation
4. Invest strategically in conservation and restoration
5. Engage your value chain to bring solutions to scale
6. Innovate in materials, processes and products
7. Build natural instead of manmade infrastructure
8. Leverage new natural capital markets and investment tools
9. Join forces

1. Assess Your Company's Impacts and Dependencies on Ecosystems

Forward-thinking companies are analyzing their interconnected web of environmental impacts and dependencies across the entire value chain—from sourcing raw materials or semi-finished goods, through manufacturing and processing, packaging and shipping, product use and the end-of-life or "re-use" phase.

Businesses that map, monitor and measure their impacts and dependencies on ecosystems can better assess materiality, mitigate impacts and identify opportunities for cost savings and new revenues. Traditional environmental management systems and due diligence tools are often ill-equipped to evaluate the full risks and opportunities arising from the use and degradation of ecosystems. Fortunately, several new tools are now available to help companies undertake this process, and leading NGOs [non-governmental organizations]—The Nature Conservancy [and] World Resources Institute among others—are partnering with companies to guide their analyses and planning. Companies can now produce reliable, predictive models connecting business and ecosystem impacts.

2. Put a Price on Nature's Value

Companies can position themselves for long-term success by working today to put a monetary value on what nature does for their businesses—and by calculating the costs of damage to healthy ecosystems. Doing so can improve business decision making by exposing significant costs and benefits that could seriously impact the bottom line but which traditional financial analyses usually miss. The first pilot project underpinning Dow Chemical's innovative collaboration with The Nature Conservancy to improve the science and practice of valuing ecosystem services is already revealing these kinds of opportunities related to Dow's Freeport, Texas site.

In addition, the valuation of "natural capital" makes financial disclosure more robust and gives companies the option of pursuing integrated reporting.

It's becoming easier to obtain the data necessary for valuation. Companies are beginning to automate systems to monitor ecosystem impacts and natural resource usage and are using database dashboards that receive feeds from remote field sensors to enable real-time observation and comparison.

This, in turn, facilitates reliable tracking of supply chains and certification chains.

3. Optimize Resource Use to Minimize Environmental Degradation

Companies that work to reduce their impacts on ecosystems often discover new opportunities to boost resource productivity and efficiency—resulting in cost savings that go straight to the bottom line. Driving resource productivity on an end-to-end basis, through supply and value chains, can create significant business benefits. Introducing stringent efficiency measures to manage water and other natural resources reduces pressure on critical systems while creating opportunities to cut costs and increase profit margins.

Waste management solutions that optimize resource reuse and recycling while keeping toxins out of circulation have the dual benefit of saving/making money while also protecting valuable ecosystems. Manufacturing companies in particular may be able to recapture valuable materials, including usable metals and minerals, while reducing harmful emissions and keeping hazardous materials out of critical land and water ecosystems. Often, the costs of investing in resource productivity and efficiency strategies are more than offset by energy and cost savings achieved—and, in some cases, by the revenues generated by selling recaptured materials.

The industries with perhaps the most to gain may be those with the biggest "footprint" on ecosystems—energy, mining, infrastructure, manufacturing and agriculture. These industries significantly impact and rely upon well-functioning ecosystems: their web of impacts and dependencies stem from the extraction of raw materials and extending through industrial processing, electricity generation and final outputs. For these industries in particular, avoiding, minimizing and offsetting impacts to natural infrastructure is simply smart business. In addition to generating cost savings, they can reduce their exposure to legal and regulatory risks, maintain their "social license" to operate and support the ecosystems on which they and their stakeholders depend.

4. Invest Strategically in Conservation and Restoration

For decades, most companies have viewed investments in ecosystem conservation and restoration as optional philanthropic acts designed to produce broad social and economic benefits. Today, however, companies increasingly see investments in "natural infrastructure" as important—sometimes mandatory—to advancing key business objectives.

For instance, companies with large carbon footprints have invested in healthy forests as a cost-effective tool to support their overall strategy to reduce their climate impacts. Brands that depend heavily on water are investing in watersheds to avert water scarcities that could drive up costs or harm communities in which they operate. Businesses that rely on affordable agricultural goods are investing in efforts to keep soils healthy and productive. Companies that operate in regions with particularly vulnerable ecosystems are working to protect them to safeguard or enhance their reputations.

5. Engage Your Value Chain to Bring Solutions to Scale

Company value chains provide opportunities for investments in natural infrastructure to have a multiplier effect, helping businesses achieve the scale needed to realize meaningful and measurable benefits, in particular in terms of minimizing supply chain risks and bottlenecks. Actively engaging affiliates, suppliers, brands, and other partners can be complex, but it is key to durable, lasting solutions— whether the challenge is sustainably sourcing raw materials, conserving and restoring precious resources such as forests and freshwater, optimizing manufacturing processes, or bolstering workers, facilities and local communities from the perils of extreme weather, flooding or fires.

6. Innovate in Materials, Processes and Products

In the years ahead, customer demand will accelerate for products and services that reduce dependence on natural resources and minimize negative impacts on ecosystems.

By anticipating and meeting customers' emerging needs in a resource-constrained world, companies can gain competitive advantage and seize new opportunities for revenue growth.

A rapidly growing number of companies are already profiting by offering solutions that save customers money through increased energy and resource efficiencies. But leading-edge companies see the benefits for today and tomorrow of making sustainability considerations part of a holistic innovation model—one that makes sustainability attributes standard among all the factors considered when developing solutions for customer needs. To be sure, many sustainability-related innovations will not generate quick payback and may require significant up-front investments with an eye towards long-term benefits. However, companies that are serious about innovating for sustainability cite many collateral business benefits produced along the journey. Their progress affords them new opportunities to differentiate their products and brands and to tap into growing markets for certified or eco-labeled products and services. Their search to anticipate future customer needs generates new ideas for delivering value to customers today. And their efforts to break barriers and forge new ground unveils opportunities for future revenue growth—perhaps involving entirely new business models—that they otherwise would not have considered until competitors got there first.

7. Build Natural Instead of Manmade Infrastructure

Strong, reliable manmade ("gray") infrastructure undergirds a healthy marketplace, and most companies depend heavily on it to operate effectively and efficiently. Yet increasingly, companies are seeing the enormous potential for "natural infrastructure" in the form of wetlands and forests, watersheds and coastal habitats to perform many of the same tasks as gray infrastructure—sometimes better and more cheaply.

For instance, investing in protection of coral reefs and mangroves can provide a stronger barrier to protect coastal operations against flooding and storm surge during extreme weather, while inland flooding can be reduced by strategic investments in catchment forests, vegetation and marshes. Forests are also crucial for maintaining usable freshwater sources, as well as for naturally regulating water flow.

Putting funds into maintaining a wetland near a processing or manufacturing plant can be a more cost-effective way of meeting regulatory requirements than building a wastewater treatment facility, as evidenced by the Dow Chemical Seadrift, Texas facility, where a 110-acre constructed wetland provides tertiary wastewater treatment of five million gallons a day. While the cost of a traditional "gray" treatment installation averages >$40 million, Dow's up-front costs were just $1.4 million.

For companies reliant on agricultural systems, improved land management of forests and ecosystems along field edges and streams, along with the introduction of more diversified and resilient sustainable agriculture systems, can minimize dependency on external inputs like artificial fertilizers, pesticides and blue irrigation water.

8. Leverage New Natural Capital Markets and Investment Tools

Over the past decade, the world has seen an acceleration of market-oriented experiments hinging on the idea of paying for once-free ecosystem services. Governments as well as private firms and NGOs are working to pioneer innovative market mechanisms that offer new incentives for economic actors to maintain and restore natural systems. Existing models for "Payments for Ecosystem Services (PES)" can be grouped into four main categories:

1. Direct payments to landowners or managers to maintain or enhance healthy ecosystems—often paid for through the issuing of forest bonds or creation of water funds that gather investments from the beneficiaries of ecosystem services.
2. Regulation-driven trading of ecosystem "credits" between buyers and sellers within a regulated market of a particular ecosystem service. For instance, the State of Victoria, Australia oversees the purchase and sale of "water shares" that give users the right to consume a set amount of water. In the United States, the Clean Water Act requires developers that damage wetlands to offset their impacts by protecting, enhancing, or restoring a similar wetland area in the same watershed—or by paying a third party to do so, either directly or by purchasing "credits" from a "wetland mitigation bank."
3. Voluntary trading of ecosystem "credits" and other direct private payments in which individuals contract directly with sellers offering ecosystem services. For instance, a landowner planting timber to sequester carbon might sell certified carbon credits to a company seeking to offset its carbon emissions.
4. Purchase of certified products or services deemed to have a neutral or positive effect on ecosystem services such as Forest Stewardship Council certified wood.

PES deals are emerging wherever businesses, public-sector agencies, and nonprofit organizations are looking for new ways to solve thorny environmental challenges. These schemes can change incentive structures and provide a new source of income for land management, restoration, conservation, and sustainable-use activities. Most transactions focus on valuation of one particular ecological service or attribute such as reducing global warming emissions or protecting habitat for an endangered species. Increasingly, transactions involve "bundling" of ecosystem services such as valuing a forest tract for its ability to soak up carbon dioxide and help purify drinking water among other things.

ForestTrends and the Ecosystem Marketplace have produced a comprehensive up-to-date (2012) matrix of the primary markets for nature's services.

9. Join Forces

Through collaboration and collective action, companies can help establish markets, get meaningful initiatives to scale and raise the bar across industries.

Taken alone, one company's effort to quantify their ecosystem dependencies or another's investment in the restoration of a particular forest or watershed may seem to make a small dent in the massive challenges before us, but collectively, they are having a significant impact—fortifying key natural infrastructure, and ushering in a sea change in how industry views its relationship to the natural world.

For companies seeking credible expert partners, a legion of expert NGOs stand at the ready to help navigate the challenges of ecosystem valuation and investment.

In September 2011, the Corporate Eco Forum and The Nature Conservancy announced a joint effort at the Clinton Global Initiative to mobilize a critical mass of major companies to initiate projects and investments ("commitments") that effectively demonstrate the need for business to protect and restore green infrastructure around the world including forests, fresh water and marine systems.

Twenty-four leading companies rose to the challenge:

Company	Industry/Sector	Commitment Name	Ecosystem Focus	Approach
Alcoa	Mining	Using Natural Systems for Sustainable Water Management	Freshwater, Watersheds	Natural Infrastructure
CH2MHILL	Infrastructure	Engaging Clients to Improve Water Stewardship with Green Infrastructure	Freshwater, Watersheds	Natural Infrastructure Investment
Clorox	Consumer Products	Water Reduction, Recapture, and Restoration	Freshwater	Optimization of Resources
The Coca-Cola Company	Food and Beverage	Engaging Bottlers in Sustaining Global Water Systems	Freshwater	Optimization of Resources
Darden Restaurants	Food Services	Catalyzing Industry to Rebuild World Fisheries	Fisheries	Value Chain Engagement
Dell	Technology	Powering the Possible for the Environment	Potentially all	Value Chain Engagement
Disney	Consumer Products/ Entertainment	Investing in Natural Solutions	Forests	Strategic Conservation/ Restoration
The Dow Chemical Company	Chemicals	Determining the Business Value of Ecosystem Services in Brazil	Freshwater, Forests, Soil	Assesment and Valuation of Ecosystem Services

Company	Industry/Sector	Commitment Name	Ecosystem Focus	Approach
Duke Energy	Energy	Restoration of Appalachian Forests with American Chestnut	Forests	Assesment and Valuation of Ecosystem Services
Ecolab	Water and Energy	Supporting the Alliance for Water Stewardship International Water Stewardship Standard	Freshwater	NGO Partnership
EKO Asset Management	Finance	NatLab—The Natural Infrastructure Innovative Financing Lab	Forests, Watersheds, Forests	Strategic Conservation/ Restoration
Enterprise Holdings	Automotive	Enterprise Rent-A-Car 50 Million Tree Pledge	Forests, Watersheds	New Market Mechanism
FEMSA	Food and Beverage	Latin American Water Funds Partnership	Freshwater, Watersheds	Strategic Conservation/ Restoration
General Motors	Automotive	Safeguarding Ecosystems Through Cost-Effective Waste Management	Freshwater, Soil	New Market Mechanism
Hanes Brands	Apparel	Introducing Innovative Products Using Sustainable Flax Fiber	Freshwater, Soil, Forests	Optimization of Resources
Kimberly-Clark	Consumer Products	Kimberly-Clark Plans To Reduce Its Forest Fiber Footprint	Forests	Material, Product, and Process Innovation
Lockheed Martin	Technology	Protecting Natural Infrastructure Through E-Waste Stewardship of Resources	Freshwater, Soil, Air	Optimization of Resources
Marriott International	Tourism and Hospitality	Amazon's Juma Reserve and the Sustainable Development of Fairfield by Marriott Hotels in Brazil	Forests	Strategic Conservation/ Restoration
Nike	Apparel	Mata no Peito Coalition for Brazil Forest Projects	Forests	Cross-Industry Coalition
Patagonia	Apparel	Protecting Ecosystems and Brand Integrity: Scaling up Patagonia's commitment to the bluesign Standard	Freshwater	Value Chain Engagement
TD Bank	Banking	Reducing Paper Use and Protecting North American Forests	Forests	Strategic Conservation/ Restoration
Unilever	Consumer Products	100% Certified Sustainably-Sourced Palm Oil	Forests	Material, Product, and Process Innovation
Weyerhaeuser	Forest Products	Driving Sustainability for Additional Value with Forest Solutions and Ecosystem Services	Forests	Valuation of Ecosystem Services/Innovative Business Model
Xerox	Technology	Rewarding Low-Impact Forest Management by Valuing Carbon Benefits	Forests	Value Chain Engagement

Source: The Corporate Eco Forum

20

THE PROBLEM OF CONSUMPTION

Peter Dauvergne[*]

Seasoned sailors avoid the clockwise vortex of calm winds and slow-moving currents of the North Pacific Gyre. And with good reason. Inside this dead zone is the Great Pacific Garbage Patch, where jellyfish ingest tiny plastic pellets in a floating graveyard of plastic at least twice the size of the US state of Texas. Here rests our empty plastic water bottles, lost footballs, and disposable cigarette lighters.

The next decade will likely see this Garbage Patch double in size as even more plastic washes out to sea. Sunlight will eventually break down much of this debris into small pellets. But this is hardly good news, as sharks, tuna, and whales feed on the pellet-eating jellyfish. Why, even with the rise over the last few decades of environmental norms, structures, organizations, policies, financing, and rules of governance, are the oceans continuing to fill with garbage? And this is only one of many possible examples of escalating global environmental problems. Why is the Arctic melting, faster and faster? Why are over half of the world's original forests and wetlands now gone?

There are, of course, many entwined reasons. One of the biggest is "the problem of consumption," not only what consumers choose and use, but more significantly how systemic drivers shape the quantities, costs, and benefits of producing, distributing, and disposing of consumer goods. At the core of this problem is the inability of environmental governance to alter, in any fundamental way, the global ecological effects of these drivers—such as advertising, economic growth, technology, income inequality, corporations, population growth, and globalization—that together are causing consumption, much of which is wasteful, to rise steadily worldwide.

*Originally published in *Global Environmental Politics* vol. 10 no. 2 (May 2010): 1–10. Reprinted with permission.

On many measures, policies, actions, and technologies to shape consumption appear to be "improving" environmental management. But too often the measures are close-up snapshots that cut out a much bigger, more complex, global picture of crisis. One common set of measures zooms in on consumer use of a product. Here, it is easy to find progress: simply compare the energy needs of a refrigerator or microwave or TV from the 1970s with a 2010 model. Another common set of measures zeros in on national consumption patterns. Here it is harder to find positive trends. Still, many exist—from higher recycling rates to more green buildings—for those who are looking for signs that capitalist economies are capable of shifting toward some form of sustainability.

Yet all of these measures need to be put into the context of a rising global population and rising per capita consumption in a globalized capitalist economy, a system that creates incentives—indeed, makes it imperative—for states and companies to "externalize externalities"[1] beyond the borders of those who are actually doing most of the consuming. The challenge for environmentalists and policymakers is therefore about much more than influencing "consumers"—much of what is happening globally is beyond their control. Rather, it is about transforming a global system that is driving unsustainable production, much of which is increasingly masking itself as sustainable consumption. Fundamentally, this means that any move toward sustainable consumption will require much better full cost accounting and more equitable distribution of income: locally, nationally, and globally.

Research in the subfield of global environmental politics [GEP] is increasingly probing this deep problem of consumption. Examples, to name just a few, include Michael Maniates on the "individualization of responsibility," Thomas Princen on "sufficiency" and "distancing," Jennifer Clapp on "distancing of waste" and "norm emergence," Doris Fuchs and Sylvia Lorek on "sustainable consumption," Paul Wapner and John Willoughby on "lifestyle change," Juliet Schor on the "new consumer culture," Jack Manno on "commoditization," Matthew Paterson on "cultural political economy," and my work on "shadows of consumption."[2]

Still, across the social sciences relatively little research has probed the full complexity and difficulty of "governing consumption globally" compared with, say, the extensive research on global environmental governance and trade agreements, international environmental negotiations, or nongovernmental organizations. One purpose of this essay is to encourage more research on this topic among GEP scholars. A second is to stress the need for international efforts to govern consumption that go beyond the current Marrakech process—an attempt to draft a 10-Year Framework on "sustainable production and consumption" for the 2011 session of the UN Commission on Sustainable Development [Editors' note: See UN Document A/CONF.216/5, 19 June 2012.] A third is to challenge the common view among international policymakers and business leaders that a greening of household consumption can significantly reduce the global costs of consumption. Here, local-to-global analysis typical of GEP scholarship has the potential to play a critical role in helping to redirect policy efforts.

The Global Costs of Consumption

The direct impact of thousands of everyday choices by 6.8 billion consumers partly explains the escalating environmental crisis. But obvious consequences—a Coke bottle floating down a smoke-colored river into the Pacific—comprise just a fraction of the real costs of consumption. Uncovering the full costs requires an accounting of the many indirect and hidden spillovers of supplying and replacing consumer products. These shadow effects of consumption can have as great, if not greater, consequences. And the globalization of corporations, trade, and financing is making these shadows longer, deeper, and harder to see.

Old IBM and Apple computers are piling up in developing countries with relatively low environmental standards, where recycling hazardous parts involve few safeguards for workers, many of them children. Inequalities are growing within and between countries, as costs spill into places with less power, from the slums of India to the aboriginal communities of North America. Wasteful and excessive consumption is increasing as consumer prices underestimate the environmental and social costs of everything from a cup of Colombian coffee on sale in Paris to a made-in-China Barbie on sale in San Francisco. And future generations are being exposed to great risks, with ignorance a green light to proceed rather than a sign for precaution.[3]

Perhaps most worrying of all, over time the costs of consumption are drifting into the world's most vulnerable ecosystems and poorest societies as powerful states and corporations externalize the environmental and social costs from the majority of consumers. This is adding to a growing crisis, for example, for the Inuit communities in the Arctic as industrial processes—from manufacturing in Europe to incinerating garbage in Asia—poison the land with persistent organic pollutants that travel up food chains and grasshopper across the globe through a process of repeated evaporation and redeposit until settling in cold climates.[4]

Such a process leaves consumers largely unaware—and corporations largely unaccountable for—the true costs of consumption. How many consumers in Tokyo, for example, would connect living in a concrete high-rise to deforestation in Papua New Guinea? Yet, over the last half-century, the most common use of the giant old-growth trees of Southeast Asia and Melanesia has been for plywood paneling to mold concrete in Japan. Called *kon pane* in Japanese, construction companies generally burned or left these panels to rot after only a few uses. Why such fantastic waste? The answer is simple: it was cheaper to buy new panels than clean the old ones.[5]

Consumers elsewhere are equally unaware of the externalities of consumption on the tropics. China's decision in 1998 to ban natural forest logging at home caused timber imports to jump. Overall timber imports have quadrupled over the last decade; and today half of all traded timber lands in China.[6]

Much of the timber entering China is illegal—as high as 80 percent from countries like Indonesia, Cambodia, and Papua New Guinea—thus depriving governments and communities of revenue. Chinese consumers are not alone in purchasing and using these wood products. Chinese exports of wooden furniture to Europe and North America, for example, have been growing rapidly in recent years, with at least some of this furniture made from illegal logs from places like Southeast Asia and eastern Russia.

Rising consumption of non-timber products is also driving tropical deforestation. On Indonesia's outer islands, for example, plantation companies are burning down degraded forests to clear land for oil palm for the rising worldwide consumption of margarine and oil for deep-frying. Raging forest fires every year in Indonesia are now one of the world's biggest sources of greenhouse gases. Another example is in the Amazon, where the primary cause of deforestation is land-clearing for cattle ranches as Brazil strives to hold onto its position as the world's largest beef exporter by volume in a global marketplace where meat consumption is rising quickly. Clearing land for soybean plantations (for export markets from animal feed to processed foods) is another core cause of deforestation in the Amazon.

Granted, this is all producing lots of cheap food—as well as lots of profits for multinational agricultural companies and the global fast-food industry.[7] But the costs for the tropics far outweigh the benefits for increasingly obese consumers. And this is only one of many possible examples of how an unbalanced global economy is displacing much of the costs of consumption onto the world's poorest peoples and most vulnerable ecosystems. Just look at the families in Manila now living inside smoking mountains of fast-food wrappers, car tires, and toxic waste drums. Or at the polar bears slipping into endangered status as their Arctic home melts away.

Governing Consumption Globally

Many factors complicate global environmental governance of consumption. A growing world population and rising per capita incomes are two of the most significant. The world population grew during the second half of the 20th century more than it had in the preceding four million years. Since the 1970s, the global economy has been expanding even faster than population, with world Gross Domestic Product (in constant US$ 1995) almost tripling from 1970–2000. The global economy grew even faster from 2001–2006: faster than during any five-year period since World War II.[8]

World economic growth slowed considerably in 2008 and 2009 during the global financial downturn. Yet the future will still see a much larger world population and, unless the world economy collapses, much higher per capita rates of consumption. By late 2009, the International Monetary Fund already saw many signs of a "recovery" of the world economy, with much higher growth predicted for 2010.[9] And most analysts still expect the global middle class to triple by 2030:

a group able to afford big-ticket items like cars and home appliances. By 2050 the world population is set to exceed 9 billion, with over 95 percent of this increase occurring in developing countries like Indonesia, India, and China. In this setting, changing the environmental choices of enough consumers fast enough to make a global difference is very hard, and getting harder.

At the same time, the world market—what some call the global consumer culture—is widening and deepening. One indicative statistic is the value of world merchandise exports, which now exceeds US$16 trillion. This is up from US$6 trillion in 2000, an amount that by then was already more than a 100 times higher than in 1948. Another revealing statistic is the flow of foreign direct investment into developing countries which, before the global financial crisis of 2007–09, had reached US$380 billion in 2006, up from US$22 billion in 1990.[10]

Economic globalization can allow new technologies or more environmentally friendly products to reach more consumers, faster and with enhanced efficiencies for resource and energy inputs. The environmental history of the automobile—including a diffusion of regulations and technologies from places like California to the rest of the world—provides one example of how the globalization of markets can ramp up global standards.[11] Still, such benefits are more than outweighed by the environmental costs spilling from the globalized production, trade, and investment chains that supply increasing numbers of consumers with goods and services.

Many other forces and factors also influence the sustainability of consumption. Advertising to influence consumer decisions is one obvious source. Worldwide, trillions of dollars are spent each year to convince consumers to buy new products and services: an amount that's growing fast under many guises, from athletes wearing brands to TV actors drinking Starbucks coffee. This is deepening a culture of consumerism, especially among high-income earners. All of the messaging is saying buy more, consume more to be happy. Advertisers creatively promote "perceived obsolescence" and imbue buying something like a car with feelings like self-worth, freedom, adventure, and success. This is hardly unique to the auto industry, however: the same is true for computers, refrigerators, cell phones, and so on.

And advertising is only one of the factors making it difficult to influence consumer decisions consistently and effectively. Others include habits, skepticism, convenience, availability, affordability, future savings, and opportunity, to name just a few. Many consumers ultimately want ease of purchase and good value; some are also inconsistent, saying one thing and doing another. Genuine and perceived uncertainty in what actually comprises "sustainable consumption" and "sustainable lifestyles" can also cause consumers to lose interest or confidence, providing a justification for some people to prioritize other factors above environmentalism.

Moreover, consumers buy products not only for personal reasons, but also in response to socioeconomic constraints, opportunities, and expectations. The choices consumers make around whether to purchase—and then when to drive—a car is one obvious example. The availability, reliability, and affordability of public transportation all affect this decision. Automakers know this well. Many of the biggest companies have a long record of opposing—and sometimes even destroying—public transportation (such as dismantling the electric trolley system in the United States).[12]

Many other more subtle structures, however, can influence consumer choices. Sports leagues for children, for example, can leave parents driving to games hours away. Carpooling is certainly possible; but, for a parent without a car, requesting weekly rides is a tough option given the expectations of the coaches, parents, and children. As these opportunities, constraints, and expectations coalesce, even committed environmentalists commonly make decisions that increase their personal ecological footprint, thereby making choices that feel frustratingly hypocritical. This, in turn, can contribute to environmental fatigue: to an environmentalist carrying home groceries in a plastic bag despite full knowledge of the potential harm.[13]

Acting Incrementally, Failing Globally

Influencing individual consumers to act more sustainably, then, is one of the most complex and difficult challenges for environmental governance. Influencing enough consumers to affect global change is an even greater challenge. And transforming major systemic drivers of consumption is still more difficult and complex. The overall system of global environmental governance is improving management on some measures, most notably by gradually expanding markets for more efficient products with less per unit environmental impacts. One example, among thousands, is the history of the increasing energy efficiency of new refrigerators since the global phase-down of CFCs [chlorofluorocarbons] beginning in the early 1990s.

But, because these advances tend to require or contribute to more consumption, and because they tend to do little to influence the drivers of consumption or mitigate the indirect costs of producing, transporting, and disposing of consumer goods, much of the so-called "progress" is incremental, local, or temporary, unable on a global scale to produce enough change to mitigate the damaging environmental consequences of buying and using most consumer products. Sometimes this progress is even causing the costs of consumption to intensify further, with environmental conditions improving in developed countries and deteriorating in developing ones that produce and import more damaging products. This helps to explain why so many global environmental efforts are failing. It also helps to explain why so many involved in the global policy process are overly optimistic about the value of incremental environmentalism, as those with more power and wealth shift many of the costs of consumption to those with less.

International environmental laws to control transboundary pollution are helping a little to mitigate the environmental damage of consumption (e.g., the 1989 Basel Convention on the Control of Transboundary Movements of Hazardous Wastes and their Disposal, and the 2001 Stockholm Convention on Persistent Organic Pollutants). So are consumer labels to certify that products are from sustainable sources (e.g., the Forest Stewardship Council and the Marine Stewardship Council). So are corporate policies to increase environmental and social accountability (e.g., Electrolux's policy to audit suppliers in developing countries like China and Brazil to monitor compliance with its corporate code of conduct). And so are incentives for manufacturers to include disposal costs into the price of consumer goods (e.g., the European Commission's End-of-Life Vehicles directive, which requires manufacturers to "de-pollute" and recycle used vehicles with their logo).

Yet the big picture is clear. Even as global environmental governance continues to strengthen incrementally, the "global environment" that is being "governed" is continuing to slide into an ever-greater crisis, creating an ever-more difficult problem to "govern." To be effective on a global scale, far more needs to be done, faster, to re-imagine and reorganize an unbalanced global economy, and to shift more of the benefits to the world's poorest people and less of the costs of producing, using, and disposing of consumer goods to the most vulnerable ecosystems. This will require international policy processes to tackle head on the systemic drivers of consumption.

Conclusion: Beyond a Greening of Consumption

Such a conclusion challenges the current thinking among policymakers and business leaders that stresses the importance of greening consumer choices and lifestyles to mitigate the effects of consumption, while sustaining economic growth.[14] This raises many questions about the predictive value of ecological modernization theory as a strand of environmental thought. The gist of this theory, which draws primarily on the histories of Western Europe after World War II, is that appropriate market-based environmental regulations can increase the competitiveness of industry and foster socioeconomic development. The theory assumes it is possible to stimulate green economic growth by creating incentives to promote markets and innovative technologies that increase efficiency, use less energy, deplete fewer resources, and recycle more waste. Governments need as well to develop a policy framework so companies see protecting the environment not as a cost, but as a business opportunity to improve competitiveness—and thereby create incentives for firms to go beyond the legal environmental rules in various jurisdictions. The theory predicts a gradual restructuring of global capitalism into a global system of sustainable economic growth.[15]

It underestimates significantly, however, the extent of the global problem of consumption, capturing instead a slice of the process of change, especially in the wealthy states of Europe. Promoting green products and sustainable lifestyles is only scratching at the surface of a problematic capitalist world order built on ever-expanding economic growth, consumption, and markets, and efficiencies and profits realized by distancing and externalizing the environmental and social costs of producing, using, and replacing consumer goods.

First called for by the 2002 World Summit on Sustainable Development's Johannesburg Plan of Action, the Marrakech process to develop a 10-year framework of programs for sustainable consumption and production has some potential to address the problem of consumption more effectively.[16] But this will require going beyond the assumptions, pathways, and measurements of an ecological modernization approach. It will require a questioning of our economic order, income inequality, and a global system sinking a disproportionate amount of the costs of consumption into the world's poorest countries and most vulnerable ecosystems. Thinking incrementally and acting locally, while beneficial, is not enough to prevent the environmental governance of consumption from continuing to fail globally. To return to the rising tide of plastics in the Pacific Ocean, succeeding globally will require far greater change than simply increasing the number of conscientious consumers refusing plastic bags, recycling plastic bottles, or sleeping contentedly on recycled plastic pillow stuffing.

REFERENCES

Ali, Saleem. 2009. *Treasures of the Earth: Need, Greed, and a Sustainable Future.* New Haven, CT: Yale University Press.

Clapp, Jennifer. 2002. Distancing of Waste: Overconsumption in a Global Economy. In Thomas Princen, Michael Maniates, and Ken Conca, eds. *Confronting Consumption,* 155–176. Cambridge, MA: MIT Press.

Clapp, Jennifer, and Doris Fuchs. 2009. *Corporate Power in Global Agrifood Governance.* Cambridge, MA: The MIT Press.

Clapp, Jennifer, and Linda Swanston. 2009. Doing Away with Plastic Shopping Bags: International Patterns of Norm Emergence and Policy Implementation. *Environmental Politics* 18 (3): 315–332.

Dauvergne, Peter. 1997. *Shadows in the Forest: Japan and the Politics of Timber in Southeast Asia.* Cambridge, MA: The MIT Press.

———. 2008. *The Shadows of Consumption: Consequences for the Global Environment.* Cambridge, MA: The MIT Press.

Downie, David Leonard, and Terry Fenge, eds. 2003. *Northern Lights against POPs: Combatting Toxic Threats in the Arctic.* Montreal, QC: McGill-Queen's University Press.

Freund, Peter, and George Martin. 1993. *The Ecology of the Automobile.* Montreal, QC: Black Rose Books.

Fuchs, Doris A., and Sylvia Lorek. 2005. Sustainable Consumption Governance: A History of Promises and Failures. *Journal of Consumer Policy* 28 (3): 261–288.

Iles, Alastair. 2004. Mapping Environmental Justice in Technology Flows: Computer Waste Impacts in Asia. *Global Environmental Politics* 4 (4): 76–107.

International Monetary Fund. 2009. *World Economic Outlook: October 2009.* Washington, DC: World Bank. Available online at: http://www.imf.org/external/pubs/ft/weo/2009/02/pdf/text.pdf.

Jackson, Tim. 2004. Negotiating Sustainable Consumption: A Review of the Consumption Debate and its Policy Implications. *Energy and Environment* 15 (6): 1027–1051.

———. 2005. Live Better by Consuming Less? Is There a Double 'Double Dividend' in Sustainable Consumption? *Journal of Industrial Ecology* 9 (1–2): 19–36.

———. 2008. The Challenge of Sustainable Lifestyles. In *2008 State of the World: Innovations for a Sustainable Economy.* New York: Norton.

Laurance, William. 2008. The Need to Cut China's Illegal Timber Imports. *Science Magazine* 29 (February): 1184–1185.

Maniates, Michael. 2001. Individualization: Plant a Tree, Buy a Bike, Save the World? *Global Environmental Politics* 1 (3): 31–52.

Manno, Jack. 2002. Commoditization: Consumption Efficiency and an Economy of Care and Connection. In Thomas Princen, Michael Maniates, and Ken Conca, eds. *Confronting Consumption,* 67–99. Cambridge, MA: MIT Press.

Mol, Arthur P. J. 2001. *Globalization and Environmental Reform: The Ecological Modernization of the Global Economy.* Cambridge, MA: The MIT Press.

———. 2002. Ecological Modernization and the Global Economy. *Global Environmental Politics* 2 (2): 92–115.

Mol, Arthur P. J., and Martin Jänicke. 2009. The Origins and Theoretical Foundations of Ecological Modernization Theory. In Arthur P. J. Mol, David A. Sonnenfeld, and Gert Spaargaren, eds. *The Ecological Modernization Reader: Environmental Reform in Theory and Practice,* 17–27. London: Routledge.

Mont, Oksana, and Andrius Plepys. 2008. Sustainable Consumption Progress: Should We Be Proud or Alarmed? *Journal of Cleaner Production* 16 (4): 531–537.

Paterson, Matthew. 2007. *Automobile Politics: Ecology and Cultural Political Economy.* Cambridge: Cambridge University Press.

Princen, Thomas. 2005. *The Logic of Sufficiency.* Cambridge, MA: The MIT Press.

Princen, Thomas, Michael Maniates, and Ken Conca, eds. 2002. *Confronting Consumption.* Cambridge, MA: The MIT Press.

Schor, Juliet B. 2004. *Born to Buy: The Commercialized Child and the New Consumer Culture.* New York: Scribner.

Vermeir, Iris, and Wim Verbeke. 2006. Sustainable Food Consumption: Exploring Consumer "Attitude-Behavioral Intention" Gap. *Journal of Agricultural and Environmental Ethics* 19 (2): 169–194.

Vogel, David. 1995. *Trading Up: Consumer and Environmental Regulation in a Global Economy.* Cambridge, MA: Harvard University Press.

Wapner, Paul, and John Willoughby. 2005. The Irony of Environmentalism: The Ecological Futility but Political Necessity of Lifestyle Change. *Ethics and International Affairs* 19 (3): 77–89.

World Bank. 2006. *Global Economic Prospects 2007: Managing the Next Wave of Globalization.* Washington, DC: World Bank.

World Business Council for Sustainable Development. 2008. *Sustainable Consumption Facts and Trends: From a Business Perspective.* Geneva: World Business Council for Sustainable Development.

Yago, Glenn. 1984. *The Decline of Transit: Urban Transportation in German and U.S. Cities, 1900–1970.* Cambridge: Cambridge University Press.

NOTES

1. I am indebted to one of the anonymous reviewers for this phrasing.

2. See Princen, Maniates, and Conca 2002; Maniates 2001; Princen 2005; Clapp 2002; Clapp and Swanston 2009; Fuchs and Lorek 2005; Wapner and Willoughby 2005; Schor 2004; Manno 2002; Paterson 2007; Mol 2001, 2002; and Dauvergne 2008.

3. For the example of computer waste, see Iles 2004.

4. See Downie and Fenge 2003.

5. See Dauvergne 1997.

6. Laurance 2008, 1184.

7. For a recent analysis of the global agriculture industry, see Clapp and Fuchs 2009.

8. World Bank 2006; World Bank, World Development Indicators Online, available at www.worldbank.org.

9. IMF 2009.

10. World Bank 2006; World Bank, World Development Indicators Online, available at www.worldbank.org.

11. See Vogel 1995.

12. Yago 1984, 59–61; and Freund and Martin 1993, 135–37.

13. Some recent literature on sustainable consumption and sustainable lifestyles includes Fuchs and Lorek 2005; Vermeir and Verbeke 2006; Jackson 2004, 2005, 2008; Mont and Plepys 2008; Ali 2009.

14. The World Business Council for Sustainable Development (2008: 5), for example, concludes: "Current global consumption patterns are unsustainable. . . . It is becoming apparent that efficiency gains and technological advances alone will not be sufficient to bring global consumption to a sustainable level; changes will also be required to *consumer lifestyles, including the ways in which consumers choose and use products and services*" (emphasis added).

15. See Mol 2001, 2002; Mol and Jänicke 2009.

16. For background on the Marrakech process, see the United Nations website at http://esa.un.org/marrakechprocess.

21

URBAN SUSTAINABILITY AND RESILIENCE: WHY WE NEED TO FOCUS ON SCALES

Thomas Elmqvist*

Two of the most debated and challenging concepts in urban development are sustainability and resilience. How are they related? Do they mean approximately the same thing or are they distinctly different and can misunderstandings lead to undesired outcomes?

In this essay I will try to clarify the concepts, discuss two common misinterpretations and reflect on the many difficulties that remain in application in urban development.

Can a city be sustainable?

Most people would answer that this is not only possible but also, given rapid urbanization, necessary for the planet to become sustainable. But my immediate answer is NO and here is the first common misconception we need to deal with. Cities are centers of production and consumption and urban inhabitants [are] reliant on resources and ecosystem services, from food, water and construction materials to waste assimilation, secured from locations around the world. Although cities can optimize their resource use, increase their efficiency, and minimize waste, they can never become fully self-sufficient. Therefore, *individual cities cannot be considered*

*Originally published 27 March 2013 as a blog posting on "The Nature of Cities," *www.thenatureofcities* *.com/.* Reprinted with permission.

"sustainable" without acknowledging and accounting for their *teleconnections*—that is, their long-distance dependence and impact on resources and populations in other regions around the world.

Sustainability is commonly misunderstood as being equal to self-sufficiency, but in a globalized world virtually nothing at a local scale is self-sufficient. To become meaningful, urban sustainability therefore has to address appropriate scales, which always would be larger than an individual city.

The classical definition of sustainable development (Brundtland Report on Sustainable Development) focuses on how to manage resources in a way that guarantees welfare and promotes equity of current and future generations, in general addressing the global scale. [Editors' note: See Part Four of this volume for a selection from the Brundtland, or WCED, report.] However, in the urban context, research and application of sustainability have so far been constrained to either single or narrowly defined issues (e.g., population, climate, energy, water) or rarely moved beyond city boundaries.

Clearly what constitutes urban sustainability needs rethinking and reformulation, taking urban teleconnections into account. We will come back to this at the end of the essay.

Can we build resilience in a single city?

Similarly, most people would answer yes to this question and that a resilient city would be highly desirable and necessary. But again, my answer is NO, at least when it comes to *general resilience,* and here we deal with the second common misconception.

Firstly, a narrow focus on a single city is often counterproductive and may even be destructive since building resilience in one city often may erode it somewhere else with multiple negative effects across the globe (this relates to the distinction between general and specified resilience explained below).

Secondly, from historical accounts we learn that while there are some cities that have actually failed and disappeared (e.g. Mayan cities), our modern-era experience is that cities rarely if ever collapse and disappear. Rather, they may enter a spiral of decline, becoming non-competitive and losing their position in regional, national and even global systems of cities. However, through extensive financial and trading networks, cities have a high capacity to avoid abrupt change and collapse and applying the resilience concept at the local city scale is thus not particularly useful.

What is resilience?

Resilience (see Resilience Alliance, www.resalliance.org/) has a long history in engineering science but the most influential ecological interpretation was developed by Canadian ecologist C.S. "Buzz" Holling in 1973. Resilience builds on two radical premises. The first is that humans and nature are strongly coupled and co-evolving, and should therefore be conceived of as one "social-ecological" system.

The second is that the long-held assumption that systems respond to change in a linear, predictable fashion is simply wrong. Complex systems are, according to resilience thinking, rarely static and linear; instead they are often in constant flux, highly unpredictable and self-organizing, with feedbacks across time and space. A key feature of complex adaptive systems is that they can settle into a number of different stability domains. A lake, for example, will stabilize in either an oxygen-rich, clear state or algae-dominated, murky one. A financial market can float on a housing bubble or settle into a basin of recession.

Historically, we have tended to view the transition between such states as gradual. But there is increasing evidence that many systems do not respond to change that way: The clear lake seems hardly affected by fertilizer runoff until a critical threshold is passed, at which point the water abruptly goes turbid. Resilience science focuses on these sorts of tipping points. It looks at *slow variables* (i.e. gradual stresses), such as climate change, as well as *fast variables* (i.e. chance events), such as storms, fires, even stock market crashes that can tip a system into another equilibrium state from which it is difficult, if not impossible, to recover.

Over the past decade, resilience science has expanded much beyond ecologists to include thinking among economists, political scientists, mathematicians, social scientists, and archaeologists. (For a general overview see this video: www.stockholmresilience.org/21/research/what-is-resilience.html.)

Resilience is now used widely in discussing urban development, but it is much more challenging than when applied to a lake, agricultur[e] or a forest system. When most people think of urban resilience it is generally in the context of response to sudden impacts, such as a hazard or disaster recovery—for example, Hurricane Katrina in New Orleans and recently [Hurricane] Sandy in New York City. How rapidly does the system recover and how much shock can it absorb before it transforms into something fundamentally different? This is often viewed as the essence of resilience thinking. However, the resilience concept goes far beyond recovery from single disturbances and it is here an important distinction is made between *general resilience* and *specified resilience*. General resilience refers to the resilience of a large-scale system to all kinds of shocks, including novel ones; specified resilience refers to the resilience "of what, to what"—that is, resilience of smaller scale-systems, a particular part of a system, related to a particular control variable, or to one or more identified kinds of shocks.

From an urban perspective, general resilience thus only makes sense on a much larger scale than individual cities (although specified resilience may be explored at a smaller scale). The concept of general resilience and scale leads us to another quite radical idea: change and transformation at the city level is necessary for maintaining resilience at the larger scale.

This may at first seem strongly counter-intuitive. Isn't resilience about keeping systems as is and avoiding change and transformations?

Transformation and resilience

To further explore this we need to put everything in a larger historical and global perspective.

The relatively stable environment of the Holocene, the current interglacial period that began about 10,000 years ago, allowed agriculture and complex societies, including current urbanization, to develop. This stable period is in contrast to the rather violent fluctuations in temperature in the preceding 90,000-year period. The stability induced humans, for the first time, to invest in agriculture and manage the environment rather than merely exploit it. Despite some natural environmental fluctuations over the past 10,000 years, complex feedback mechanisms involving the atmosphere, the terrestrial biosphere and the oceans have kept variation within the narrow range associated with the Holocene state. However, since the industrial revolution (the advent of the Anthropocene), humans are believed to have effectively begun pushing the planet outside the Holocene range of variability for many key Earth System processes (for full reference see http://www.ecologyandsociety.org/vol14/iss2/art32/), including introduction of the concept of planetary boundaries). Urbanization represents one of the major processes contributing to this pushing pressure through, for example, greenhouse gas emissions, massive land use change and increased resource consumption.

FIGURE 21.1 The last glacial cycle of 18O (an indicator of temperature) and selected events in human history

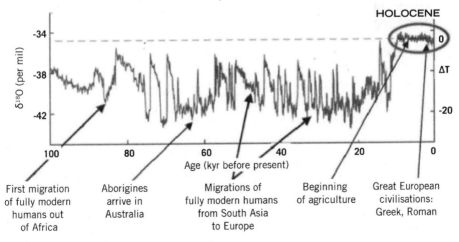

Source: Rockström et al. 2009

Maintaining resilience at the global scale—that is, avoiding that the planet passes a threshold and again enters into a new period of violent climate fluctuations—is therefore believed to require massive transformations at the level of cities. But what are these transformations, and what would trigger urban regions to employ them?

Coping vs. transformation

To explore this we will return to the basic principle in resilience thinking: a slow variable (like urbanization) may invisibly push the larger system closer and closer to a threshold (beyond which there would be radical change toward a new equilibrium) and . . . disturbances that previously could have been absorbed become the straws that break the camel's back. However, urbanization does not just represent a slow variable. At the same time it is a process leading to higher intensity/frequency of disturbances through, for example, its impact on both global and regional climate change. Urbanization therefore represents a double-arrowed process and complex interaction between slow and fast variables. Conventional urban responses to disturbances such as coping and adaptive strategies may not only over time be insufficient at the city scale, they may also be counterproductive when it comes to maintaining resilience at the global scale.

A *coping strategy* is often used to describe the ability at the local scale and often at the level of individuals (such as having savings [in] a bank account) to deal effectively with a single disturbance, with the understanding that a crisis is rare and temporary and that the situation will quickly normalize when the disturbance recedes. *Adapting* to change is defined as an adjustment at somewhat larger scales in natural and human systems, in response to actual or expected disturbances when frequencies tend to increase (e.g. building higher and higher levees in response to increasing risks of flooding) (Figure 21.2).

Transformation strategies are employed when coping and adaptation strategies are insufficient and outcomes are perceived to be highly undesirable. A *transformation* is thus defined as a response that differs from both coping and adaptation strategies in that the decisions made and actions taken change the identity of the system itself, creat[ing] a fundamentally new system when ecological, economic, or social structures make the existing system untenable. It also and most importantly must address the causes of the increasing intensity/frequency of disturbance, which necessarily may not be the case with coping and adaptation. There are numerous examples of urban regions already engaged in developing both coping and adaptive strategies in response to, for example, sea level rise, demographic changes, and shortage of natural resources. However, when intensities and frequencies of disturbances increase, building larger dams or higher levees may no longer protect a city from flooding or sea level rise. Instead, a transformation to, say, a floating city may be the only viable option.

FIGURE 21.2 Coping, adaptive, transformative strategies in relation to spatial scales and intensity/frequency of disturbances and anthropogenic impacts

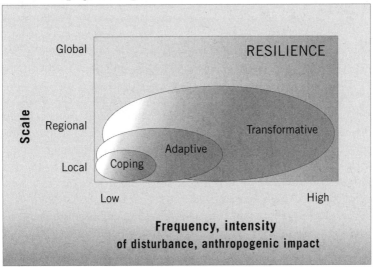

Source: www.thenatureofcities.com

However, even if we would agree that a myriad of transformations at the local/ regional scale is important for maintaining resilience at the global scale, current coping and adaptive strategies need our attention since they may be counterproductive, lead to lock-in and prevent a transformation [from being] initiated. For example, this would include exploring the local-global synergies or tradeoffs of different re-designing schemes of the supply and consumptions chains, evaluating different modes of re-designing urban morphology and transport and [evaluating] different modes of stewardships of ecosystem services within and outside city boundaries.

Resilience and sustainability: What is the difference?

So where does this take us when it comes to understanding urban resilience and sustainability?

First of all, for both concepts the local city scale is too narrow. Urban sustainability must include teleconnections and urban dependence and impacts on distal populations and ecosystems. Similarly, when building resilience at the global scale (i.e. general resilience), urban regions must take increased responsibility for implementing transformative solutions and, through collaboration across a global system of cities, provide a transformative framework to manage resource chains.

However, how do we then distinguish between the two concepts? Isn't there still a substantial overlap? My view is that we may accept that the concepts are quite similar when addressing the global scale, but we may give them a distinctly different meaning when addressing other scales. At regional and local scales resilience could more be seen as an approach (non-normative process) to meet the challenges of sustainable development (normative goal). Treating resilience as non-normative at these scales is preferable since knowledge about the components of resilience could be used to either build or erode resilience depending on whether a transformation is desirable or not in a specific context.

I have above outlined some of the challenges with the two concepts, but there are many more. We will need a lively debate exploring even further the meaning of the concepts in an urban context and how cities may contribute to global sustainability and resilience through transformative actions redefining their role and become more of sources of ecosystem services rather than sinks and increasingly provide better stewardship of marine, terrestrial and freshwater ecosystems both inside and outside city boundaries.

It would be important to feed such a lively debate into the current efforts to develop a framework for the Sustainable Development Goals (for example, see http://sustainabledevelopment.un.org/):

- Can we agree that the city-scale is too narrow for both sustainability and resilience analyses and policies implementing them?
- How should SDGs [sustainable development goals] become relevant for urban development? How could scales be addressed in the SDGs? For example, how do we design scalable targets and indicators that link the local and the global scale?
- How should we use the resilience concept in relation to urban development? Could and should resilience be used in both a normative and a non-normative sense depending on scale?

I invite all readers to give their view!

PART FIVE

FROM ECOLOGICAL CONFLICT TO ENVIRONMENTAL SECURITY?

As seen in the previous section, the concept of sustainability has emerged as a powerful paradigm shaping the interpretations, goals, and behavior of a broad range of actors on the global environmental stage. But the global environmental debate of the past four decades has engaged not only economic issues of welfare, production, and livelihood but also political questions of international conflict, violence, and geopolitics. The control of natural resources is also highly contested, leading some to frame natural-resource management as conflict management. In such divisive circumstances, it is not surprising that paradigms focused on the conflictual dimensions of environmental problems also have emerged.

One attempt to grapple with these intensely political themes is the paradigm of "environmental security." Like sustainability, environmental security offers a potentially powerful but also controversial way to think about the social dimensions of environmental problems. The environmental security paradigm rests on a series of claims: that environmental change is an important source of social conflict, that many societies face graver dangers from environmental change than from traditional military threats, and that both environmental and security policies must be redefined to take account of these new realities. We saw an early articulation of this position from Lester Brown in Part One.

We begin the environmental security section with a look back at the historical roots of the environmental security paradigm by Geoffrey Dabelko (Chapter 22). This multidimensional story illustrates the diversity of the paradigm's origins and focus areas. It also highlights the difficulties of placing environmental security concerns on the international agenda and keeping them there. Looking to the future, Dabelko points hopefully toward the emergence of a new generation of more careful analytic scholarship and growing recognition of the peacebuilding potential inherent in environmental relationships, as opposed to a narrower view of the environment as simply a potential trigger for conflict. His chapter also highlights the strong influence of environmental security ideas from outside the United States, contrary to the common perception that the United States (and specifically its military) is the dominant and original proponent.

Chapter 23, excerpted from the United Nations report *From Conflict to Peacebuilding*, characterizes a diverse set of connections among environmental change, natural-resource use, and violent conflict. Prepared by the UN Environment Programme (UNEP) as a "policy justification" for its activities, the excerpt presented here outlines pathways forward for practitioners to respond to the complex set of dynamics associated with the environment, violence, and peacebuilding. Scholars concerned with an environment-conflict link initially focused their attention largely on problems of increasing natural-resource scarcity. A growing body of research suggested that scarcity of renewable resources—principally water, fish stocks, forests, and fertile land—could contribute to social instability, civil strife, and violent conflict, particularly when coupled with population growth and inequitable division of resources.[1] More recently, scholars focused on the violence potential of resource abundance, which may create incentives for actors to capture "lootable" resources, to extend the duration of conflict in order to profit from war economies, or to promote distorted patterns of economic development that yield weak and brittle governments.[2] UNEP's analysis suggests that both scarcity and abundance may trigger violent conflict, particularly in the context of weak, illegitimate, or predatory political institutions. These mechanisms may originate in the grievances of local communities or when "violence entrepreneurs" exploit real or perceived scarcities between groups. UNEP also works on post-conflict peacebuilding, and has produced a series of post-conflict assessments of the environmental challenges facing war-torn societies.[3]

Given such conflict potential, some proponents of environmental security have argued that there is an urgent, compelling need to "redefine" the concept of security.[4] In this view, environmental security is more than just an effort to reconceptualize threats or to document empirical patterns of environmental degradation and violence. It is also a political agenda aimed at mobilizing the state and society toward a new set of goals and at redirecting resources and energies away from traditional, narrowly military concerns. Some proponents argue that only by framing the environmental problematique in security terms can the necessary level of governmental attention and social mobilization be ensured.[5] Others argue that security institutions could contribute directly to environmental protection, given their financial resources, monitoring and intelligence-gathering capabilities, and scientific and technological expertise.[6]

Thus, although the origins of the environmental security paradigm can be traced at least to the early post–World War II period,[7] it is surely no accident that the idea of rethinking security policy in ecological terms flourished in the post–Cold War era. Policymakers, military institutions, and entire societies began to reconsider the character of the threats they face. Many proponents of environmental security were driven by the belief that the end of the Cold War opened a window of opportunity for fundamental changes in security policies and a reordering of social priorities.

Among the many controversies surrounding the paradigm of environmental security, two are central. First, is there enough evidence to support the claim that ecological change is, or will be, a major new source of conflict? Although a growing body of research points to specific cases in which environmental change seems to have played a role in promoting or exacerbating social conflict, many questions remain. Why does environmental stress produce such conflict in some cases but not in others? Is it possible that environmental problems are a symptom of conflict-prone social systems rather than a root cause of conflict? A second set of questions involves the more nebulous concept of security. Are the advantages of linking environmental problems to security concerns worth the risk of militarizing a society's responses to environmental problems?

Daniel Deudney (Chapter 24) raises both sets of questions in an essay that remains the seminal critique more than two decades after he penned it. Deudney is skeptical that environmental change precipitates acute conflict, at least in the form of war; he argues that environmental problems have little in common with the traditional security problem of interstate violence.[8] He is also wary of evoking the powerful concept of security to mobilize society: "For environmentalists to dress their programs in the blood-soaked garments of the war system betrays their core values and creates confusion about the real tasks at hand." Others have voiced stronger criticisms, suggesting that the powerful association between the concept of security and the use of military force creates the danger of turning environmental problems into sources of military tension and conflict.[9] These critics share Deudney's view that the conflictual mind-set and the military tools of security institutions are poorly suited to the global environmental problematique. To paraphrase a book title from the early 1990s, will these efforts green security or militarize the environment?[10]

There is also the danger that environment-conflict linkages tell only part of the story. If tensions over environment and natural resources can trigger conflict, may they not also trigger cooperation? If actors recognize the conflict potential, might they not work to enhance capacities for peaceful dispute resolution? Arguably this has been the case with regard to water, a resource around which there are many social tensions—but also many initiatives for cooperation, institution building, and shared resource governance. It would be a mistake to view only the conflictual side of social responses. As Kader Asmal, then a South African government official who chaired the World Commission on Dams (see Chapter 14 by Bissell in this volume), has argued, for all the gloom-and-doom talk from politicians and journalists about water scarcity triggering "water wars" in the near future, the historical record around water has overwhelmingly been one of cooperation and negotiation, not conflict and violence:

With all due respect to my friends, *have* battles been fought over water? Is water scarcity a *casus belli*? Does it in fact divide nations? My own answer is no, no and no. I recognize the obvious value to sensational "Water War." Alarmists awaken people to the underlying reality of water scarcity, and rally troops to become more progressive and interdependent. By contrast, to challenge or dispute that rhetoric is to risk making us passive or smug about the status quo, or delay badly needed innovations or co-operation against stress. And yet I do challenge "Water War" rhetoric. For there is no hard evidence to back it up.[11]

While there is little evidence for wars between countries over water, there is emerging evidence that local water issues can be a force for cooperation in the face of wider conflict. Chapter 25 presents an excerpt from a report by the civil-society organization EcoPeace/Friends of the Earth Middle East (FOEME) that outlines its practical approach to using environmental interdependencies to build trust between parties to a conflict. FOEME's Good Water Neighbors project brings together Israeli, Palestinian, and Jordanian communities living side by side and suffering jointly from poor water quality. Partnering with schools and mayors, FOEME works to improve water quality, hygiene, and access in ways that bring communities and leaders together to cooperate on a wider agenda despite the on-going conflict. They then proactively build on this local cooperation to support cooperation at higher levels of political organization while serving as a model for other potential environmental peacebuilders around the world.

In weighing both the conflictual and cooperative potential of ecological inter-dependence, it is also important not to limit our analysis to the level of interstate, intergovernmental relations. Balakrishnan Rajagopal (Chapter 26) provides a dra-matic portrayal of the violence against people and communities that often accom-panies natural-resource development, particularly when such projects occur in the absence of human rights guarantees and a voice for local, affected communi-ties. He points to a different kind of violence problem: the "structural violence" of forced displacement of tens of millions of people around the world, to make way for large dams, agricultural colonization schemes, and other large-scale resource development projects. This critique suggests that the environmental security frame must be broadened to encompass human security concerns, rather than simply the question of interstate or intergroup violent conflict.

Social science may lack the tools to tell us exactly when and where environmen-tal problems may produce violence. Nevertheless, the capacity of environmental change to disrupt people's lives, erode standards of living, and threaten established interests tells us that the possibility of widespread violent conflict must be taken seriously. Research that helps us understand when and where such conflict is likely to occur could be an important tool for avoiding conflict, building international confidence, and resolving nonviolent conflict.

The environmental security debate is further complicated by the way in which it intersects the North-South axis in world politics. The focus of ecological conflict research tends to be on the economically less-developed regions of the planet; most analysts emphasize these regions when identifying likely sites of future environ-mentally induced conflicts. There are many reasons for this focus on the South: its limited financial and technological resources, high population growth rates, pre-existing political instability, and day-to-day struggles for survival that engulf large segments of the population.

However, even if it is plausible to claim that the South will be the site of conflicts with significant environmental dimensions, this concern cannot be divorced from the broader pattern of North-South relations. Many Southern governments and activists have viewed the North's concern for "security" in the South, environmen-tal or otherwise, with skepticism if not outright suspicion. They see the rhetoric of environmental security as an excuse to continue the North's long-standing practice of military and economic intervention, while also providing a way for the North to deny its own overwhelming responsibility for the deteriorating state of the planet. Calls for changes in security policies may seem like a way to break the cycle of violence, suspicion, and zero-sum thinking; but given the purposes that security policies have served in the past, such calls also raise deep suspicions about ulterior motives.

These objections, and an uncompromising devotion to the principle of sovereign control of natural resources, are at the heart of controversy over the recent climate change and security debates at the UN Security Council (UNSC). Climate change, on the back burner in the 1990s debates on environmental security, dominates the paradigm today. This prominent role was illustrated in July 2011 when the German government, in its role as monthly president of the Security Council, put climate on the agenda for discussion, for just the second time in the Council's history. Member-states presented very different views regarding the efficacy and appropriateness of the United Nations' top security body taking up climate change. The essay by Joe Thwaites (Chapter 27) presents these diverse arguments with illustrative excerpts from member-state speeches.

The paradigm of environmental security remains controversial because it links plausible claims about conflict to the symbolically powerful and highly charged concept of security. At best, linking environment and security could be a way to build trust among nations and make security a cooperative, global endeavor, while at the same time steering resources and public energy toward resolving environmental problems.[12] At worst, tying environmental concerns to militarized approaches to social conflict could undercut environmental cooperation or itself be a recipe for greater violence.

Thinking Critically

1. What are the different strands of environmental security outlined in Dabelko's "Uncommon Peace" essay? Why do you think some dimensions dominate today's environmental security debates? Which issues deserve the most attention in the current debate?

2. Can you think of examples that run counter to the environmental conflict argument—that is, cases where the conditions for environmentally induced violent conflict seem to exist but violence does not occur? What social institutions or other conditions are likely to influence whether violence occurs? Is the connection between environment and conflict solely a problem for the developing world?

3. Which seems more likely: the "greening" of security policy or the militarization of environmental policy? Do you consider Deudney's concerns about the mismatched tools of traditional security institutions to be well

founded? Is it possible to generalize across countries in answering this question?

4. Can you think of other places where the "Good Water Neighbors" peace-building strategy could be tried at the local level? How would you connect such cooperation to areas of conflict as a way to build trust or lessen tensions?

5. Might environmental cooperation also cause environmental conflict? Can international cooperation cause the sort of violence discussed by Rajagopal? If countries in a shared river basin agree to build a dam instead of fighting over the water, is that "environmental peacebuilding" or merely a shifting of violence from interstate affairs onto local communities in the basin? Is it possible to develop strategies that work for peace on both levels at once?

6. Do you think the UN Security Council is an appropriate forum for debating climate change and security links? Which of the specific arguments for or against Security Council involvement do you find most persuasive, and why? What practical benefits, if any, do you think will flow from its debating climate change and security links?

NOTES

1. See, for example, Thomas Homer-Dixon, "Environmental Scarcities and Violent Conflict: Evidence from Cases," *International Security* 19, no. 1 (1994): 5–40.

2. For an overview of this literature, see Michael L. Ross, "What Do We Know About Natural Resources and Civil War?" *Journal of Peace Research* 41, no. 3 (May 2004): 337–356. See also Michael L. Ross, *The Oil Curse* (Princeton: Princeton University Press, 2012).

3. See the multipartner effort on environmental peacebuilding that features UNEP country-level assessments as well as a six-volume set of case studies, available at http://www.environmentalpeacebuilding.org/.

4. See, for example, Jessica Tuchman Mathews, "Redefining Security," *Foreign Affairs* 67 (1989): 162–177; Norman Myers, "Environment and Security," *Foreign Policy* 74 (Spring 1989): 23–41; and Chapter 4 of this volume, by Lester Brown.

5. Former vice president Al Gore discusses this theme in his first book on the global environment, *Earth in the Balance: Ecology and the Human Spirit* (New York: Houghton Mifflin, 1992).

6. Kent Hughes Butts, "Why the Military Is Good for the Environment," in Jyrki Käkönen, ed., *Green Security or Militarized Environment* (Aldershot, UK: Dartmouth Publishing, 1994). For a discussion of how the US government has operationalized environmental security ideas in a variety of ways, see Geoffrey D. Dabelko and P. J. Simmons, "Environment and Security: Core Ideas and U.S. Government Initiatives," *SAIS Review* 17 (Winter–Spring 1997): 127–146. See also all issues of the *Environmental Change and Security Project Report*, published by the Washington-based Woodrow Wilson International Center for Scholars.

7. Early examples include Fairfield Osborn, *Our Plundered Planet* (Boston: Little, Brown, 1953); and Harrison Brown, *The Challenge of Man's Future* (New York: Viking, 1954).

8. For a similar critique regarding the role of the environment in causing conflict, see Marc A. Levy, "Is the Environment a National Security Issue?" *International Security* 20, no. 2 (Fall 1995): 35–62; and Thomas F. Homer-Dixon and Marc A. Levy, "Correspondence: Environment and Security," *International Security* 20, no. 3 (Winter 1995–1996): 189–194. More recently these critiques have focused on climate and conflict links; see the January 2012 special issue of *Journal of Peace Research.*

9. See, for example, Ken Conca, "In the Name of Sustainability: Peace Studies and Environmental Discourse," *Peace and Change* 19, no. 2 (April 1994): 91–113.

10. Jyrki Käkönen, ed., *Green Security or Militarized Environment* (Aldershot, UK: Dartmouth Publishing, 1994).

11. Kader Asmal, Speech to the 10th Stockholm Water Symposium, Stockholm, Sweden, August 14, 2000.

12. See, for example, Ken Conca and Geoffrey D. Dabelko, eds., *Environmental Peacemaking* (Washington, DC, and Baltimore: Woodrow Wilson Center Press and Johns Hopkins University Press, 2002).

22

AN UNCOMMON PEACE: ENVIRONMENT, DEVELOPMENT, AND THE GLOBAL SECURITY AGENDA

Geoffrey D. Dabelko[*]

In 1988, nuclear war was "undoubtedly the gravest" threat facing the environment, according to *Our Common Future,* commonly known as the Brundtland report.[1] The possible environmental consequences of thermonuclear war—radioactive contamination, nuclear winter, and genetic mutations—were widely feared during the Cold War, especially by citizens of the United States and Soviet Union, which the report called "prisoners of their own arms race."[2]

Thankfully, these nightmare scenarios did not come to pass. . . . However, in the 20 years since the report's publication, the specter of nuclear destruction has not yet been "removed from the face of the Earth,"[3] as the report called for, but has merely changed scale: the threat of the mushroom cloud has been replaced by the threat of the dirty bomb—a crude device that a terrorist cell could fashion out of pilfered nuclear material. Setting off such a bomb in a world city—a major hub in the global economy—could create more disruption than the paradigm-shifting attacks of September 11, 2001, although the radioactivity would impact far fewer people than the feared global nuclear winter of old.

Since the end of the Cold War in 1989, the security community's focus has shifted from the global clash of superpowers to fragmented groups of stateless actors

*Originally published in *Environment* vol. 50, no. 3, pp. 32–45, May 2008. Reprinted with permission of the Helen Dwight Reid Educational Foundation. Published by Heldref Publications, 1319 Eighteenth St. N.W., Washington, D.C. 20036–1802. © 2008.

fomenting civil war and terrorism. The end of the Cold War also opened greater political space for analyzing a range of diverse threats to both individuals and the world beyond using the traditional state-centered approach. The environment—along with the related challenges of health and poverty—has become a key area of focus within that new space.

Our understanding of the links between environment and security has evolved in the last 20 years to reflect these changing threat scenarios. Today, "environmental security" has become a popular phrase used to encompass everything from oil exploration to pollution controls to corn subsidies. The Brundtland report, in an underappreciated chapter entitled "Peace, Security, Development, and the Environment," set the agenda for understanding these multiple links between environment and security. . . .

Redefining Security in *Our Common Future*

Our Common Future, produced by the World Commission on Environment and Development (WCED), is best known for its definition of sustainable development.[5] Yet the so-called Brundtland Commission, named after its chair, former Norwegian Prime Minister Gro Harlem Brundtland, also called for a broader conception of security that included instability caused in part by environmental factors. Conflict, attendant military spending, and the ultimate threat of nuclear exchange were highlighted as direct and indirect impediments to achieving sustainable development. As was to become the habit of many subsequent environmental security advocates, *Our Common Future* called for fundamentally broadening security definitions to accommodate these wider threats while simultaneously employing environment and conflict arguments that fell comfortably within the traditional confines of security.[6]

In the introductory chapter, the commissioners stated, "The whole notion of security as traditionally understood—in terms of political and military threats to national sovereignty—must be expanded to include the growing impacts of environmental stress—locally, nationally, regionally, and globally."[7] While acknowledging these linkages were "poorly understood," the commission held that "a comprehensive approach to international and national security must transcend the traditional emphasis on military power and armed competition."[8] . . .

While by no means the first advocate for this expanded notion of security,[10] the Brundtland Commission was a key legitimizing voice. Its influence was felt in the United Nations Development Programme's (UNDP) "human security" frame, which gained traction in UN forums and was championed by select national leaders such as Canada's Foreign Minister Lloyd Axworthy.[11] Even as it called for altering the security paradigm, the Brundtland Commission made arguments firmly ensconced in a traditional statist security perspective. The report flagged "environmental stress as both a cause and an effect of political tension and military conflict" and recognized that "environmental stress is seldom the only cause of major conflicts within or among nations" but could be "an important part of the web of causality associated with any conflict and can in some cases be catalytic."[12]

The commissioners identified climate change, loss of arable land, fisheries, and water as factors likely to contribute to conflict and spur other security-related problems, such as migration and economic dislocation. It also highlighted poverty, inequality, and lost development opportunities as key factors in creating insecurity. However, these factors were not consistently addressed in the early research on environmental stress and conflict that followed in the early 1990s, possibly due to relatively low levels of developing-country participation in these research efforts. Had more researchers adopted the Brundtland Commission's broader lens, analyses of environment-conflict links might have better integrated more robust analysis of poverty concerns and the physically remote, yet highly relevant role of international markets for natural resources.[13]

The Brundtland Commission also identified political capacity as an important element in environment-conflict links 10 years before it was hailed "the missing ingredient" by the field's researchers.[14] The commissioners stated that environmental stress could contribute to interstate or subnational conflict "when political processes are unable to handle the effects of environmental stress resulting, for example, from erosion and desertification."[15] *Our Common Future*'s focus on environment and conflict provided a legitimizing foundation for what, just a few years later, became an explosion of analytical work within and outside of governments.[16] During the 20 years that followed the release of *Our Common Future*, scholarly and policy interest in the linkages it highlighted has risen, fallen, and risen again.[17] . . .

No Room for Environmental Security on the Rio Agenda

The environment, peace, and security chapter of *Our Common Future* did not receive extensive formal treatment at the 1992 UN Conference on Environment and Development in Rio de Janeiro. The developing world did not endorse a global dialogue on environmental issues within the context of conflict and security, reacting negatively to formal environmental security proposals in UN forums.[20] The coalition of developing nations, the Group of 77, perceived the security frame as a Pandora's box that, once opened, could dilute their claims of absolute sovereign control over their resources. The United States was equally wary, fearing environmental issues might dilute and undermine military-focused security definitions in the midst of the Cold War. More practically, the environment, conflict, and security issues raised in *Our Common Future* did not easily lend themselves to resolution in a multilateral environmental treaty, the preferred mechanism at Rio and of the international environmental community in general.[21]

The Soviet Union attempted—and failed—to institutionalize environment and security links at the United Nations prior to the Rio conference. In October 1987, in the wake of the Chernobyl accident, Mikhail Gorbachev launched his "Murmansk Initiatives" in a speech in that northern city on the Kola Peninsula.[22] Calling for *glasnost* and greater cooperation (particularly among the Arctic states) in trade, environment, culture, and arms control, he proposed "ecological security" as a top global priority for both bilateral relationships and international institutions.[23] While aimed at environmental challenges, the Murmansk Initiatives were a de facto forum for moving beyond environmental goals to broader confidence-building efforts across the Cold War divide.

Gorbachev and then–Soviet Foreign Minister Eduard Shevardnadze, in speeches to the United Nations in 1988 and 1989, proposed creating ecological security institutions because, in Shevardnadze's words, "Overcoming the global threat to the environment and ensuring universal environmental security through prompt and effective action is an imperative of our times."[24] In early May 1989, Shevardnadze called for the creation of a "UN Center for Emergency Environmental Assistance," commonly referred to as the "Green Helmets," to be headed by a UN undersecretary-general.

The foreign minister asked all member states to discuss this idea, in which a group of environmental experts would comprise a rapid-response force, "at a time when countries are starting preparation for a UN-sponsored conference on environment and development planned for 1992."[25] He also called on the UN General Assembly to create a UN Environmental Security Council. These specific proposals were predicated on the more fundamental premise that security had to be redefined: "For the first time we have understood clearly what we just guessed: that the traditional view of national and universal security based primarily on military means of defense is now totally obsolete and must be urgently revised."[26] . . .

The reaction to the Murmansk Initiatives and the subsequent UN proposals was mixed. The U.S. government response was "reserved," perceiving the Soviet ideas as posturing and rhetoric designed to play to the developing country galleries at the UN General Assembly.[27] Environment was not yet widely linked with security in U.S. diplomatic circles, with then–U.S. Senator Al Gore one of the few politicians regularly promoting the connection.[28] With the concurrent collapse of communism in Central and Eastern Europe, the rest of the world glimpsed the massive toxic legacy lurking behind the Iron Curtain, which damaged the credibility of Soviet environmental decisionmaking. Shevardnadze's 27 September 1988 call for the United States and others to transfer funds from military programs to environmental efforts echoed similar efforts in the 1970s and 1980s by the Soviets to slow or constrain NATO weapons development by promoting international environment regimes.[29]

The Green Helmets proposal was highly unpopular with developing countries and became a political nonstarter. Countries such as Brazil feared (and continue to fear) developed-country intervention seeking to stop exploitation of natural resources such as those in the Brazilian Amazon.[30] The sovereign right of nonintervention was employed as an argument against the Green Helmets proposal, cutting off UN General Assembly discussion of further ecological security proposals. This dynamic repeated itself 10 years later in the UN context when then–UN Environment Programme Executive Director Klaus Toepfer reintroduced the Green Helmets idea, which was once again quickly rejected by the Group of 77 countries due to sovereignty concerns.

Environmental Security Takes Root

This failure to achieve high-profile traction on environmental security linkages at the United Nations in the 1990s did not imply a commensurate lack of interest among certain individual nations and regional organizations. The end of the Cold War did not produce the expected peace dividends, as hostilities held in check by the superpower competition were unleashed and the number of conflicts actually spiked in the 1990s. For some, such as Al Gore, by then U.S. vice president, the rise in civil conflicts—such as those in Liberia, Somalia, Rwanda, and Haiti—indicated that governments should pay greater attention to the underlying demographic, environmental, and distributional origins of these conflicts. These concerns led to a raft of analytical and policy initiatives which were prominent in, but by no means limited to, the United States.[31]

While environmental advocates and security actors remained wary of each other's focus, means, and ends, both analysts and policymakers sought to understand these linkages. Journalist Robert Kaplan captured the policy community's attention (and fears) in his 1994 *Atlantic Monthly* article entitled "The Coming Anarchy."[32] Kaplan held up demographic and natural resource pressures as primary explanations for West Africa's failing states, drawing heavily on the work of peace researcher Thomas Homer-Dixon from the University of Toronto. Many critics thought Kaplan oversold the environment as the national security issue of the twenty-first century, and his claims that West Africa's fundamental challenges were widely applicable to other regions of the world provoked an analytical and policy backlash when environmental scarcity did not prove to be the ultimate threat in the post–Cold War era. Environmental security would not provide an all-encompassing alternative security paradigm. Nevertheless, the contributions of natural resource scarcity and abundance to conflict—as well as larger environmental challenges to traditional definitions of security—became institutionalized concerns for foreign, development, and security communities.

In 1994—a key year in our understanding of the links between environment, development, and security—the UNDP dedicated its annual *Human Development Report* to human security, suggesting that environmental security was one of seven areas that should constitute a new global security paradigm.[33] Japan, Canada, and a wide range of UN bodies now commonly use this frame, and small island states commonly invoke it to dramatize the threat to survival posed by climate change–induced sea-level rise. Although its critics bemoan its lack of precision,[34] human security was prominently deployed in nonenvironmental successes such as the establishment of the 1997 Convention to Ban Landmines and the International Criminal Court in 2002.

In the late 1990s, climate change and the 1997 Kyoto Protocol captured the attention of most of the global environmental community. Climate change had not featured prominently in the debates over whether the environment is a contributing cause of conflict, and it had not yet been framed as an existential global security threat. The heavy focus on the multilateral environmental treaty mechanism and the all-country negotiations to reach a global agreement was not well suited to addressing the intertwined and site-specific social, political, economic, and environmental challenges of climate change. Scholars were mired in a set of testy methodological logjams that have only begun to break up in recent years due to innovative qualitative and quantitative work. In the policy realm, program implementation suffered from the reluctance of donors to integrate conflict considerations into their antipoverty or livelihoods efforts. At the same time, many developing countries and donors remained suspicious of environmental issues, considering them luxury items for wealthy countries rather than life-and-death livelihood problems for the world's poor. However, by the early twenty-first century, many overcame their hesitation to integrate environment, development, and conflict efforts, as evidenced by greater willingness to analyze these natural resource linkages and address them with local, field-based programs.

The reaction to the September 11 attacks certainly set back efforts to address environment and security linkages. Just as the superpower confrontation of the Cold War provided little political space for a broader array of security concerns, the "war on terror" kicked other threats off policymakers' priority lists. . . . And the antipathy of U.S. President George W. Bush's administration to anything dubbed "environmental" set back efforts in international forums and pushed much of the official U.S. work on environmental security behind the scenes, or forced it to be relabeled as disaster relief. Yet interest in environment, peace, and security linkages continues to grow within the UN system, the bilateral development and security communities, and in countries experiencing conflict. As the "force-only" responses to the September 11 attacks have fallen short of achieving either military or human security objectives, policymakers and practitioners have been returning to more inclusive notions of security.[36] . . .

The Future of Environment, Peace, and Security

. . . The sheer diversity of environment-security links, as complex today as they were 20 years ago, will continue to frustrate those in the policy and analytical realms who want more analytical precision and a narrower lens for a term as broad as "environmental security." Yet the failure of one set of environment and security linkages to achieve dominance has guaranteed that no avenues have been prematurely closed off. The temptation to crown one set of linkages the top priority or the only legitimate definition of environmental security ignores the diversity of valid concerns that arise in different contexts and sets up a false all-or-nothing choice.

Efforts to broaden the definition of security are again gaining traction, boosted by the widespread concern with the potential impacts of climate change and the perception that using force as the only approach to conflict is counterproductive. A few prominent scientists even claim that climate change is a bigger threat than terrorism.[39] These environment and security links have helped break down the stereotype that environmental issues are the province of wealthy advocates interested in saving charismatic wildlife. Instead, policymakers and practitioners are increasingly viewing these natural resources as critical to the day-to-day livelihoods of literally billions of people. By awarding recent peace prizes to Al Gore and the Intergovernmental Panel on Climate Change, as well as environmental activist Wangari Maathai, the Nobel Committee has helped push environmental security back into the limelight, 20 years after the Brundtland Commission brought it to the fore. A few areas, discussed below, illustrate the field's budding progress and the great potential for meaningful analytical development and practical action.

Down on the Ground: Subnational Analysis

Although there has been a dramatic decline in the number of conflicts over the past decade, persistent ones—including those in the Democratic Republic of the Congo, Nigeria, the Philippines, the Horn of Africa, and Nepal—often have strong environmental components.[40] Whether it is the abundance of valuable resources such as oil, forests, or minerals, or the scarcity of resources such as land or water, these underlying factors are increasingly viewed as central to spurring, prolonging, ending, and resolving these conflicts.[41] Analyzing the multiple roles environmental factors play before, during, and after conflict supports a much more robust research and policy agenda than does focusing exclusively on the environment's potential to cause conflict. This wider lens also helps address the misperception that environment is *the* factor causing conflict; those who analyze environment, conflict, and security issues seek only to be included in the larger conflict discussion.

New analytical developments are bolstering policymakers' and practitioners' interest in practical ways to break the links between environment and conflict. In particular, the increasing ability to analyze georeferenced environmental and conflict data at much more local levels will improve the historically limited quantitative evaluations of these linkages. Preliminary research funded by the National Science Foundation, for example, has found statistically significant correlations between rainfall and civil conflict, strongly suggesting the value of robust analytical work.[42] And while violent conflict continues to garner the most attention, broadening the definition of "conflict" to include nonviolent or less organized violent conflict has increased the range of cases under discussion. For example, the social protests that have met water privatization megaprojects (such as large dams), international markets for natural resources, or conservation areas that limit community usage, expand the range (and relevance) of environmental security analysis.[43]

Climate Change and Security

The recent rise of concern over climate change has both spurred—and been spurred by—climate-security connections. Prominent reports in the European Union, United States, United Kingdom, and Germany aimed at garnering more policy attention to climate change have emphasized its security linkages.[44] With a push from the United Kingdom, the UN Security Council devoted an April 2007 session to climate change, peace, and security, the first Security Council session on an environmental topic.[45] UN Secretary-General Ban Ki-moon subsequently linked UN efforts to battle climate change with its mission to address the underlying causes of conflict in Darfur, Sudan.[46] In March 2008, European Union High Representative for the Common Foreign and Security Policy Javier Solana presented to the European Council a short climate change and security paper responding to pressure (particularly from Germany) to raise the profile of climate-security connections. Mirroring some of the language used in prominent reports from German, British, and U.S. nongovernmental organizations, the brief called climate change a "threat multiplier which exacerbates existing trends, tensions and instability" that could "overburden states and regions which are already fragile and conflict prone," posing "political and security risks that directly affect European interests."[47]

The 2007 Nobel Peace Prize, awarded to Al Gore and the Intergovernmental Panel on Climate Change, most prominently linked climate change and security. In announcing the award, the Norwegian Nobel Committee called climate change both a fundamental threat to human well-being and a contributing factor to more traditional violent conflict. In 1987, the Brundtland Commission argued, "Slowing, or adapting to, global warming is becoming an essential task to reduce the risks of conflict."[48] In 2007, the Norwegian Nobel Committee echoed those words:

> Extensive climate changes may alter and threaten the living conditions of much of mankind. They may induce large-scale migration and lead to greater competition for the earth's resources. Such changes will place particularly heavy burdens on the world's most vulnerable countries. There may be increased danger of violent conflicts and wars, within and between states.[49]

The heightened attention to climate change boosts the prospects for constructively addressing environment, development, and security linkages. The wide range of potential climate impacts is reenergizing broader debates over human security that suggest redefining security beyond purely militaristic terms. At the same time, the traditional security community's concern with climate change (and the social reactions it may produce, such as migration) has helped garner wider attention. For example, examining its implications for desertification, precipitation, and crops in vulnerable areas such as the Sahel may also help illuminate the preexisting but neglected connections between these environmental variables and social conflict. Ironically, climate change mitigation efforts, such as increasing the use of biofuels, are arguably creating new natural resource and conflict links, as more forests are cleared for palm oil plantations and food prices are rising as we choose to grow our fuel supplies. These "knock-on effects" present a new research agenda for environment, development, and conflict scholars and practitioners.

Environmental Peacemaking

. . . A growing number of conflict-prevention and post-conflict scholars and practitioners argue that natural resource management can be a key tool for helping prevent or end conflict and for building peace in a post-conflict setting.[50] The cooperation imperative spurred by environmental interdependence and the long-term need for iterated interaction can be used as the basis for confidence building rather than merely engendering conflict.[51]

The Nile Basin is an unlikely example of conflict prevention. Many of the countries in this volatile region are beset by high levels of civil conflict, and their widespread dependence on the Nile's waters have led many to flag this river basin as the most likely to experience international water wars.[52] Yet for the past nine years, the basin's riparian states—Burundi, the Democratic Republic of the Congo, Egypt, Eritrea, Ethiopia, Kenya, Rwanda, Sudan, Tanzania, and Uganda—have convened the ministerial-level Nile Basin Initiative (NBI) to develop a shared vision of sustainable use of those waters.[53] The initiative centers around eight "Shared Vision" projects—including the Regional Power Trade, Water Resources Management, and Efficient Water Use for Agriculture projects—meant to foster trust and encourage investment. While formally framed as a development enterprise,[54] these efforts also implicitly serve as a means to prevent conflict predicated on environmental interdependence.[55] However, the NBI process is not without its critics, and issues of transparency and wider stakeholder participation remain concerns.[56]

In times of active conflict, management of a shared natural resource across lines of conflict can serve as a communication lifeline when other aspects of the relationship remain highly volatile. The "Picnic Table Talks"—in which Israeli and Jordanian water managers met at a picnic table to jointly manage their water resources while their countries were formally at war—are a vivid example. These technical exchanges helped build trust and personal connections that contributed to achieving the larger peace treaty between the countries in 1994.[57] More recently, Friends of the Earth launched the Good Water Makes Good Neighbors Middle East initiative to promote cooperation among Israelis, Palestinians, and Jordanians on shared water problems.

In this fashion, environmental management serves as a way to develop confidence that may carry over to other aspects of a relationship. Transboundary protected areas or "peace parks" are also an emerging—if still controversial—means to capitalize on shared ecological boundaries to build trust between parties in conflict.[58]

Finally, assessing post-conflict environmental conditions can serve as a necessary first step to building a sustainable peace. The UN Environment Programme's Post-Conflict and Disaster Management Branch (PCDMB) is leading the way on this post-conflict stage with what it calls "environmental diplomacy."[59] PCDMB's objective scientific assessments of war-time environmental damage in countries as diverse as Bosnia, Sudan, Liberia, Iraq, and Afghanistan (and forthcoming, in Nigeria, Nepal, Rwanda, and the Democratic Republic of the Congo) have become a foundation for efforts to strengthen environmental management institutions in ways that contribute to reconciliation and capacity building across lines of conflict. These steps toward "environmental diplomacy," like most efforts to capitalize on environmental peacemaking, are modest, small-scale, and remain to be fully tried and tested. Yet this robust analysis may soon be possible, as other parts of the United Nations focused on development and conflict issues move to capitalize on the environmental confidence building that can be fostered by addressing natural resource and pollution connections to livelihoods in post-conflict settings. Bilateral aid agencies are also pursuing similar practical steps by incorporating natural resource management into their peacemaking toolboxes.

Many hurdles remain, beginning with the imposing bureaucratic and institutional impediments to collaboration facing environment, development, and security actors, who speak different languages, use different tools, and often have very different bottom-line goals. But pushed by on-the-ground realities, researchers and practitioners are trying to navigate these complex linkages and find ways to work together. Environmental peacemaking efforts have limited use for unwieldy multilateral environmental agreements, the UN's go-to tool, which are poorly matched to the day-to-day intersections of environment, peace, and security issues at the intrastate level. Instead, parties seeking to break the negative links between environment and conflict must focus on local, national, and regional instruments that can grapple more effectively with the integrated problems of poverty, environment, and conflict.

Twenty years after the release of the Brundtland Report, our common future still depends on the health of our environment. It is increasingly clear that our common peace may rely on it as well. Preparing for and waging war often destroys the environment and diverts resources better deployed for sustainability. And a devastated environment can spur new conflicts over resources. Climate change threatens to destabilize not only our atmosphere, but also nations. But it is also garnering the attention of the wide range of actors necessary to tackle these fundamental challenges. Even as we become more attentive to the ways in which the environment can contribute to conflict, we must remain open to opportunities for environmental peacemaking to help us secure our environment—and ourselves.

NOTES

1. World Commission on Environment and Development (WCED), *Our Common Future* (New York: Oxford University Press, 1987), 290.

2. Ibid., page 304.

3. Ibid., page 304.

5. Portions of this and subsequent sections are drawn from G. D. Dabelko, "Tactical Victories and Strategic Losses: The Evolution of Environmental Security," PhD diss., Department of Government and Politics (College Park, MD: University of Maryland, 2003).

6. J. Mathews, "Redefining Security," *Foreign Affairs* 68, no. 2 (1989): 162–77; and N. Myers, "Environment and Security," *Foreign Policy* 74 (Spring 1989): 23–41.

7. WCED, note 1 above, page 19.

8. WCED, note 1 above, page 290.

10. L. Brown, "Redefining Security," Worldwatch paper no. 14 (Washington, DC: Worldwatch Institute, 1977).

11. UN Development Programme (UNDP), Human Development Report 1994 (New York: Oxford University Press, 1994); R. Paris, "Human Security: Paradigm Shift or Hot Air?" *International Security* 26, no. 2 (2001): 87–102; and L. Axworthy, "Introduction," in R. McRae and D. Hubert, eds., *Human Security and the New Diplomacy: Protecting People, Promoting Peace* (Montreal: McGill–Queen's University Press, 2001), 3–13.

12. WCED, note 1 above, pages 290–91.

13. N. L. Peluso and M. Watts, eds., *Violent Environment* (Ithaca, NY: Cornell University Press, 2001); and J. Barnett, *The Meaning of Environmental Security: Ecological Politics and Policy in the New Security Era* (London: Zed Books, 2001).

14. T. F. Homer-Dixon, *The Ingenuity Gap* (New York: Alfred A. Knopf, 2000); G. D. Dabelko and R. Matthew, "Environment, Population, and Conflict: Suggesting a Few Steps Forward," *Environmental Change and Security Project Report* 6 (2000): 99–103; and S. D. VanDeveer and G. D. Dabelko, "It's Capacity, Stupid: International Assistance and National Implementation," *Global Environmental Politics* 1, no. 2 (2001): 18–29.

15. WCED, note 1 above, page 291.

16. T. F. Homer-Dixon, "On the Threshold: Environmental Changes as Causes of Acute Conflict," *International Security* 16, no. 2 (1991): 76–116; T. F. Homer-Dixon, "Environmental Scarcities and Violent Conflict: Evidence from Cases," *International Security* 19, no. 1 (1994): 5–40; T. F. Homer-Dixon, *Environment, Scarcity, and Violence* (Princeton, NJ: Princeton University Press, 1999); G. Baechler, *Violence through Environmental Discrimination: Causes, Rwanda Arena, and Conflict Model* (Dordrecht, The Netherlands: Kluwer Academic Publishers, 1989); N. P. Gleditsch, ed., *Conflict and the Environment* (Dordrecht, The Netherlands: Kluwer Publications, 1989); P. F. Diehl and N. P. Gleditsch, eds., *Environmental Conflict* (Boulder, CO: Westview Press, 2001); D. H. Deudney and R. Matthew, eds., *Contested Grounds: Security and Conflict in the New Environmental Politics* (Albany, NY: State University of New York Press, 1999); UN Environment Programme (UNEP), *Understanding Environment, Conflict, and Cooperation* (Nairobi: UNEP, 2003); and C. Kahl, States, *Scarcity and Civil Strife in the Developing World* (Princeton, NJ: Princeton University Press, 2006).

17. R. Matthew, B. McDonald, and M. Brklacich, "Analyzing Environment, Conflict, and Cooperation," in UNEP, ibid., pages 5–15; and G. D. Dabelko, "The Environmental Factor," *Wilson Quarterly* 23, no. 4 (1999): 14–19.

20. J. M. Trolldalen, *International Environmental Conflict Resolution: The Role of the United Nations* (Washington, DC: World Foundation for Environment and Development, 1992).

21. The 1976 Convention on the Prohibition of Military or Any Other Hostile Use of Environmental Modification Techniques (ENMOD) and subsequent international law aimed at reducing the intentional use of the environment as a tool of war are exceptions to the global level agreement in this area. See J. E. Austin and C. E. Bruch, *The Environmental Consequences of War: Legal, Economic, and Scientific Perspectives* (Cambridge: Cambridge University Press, 2000).

22. See D. Scrivener, *Gorbachev's Murmansk Speech: The Soviet Initiative and Western Response* (Oslo: The Norwegian Atlantic Committee, 1989), for a discussion of Gorbachev's 1987 Murmansk Initiatives and the Western response.

23. "Ecological security" as opposed to "environmental security" is a closer translation of the Russian *ekologicheskaia bezopastnost*. It appears to be used interchangeably with no special distinction between "ecological" and "environmental." Others do use the term "ecological security" to connote the balance between Homo sapiens and other species. See D. Pirages and T. M. DeGeest, *Ecological Security: An Evolutionary Perspective on Globalization* (Lanham, MD: Rowman & Littlefield Publishers, 2003).

24. "Soviet Union Proposes Center for Emergency Environmental Aid," Reuters, 5 May 1989.

25. "Shevardnadze Calls for Steps to Protect Environment," Information Telegraph Agency of Russia (ITAR-TASS), 3 May 1989.

26. E. Shevardnadze, Speech to the 43rd session of the UN General Assembly, 27 September 1988.

27. B. Jancar-Webster and V. I. Sokolov, "Environmental Security: Challenges for the United States and Russia," in S. Cross, I. A. Zevelev, V. A. Kremenyuk, and V. Gevorgian, eds., *Global Security Beyond the Millennium: American and Russian Perspectives* (New York: MacMillan Press, 1999), 131.

28. F. Lewis, "Environment Is Security," *New York Times* (24 May 1989).

29. This call for the transfer of funds is also found in Trolldalen, note 20 above.

30. T. G. da Costa, "Brazil's SIVAM: Will It Fulfill Its Human Security Promise?" *Environmental Change and Security Project Report* 7 (2001): 47–58.

31. Dabelko, note 5 above; G. D. Dabelko and P. J. Simmons, "Environment and Security: Core Ideas and U.S. Government Initiatives," *SAIS Review* 17, no. 1 (1997): 127–46; R. Floyd, "Typologies of Securitisation and Desecuritisation: The Case of US Environmental Security 1993–2006," PhD diss., University of Warwick, 2007; and D. C. Esty et al., *State Failure Task Force Report: Phase II Findings* (McLean, VA: Science Applications International Corporation, 31 July 1998).

32. R. D. Kaplan, "The Coming Anarchy," *Atlantic Monthly* 273, no. 2 (February 1994): 45–76.

33. UNDP, note 11 above. The seven securities were economic, food, health, environmental, personal, community, and political.

34. Paris, note 11 above.

36. J. Wolfensohn, Speech at the Woodrow Wilson International Center for Scholars, Washington, DC, 6 March 2002.

39. U.K. Science Adviser Sir David King claimed, "[C]limate change is the most severe problem that we are facing today—more serious even than the threat of terrorism." D. A. King, "Climate Change Science: Adapt, Mitigate, or Ignore?" *Science* 303, no. 5655 (9 January 2004): 176.

40. Uppsala Conflict Data Program, *Uppsala Conflict Database*, http://www.pcr.uu.se /database/.

41. UNEP, *Sudan Post-Conflict Environmental Assessment* (Geneva: UNEP, 2007); U.S. Agency for International Development (USAID), *Forests and Conflict: A Toolkit for Intervention* (Washington, DC: USAID, 2005); and USAID, *Land and Conflict: A Toolkit for Intervention* (Washington, DC: USAID, 2005).

42. M. A. Levy, "Is the Environment a National Security Issue?" *International Security* 20, no. 2 (1995): 35–62; and M. Levy, C. Thorkelson, C. Vörösmarty, E. Douglas, and M. Humphreys, "Freshwater Availability Anomalies and Outbreak of Internal War: Results from a Global Spatial Time Series Analysis," paper presented at Human Security and Climate Change, Oslo, Norway (21–23 June 2005).

43. K. Conca, *Governing Water: Contentious Transnational Politics and Global Institution Building* (Cambridge, MA: MIT Press, 2005).

44. Military Advisory Board, *National Security and the Threat of Climate Change* (Washington, DC: CNA Corporation, 2007); German Advisory Council on Global Change, *World in Transition: Climate Change as a Security Risk* (London: Earthscan, 2007); J. W. Busby, *Climate Change and National Security: An Agenda for Action*, Council Special Report no. 32 (New York: Council on Foreign Relations Press, 2007); and K. M. Campbell et al., *The Age of Consequences: The Foreign Policy and National Security Implications of Global Climate Change* (Washington, DC: Center for Strategic and International Studies and Center for a New American Security, 2007).

45. See "Security Council Holds First-Ever Debate on Impact of Climate Change on Peace, Security, Hearing Over 50 Speakers," UN Security Council press release SC/9000, 17 April 2007, http://www.un.org/News/Press/docs/2007/sc9000.doc.htm.

46. K. Ban, "A Climate Culprit in Darfur," *Washington Post* (16 June 2007).

47. EU Commission and the Secretary-General/High Representative, *Climate Change and International Security* (Brussels, Belgium: Council of the European Union, 3 March 2008), 2.

48. WCED, note 1, page 294.

49. The text of the announcement of the 2007 Nobel Peace Prize winners is available at http://nobelpeaceprize.org/eng_lau_announce2007.html.

50. K. Conca and G. D. Dabelko, eds., *Environmental Peacemaking* (Washington, DC, and Baltimore, MD: Woodrow Wilson Press and Johns Hopkins University Press, 2002); K. Conca, A. Carius, and G. D. Dabelko, "Building Peace Through Environmental Cooperation," *State of the World 2005: Redefining Global Security* (Washington, DC: Worldwatch Institute, 2005); E. Weinthal, "From Environmental Peacekeeping to Environmental

Peacemaking," *Environmental Change and Security Program Report* 10 (2004): 19–23; and A. Carius, "Environmental Peacebuilding: Conditions for Success," *Environmental Change and Security Program Report* 12 (2006–2007): 59–75.

51. K. Conca, "The Case for Environmental Peacemaking," in K. Conca and G. D. Dabelko, eds., *Environmental Peacemaking* (Washington, DC, and Baltimore, MD: Woodrow, Wilson Press and Johns Hopkins University Press, 2002), 1–22.

52. For example, World Bank Vice President Ismail Serageldin claimed in 1995 that "the wars of the next century will be about water," and Egyptian President Anwar Sadat said in 1979, "The only matter that could take Egypt to war again is water." Egyptian Minister of State for Foreign Affairs Boutros Boutros-Ghali echoed this statement when he predicted in 1985, "The next war in the Middle East will be fought over water, not politics." See "Talking Point: Ask Boutros Boutros-Ghali," BBC News, 10 June 2003, http://news.bbc.co.uk/2/hi/talking_point/2951028.stm.

53. See *Nile Basin Initiative*.

54. C. W. Sadoff and D. Grey, "Beyond the River: The Benefits of Cooperation on International Rivers," *Water Policy* 4, no. 5 (2002), 389–404.

55. Anecdotally, policy efforts from a range of geographical settings (Central Asia, the Caucasus, and East Africa) suggest that making the conflict prevention or post-conflict reconciliation goals of environmental peacemaking implicit or unstated is advantageous. Stating the conflict prevention goals explicitly makes the environmental and security cooperation more difficult to achieve in some settings, suggesting practitioners must find a way to capitalize on the peacemaking gains without overtly framing the goal of such efforts as peace rather than environmental sustainability.

56. P. Kameri-Mbote, "Water Conflict and Cooperation: Lessons from the Nile Basin Initiative," Navigating Peace Initiative Policy Brief 4 (Washington, DC: Environmental Change & Security Program, Woodrow Wilson International Center for Scholars, 2007), available at *http://www.wilsoncenter.org/topics/pubs/NavigatingPeaceIssuePKM.pdf*.

57. See A. Wolf, *Hydropolitics along the Jordan River: The Impact of Scarce Water Resources on the Arab-Israeli Conflict* (Tokyo: United Nations University Press, 1995).

58. Peace parks are also highlighted as means to (re)open political boundaries and stimulate economic growth from tourism in post-conflict environments. Early peace park efforts in southern Africa in particular have been widely criticized for not sharing benefits with local people and actually creating new human-animal conflicts. For an overview of perspectives, see S. Ali, ed., *Peace Parks: Conservation and Conflict Resolution* (Cambridge, MA: MIT Press, 2007).

59. For the UN Environment Programme's Post-Conflict and Disaster Management Branch, see *http://postconflict.unep.ch/*. See also J. Karensen, "Environmental Needs in Post-Crisis Assessments and Recovery: Interview with David Jensen," in *European Commission, Early Warning, Early Action? The Debate on EU's Crisis Response Continues* (Brussels, Belgium: European Commission, forthcoming 2008).

23

FROM CONFLICT TO PEACEBUILDING: THE ROLE OF NATURAL RESOURCES AND THE ENVIRONMENT

UNITED NATIONS ENVIRONMENT PROGRAMME*

Introduction

Since the end of the Cold War, two fundamental changes have shaped the way the international community understands peace and security. First, the range of potential actors of conflict has expanded significantly to include a number of non-state entities. Indeed, security is no longer narrowly conceived in terms of military threats from aggressor nations. In today's world, state failure and civil war in developing countries represent some of the greatest risks to global peace. War-torn countries have become havens and recruiting grounds for international terrorist networks, organized crime, and drug traffickers, and tens of millions of refugees have spilled across borders, creating new tensions in host communities. Instability has also rippled outward as a consequence of cross-border incursions by rebel groups, causing disruptions in trade, tourism and international investment.

Second, the potential causes of insecurity have also increased and diversified considerably. While political and military issues remain critical, conceptions of conflict and security have broadened: economic and social threats including poverty, infectious diseases and environmental degradation are now also seen

*Excerpted from United Nations Environment Programme, *From Conflict to Peacebuilding: The Role of Natural Resources and the Environment*, February 2009. © 2009 United Nations. Reprinted with the permission of the United Nations.

as significant contributing factors. This new understanding of the contemporary challenges to peace is now being reflected in high-level policy debates and statements. The 2004 report of the UN Secretary-General's High-Level Panel on Threats, Challenges and Change highlighted the fundamental relationship between the environment, security, and social and economic development in the pursuit of global peace in the 21st century,[1] while a historic debate at the UN Security Council in June 2007 concluded that poor management of "high-value" resources constituted a threat to peace.[2]

More recently, UN Secretary-General Ban Ki-moon confirmed that "the basic building blocks of peace and security for all peoples are economic and social security, anchored in sustainable development, [because they] allow us to address all the great issues—poverty, climate, environment and political stability—as parts of a whole."[3]

The potential for conflicts to be ignited by the environmental impacts of climate change is also attracting international interest in this topic. A recent high-level brief by the European Union, for instance, called climate change a "threat multiplier which exacerbates existing trends, tensions and instability," posing both political and security risks.[4] As a result, no serious discussion of current or emerging threats to security can take place without considering the role of natural resources and the environment.

This changing security landscape requires a radical shift in the way the international community engages in conflict management. From conflict prevention and early warning to peacemaking, peacekeeping and peacebuilding, the potential role of natural resources and the environment must be taken into consideration at the onset. Indeed, deferred action or poor choices made early on are easily "locked in," establishing unsustainable trajectories of recovery that can undermine the fragile foundations of peace. In addition, ignoring the environment as a peacebuilding tool misses an important opportunity for dialogue and confidence-building between former conflicting parties: some of the world's greatest potential tensions over water resources, for example—including those over the Indus River system and Nile Basin—have been addressed through cooperation rather than violent conflict.[5, 6] Integrating environmental management and natural resources into peacebuilding, therefore, is no longer an option—it is a security imperative. . . .

The Role of Natural Resources and the Environment in Conflict

Rationale

Environmental factors are rarely, if ever, the sole cause of violent conflict. Ethnicity, adverse economic conditions, low levels of international trade and conflict in neighboring countries are all significantly correlated as well. However, it is clear that the exploitation of natural resources and related environmental stresses can become significant drivers of violence.

Since 1990, at least eighteen violent conflicts have been fuelled by the exploitation of natural resources. . . . [9] Looking back over the past sixty years, at least forty percent of all intrastate conflicts can be associated with natural resources.[10] Civil wars such as those in Liberia, Angola and the Democratic Republic of Congo have centered on "high-value" resources like timber, diamonds, gold, minerals and oil. Other conflicts, including those in Darfur and the Middle East, have involved control of scarce resources such as fertile land and water.

As the global population continues to rise, and the demand for resources continues to grow, there is significant potential for conflicts over natural resources to intensify. Demographic pressure and urbanization, inequitable access to and shortage of land, and resource depletion are widely predicted to worsen, with profound effects on the stability of both rural and urban settings. In addition, the potential consequences of climate change for water availability, food security, the prevalence of disease, coastal boundaries, and population distribution are also increasingly seen as threats to international security, aggravating existing tensions and potentially generating new conflicts.[11]

The relationship between natural resources, the environment and conflict is thus multi-dimensional and complex, but three principal pathways can be drawn:

a. Contributing to the outbreak of conflict
b. Financing and sustaining conflict
c. Undermining peacemaking

Contributing to the Outbreak of Conflict

Many countries currently face development challenges relating to the unsustainable use of natural resources and the allocation of natural wealth. At a basic level, tensions arise from competing demands for the available supply of natural resources. In some cases, it is a failure in governance (institutions, policies, laws) to resolve these tensions equitably that leads to specific groups being disadvantaged, and ultimately to conflict. In others, the root of the problem lies in the illegal exploitation of resources.

Research and field observation indicate that natural resources and the environment contribute to the outbreak of conflict in three main ways. First, conflicts can occur over the fair apportioning of wealth derived from "high-value" extractive resources like minerals, metals, stones, hydrocarbons and timber.[12] The local abundance of valuable resources, combined with acute poverty or the lack of opportunity for other forms of income, creates an incentive for groups to attempt to capture them by taking control of resource-rich territories or violently hijacking the state. The potential for "high-value" natural resources to contribute to conflict is a function of global demand and depends largely on their market price.

Second, conflicts also occur over the direct use of scarce resources including land, forests, water and wildlife. These ensue when local demand for resources exceeds the available supply or when one form of resource use places pressure on other uses.[13] This can result either from physical scarcity or from governance and distribution factors. Such situations are often compounded by demographic pressures and disasters such as drought and flooding. Unless local institutions or practices mitigate competing interests, these tensions can lead to forced migration or violent conflict at the local level. . . .

Third, countries whose economies are dependent on the export of a narrow set of primary commodities are more likely to be politically fragile.[27] Not only are their economic fortunes held hostage to the fluctuating price of the commodity on international markets, but it can be difficult for developing countries to add value or generate widespread employment from such exports. Moreover, governments whose revenues are generated from the export of commodities rather than from taxation tend to be alienated from the needs of their constituents. The combination of the problems of currency appreciation and the opaque revenue management and corruption that have developed in many resource-rich countries is known as the "resource curse."[27]

The common trait in these three situations is the inability of weak states to resolve resource-based tensions peacefully and equitably. Indeed, conflict over natural resources and the environment is largely the reflection of a failure of governance, or a lack of capacity. As demands for resources continue to grow, this conclusion highlights the need for more effective investment in environmental and natural resource governance.

Financing and Sustaining Conflict

Regardless of whether or not natural resources play a causal role in the onset of conflict, they can serve to prolong and sustain violence. In particular, "high-value" resources can be used to generate revenue for financing armed forces and the acquisition of weapons. Capturing such resources becomes a strategic objective for military campaigns, thereby extending their duration.

In the last twenty years, at least eighteen civil wars have been fuelled by natural resources. . . . Diamonds, timber, minerals and cocoa have been exploited by armed groups from Liberia and Sierra Leone, Angola and Cambodia. Indeed, the existence of easily captured and exploited natural resources not only makes insurgency economically feasible[28] (and, therefore, war more likely); it may also alter the dynamics of conflict itself by encouraging combatants to direct their activities towards securing the assets that enable them to continue to fight. Thus revenues and riches can alter the mindset of belligerents, transforming war and insurgency into an economic rather than purely political activity, with violence resulting less from grievance than from greed.

Undermining Peacemaking

Economic incentives related to the presence of valuable natural resources can hinder the resolution of conflict and complicate peace efforts. As the prospect of a peace agreement appears closer, individuals or splinter groups who stand to lose access to the revenues gained from resource exploitation can act to spoil peacemaking efforts. Indeed, real or perceived risks of how peace may alter access to and regulation of natural resources in ways that damage some actors' interests can be a major impediment. At the same time, natural resources can also undermine genuine political reintegration and reconciliation even after a peace agreement is in place, by providing economic incentives that reinforce political divisions. . . .

Furthermore, preliminary findings from a retrospective analysis of intrastate conflicts over the past sixty years indicate that conflicts associated with natural resources are twice as likely to relapse into conflict within the first five years.[29]

Impacts of Conflict on Natural Resources and the Environment

Rationale

The environment has always been a silent casualty of conflict. To secure a strategic advantage, demoralize local populations or subdue resistance, water wells have been polluted, crops torched, forests cut down, soils poisoned, and animals killed. In some cases, such as the draining of the marshlands of the Euphrates-Tigris Delta by Saddam Hussein during the 1980s and 1990s, ecosystems have also been deliberately targeted to achieve political and military goals. During the Vietnam War, nearly 72 million liters[47] of the dioxin-containing defoliant Agent Orange were sprayed over the country's forests, resulting in entire areas being stripped of all vegetation. Some of these areas remain unsuitable for any form of agricultural use today. Recent examples of intentional environmental damage include the 1991 Gulf War, during which Kuwait's oil wells were set on fire and millions of tons of crude oil were discharged into waterways. In this instance, the environment itself was used as a weapon of mass destruction.

While numerous other examples of natural resources being used as a weapon of war exist, the majority of the environmental damage that occurs in times of conflict is collateral, or related to the preparation and execution phases of wars and to the coping strategies of local populations. In this regard, impacts of conflict on the environment can be divided into three main pathways:

a. Direct impacts
b. Indirect impacts
c. Institutional impacts

Direct Impacts

Often presenting acute risks for human health and livelihoods, the direct impacts of conflict on the environment are the most visible and well understood. This type of impact is largely due to chemicals and debris generated by bomb damage to settlements, rural areas and infrastructure. . . . In some situations, natural resources such as oil wells, forests and water can also be targeted. The direct effects of war are not limited to the countries in which they are waged, as air and water pollution can be carried across borders, threatening the health of populations in neighboring regions. Direct damage to the environment can also result from the movement of troops, landmines and other unexploded ordnance, weapons containing depleted uranium, and the production, testing, stockpiling and disposal of weapons.

Indirect Impacts

By disrupting normal socio-economic patterns, wars force populations to adopt coping strategies, and often lead to internal displacement or migration to neighboring countries. In the refugee camps that are established to provide basic shelter, food and protection, natural resources are critical assets, providing land, water, construction materials, and renewable energy. Damage to natural resources not only undermines the delivery of humanitarian aid, but can also cause conflict with host communities.

Conversely, vulnerable populations that do not flee must find alternative strategies to survive the breakdown of governance, social services and economic opportunities. Despite the long-term consequences, converting natural resources into capital is often a key coping mechanism and lifeline. . . .

Once conflict has diminished, the resettlement of refugees and the restoration of economic activities can put intense pressure on natural resources. The indirect environmental impacts of war-time survival strategies and post-conflict reconstruction can be more persistent and widespread than the direct impacts of war.

Institutional Impacts

Weak governance institutions and expressions of authority, accountability and transparency are frequently eroded by conflict. When tensions intensify and the rule of law breaks down, the resulting institutional vacuum can lead to a culture of impunity and corruption as public officials begin to ignore governance norms and structures, focusing instead on their personal interests. This collapse of governance structures contributes directly to widespread institutional failures in all sectors, allowing opportunistic entrepreneurs to establish uncontrolled systems of resource exploitation. Conflict also tends to confuse property rights, undercut positive environmental practices, and compromise dispute resolution mechanisms. At the same time, public finances are often diverted for military purposes, resulting in the decay of, or lack of investment in, water, waste and energy services, with corresponding health and environmental contamination risks. . . .

The Role of Natural Resources and the Environment in Peacebuilding

Rationale

Whether a war-torn society can maintain peace after a conflict ceases depends on a broad range of factors, including the conditions that led to the onset of war, the characteristics of the conflict itself, the nature of the peace settlement, and the influence of external forces (i.e. global economic or political pressures).

The previous sections have shown that natural resources can be an important contributing factor in the outbreak of conflict, in financing and sustaining conflict, and in spoiling peacemaking prospects. Increasing demand for resources, population growth and environmental stresses, including climate change, will likely compound these problems. At the same time, conflicts cause serious environmental impacts, which need to be addressed to protect health and livelihoods.

In peacebuilding, it is therefore critical that the environmental drivers and impacts of conflict are managed, that tension are defused, and that natural assets are used sustainably to support stability and development in the longer term.[60] Indeed, there can be no durable peace if the natural resources that sustain livelihoods and ecosystem services are damaged, degraded or destroyed. As mentioned above, conflicts associated with natural resources are twice as likely to relapse into conflict in the first five years. Despite this, fewer than a quarter of peace negotiations aiming to resolve conflicts linked to natural resources have addressed resource management mechanisms.[61]

Furthermore, the UN has not effectively integrated environment and natural resource considerations into its peacebuilding interventions. Priorities typically lie in meeting humanitarian needs, demobilization, disarmament and reintegration, supporting elections, restoring order and the rule of law, and opening the economy to foreign investment. The environment and natural resources are often framed as issues to be addressed at a later stage.

This is a mistaken approach, which fails to take into account the changing nature of the threats to national and international security. Rather, integrating these issues into peacebuilding should be considered a security imperative, as deferred action or poor choices made early on often establish unsustainable trajectories of recovery that may undermine long-term peace and stability.

To ensure that environmental and natural resource issues are successfully integrated across the range of peacebuilding activities . . . , it is critical that they are not treated in isolation, but instead form an integral part of the analyses and assessments that guide peacebuilding interventions. Indeed, it is only through a cross-cutting approach that these issues can be tackled effectively as part of peacebuilding measures to address the factors that may trigger a relapse of violence or impede the peace consolidation process. The following section provides three compelling reasons . . . to demonstrate how environment and natural resources can concretely contribute to peacebuilding:

a. Supporting economic recovery
b. Developing sustainable livelihoods
c. Contributing to dialogue, cooperation and confidence-building

Supporting Economic Recovery

Recreating a viable economy after a prolonged period of violent conflict remains one of the most difficult challenges of peacebuilding.[69] A post-conflict state faces key policy questions on how to ensure macro-economic stability, generate employment and restore growth. It must therefore seek to immediately (re)establish systems for the management of public finances, as well as monetary and exchange rate policies. This is complicated by the fact that conflict reverses the process of development, impacting institutions, foreign investment, capital and GDP [Gross Domestic Product].[70]

Authorities typically need to identify quick-yielding revenue measures and priority expenditures aimed at supporting economic recovery and restoring basic infrastructure and services. In a post-conflict situation, governments are also faced with high unemployment rates that can result in social instability. Extractable natural resources are often the obvious (and only) starting point for generating rapid financial returns and employment. However, as illustrated by the cases of Sierra Leone and Liberia, the exploitation of natural resources and the division of the ensuing revenues can also create the conditions for renewed conflict. It is therefore vital that good management structures are put in place, and that accountability and transparency are ensured. . . .

Developing Sustainable Livelihoods

The ability of the environment and resource base to support livelihoods, urban populations and economic recovery is a determining factor for lasting peace. In the aftermath of war, people struggle to acquire the clean water, sanitation, shelter, food and energy supplies on which they depend for their well-being and livelihoods. A failure to respond to the environmental and natural resource needs of the population as well as to provide basic services in water, waste and energy can complicate the task of fostering peace and stability.

Sustainable livelihoods approaches provide a framework for addressing poverty and vulnerability in all contexts. They have emerged from the growing realization of the need to put the poor and all aspects of their lives and means of living at the center of development and humanitarian work, while maintaining the sustainability of natural resources for present and future generations.

Collapse of livelihoods from environmental stresses, overuse of assets or poor governance results in three main coping strategies: innovation, migration and competition. Combined with other factors, the outcome of competition can be violent. For this reason, developing sustainable livelihoods should be at the core of any peacebuilding approach. . . .

Contributing to Dialogue, Confidence-building and Cooperation

The collapse of social cohesion and public trust in state institutions is a crippling legacy of war.[71] Irrespective of the genesis of the violence, creating the space for, and facilitating, national and local dialogue in ways that rebuild the bonds of trust, confidence and cooperation between affected parties is an immediate post-conflict task. Peacebuilding practitioners are currently discovering new or unseen pathways, linkages and processes to achieve these goals.

Experience and new analysis alike suggest that the environment can be an effective platform or catalyst for enhancing dialogue, building confidence, exploiting shared interests and broadening cooperation. The approach can be applied at multiple levels, including between local social groups (across ethnic or kinship lines of conflict), between elite parties or leadership in conflict factions, and at the transnational and international levels.

The premise lies in the notion that cooperative efforts to plan and manage shared natural resources can promote communication and interaction between adversaries or potential adversaries, thereby transforming insecurities and establishing mutually recognized rights and expectations. Such efforts attempt to capitalize on parties' environmental interdependence, which can serve as an incentive to communicate across contested borders or other dividing lines of tension.

The shared management of water, land, forests, wildlife and protected areas are the most frequently cited examples of environmental cooperation for peacebuilding, but environmental protection (in the form of protected areas, for example) has also been used as a tool to resolve disputes over contested land or border areas. . . . Meanwhile, constitutional processes or visioning exercises that aim to build national consensus on the parameters of a new system of governance can include environmental provisions. Issues such as the right to clean air, water and a healthy environment are often strong connecting lines between stakeholder groups with diverging interests. The need for communities to identify risks from climate change and to develop adaptation measures could also serve as an entry point. Finally, as many post-conflict states are parties to international regimes, regional political processes and multilateral environmental agreements, opportunities and support may also exist through these mechanisms.

Conclusions and Policy Recommendations

Three main conclusions can be drawn from the arguments and cases presented in this report:

a. Natural resources and the environment can be implicated in all phases of the conflict cycle, contributing to the outbreak and perpetuation of violence and undermining prospects for peace. In post-conflict countries, they can also contribute to conflict relapse if they are not properly managed from the outset. The way that natural resources and the environment are managed has a determining influence on peace and security.
b. The environment can itself fall victim to conflict, as direct and indirect environmental damage, coupled with the collapse of institutions, can lead to environmental risks that threaten health, livelihoods and security. These risks should be addressed as a part of the recovery process.
c. Natural resources and the environment can contribute to peacebuilding through economic development, employment generation and sustainable livelihoods. Cooperation over the management of natural resources and the environment provides new opportunities for peacebuilding that should also be pursued.

As a result, UNEP's Expert Advisory Group on Environment, Conflict and Peacebuilding recommends that the UN Peace-building Commission and the wider international community consider the following six areas for priority action [Editors' note: The editors are members of this advisory group]:

1. *Further develop UN capacities for early warning and early action*

The UN system needs to strengthen its capacity to deliver early warning and early action in countries that are vulnerable to conflicts over natural resources and environmental issues. At the same time, the effective governance of natural resources and the environment should be viewed as an investment in conflict prevention within the development process itself:

- Prioritize capacity-building for dispute resolution, environmental governance and land administration in states that are vulnerable to conflicts over natural resources and the environment.
- Include environmental and natural resource issues in international and regional conflict early warning systems and develop expertise for preventive action.
- Build international capacity to conduct mediation between conflicting parties where tensions over resources are rising.
- Support research on how the impacts of climate change could increase vulnerability to conflict and how early warning and adaptation projects could address this issue.
- Ensure that all development planning processes are conflict-sensitive and consider potential risks from the mismanagement of natural resources and the environment.

2. Improve oversight and protection of natural resources during conflicts

The international community needs to increase oversight of "high-value" resources in international trade in order to minimize the potential for these resources to finance conflict.

International sanctions should be the primary instrument dedicated to stopping the trade in conflict resources and the Security Council should require Member States to act against sanctions violators. At the same time, new legal instruments are required to protect natural resources and environmental services during violent conflict:

- Develop international certification mechanism to ensure that natural resources can be tracked more effectively.
- A high-level report by the Secretary-General examining the UN's experience in addressing the role of natural resources in conflict and peacebuilding, recommending ways in which existing UN approaches may be strengthened, and clarifying what constitutes a "conflict resource," would help improve coordination, increase oversight and provide a basis for the identification of cases that require action by the Security Council.
- Make secondary sanctions systematic and uniform, so that individuals and companies violating sanctions are subject to criminal prosecution, no matter which state they are based in.
- Support and strengthen current processes to develop new international legal instruments against targeting natural resources and ecosystems during conflicts.

3. Address natural resources and the environment as part of the peacemaking and peacekeeping process

During peace mediation processes, wealth-sharing is one of the fundamental issues that can "make or break" a peace agreement. In most cases, this includes the sharing of natural resources, including minerals, timber, land and water. It is therefore critical that parties to a peace mediation process are given sufficient technical information and training to make informed decisions on the distribution and sustainable use of natural resources. Subsequent peacekeeping operations need to be aligned with national efforts to improve natural resource and environmental governance:

- Strengthen UN capacity to provide technical information on the status of natural resources and the environment, and to make recommendations for sustainable use during mediation processes.
- Ensure that there are processes in place within peace agreements for the transparent, equitable and legitimate definition and realization of property rights and resource revenues and tenure.
- Mandate UN peacekeeping operations, where appropriate, to monitor natural resource extraction and management, or certain environmental issues that have the potential to re-ignite conflict or finance rebel groups. In particular, the UN should make efforts, in conjunction with regional organizations and states, to prohibit smuggled resources from being exported from sanctioned countries and to prevent the trade in conflict resources.

4. *Integrate natural resource and environmental issues into post-conflict planning*
The UN often undertakes post-conflict operations with little or no prior knowledge of what natural resources exist in the affected country, or of what role they may have played in fuelling conflict. In many cases it is years into an intervention before the management of natural resources receives sufficient attention. A failure to respond to the environmental and natural resource needs of the population, including the gender dimension of resource use, can complicate the task of fostering peace and even contribute to conflict relapse:

- Ensure that a conflict analysis is conducted at the operational planning stage of what natural resources exist in the country, the role that they may have played in fuelling conflict, and the potential risks they pose to the peace process if they are mismanaged or poorly governed. This conflict analysis should directly inform the wider post-conflict needs assessment process.
- Systematically conduct post-conflict environmental assessments that identify environmental risks to human health, livelihoods and security and prioritize needs in the short and medium term.
- Consider environmental sustainability when planning relief and recovery operations, so as to make sure that the projects are not contributing to the risk of future conflict.
- Integrated peacebuilding strategies should include a selection of environmental and natural resource indicators to monitor the peacebuilding trajectory and any potential destabilizing trends.

5. Carefully harness natural resources for economic recovery

Natural resources can only help strengthen the post-war economy and contribute to economic recovery if they are managed well. The international community should be prepared to help national authorities manage the extraction process and revenues in ways that do not increase risk of further conflict, or are unsustainable in the longer term. This must go hand in hand with ensuring accountability, transparency and environmental sustainability in their management:

- Prioritize weaknesses in natural resource and environmental governance structures for capacity-building when these may contribute to a conflict relapse or human insecurity.
- UN bodies should help assess the legitimacy and fairness of existing concession agreements, as inequitable contracts may themselves become a source of conflict. UN agencies or international financial institutions could also provide technical assistance to public officials to help negotiate equitable concessions and contracts on natural resources.
- International organizations should promote the transparent management of revenues from natural resource extraction. Where applicable, efforts should be made from an early stage to bring the country into compliance with international standards of revenue transparency and trade controls such as the Extractive Industries Transparency Initiative, the Kimberley Process, and the Forest Law Enforcement, Governance and Trade initiative.
- At the national level, independent monitoring bodies should be established to carry out regular inspections of logging, mining and other forms of resource extraction.
- Gather lessons learned on best and worst practices in terms of natural resource and environmental management in conflict-affected countries, with a view to developing a database, guidance materials and training for UN Country Teams and peacekeeping operations.
- More systematic efforts are needed by the UN and national governments to engage the private sector in the development of policies on natural resources and the environment.

6. Capitalize on the potential for environmental cooperation to contribute to peacebuilding

Every state needs to both use and protect vital natural resources such as forests, water, fertile land, energy and biodiversity. Environmental issues can thus serve as an effective platform or catalyst for enhancing dialogue, building confidence, exploiting shared interests and broadening cooperation between divided groups, as well as between states:

- At the outset of peacebuilding processes, identify locations or potential "hotspots" where natural resources may create tension between groups, as well as opportunities for environmental cooperation to complement and reinforce peacebuilding efforts.

- Conversely, make dialogue and confidence-building between divided communities an integral part of environmental projects, so that peacebuilding opportunities are not missed.
- Include environmental rights in national constitutional processes as a potential connecting line between diverging interests.
- Build on existing community-based systems and traditions of natural resource management as potential sources for post-conflict peacebuilding, while working to ensure that they are broadly inclusive of different social groups and interests.

NOTES

1. UN Secretary-General's High-Level Panel on Threats, Challenges and Change. (2004). A more secure world: Our shared responsibility: Report of the Secretary-General's High-Level Panel on Threats, Challenges and Change. United Nations General Assembly. New York.

2. UN Security Council. (2007, 25 June). Statement 2007/22 by the President of the Security Council. United Nations Security Council. New York.

3. Ban, K. (2008, 16 April). "A green future—The right war." *Time.*

4. EU Commission and High Representative. (2008). Climate change and international security: Paper to the European Council. S113/8. European Council. Brussels.

5. Conca, K. & Dabelko, G. (Eds.) (2002*). Environmental peacemaking.* Woodrow Wilson Center Press & John Hopkins University Press. Washington, D.C., pp. 61–62, 65–67.

6. Kameri-Mbote, P. (2007). *Navigating peace: Water, conflict and cooperation: Lessons from the Nile River Basin.* Woodrow Wilson International Center for Scholars. Washington, D.C.

9. Ross, M. (2004). "The natural resource curse: How wealth can make you poor". In I. Bannon & P. Collier (Eds.) *Natural resources and violent conflict.* World Bank. Washington, D.C.

10. Uppsala Conflict Data Program & Centre for the Study of Civil War. (2008). UCDP/PRIO Armed Conflict Dataset version 4.0. In Binningsbø, H. & Rustad, S. A. (2008). *PRIO working paper: Resource conflicts, resource management and post-conflict peace.* Uppsala University & International Peace Research Institute, Oslo.

11. Deutsche Gesellschaft für Technische Zusammenarbeit (GTZ) GmbH. (2008). *Climate change and security: Challenges for German development cooperation.* Federal Ministry for Economic Cooperation and Development, Germany.

12. Ross, M. (2004). "What do we know about natural resources and civil war?" *Journal of Peace Research.* 41(3), pp. 337–356.

13. These conflicts are mostly too local and small-scale to be included in conflict datasets. UNEP found 41 small-scale conflicts over natural resources such as water in the Darfur region 1930 to 2000. UN Environment Programme. (2007). Sudan post-conflict environmental assessment. UNEP. Geneva.

27. [Editor's note: Note 27 appears twice in the original.] For an introduction to the extensive literature on this subject see: Collier, P. (2007). *The bottom billion.* Oxford University Press. Oxford.

28. Collier, P. (2000). *Economic causes of civil conflict and their implications for policy.* World Bank. Washington, D.C.

29. Uppsala Conflict Data Program & Centre for the Study of Civil War. (2008). UCDP/PRIO Armed Conflict Dataset version 4.0. In Binningsbø, H. & Rustad, S. A. (2008). *PRIO working paper: Resource conflicts, resource management and post-conflict peace.* Uppsala University & International Peace Research Institute, Oslo.

47. US Department of Veteran Affairs. (2003). Agent Orange: Information for veterans who served in Vietnam. Retrieved July 2008 from http://www1.va.gov./agentorange/docs/AOIB10-49JUL03.pdf

60. Nitzschke, H. & Studdard, K. (2005). "The legacies of war economies: Challenges and options for peacemaking and peacebuilding." *International Peacekeeping.* 12(2), pp. 222-239.

61. According to preliminary findings from a retrospective analysis of post-conflict situations in the Uppsala-PRIO database (1946–2006), fewer than a quarter (26 from 137) of post-conflict countries where natural resources played a role in the conflict implemented some kind of resource management. Binningsbø, H. & Rustad, S. A. (2008). *PRIO working paper: Resource conflicts, resource management and post-conflict peace.* Uppsala University & International Peace Research Institute, Oslo.

69. UN Peacebuilding Support Office. (2008). *PBSO briefing paper: Measuring peace consolidation and supporting transition.* UN Peacebuilding Support Office. New York.

70. Collier, P. (2007). *The bottom billion.* Oxford University Press. Oxford.

71. Pruitt, D.G. & Kim, S.H. (2004). *Social conflict: Escalation, stalemate and settlement,* 3rd edition. McGraw-Hill. New York.

24

THE CASE AGAINST LINKING ENVIRONMENTAL DEGRADATION AND NATIONAL SECURITY

Daniel Deudney*

Introduction

... Environmental issues are likely to become an increasingly important dimension of political life at all levels—locally, inside states, as well as internationally. How institutions respond to these emerging constraints is likely to shape politics in a profound manner. Because state and interstate conflict are such central features of both world politics and geopolitical theory, there is a strong tendency for people to think about environmental problems in terms of national security and to assume that environmental conflicts will fit into the established patterns of interstate conflict.

The aim of this essay is to cast doubt upon this tendency to link environmental degradation and national security. Specifically, I make three claims. First, it is analytically misleading to think of environmental degradation as a national security threat, because the traditional focus of national security—interstate violence—has little in common with either environmental problems or solutions. Second, the effort to harness the emotive power of nationalism to help mobilize environmental awareness and action may prove counterproductive by undermining globalist political sensibility. And third, environmental degradation is not very likely to cause interstate wars.

*Originally published as Daniel Deudney, "The Case Against Linking Environmental Degradation and National Security," *Millennium* 19, no. 3. Copyright © 1990 by SAGE. Reprinted by permission of SAGE.

The Weak Analytical Links Between Environmental Degradation and National Security

One striking feature of the growing discussion of environmental issues in the United States is the attempt by many liberals, progressives and environmentalists to employ language traditionally associated with violence and war to understand environmental problems and to motivate action. Lester Brown, Jessica Tuchman Matthews, Michael Renner and others have proposed "redefining national security" to encompass resource and environmental threats.[1] More broadly, Richard Ullman and others have proposed "redefining security" to encompass a wide array of threats, ranging from earthquakes to environmental degradation.[2] Hal Harvey has proposed the concept of "natural security,"[3] and US Senator Albert Gore has spoken extensively in favor of thinking of the environment as a national security issue.[4] During the renewed Cold War tensions of the late 1970s and early 1980s, such concepts were advanced to prevent an excessive focus on military threats. As the Cold War winds down [Editors' note: Deudney wrote this essay in 1990, after the fall of the Berlin Wall but before the formal dissolution of the Soviet Union], such links are increasingly popular among national security experts and organizations looking for new missions. . . .

Historically, conceptual ferment of this sort has often accompanied important changes in politics.[5] New phrases are coined and old terms are appropriated for new purposes. Epochal developments like the emergence of capitalism, the growth of democracy and the end of slavery were accompanied by shifting, borrowing and expanding political language. The wide-ranging contemporary conceptual ferment in the language used to understand and act upon environmental problems is therefore both a natural and an encouraging development.

But not all neologisms and linkages are equally plausible or useful. Until this recent flurry of reconceptualizing, the concept of "national security" (as opposed to national interest or well-being) has been centered upon *organized violence*.[6] As is obvious to common sense and as Hobbes argued with such force, security from violence is a primal human need, because loss of life prevents the enjoyment of all other goods. Of course, various resource factors, such as access to fuels and ores, were understood as contributing to states' capacities to wage war and achieve security from violence.

Before either "expanding" the concept of "national security" to encompass both environmental and violence threats, or "redefining" "national security" or "security" to refer mainly to environmental threats, it is worth examining just how much the national pursuit of security from violence has in common with environmental problems and their solutions.

Military violence and environmental degradation are linked directly in at least three major ways. First, the pursuit of national-security-from-violence through military means consumes resources (fiscal, organizational and leadership) that could be spent on environmental restoration. Since approximately one trillion US dollars is spent worldwide on military activities, substantial resources are involved. However, this relationship is not unique to environmental concerns, and unfortunately there is no guarantee that the world would spend money saved from military expenditures on environmental restoration. Nor is it clear that the world cannot afford environmental restoration without cutting military expenditures.

Second, war is directly destructive of the environment. In ancient times, the military destruction of olive groves in Mediterranean lands contributed to the long-lasting destruction of the lands' carrying capacities. More recently, the United States' bombardment and use of defoliants in Indochina caused significant environmental damage. Further, extensive use of nuclear weapons could have significant impacts on the global environment, including altered weather (i.e., "nuclear winter") and further depletion of the ozone layer. Awareness of these environmental effects has played an important role in mobilizing popular resistance to the arms race and in generally delegitimizing use of nuclear explosives as weapons.

Third, preparation for war causes pollution and consumes significant quantities of resources. In both the United States and the Soviet Union, significant quantities of radioactive waste have been produced as a by-product of the nuclear arms race, and several significant releases of radiation have occurred—perhaps most disastrously when a waste dump at a Soviet nuclear weapons facility exploded and burned, spreading radioactive materials over a large area near the Urals. Military activities have also produced significant quantities of toxic wastes.

In short, war and the preparation for war are clearly environmental threats and consume resources that could be used to ameliorate environmental degradation. In effect, these environmental impacts mean that the war system has costs beyond the intentional loss of life and destruction. Nevertheless, most of the world's environmental degradation is not caused by war and the preparation for war. Completely eliminating the direct environmental effects of the war system would leave most environmental degradation unaffected. Most of the causes and most of the cures of environmental degradation must be found outside the domain of the traditional national security system related to violence.

The war system is a definite but limited environmental threat, but in what ways is environmental degradation a threat to "national security"? Making such an identification can be useful if the two phenomena—security from violence and security from environmental threats—are similar. Unfortunately, they have little in common, making such linkages largely useless for analytical and conceptual purposes. Four major dissimilarities . . . deserve mention.

First, environmental degradation and violence are very different types of threats. Both violence and environmental degradation may kill people and may reduce human well-being, but not all threats to life and property are threats to security. Disease, old age, crime and accidents routinely destroy life and property, but we do not think of them as "national security" threats or even threats to "security." (Crime is a partial exception, but crime is a "security" threat at the individual level, because crime involves violence.) And when an earthquake or hurricane strikes with great force, we speak about "natural disasters" or designate "national disaster areas," but we do not speak about such events threatening "national security." If everything that causes a decline in human well-being is labeled a "security" threat, the term loses any analytical usefulness and becomes a loose synonym of "bad."

Second, the scope and source of threats to environmental well-being and national-security-from-violence are very different. There is nothing about the problem of environmental degradation which is particularly "national" in character. Since environmental threats are often oblivious of the borders of the nation-state, they rarely afflict just one nation-state. Nevertheless, this said, it would be misleading to call most environmental problems "international." Many perpetrators and victims are within the borders of one nation-state. Individuals, families, communities, other species and future generations are harmed. A complete collapse of the biosphere would surely destroy "nations" as well as everything else, but there is nothing distinctively national about either the causes, the harms or the solutions that warrants us giving such privileged billing to the "national" grouping.

A third misfit between environmental well-being and national-security-from-violence stems from the differing degrees of intention involved. Violent threats involve a high degree of intentional behavior. Organizations are mobilized, weapons procured and wars waged with relatively definite aims in mind. Environmental degradation, on the other hand, is largely unintentional, the side effects of many other activities. No one really sets out with the aim of harming the environment (with the so far limited exception of environmental modification for military purposes).

Fourth, organizations that provide protection from violence differ greatly from those in environmental protection. National-security-from-violence is conventionally pursued by organizations with three distinctive features. First, military organizations are secretive, extremely hierarchical and centralized, and normally deploy vastly expensive, highly specialized and advanced technologies. Second, citizens typically delegate the goal of achieving national security to remote and highly specialized organizations that are far removed from the experience of civil society. And third, the specialized professional group staffing these national security organizations are trained in the arts of killing and destroying.

In contrast, responding to the environmental problem requires almost exactly opposite approaches and organizations. Certain aspects of virtually all mundane activities—for example, house construction, farming techniques, sewage treatment, factory design and land use planning—must be reformed. The routine everyday behavior of practically everyone must be altered. This requires behavior modification in situ. The professional ethos of environmental restoration is husbandmanship—more respectful cultivation and protection of plants, animals and the land.

In short, national-security-from-violence and environmental habitability have little in common. Given these differences, the rising fashion of linking them risks creating a conceptual muddle rather than a paradigm or world view shift—a *de-definition* rather than a *re-definition* of security. If we begin to speak about all the forces and events that threaten life, property and well-being (on a large scale) as threats to our national security, we shall soon drain the term of any meaning. All large-scale evils will become threats to national security. To speak meaningfully about actual problems, we shall have to invent new words to fill the job previously performed by the old spoiled ones.

The Risks in Harnessing the Rhetorical and Emotional Appeals of National Security for Environmental Restoration

Confronted with these arguments, the advocate of treating environmental degradation as a national security problem might retort:

Yes, some semantic innovation without much analytical basis is occurring, but it has a sound goal—to get people to react as urgently and effectively to the environmental problem as they have to the national-security-from-violence problem. If people took the environmental problem as seriously as, say, an attack by a foreign power, think of all that could be done to solve the problems!

In other words, the aim of these new links is not primarily descriptive, but polemical. It is not a claim about fact, but a rhetorical device designed to stimulate action. Like William James, these environmentalists hope to find a "moral equivalent to war" to channel the energies behind war into constructive directions. . . . [Editors' note: See the philosopher William James's classic 1906 essay "The Moral Equivalent of War," based on a speech he gave at Stanford University.]

At first glance, the most attractive feature of linking fears about environmental threats with national security mentalities is the sense of urgency engendered, and the corresponding willingness to accept great personal sacrifice. If in fact the basic habitability of the planet is being undermined, then it stands to reason that some crisis mentality is needed. Unfortunately, it may be difficult to engender a sense of urgency and a willingness to sacrifice for extended periods of time. . . . A second apparently valuable similarity between the national security mentality and the environmental problem is the tendency to use worst-case scenarios as the basis for planning. However, the extreme conservatism of military organizations in responding to potential threats is not unique to them. The insurance industry is built around preparations for the worst possibilities, and many fields of engineering, such as aeronautical design and nuclear power plant regulation, routinely employ extremely conservative planning assumptions. These can serve as useful models for improved environmental policies.

Third, the conventional national security mentality and its organizations are deeply committed to zero-sum thinking. "Our" gain is "their" loss. Trust between national security organizations is extremely low. The prevailing assumption is that everyone is a potential enemy, and that agreements mean little unless congruent with immediate interests. If the Pentagon had been put in charge of negotiating an ozone layer protocol, we might still be stockpiling chlorofluorocarbons as a bargaining chip.

Fourth, conventional national security organizations have short time horizons. The pervasive tendency for national security organizations to discount the future and pursue very near-term objectives is a poor model for environmental problem solving.

Finally, and perhaps most importantly, is the fact that the "nation" is not an empty vessel or blank slate waiting to be filled or scripted, but is instead profoundly linked to war and "us vs. them" thinking. The tendency for people to identify themselves with various tribal and kin groupings is as old as humanity. In the last century and a half, however, this sentiment of nationalism, amplified and manipulated by mass media propaganda techniques, has been an integral part of totalitarianism and militarism. Nationalism means a sense of "us vs. them," of the insider vs. the outsider, of the compatriot vs. the alien. The stronger the nationalism, the stronger this cleavage, and the weaker the transnational bonds. Nationalism reinforces militarism, fosters prejudice and discrimination and feeds the quest for "sovereign" autonomy. . . .

Thus, thinking of national security as an environmental problem risks undercutting both the globalist and common fate understanding of the situation and the sense of world community that may be necessary to solve the problem. In short, it seems doubtful that the environment can be wrapped in national flags without undercutting the "whole earth" sensibility at the core of environmental awareness.

If pollution comes to be seen widely as a national security problem, there is also a danger that the citizens of one country will feel much more threatened by the pollution from other countries than by the pollution created by their fellow citizens. This could increase international tensions and make international accords more difficult to achieve, while diverting attention from internal cleanup. Citizens of the United States, for example, could become much more concerned about deforestation in Brazil than in reversing the centuries of North American deforestation. Taken to an absurd extreme—as national security threats sometimes are—seeing environmental degradation in a neighboring country as a national security threat could trigger various types of interventions, a new imperialism of the strong against the weak.

Instead of linking "national security" to the environmental problem, environmentalists should emphasize that the environmental crisis calls into question the national grouping and its privileged status in world politics. The environmental crisis is not a threat to national security, but it does challenge the utility of thinking in "national" terms. . . .

Environmental Degradation and Interstate War

Many people are drawn to calling environmental degradation a national security problem, in part because they expect this phenomenon to stimulate interstate conflict and even violence. States often fight over what they value, particularly if related to "security." If states begin to be much more concerned with resources and environmental degradation, particularly if they think environmental decay is a threat to their "national security," then states may well fight resource and pollution wars. . . . In general, I argue that interstate violence is not likely to result from environmental degradation, because of several deeply rooted features of the contemporary world order—both material and institutional—and because of the character of environmental and resource interests.

Few ideas seem more intuitively sound than the notion that states will begin fighting each other as the world runs out of usable natural resources. The popular metaphor of a lifeboat adrift at sea with declining supplies of clean water and rations suggests there will be fewer and fewer opportunities for positive-sum gains between actors. . . .

There are, however, three strong reasons for concluding that the familiar scenarios of resource war are of diminishing plausibility for the foreseeable future. First, the robust character of the world trade system means that states no longer experience resource dependency as a major threat to their military security and political autonomy. During the 1930s, the world trading system had collapsed, driving states to pursue autarkic economies. In contrast, the resource needs of contemporary states are routinely met without territorial control of the resource source, as Ronnie Lipschutz has recently shown.[7]

Second, the prospects for resource wars are diminished, since states find it increasingly difficult to exploit foreign resources through territorial conquest. Although the invention of nuclear explosives has made it easy and cheap to annihilate humans and infrastructure in extensive areas, the spread of small arms and national consciousness has made it very costly for an invader, even one equipped with advanced technology, to subdue a resisting population—as France discovered in Indochina and Algeria, the United States in Vietnam and the Soviet Union in Afghanistan. . . .

Third, the world is entering what H. E. Goeller and Alvin M. Weinberg have called the "age of substitutability," in which industrial civilization is increasingly capable of taking earth materials such as iron, aluminum, silicon and hydrocarbons (which are ubiquitous and plentiful) and fashioning them into virtually everything needed.[8] The most striking manifestation of this trend is that prices for virtually every raw material have been stagnant or falling for the last several decades, despite the continued growth in world output. In contrast to the expectations voiced by many during the 1970s—that resource scarcity would drive up commodity prices to the benefit of Third World raw material suppliers—prices have fallen, with disastrous consequences for Third World development.

In a second scenario, increased interstate violence results from internal turmoil caused by declining living standards. . . . Faced with declining living standards, groups at all levels of affluence can be expected to resist this trend by pushing the deprivation upon other groups. Class relations would be increasingly "zero-sum games," producing class war and revolutionary upheavals. Faced with these pressures, liberal democracy and free-market systems would increasingly be replaced by authoritarian systems capable of maintaining minimum order.[9]

The international system consequences of these domestic changes may be increased conflict and war. If authoritarian regimes are more war-prone because of their lack of democratic control and if revolutionary regimes are more war-prone because of their ideological fervor and lack of socialization into international norms and processes, then a world political system containing more such states is likely to be an increasingly violent one. The historical record from previous economic depressions supports the general proposition that widespread economic stagnation and unmet economic expectations contribute to international conflict.

Although initially compelling, this scenario has flaws as well. First, the pessimistic interpretation of the relationship between environmental sustainability and economic growth is arguably based on unsound economic theory. Wealth formation is not so much a product of cheap natural resource availability as of capital formation via savings and more efficient ways of producing. The fact that so many resource-poor countries, like Japan, are very wealthy, while many countries with more extensive resource endowments are poor, suggests that there is no clear and direct relationship between abundant resource availability and national wealth. Environmental constraints require an end to economic growth based on increasing raw material throughputs, rather than an end to growth in the output of goods and services.

Second, even if economic decline does occur, interstate conflict may be dampened, not stoked. . . . How societies respond to economic decline may in large measure depend upon the rate at which such declines occur. An offsetting factor here is the possibility that as people get poorer, they will be less willing to spend increasingly scarce resources for military capabilities. In this regard, the experience of economic depressions over the last two centuries may not be relevant, because such depressions were characterized by underutilized production capacity and falling resource prices. In the 1930s, increased military spending had a stimulative effect, but in a world in which economic growth had been retarded by environmental constraints, military spending would exacerbate the problem. . . .

Environmental degradation in a country or region could become so extreme that the basic social and economic fabric comes apart. Should some areas of the world suffer this fate, the impact of this outcome on international order may not, however, be very great. If a particular country, even a large one like Brazil, were tragically to disintegrate, among the first casualties would be the capacity of the industrial and governmental structure to wage and sustain interstate conventional war. As Bernard Brodie observed in the modern era, "the predisposing factors to military aggression are full bellies, not empty ones."[10] The poor and wretched of the earth may be able to deny an outside aggressor an easy conquest, but they are themselves a minimal threat to outside states. Offensive war today requires complex organizational skills, specialized industrial products and surplus wealth.

In today's world everything is connected, but not everything is tightly coupled. Regional disasters of great severity may occur, with scarcely a ripple in the rest of the world. After all, Idi Amin drew Uganda back into savage darkness, the Khmer Rouge murdered an estimated two million Cambodians and the Sahara has advanced across the Sahel without the economies and political systems of the rest of the world being much perturbed. Indeed, many of the world's citizens did not even notice.

A fourth possible route from environmental degradation to interstate conflict and violence involves pollution across state borders. It is easy to envision situations in which country A dumps an intolerable amount of pollution on a neighboring country B (which is upstream and upwind), causing country B to attempt to pressure and coerce country A into eliminating its offending pollution. We can envision such conflict of interest leading to armed conflict.

Fortunately for interstate peace, strongly asymmetrical and significant environmental degradation between neighboring countries is relatively rare. Probably more typical is the situation in which activities in country A harm parts of country A and country B, and in which activities in country B also harm parts of both countries. This creates complex sets of winners and losers, and thus establishes a complex array of potential intrastate and interstate coalitions. In general, the more such interactions are occurring, the less likely it is that a persistent, significant and highly asymmetrical pollution "exchange" will result. The very multitude of interdependency in the contemporary world, particularly among the industrialized countries, makes it unlikely that intense cleavages of environmental harm will match interstate borders, and at the same time not be compensated and complicated by other military, economic or cultural interactions. Resolving such conflicts will be a complex and messy affair, but the conflicts are unlikely to lead to war.

Finally, there are conflict potentials related to the global commons. Many countries contribute to environmental degradation, and many countries are harmed, but since the impacts are widely distributed, no one country has an incentive to act alone to solve the problem. Solutions require collective action, and with collective action comes the possibility of the "free rider." . . .

It is difficult to judge this scenario, because we lack examples of this phenomenon on a large scale. "Free-rider" problems may generate severe conflict, but it is doubtful that states would find military instruments useful for coercion and compliance. . . .

Conclusion

The degradation of the natural environment upon which human well-being depends is a challenge of far-reaching significance for human societies everywhere. But this challenge has little to do with the national-security-from-violence problem that continues to plague human political life. Not only is there little in common between the causes and solutions of these two problems, but the nationalist and militarist mindsets closely associated with "national security" thinking directly conflict with the core of the environmentalist world view. Harnessing these sentiments for a "war on pollution" is a dangerous and probably self-defeating enterprise. And fortunately, the prospects for resource and pollution wars are not as great as often conjured by environmentalists.

The pervasive recourse to national security paradigms to conceptualize the environmental problem represents a profound and disturbing failure of imagination and political awareness. If the nation-state enjoys a more prominent status in world politics than its competence and accomplishments warrant, then it makes little sense to emphasize the links between it and the emerging problem of global habitability.[11] Nationalist sentiment and the war system have a long-established logic and staying power that are likely to defy any rhetorically conjured "re-direction" toward benign ends. The movement to preserve the habitability of the planet for future generations must directly challenge the tribal power of nationalism and the chronic militarization of public discourse. Environmental degradation is not a threat to national security. Rather, environmentalism is a threat to "national security" mindsets and institutions. For environmentalists to dress their programs in the blood-soaked garments of the war system betrays their core values and creates confusion about the real tasks at hand.

NOTES

1. Lester Brown, *Redefining National Security* (Washington, DC: Worldwatch Paper, No. 14, October 1977); Jessica Tuchman Mathews, "Redefining Security," *Foreign Affairs* (Vol. 68, No. 2, 1989), pp. 162–77; Michael Renner, *National Security: The Economic and Environmental Dimensions* (Washington, DC: Worldwatch Paper, No. 89, May 1989); and Norman Myers, "Environmental Security," *Foreign Policy* (No. 74, 1989), pp. 23–41.

2. Richard Ullman, "Redefining Security," *International Security* (Vol. 8, No. 1, Summer 1983), pp. 129–53.

3. Hal Harvey, "Natural Security," *Nuclear Times* (March/April 1988), pp. 24–26.

4. Philip Shabecoff, "Senator Urges Military Resources to Be Turned to Environmental Battle," *The New York Times,* 29 June 1990, p. 1A.

5. Quentin Skinner, "Language and Political Change," and James Farr, "Understanding Political Change Conceptually," in Terence Ball et al. (eds.), *Political Innovation and Conceptual Change* (Cambridge: Cambridge University Press, 1989).

6. For a particularly lucid and well-rounded discussion of security, the state and violence, see Barry Buzan, *People, States, and Fear: The National Security Problem in International Relations* (Chapel Hill, NC: University of North Carolina Press, 1983), particularly pp. 1–93.

7. Ronnie D. Lipschutz, *When Nations Clash: Raw Materials, Ideology and Foreign Policy* (New York: Ballinger, 1989).

8. H. E. Goeller and Alvin Weinberg, "The Age of Substitutability," *Science* (Vol. 201, 20 February 1967). For some recent evidence supporting this hypothesis, see Eric D. Larson, Marc H. Ross and Robert H. Williams, "Beyond the Era of Materials," *Scientific American* (Vol. 254, 1986), pp. 34–41.

9. For a discussion of authoritarian and conflictual consequences of environmentally constrained economies, see William Ophuls, *Ecology and the Politics of Scarcity* (San Francisco, CA: Freeman, 1976), p. 152. See also Susan M. Leeson, "Philosophical Implications of the Ecological Crisis: The Authoritarian Challenge to Liberalism," *Polity* (Vol. 11, No. 3, Spring 1979); Ted Gurr, "On the Political Consequences of Scarcity and Economic Decline," *International Studies Quarterly* (No. 29, 1985), pp. 51–75; and Robert Heilbroner, *An Inquiry into the Human Prospect* (New York: W. W. Norton, 1974).

10. Bernard Brodie, "The Impact of Technological Change on the International System," in David Sullivan and Martin Sattler (eds.), *Change and the Future of the International System* (New York: Columbia University Press, 1972), p. 14.

11. For a particularly lucid argument that the nation-state system is overdeveloped relative to its actual problem-solving capacities, see George Modelski, *Principles of World Politics* (New York: The Free Press, 1972).

25

ENVIRONMENTAL PEACEBUILDING: THE GOOD WATER NEIGHBORS PROJECT

EcoPeace/Friends of the Earth Middle East*

[Editors' note: The environmental peacebuilding efforts described here have grown in breadth and depth since EcoPeace/Friends of the Earth Middle East published this report. Readers are urged to access up-to-date details at www.foeme.org.]

1. Introduction

. . .

Environmental cooperation is part of a long-time solution to conflict. It offers sustainable solutions for the future. It contributes to the improvement of living conditions, such as for instance the supply of water, and it fosters the building of confidence and trust among adverse societies. Environmental issues and the mutual ecological dependence across territorial borders facilitate and encourage cooperation, cooperation that often is a first step toward the initiation of an on-going dialogue, which would be difficult to mediate through political channels. As shared management of environmental resources develops and parties to a conflict are integrated in cooperative negotiation processes[,] political tensions can be overcome through the establishment of mutual trust. [The] creation of

---

* Excerpted from EcoPeace/Friends of the Earth Middle East, *Environmental Peacebuilding Theory and Practice: A Case Study of the Good Water Neighbors Project and In-Depth Analysis of the Wadi Fukin/Tzur Hadassah Communities*, January 2008. Reprinted with permission.

a common regional identity and the idea of mutual rights and expectations are likely to emerge (Carius 2006:11).

The Israeli-Palestinian conflict has no specific ecological cause. Nevertheless, ecological issues such as water supply, pollution of groundwater, solid waste management and others are of major importance to the region and are a shared burden on both societies. Solving these common ecological challenges through cooperative solutions offers therefore an outstanding opportunity to bring about an initial dialogue between the parties to conflict, a dialogue which for once is not directed at political issues but in fact at shared problems and concerns. This interaction has the potential to converge the two adverse societies and consequently is an essential first step to foster and build sustainable peace in the region.

In the area of Israel, Jordan and the Palestinian Authority[,] different approaches and efforts are taken by different organizations in the field of environmental peacebuilding. Although they share the idea that nature ignores political boundaries and therefore has great potential to contribute to the building of peace in the Middle East[,] they all have their own modus operandi and a history of success, progress and failure. One outstanding and promising example for environmental cooperation is the Good Water Neighbors project led by the trilateral non-governmental organization EcoPeace/Friends of the Earth Middle East. An insight into the project and its achievements provides us with valuable data and information on how to successfully manage a cross-border environmental project in an area of protracted conflict.

. . .

5. EcoPeace/Friends of the Earth Middle East

5.1 The Role of an NGO as Peacemaker

In the aftermath of international war, post-conflict peace-building may take the form of concrete cooperative projects which link two or more countries in a mutually beneficial undertaking that can not only contribute to economic and social development but also enhance the confidence that is so fundamental to peace. I have in mind, for example, projects that bring States together to develop agriculture, improve transportation or utilize resources such as water or electricity that they need to share, or joint programs though which barriers between nations are brought down by means of freer travel, cultural exchanges and mutually beneficial youth and educational projects. Reducing hostile perceptions through educational exchanges and curriculum reform may be essential to forestall a re-emergence of cultural and national tensions which could spark renewed hostilities. (UN Agenda for Peace 1992:5)

The UN Agenda for Peace highlights the essential elements of peacebuilding which are also of main importance to the concept of environmental peacebuilding: the establishment of concrete cooperative projects and the utilization of common resources within these, the enhancement of confidence and the development of mutual understanding and trust through educational exchanges.

The work of FoEME takes these pivotal elements into account and therefore offers a good example for how to successfully implement projects in the field of environmental peacebuilding in an area of protracted conflict. The NGO helps to advance the peace potential in the region through the empowerment of Palestinian, Jordanian and Israeli communities and the support of shared dialogue and cooperation between them. It builds up community partnerships with the aim of raising the awareness of shared environmental issues and developing common solutions. Education and the creation of cooperative knowledge on common environmental threats play a central role in the design of every project. The final aim is not only to produce a feeling of a shared region and responsibility—neglecting for once political issues and boundaries—but to change the environmental behavior and create shared gains and benefits. These efforts build linkages between societies that are the cornerstone for confidence and trust-building between parties to a conflict.

Lederach (1997:66) emphasizes that " . . . peacebuilding . . . should be understood as a process made up of roles and functions rather than as an activity that resides in the person of the mediator or intermediary team." Using the definition composed by Mitchell (1993:147) concerning roles and functions of external peacemakers[,] the following four roles may be ascribed to the NGO Friends of the Earth Middle East:

- "Enskiller (empowerer): Develops or equalizes skills and competencies needed to enable parties to reach a mutually acceptable and sustainable solution.
- Envisioner (fact finder): Provides new data, ideas, theories, and options for adversaries to select or adapt. Develops fresh thinking on [a] range of possible options or outcomes that might lead to a solution.
- Enhancer (developer): Provides additional resources to assist adversaries reach a positive-sum solution.
- Reconciler: Undertakes long-term actions to alter negative attitudes, stereotypes, and images held at large within adversaries. Builds new relationships across remaining divisions."

As an Enskiller FoEME creates knowledge and abilities to improve the environmental situation in Israel, Jordan and the Palestinian Authority and proposes sustainable solutions from which all the societies may benefit. As an Envisioner FoEME provides different new ideas and options for solving environmental threats within and in cooperation with partnering communities. As an Enhancer FoEME allocates the communities on the one hand with financial resources and on the other hand with knowledge on their own and the other's situation, their future prospects and possibilities. And finally, as a Reconciler FoEME fosters the change of negative perceptions and images and the establishment of long-lasting relationships and cooperation between the societies. The building of new relationships is seen as one of the core elements of peacebuilding as relationships "in their totality form new patterns, processes and structures" (Lederach 1997:85) which means that they have the potential to alter existing schemes and effectuate changes within societies, and generate processes of social change. A pivotal condition for the creation of a long-lasting relationship between adversaries is the common "need to move . . . toward a desired and shared vision of increased interdependence" (Lederach 1997:84).

5.1.1 Capacity and Relationship Building

As an Enskiller FoEME does what Lederach is calling "capacity building." "The word 'capacity' . . . is linked to a concept of empowerment. . . . [E]mpowerment is related to a fundamental challenge of peacebuilding: How to create and sustain within individuals and communities the movement from 'I/we cannot effect desired change' to 'I/we can.' . . . [C]apacity building therefore refers to the process of reinforcing the inherent capabilities and understandings of people related to the challenge of conflict in their context, and to a philosophy oriented toward the generation of new, proactive, empowered action for desired change in those settings" (Lederach 1997:108–109). Capacity building is a first fundamental step in the long-term process of developing understanding and abandoning negative stereotypes and has a greater impact if it is applied in and by groups and communities.

Empowering communities is one of the main efforts taken by FoEME. Local field staff (teachers, social workers and others) are appointed to work within the communities, involving youth, adults, schools and different local stakeholders such as mayors in different projects. The success of the projects emerges on the one hand from the realization of concrete environmental and educational projects within the communities and on the other hand from cooperation with partnering communities which suffer from similar environmental hazards and therefore have shared intentions to improve the present situation.

With the example of FoEME it becomes apparent how capacity building is closely related to relationship building. It is essential not only to develop an individual's capacity and skill but also to build relationships in and across the lines of the division in a context of protracted conflict (Lederach 1997:109).

Sustainable peacebuilding requires a change in relationships in which the vision of a shared future is created and an understanding of, and practical responses to, the existing realities and crises are established (Lederach 1997:112). FoEME has devised an infrastructure for its projects that both fosters the development of a common vision for the future and realizes improvements in the environmental situation of the communities.

5.1.2 Grassroots, Middle-Range and Top-level Leadership

FoEME combines bottom-up community work with top-down advocacy which to-gether lead to a successful implementation of projects. Lederach (1997:137) mentions the importance of the horizontal and the vertical integration of people and processes for the emergence of social change and the establishment of a sustainable peace.

Nevertheless in recent times more and more emphasis is put on the grassroots which often turn the balance for ending conflict. "One could argue that virtually all of the recent transitions toward peace—such as those in El Salvador and Ethiopia, as well as the earlier one in the Philippines—were driven largely by the pressure for change that was bubbling up from the grassroots. In fact, at times it seems that ex-haustion, rather than innovative planned transformation, is chiefly responsible for ending conflicts" (Lederach 1997:52). Special attention may be given therefore to the empowerment of the grassroots in projects such as the Good Water Neighbors that strengthen the bottom of a society and facilitate action.

Not less important than the grassroots level is the middle-range leadership. Middle-level leaders are positioned so that they are connected both to the top and the grassroots level. They have the advantages of not being controlled by the au-thority and knowing the context and the experiences of people living at the grass-roots level. Furthermore middle-range leaders do not seek to capture any political or military power but instead they derive their status and influence from ongoing relationships. As they are neither in the international nor the national limelight they tend to have greater flexibility of movement and action than top-level lead-ers. This flexibility is useful for making vertical and horizontal connections that are necessary to sustain a process of change (Lederach 1997:41–42/81). Believing that middle-range leaders exhibit a determinant location in a conflict situation and might be part of achieving and sustaining peace, FoEME closely works with the mayors of the communities and regions involved in the Good Water Neighbors project. The mayors of the partnering communities sign Memorandums of Un-derstanding in which they adhere to cooperation and the common engagement for shared environmental problems. Although these Memorandums of Under-standing are not official agreements they are a first step in the establishment of a long-lasting bond and trust between communities and a statement to the outside world that will and belief for cooperation and a peaceful coexistence do exist. Moreover with signing this document the mayors are showing their residents that cooperation with the former adversaries is the desirable and right pathway to the resolution of the conflict and the building of sustainable peace in the region.

5.2 Approach of EcoPeace/Friends of the Earth Middle East

. . . FoEME combines two types of work which together help the NGO to meet all the criteria of peacebuilding: bottom-up community work and top-down advocacy.

An important part of the top-down advocacy is the composition of academic and policy papers which aim at displaying in detail the severity of the cross-border environmental problems. Written by experts from the relevant societies the policy papers have the potential to gain credibility and support of local and regional stakeholders. The policy papers, based on common research, are designed to create a single regional vision concerning the solution to the cross-boundary problem at hand. Policy papers focus on transboundary eco-systems such as the Jordan River, Dead Sea and Mountain Aquifer and highlight the importance and necessity of a common management and vision as a solution for the environment and conflict situation in the region. Each office led by their director and local staff then advocate/educate decision makers and their respective public, the common vision espoused. The strength of this approach is that Jordanians advocate the position to Jordanians, Palestinians to Palestinians and Israelis to Israelis. In each case it is the same position, but in the cultural context and manner that maximizes local influence. Furthermore the NGO includes Israeli, Jordanian and Palestinian media in its endeavors[,] using media coverage as a means of creating political pressure and placing shared environmental issues on the daily political agenda. A successful example is the large public and media attention raised for the public hearing of the World Bank, concerning the Red-Dead Canal, which brought about that the alternative of the Jordan River may be included in the Terms of References of the World Bank feasibility study. The establishment of a shared academic and policy vision is essential for the development of community understanding and leadership as people may use scientific knowledge to both diffuse and defend their undertakings. Moreover it creates an overall accepted vision for a better common future which generates a process of trust-building, the cornerstone of peacebuilding.

Consistency, creativity and flexibility constitute the fundament for the strength and success of the NGO. Although FoEME has been focusing on the same issues for over [22] years its work is characterized by the steady generation of new ideas which often originate from one community and are then applied to other communities all over the region (see 5.3 The Neighbors' Path). In contrast to any governmental organization the NGO has a very broad room for maneuver and can gain community belief and support though the realization of concrete projects such as for instance the successful introduction of gray water/rain water harvesting systems in schools and municipal buildings of the communities participating in the Good Water Neighbors project.

5.3 Good Water Neighbors Project

The Good Water Neighbors (GWN) project is one outstanding example of a successful effort in the field of environmental peacebuilding in the Middle East. The general idea behind the project is that the dependence on the same water resources can create one community out of adverse users and stakeholders. This community on the one hand benefits environmentally and economically from cooperative management and on the other hand builds up long-lasting relationships which will, in a long-term perspective, facilitate the establishment of trust and the feeling of a shared collective identity. Basically the project strives for achieving two main goals. First, a change of perception towards the environment and at a later stage towards cooperation and peace and second a definite change in behavior towards the aforesaid issues which will assure sustainability and endurance.

The Good Water Neighbors project was established in 2001 working until 2005 (Phase I of the project) with 11 Israeli, Palestinian and Jordanian Communities, expanding in the present Phase II, 2005–2008, to 17 communities [Editor's note: Phase III featured 28 communities in 2013]. The intention is to further increase the number of communities until a critical mass is achieved. Not surprisingly when the project was first launched it was difficult to convince communities to join. Today, however, there is demand from new communities to come on board but sadly lack of funding is the current impediment.

Each community has a neighboring partner community which is located on the other side of the political divide/border and shares and depends on the same water resource. A local staff person, coming from the community, is hired to work for FoEME and carry out the project activities. Local staff [are] chosen on the basis of their ability to work with the community and their acceptance in the community. Peace activists and environmentalists are not sought for this position but rather an individual that knows how to speak in the local community context. The project aims at raising environmental awareness and developing initiatives for the improvement of the environmental situation within and between the partnering communities.

Led by the local staff person, the project works with three groups of stakeholders: youth, adults and mayors. In each community, local field staff works in close partnership with youth and adults, through local schools, youth clubs, community centers and community based organizations. The program benefits from a common text book on shared water issues, called WaterCare. It is a text book written by Israeli, Palestinian and Jordanian teachers as part of the Multilateral EXACT program. It is the same text book in Arabic and Hebrew. The use of the WaterCare text book combined with field visits in the community, across to the neighboring community and regional tours held, helps participating youth understand the water issues of their community and their neighbors' community. One youth group decided to initiate a petition calling for action to improve the water reality in their and their neighbor's community. This led to all youth water trustees developing petitions specific to their cross-border issues and collecting in total over 15,000 signatures from local residents.

To both gain the trust of the community and empower youth that they can be themselves the catalyst for change, concrete projects are undertaken in each community, led by the youth. In each community school buildings were transformed into wise-water buildings re-using grey or rainwater for the flushing of toilets and watering of school gardens, being able to cut by a third the amount of water used in the buildings. Furthermore ecological gardens were built, creating a common environmental learning process and training among youth and serving as an example of how to handle scarce water resources. Another educational program, the building of ecological wetlands, was introduced in 2007, an effective way of cleaning sewage and other wastewater in small communities or single households. All these efforts on the one hand empower the youth to improve the environmental reality in their community by establishing the necessary knowledge and tools and on the other hand facilitate dialogue and the creation of a cooperative knowledge on environmental hazards and possible solutions.

The next group of stakeholders is the adults of the respective communities whose support and belief in the project is essential for its success. Their involvement in the project makes them not only partners of the NGO but in fact defenders of cooperation and of reconciliation efforts. Adult forums have been created, offering a platform for discussion with local professionals and planners on environmental problems and possible solutions. In the partnering communities Tulkarem and Emek Hefer the received support of the local community by the mayors was fundamental for their motivation to move forward in the issue of sewage cooperation. In the communities around the Dead Sea the shared problem of the fly plague is being discussed and the idea of composting manure has been developed. The Jordan River communities are very much involved in the process of establishing a Peace Park in the area of the former Rotenberg hydropower station whose cross-border management will not only improve and deepen the relationships across the border but also bring eco-tourism and therewith economic development to the region. The concrete realization of ideas, visible to the whole community, is of main importance within the project framework. Prosperities play an important role in the building of trust first of all in the NGO, the project, its ideas and ideals and later within and between the communities. Through exchange and ongoing cooperation between the locals of the neighboring communities a common dedication to the solution of shared environmental problems is established which fosters the creation of a desired common responsibility and vision for the future.

The idea of the Neighbors' Path was developed by the adult's forum in one of the communities of the GWN project, Tzur Hadassah, and is today implemented in all the other 16 communities participating in the project. A trail is established during whose visit the natural and cultural heritage of each one of the GWN communities is shown. Following the path of water, ending at the border, the trail highlights the connection between the communities and their water resources, revealing degradation and pollution, and provides insights to the water reality across the political divide. The Neighbors' Path emphasizes the need for cross-border solutions in protecting water resources by displaying the mutual dependence on and interrelation between the water resources. The idea behind the project is to mobilize the local community in support of cross-border cooperation and the protection of the local ecosystem and to promote local entrepreneurship. The involvement of local businesses not only deepens the locals' involvement in the GWN project but also generates alternative income from the tourism visitation of the path. The Neighbors' Path aims at attracting local, national and foreign tourists showcasing the benefits of cooperation. At this stage of the project the main focus lies in getting local residents, students and adults, and people from the big cities to undertake tours in their own country to get to know the water and environment reality of their own and the neighboring societies. The goal is to carry out 30 tours in each and every community over the coming two years [2009–2010]. At the same time interested groups from Europe and the USA will visit the different communities' paths while participating in a regional cross-border tour. The communities will be able to benefit economically from these visitations.

Stemming from the grassroots the Neighbors' Path has the potential to develop into a nation-wide example for successful cross-border cooperation. It includes many of the different aspects of environmental peacebuilding: Firstly, it highlights the interdependence of environmental issues and creates cooperative knowledge on environmental issues whereby it establishes a feeling of a shared region and a shared responsibility for the present and future situation. Secondly, it strengthens the linkages between the partnering communities by creating shared gains and benefits. And finally it educates local and foreign people on the environment and cooperation and supports the process of changing perceptions towards these issues.

The third group of stakeholders is the mayors. The importance of the involvement of mid-range leaders has been mentioned already in chapter 5.1.2. Being located in a position between the grassroots and the top-level leaders they are not only able to make political statements and raise political attention for the joint efforts but also they act as ambassadors for the vision of a shared future. Events such as the Big Jump—mayors of the Jordan River Valley jumping together in the waters of the Yarmouk River—are on the one hand very effective in raising public awareness and interest in the ongoing disappearance of the Jordan River and the urgent necessity of its rehabilitation and on the other hand act as an official and operative statement that cooperation and a peaceful get-together in fact is possible.

[In 2008] for the first time the partnering municipalities Tulkarem and Emek Hefer are cooperating on the issue of olive mill waste. Until now the waste from the olive mills located in the Tulkarem area was dumped into the Alexander River which flows from Tulkarem through Emek Hefer into the Mediterranean, polluting not only the river and killing flora and fauna in the river bed but also the sea and the coastline. Today the waste from the mills is placed in a truck and taken to Israel for treatment[,] reducing to a big extent the pollution of the shared water resource.

The success of this endeavor is owed on the one hand to the initiative of the local field staff, the project coordinators and planners but moreover also to the local stakeholders within the municipalities. Due to ongoing cooperation between the neighboring communities trust has been built over the years, mutual trust that facilitates and simplifies the implementation of such a cross-border project and is the cornerstone for its success. People from both communities were committed to realize shared goals and now mutually benefit from the reached gains. The recognition of the shared responsibility for the present and future situation has been fruitful.

5.3.1 Evaluation of the GWN Project

In order to assess the GWN project from a more internal perspective a questionnaire was handed out to the Palestinian, Jordanian and Israeli field staff and to the water trustees (youth). The results help to evaluate the project and its contribution to the building of peace in the area and provide us with valuable local suggestions and inputs on how to possibly upgrade the project framework.

The field staff questionnaire was answered by 13 people, all working locally in the different communities of the GWN project. The 13 are made up of five Jewish Israelis, four Palestinians, three Jordanians and one Arab-Israeli. The youth questionnaire was answered by 27 water trustees, 9 Jordanians, 3 Arab-Israelis, 5 Palestinians and 10 Jewish Israelis.

In general all the field staff agree that the GWN project has led to a better understanding of environmental problems within his/her community. More efforts have to be taken to actually improve the environmental situation satisfyingly in each and every community, only half of the field staff assuring that the environmental situation in her/his community was very much changed indeed since the involvement in the project. However this is partly to trace back to the fact that six of the communities have been integrated in the GWN project only since 2005. Asking about the actual changes and improvements that have been taking place in the communities[,] all the field staff mentions the "green thinking" that has been dispersed in the communities. Children, adults and even the municipalities have much greater awareness of nature in general and particular environmental issues that constitute a risk for the community. Moreover they are all involved in concrete environmental projects and therefore carry a certain kind of responsibility. Many field staff emphasize the importance of the improved water supply in schools and the ecological gardens that support the environmental education and contribute to the understanding of the water reality. Other noted improvements are for instance the prevention from further environmental destruction by Israeli communities in Wadi Fukin, the coordination of waste disposal in Baqa, the improvement of the water quality of the shared Alexander River, the advancement of agriculture, wise water use (farmers, schools) and many others.

Asking about the difficulties to change people's attitudes towards the environment, opinions diverge. [I]t is mostly the Palestinian field staff that considers it difficult; most Jordanians and Israelis don't and therefore the NGO is seen as an essential stakeholder in this fundamental process. Everyone agrees that the project activities, the meetings between the communities, the workshops, the distribution of papers help a lot to change people's attitudes. Still most of the field staff believes that if the activities were even more numerous it would be able to reach more individuals and hence be more effective.

Changing the behavior towards the environment is a long-winded process; achievements are visible only after a certain period of time. This is definitely being felt in all the communities. Still the field staff is optimistic, especially because environmental issues are becoming part of the public discourse and environmental friendly ideas are being produced within the communities. Positive changes are obvious especially with schoolchildren as they are enjoying environmental education and participating in different projects. Children's awareness and action may furthermore have positive impacts on the whole family and household.

The GWN project definitely leads to a better understanding of the communities' shared environmental problems and offers appropriate arrangements to solve them. Most of the field staff thinks that the project very much offers solutions to common environmental hazards. Moreover its activities indeed build connections between adverse societies, most of the respondents saying that the project helps to build trust between neighboring communities. According to the field staff the most effective activities are the development of common projects and businesses, the meetings of children and adult groups and the cooperation between the mayors.

Whether the connection between the communities will last in the future seems to be controversial although half of the field staff is positive about this. Still, the rest argues that it very much depends on the political situation. It's obvious that the newly built harmonious relationships are still contingent on political events despite cooperation and trust-building. Therefore the communities are in the need of an ongoing support, an institutional structure, as long as the conflict is there, otherwise the conflict will overpower them. The GWN project is one possibility, as a stable institution it supports the communities and fosters the institutionalization of cooperation.

Most of the respondents agree that the current political situation complicates or forms an obstacle to cooperation and that political events very much influence the possibility of building trust between the communities. Still on the whole people are convinced that the project does contribute to the building of peace in the area and that their communities are much more involved in the process of building peace since their participation in the GWN project. Very important to everyone is the process of getting to know each other, the establishment of amicable relationships, the recognition of the other side's problems and fears and the loosing of the own fears towards cooperation. Through the GWN project the other side, the neighbor becomes a face of a human or even a friend with whom cooperation becomes possible or even desirable.

5.3.2 Water Trustees–Youth

The significance and the achievements of the GWN project become particularly apparent through the evaluation of the youth questionnaire. By learning about their own and the neighbor's water reality the youth becomes sensitized to the mutual dependence on the same water resources and the necessity for a cooperative management and shared solutions. Furthermore during youth camps the water trustees have the opportunity to get to know their counterparts, being able to establish amicable relationships and to realize that they resemble them much more than they were actually thinking. Negative stereotypes are abolished, convergence is taking place and the idea of a common future becomes imaginable. The GWN project empowers Palestinian, Jordanian and Israeli youth to influence not only the present and future environmental situation in the region but also to head for a common reconciliation process. With this the project follows the demand of sustainable development to enable future generations to meet their own needs.

In general the water trustees have a very broad knowledge of the different environmental problems their own and the other communities are facing. Most of them mention water shortage, environmental pollution, especially the pollution of rivers, wadis and groundwater and uncontrolled sewage disposal. The youth living in the Jordan River Valley and around the Dead Sea are very much concerned about the declining water level there. Many children state that due to the youth camp and the visits to different affected places they started to understand the severity of the situation and the need to take action.

The youth camps were very successful in building up relationships between the youth of the different societies, language seems to have been the main obstacle they had to overcome. All the water trustees understand the importance of cooperation if an improvement of the present situation shall be achieved.

A few citations of the water trustees may demonstrate the thoughts of the youth, what they have learned during the camp and how they want to apply this knowledge in the future.

We should organize meetings and workshops to educate and guide people how to use the water and manage it properly.

—Palestinian boy, 15 years old.

God has given us all this good and all this beauty, we have to protect this and we should even make it more beautiful.

—Arab-Israeli boy, 14 years old.

We should introduce more ideas that will bring benefits to all societies.

—Jordanian boy, 15 years old.

It is important that communities work together because only like that you can stop wars and solve problems.

—Jewish Israeli girl, 14 years old.

We should love to work together hand in hand and increase the endurance and patience.

—Jordanian boy, 15 years old.

I have learned that we, Israelis and Palestinians, are not significantly different and that to build connections between us can be a great pleasure.

—Jewish Israeli boy, 15 years old.

We should put signs to guide people how to protect our nature.

—Palestinian boy, 15 years old.

We should keep our eyes on how we are using our water at home and we should be using it in a wise way.

—Jordanian boy, 16 years old.

Conclusion

This paper deals with the concept of environmental peacebuilding as one possible element of building peace in regions of protracted conflict. Compared to other possible—social, political, economic or cultural—efforts in the field of peacebuilding[,] the environment has certain characteristics which turn it into an important stakeholder in the process of settling down conflict.

As environmental issues are an integral part of the basic needs of every human being, an insecure and unhealthy environment is a mutual harm borne by all the societies living together in the same ecological region. Environmental depletion and the mutual dependence on shared resources can therefore be used as a connecting element between parties to a conflict, regarding the improvement of the environmental situation as a common benefit to all the societies. Obviously nature knows no boundaries, the interdependence of natural resources requires a region-wide, cross-border management, otherwise common urgent matters such as water scarcity and the pollution of water resources may not be solved. Here lies the potential of environmental peacebuilding to contribute to the process of building peace in a region of protracted conflict. Initiating cooperation on shared environmental issues implicates ongoing dialogue between parties to a conflict, a dialogue which offers the opportunity to exchange different perceptions and perspectives and is a cornerstone of trust-building between societies. The establishment of cross-border societal linkages, such as the ones between the partner communities of FoEME's Good Water Neighbors project, facilitates the creation of shared practices, values and norms which in the long-run lead to the development of a mutual responsibility for the common ecological region, neglecting political and highlighting natural borders. In order that environmental cooperation can develop into broader forms of political cooperation and generate a social and political dialogue going beyond environmental issues[,] bottom-up community work has to be combined with top-down advocacy, incorporating the grassroots, the middle-range and the top-level leadership. The NGO EcoPeace/Friends of the Earth Middle East offers a good example on how to implement this holistic approach successfully.

Environmental peacebuilding is a very new subject in the field of development and cooperation, neither a broad selection of profound theories nor case studies are available for being able to assess the potential of cooperative management of shared resources to initiate a process of amicable dialogue and reconciliation in regions of protracted conflict in general. Moreover long-time experience and research are necessary to review the results of projects in terms of building peace.

Nevertheless efforts such as the Good Water Neighbors project may be used as a showcase of a six-year-old successful implementation of the concept of environmental peacebuilding and serve as an example for environmental security, reconciliation and peace in other regions of protracted conflict on our planet.

BIBLIOGRAPHY

Carius, Alexander (2006): Environmental Peacebuilding. Environmental Cooperation as an Instrument of Crisis Prevention and Peacebuilding: Conditions for Success and Constraints. Adelphi Report. Berlin, p. 11.

Lederach, John Paul (1997): *Building Peace. Sustainable Reconciliation in Divided Societies.* United States Institute for Peace, Washington.

Mitchell, Christopher (1993): The Process and Stages of Mediation: The Sudanese Cases. In: Smock, David R. ed., *Making War and Waging Peace.* Washington DC: United States Institute of Peace Press, p. 147.

United Nations (1992): An Agenda for Peace. Preventive diplomacy, peacemaking and peacekeeping. Report of the Secretary-General.

26

THE VIOLENCE OF DEVELOPMENT

Balakrishnan Rajagopal[*]

"Ethnic cleansing"—the forcible dislocation of a large number of people belonging to particular ethnic groups—is an outlawed practice. Individuals who are accused of ethnic cleansing are subjected to indictment by international criminal tribunals, and even domestic courts are increasingly used in the West to prosecute those who commit mass violence abroad.

Yet most large forced dislocations of people do not occur in conditions of armed conflict or genocide but in routine, everyday evictions to make way for development projects. A recent report by the World Commission on Dams estimates that 40 million to 80 million people have been physically displaced by dams worldwide, a disproportionate number of them being indigenous peoples. [Editors' note: See Bissell's essay on the WCD in Part Three of this volume.] Indeed, this "development cleansing" may well constitute ethnic cleansing in disguise, as the people dislocated so often turn out to be from minority ethnic and racial communities.

In the Philippines, almost all the large dam schemes are on the land of the country's 6 million to 7 million indigenous people. In India, 40 percent to 50 percent of those displaced by development projects—a total estimated at more than 33 million since 1947—are tribal people, who account for just 8 percent of the country's 1 billion population.

Still, international human rights monitors remain oblivious to the violence of development. A biased focus on international criminal justice—the pursuit of a Milosevic, for example—has blinded the world's conscience to mass crimes that are often as serious as those that occurred in Rwanda and the former Yugoslavia.

The millions of people forcibly dislocated from their lands are usually from among the poorest and most vulnerable sections of populations. Upon dislocation,

---

*Originally published in *The Washington Post*, August 8, 2001. Reprinted with permission of the author.

these communities are pushed into further poverty and violence. These conditions are themselves grave human rights violations, but they also lead to further violations—for example, by exacerbating conflicts between large communities that lose land and are resettled and the communities into which they move.

Forcible dislocation destroys the livelihoods of entire communities as large dams and inappropriate agricultural projects alter the land-use patterns that traditionally support farming, grazing and fishing. And the number of people forcibly dislocated is probably far larger than reported, as the displaced are systematically undercounted—for example, by as much as 47 percent in the case of the projects funded by the World Bank. In China's Western Poverty Reduction Project in Qinghai, the World Bank Complaints Panel found that entire towns of thousands of Tibetan and Mongol minorities were not counted as affected.

The United Nations has declared mass eviction to be a violation of the human right to housing. And because of growing conflicts over water and natural resources, the World Commission on Dams was established in 1998 by the World Bank, the International Conservation Union and others. But despite these efforts, human rights violations continue in the name of development.

For instance, a judgment by the Indian Supreme Court in October 2000 will allow the construction of a mega-dam on the Narmada River to go forward. This is deeply disappointing given the Indian judiciary's history as the protector of the rights of the underprivileged. It is also tragic because the project will lead to the displacement of more than 200,000 people and the elimination of the rich ecological resources in the Narmada Valley, one of India's most fertile.

The Narmada Valley dam project is the second largest in the world, after the Three Gorges dam project in China, which is known for its excessive human and environmental costs. The World Bank, which originally was to have funded the Narmada project, withdrew funding in 1993 after being criticized for violating its own internal regulations on resettlement and rehabilitation and environmental clearance. Every funder since then—Japanese and Germans included—has withdrawn after running into criticism, and the project is now being funded by Indian state governments, redirecting scarce funds from much-needed health and education projects.

A broad coalition opposing the dam, consisting of the people of the Narmada Valley as well as domestic and foreign intellectuals, social activists, journalists, judges and lawyers, has repeatedly pointed out technological alternatives for producing power and providing water, but these have been dismissed by the Indian Supreme Court.

On the other side is the developmental nationalism displayed by Indian Home Minister L. K. Advani, who says opponents of such projects are working at the behest of "foreign nations"—a response commonly given by governments that commit gross human rights abuses.

It is clear that international indifference toward the violence of development projects needs to end.

27

CLIMATE CHANGE AT THE UN SECURITY COUNCIL: CONCEPTUAL AND PROCEDURAL CONTROVERSIES

Joe Thwaites

On July 20, 2011, the United Nations Security Council held a thematic debate on the implications of climate change for international security. It was the second time the Council had dedicated a meeting to the topic of climate change, and both sessions proved to be controversial, for both conceptual and procedural reasons.[1] This article examines the main arguments put forward by UN member-states for and against the Security Council considering the issue.

The primary body for addressing climate change within the UN system is the Framework Convention on Climate Change (UNFCCC), formed in 1992.[2] Almost every UN member-state is a party to the Convention. The 1997 Kyoto Protocol was agreed to under the auspices of the UNFCCC, and it is the current setting for negotiations on a future global climate agreement. However, progress has been sclerotic, and as a result some states have attempted to raise the issue in other international settings. The UN Security Council is one of them.

Under the terms of the UN Charter, the Security Council is charged with "primary responsibility for the maintenance of international peace and security."[3] It is arguably the most powerful body within the UN system due to its legal ability to approve sanctions, both economic and military, if it deems this necessary "to maintain or restore international peace and security."[4] By virtue of the power vested in the body, discussion of a topic by the Security Council raises its diplomatic and media profile well above that of the myriad issues the United Nations deals with in its daily activities. However, the Council's exceptional power, along with its narrow membership and rules of procedure, has made it the source of much controversy. Only five states—China, France, Russia, the United Kingdom, and the United States (the "P5")—possess permanent Security Council seats, and a further ten are elected as nonpermanent members for two-year terms. Council resolutions may be vetoed by any of the P5. While vetoes are cast infrequently, the power to do so constrains what is discussed and what may be considered for serious action. Where it is not possible to pass a resolution, the Council may choose to approve a nonbinding Presidential Statement. Such statements lack the legal force of a resolution, but because they express a unified Council opinion on an issue, they require the consensus of all members.[5]

The first UN Security Council debate on climate-related issues, held in 2007, was highly contentious. Some states argued that climate change posed a clear security threat—Tuvalu portrayed climate change as a "conflict . . . not being fought with guns and missiles but with weapons from everyday life—chimney stacks and exhaust pipes" while Namibia likened it to "low-intensity biological or chemical warfare." Many other states, however, argued that the discussion was outside of the Council's purview. As India put it, "The Security Council does not have the expertise and may not have the mandate: to make an uncertain long-term prospect a security threat amounts to an informal amendment of the Charter."[6] Council members were unable to agree upon any formal outcome. When Germany, as the monthly rotating President of the Council, proposed the subsequent 2011 debate, it had no expectation of passing a binding resolution; but it hoped to obtain support for a Presidential Statement on the issue and engaged in much public and private diplomacy toward this goal in the months leading up to the debate.[7]

Framing the Debate: Climate Change as a Threat to International Peace and Security?

In advance of the debate, Germany circulated a concept note to member-states setting out its rationale for holding a debate and posing questions on the UN system's preparedness for potential security implications of climate change, such as sea-level rise, statelessness, food insecurity, extreme weather events, reduced water access, and migration. The concept note asked states to consider how the Security Council, other UN bodies, and regional organizations can work together to respond to these challenges, and how the security implications of climate change can be incorporated into conflict prevention and peacebuilding work.[8]

The Security Council debate opened with some pointed remarks by UN Secretary-General Ban Ki-Moon:

> We must make no mistake. The facts are clear. Climate change is real, and it is accelerating in a dangerous manner. It not only exacerbates threats to international peace and security, it is a threat to international peace and security. . . .

Around the world, hundreds of millions of people are in danger of going short of food and water. That undermines the most essential foundations of local, national and global stability. Competition between communities and countries for scarce resources, especially water, is increasing, exacerbating old security dilemmas and creating new ones. Environmental refugees are reshaping the human geography of the planet, a trend that will only increase as deserts advance, forests are felled and sea-levels rise. Mega-crises may well become the new normal. Those are all threats to human security, as well as to international peace and security. . . .

The Security Council can play a vital role in making clear the link between climate change, peace and security. The members of the Council bear a unique responsibility to mobilize national and international action to confront the very real threat of climate change and the specific threats to international peace and security that derive from it. Of course, nothing would build a more lasting foundation for a peaceful world than securing sustainable development for all of our citizens.[9]

The Executive Secretary of the UN Environment Programme, Achim Steiner, also addressed the Council, stressing the historic nature of the challenge:

I hope that historians in 50 years looking back at the decisions we are making today will see an international community using the knowledge available—including un-avoidable uncertainties—to address cooperatively a phenomenon that, as I said earlier, is unprecedented in its implications for civilization. . . . If we take into account food insecurity, natural disasters and the potential for conflict and tensions over ever more scarce resources, together with displacement and the potential disappearance of entire nation states from our world map—including their culture, identity and sovereignty—within a time span of 50 to 100 years, we have to recognize that climate change is an issue that needs to be viewed not just from a scientific and technological perspective of managing carbon emissions, but truly from a geopolitical and security perspective. Our response will either unite us in cooperative action or divide us and lead us into chaos, tension and potential conflict.

Concept: Is Climate Change a Security Threat?

Several member-states embraced the idea that climate change presents a security challenge. The president of Nauru, who came to New York to address the Council in person, stressed the existential security threat that climate change poses for Small Island Developing States:

Solidarity demands more than sympathetic words demonstrated by formally rec-ognizing that climate change is a threat to international peace and security. It is a threat as great as nuclear proliferation or terrorism, and it carries the potential to destabilize Governments and ignite conflict. Neither nuclear proliferation nor terrorism has ever led to the disappearance of an entire nation, though that is what we are confronted with today.

Bangladesh, a country with much low-lying land at particular risk of flooding, highlighted numerous extreme climate-related weather events that have undermined security:

> Recently, we have seen how wildfires in Russia and Australia; floods in Pakistan; earthquakes in Haiti, Chile and New Zealand; the tsunami in Japan; tornados and twisters in the United States and drought in Africa have affected developed and developing countries alike. It is true that climate change–induced food insecurity, the uprooting of populations and related adversity constitute a threat to international peace and security.

A number of European nations also spoke about less proximate security implications of climate change. France, for example, stressed the risk of destabilizing impacts on agricultural productivity and water resource availability. However, some countries questioned the certainty of such pronouncements. As India put it:

> Climate change, in an overarching sense, is beginning to impact the security of the global community in the same way as poverty, food security and underdevelopment continue to undermine international well-being. Sweeping generalizations about climate change leading to droughts, floods, changes in weather patterns, water and food scarcity, and violent conflicts are, however, yet to be fully tested against empirical and scientific analyses.

Russia argued that in light of such uncertainties, Council consideration of the issue was inappropriate:

> Russia is skeptical about the repeated attempts that have been made to place on the agenda of the Security Council the issue of the threat posed by climate change to international peace and security. . . .
>
> The report of the General Assembly[10] . . . does not contain serious arguments to support the position of those States advocating that this issue be placed on the Council's agenda. The report refers only to hypothetical impacts of climate change on security and is not able to precisely predict them. It fails to provide empirical data establishing any correlation between these phenomena. Although it contains very balanced conclusions and recommendations on further work in this area, it is very telling that the Security Council is not once referred to in the report.

Brazil likewise questioned the wisdom of adopting a security approach:

> The links between climate change and development and between security and development are clear and have been explicitly recognized by the United Nations. The possible

security implications of climate change, however, are far less obvious. Environmental impacts do not threaten international peace and security on their own. In certain circumstances, the adverse effects of climate change may contribute to aggravating existing threats to international peace and security. . . .

Security tools are appropriate to deal with concrete threats to international peace and security, but they are inadequate to address complex and multidimensional issues such as climate change.

Legitimacy: Does the Security Council Have a Mandate to Discuss Climate Change?

The debate also touched on an ongoing point of contention about the Council itself: how broadly or narrowly to interpret its mandate for action. Many states made clear that their opposition was based on their view that an issue such as climate change was outside the Council's mandate. Argentina made this point on behalf of the Group of 77 developing countries (G-77, a developing-country caucus within the United Nations that now includes over 130 member-states):

The Council's primary responsibility is the maintenance of international peace and security, as set out in the Charter of the United Nations. Other issues, including those related to economic and social development, are assigned by the Charter to the Economic and Social Council and the General Assembly. The ever-increasing encroachment by the Security Council on the roles and responsibilities of other principal entities of the United Nations represents a distortion of the principles and purposes of the Charter, infringes on their authority and compromises the rights of the general membership of the United Nations. . . .

We maintain that the United Nations Framework Convention on Climate Change (UNFCCC) is the primary international intergovernmental forum for negotiating the global response to climate change.

Egypt, speaking on behalf of the 120 members of the Non-Aligned Movement (NAM, a political coalition of states that originated in the 1960s to oppose the geopolitical polarization of the Cold War), expressed similar sentiments:

The Non-Aligned Movement stresses that the Security Council must fully observe all provisions of the Charter establishing the delicate balance among the competencies of all principal organs. . . .

The Non-Aligned Movement therefore emphasizes that the Council's decision to hold this debate should not be considered a precedent, and that this debate should not result in any form of outcome that undermines the authority or mandate of the relevant bodies, processes and instruments of wider membership that already address climate change.

A number of developed countries expressed their frustration that discussion was being opposed with what they saw as bureaucratic technicalities. Australia argued that the Council, like all UN bodies, must have a role given the urgency of the challenge:

> Ultimately, the question as to where the responsibility for the issue of climate change lies is an easy one. The overwhelming nature of the challenge of climate change means that the responsibility lies with all of us, in every forum.

The United States was unusually blunt in condemning what it saw as obstructionism:

> We have dozens of countries represented in this body and in this very Chamber whose very existence is threatened. They have asked the Council to demonstrate our understanding that their security is profoundly threatened. Instead, because of the refusal of a few to accept our responsibility, by its silence the Council is saying in effect "tough luck." That is more than disappointing; it is pathetic, short-sighted and, frankly, a dereliction of duty.

Interestingly, while aligning themselves with the G-77 and NAM statements, several members of these blocs advanced more nuanced positions that did allow some role for Security Council discussion of the issue. Papua New Guinea pointed out that the Council has addressed other "nontraditional" security issues without dominating the discussion or undermining other UN entities:

> We observe that the Council has been previously called upon to exercise its mandate to address issues such as development, HIV/AIDS, children in armed conflict, women in conflict and other issues. While these issues have remained on the agenda of the Council, that has not diluted the primacy of those relevant United Nations organs and agencies that have direct oversight—for example, the Economic and Social Council over the development agenda.

In a statement representative of many Small Island Developing States, Palau argued that while climate change was not a conventional military threat, the fact that it threatens the existence of entire states places it clearly within the Council's mandate:

> The Security Council is responsible for carrying out the most crucial international tasks and is, as a result, accorded extraordinary powers by the Charter. When a threat to international peace and security arises, the Security Council has the mandate and limitless ability to act. That basic function under the Charter should be uncontroversial. Palau is surprised and disappointed, therefore, to hear any opposition whatsoever to an outcome from this debate. . . . While the causes of this threat are novel, the effects, which endanger the sovereignty and territorial integrity of Member States, fit squarely within the Council's traditional mandate.

Capability: is the Security Council a Competent and Representative Body to Address Climate Change?

Alongside the question of legitimacy lies an equally sharp debate about whether the Security Council is competent to do anything useful. Most developed countries argued that considering climate change among the range of potential causes of conflict would strengthen the Security Council's capacity to prevent and resolve conflicts. As the United Kingdom, which had organized the first debate in 2007, reasoned:

> The Council is tasked with the maintenance of international peace and security. It can and indeed should, therefore, consider emerging threats. Conflict prevention is a key element in the Council's work. The United Kingdom believes that it is through discussion and better awareness of new and cross-cutting security challenges, including the effects of climate change, that the Council can best fulfill its responsibility to prevent future conflict....
>
> History will not judge us kindly if, through complacency or ideology, we duck this important responsibility.

Other states argued that the Council's deliberations would have the benefit of injecting political momentum into the climate debate. As Singapore outlined:

> The Security Council can also make an important contribution to the climate change discussion in two ways. First, it can help to build greater awareness of the catastrophic long-term consequences of climate change, including the possible security consequences. Secondly, the Security Council can help to reinforce ongoing efforts to inject political momentum into the UNFCCC negotiating process....
>
> Let me conclude with a quote from Ralph Waldo Emerson, who once said that "What you do speaks so loudly that I cannot hear what you say." I hope the debate today will not become a substitute for action, but will be a prelude to action.

Many countries, however, argued that the Security Council was poorly placed to address climate change. China's statement was representative:

> Climate change may affect security, but it is fundamentally a sustainable development issue. The Security Council lacks expertise in climate change and the necessary means and resources. Moreover, the Council is not a forum for decision-making with universal representation. Its discussions are not aimed at putting together a broadly accepted programme, nor can they take the place of the UNFCCC negotiations among the 193 United Nations Member States.
>
> It is the general belief of the majority of developing countries that the Council's discussion on climate change will neither contribute to the mitigation efforts of countries nor assist affected countries in effectively responding to climate change.

China's statement underscored the fact that the Council's ability to act is not simply one of technical capacity but of political legitimacy as well, something India also emphasized:

> We must not confuse political motion with action. Climate change needs the collective understanding and support of all Member States. Action must therefore lie in the UNFCCC.

Bolivia pressed this theme even more strongly, raising pointed questions not only about the Council's unrepresentative nature but also about the culpability of the particular states wielding the most power within the Council:

> While we recognize the security dimension of this issue, we do not believe that the issue should be addressed by the Security Council because the representatives of the largest emitters of greenhouse gases are precisely those States with permanent seats in the Council and the right to veto. Given those conditions, is it possible for the Security Council to adopt resolutions on sanctions or reparations that effectively hold those countries responsible for the damage they are causing?
>
> The security aspect of climate change should be dealt with in a forum where the guilty States do not possess permanent seats or the right to veto. It should be discussed in a forum where the main victims are adequately represented: the island States threatened with disappearance, countries with glaciers, the countries of Africa, and all of the developing countries that have to pay for damage that they did not cause. Today, the only forum with this level of participation is the General Assembly. For that reason, all aspects of climate change should be addressed comprehensively by that body.

Russia was similarly skeptical of the value the Council would bring to addressing climate change:

> We believe that involving the Security Council in a regular review of the issue of climate change would bring no added value whatsoever and would merely lead to a further politicization of the issue and increased disagreements among countries, which would be an extremely undesirable outcome.

Action: What Could the Security Council Actually Do?

Although the debate was dominated by discussion of whether the Security Council should even be discussing climate change, a few countries did suggest concrete actions the Council could take. The Pacific Small Island Developing States laid out a series of recommendations, which the president of Nauru presented:

The Security Council has also asked us what concrete steps it can take to address the issue. Allow me to tell it.

The Council should start by requesting the immediate appointment of a special representative on climate and security. That individual's primary responsibility should be to analyse the projected security impacts of climate change so that the Council and all Member States can understand what lies ahead. The Council should also request an assessment of the capacity of the United Nations system to respond to such impacts so that vulnerable countries can be assured that it is up to the task.

These proposals are the absolute minimum required to move the international community from a culture of reaction to one of preparedness.

Belgium also offered recommendations on possible preventive action:

It would be irresponsible to reduce climate change to its negotiating aspect. An overall framework for preventive diplomacy is indispensable to alleviate the consequences outlined in the reports of the Intergovernmental Panel on Climate Change, especially for the most vulnerable countries.

We have to take concrete steps towards a coherent approach within the United Nations system. Our international institutions should be prepared to respond to the impacts of climate change and the scarcity it will cause.

Finally, although Hungary raised the issue of providing climate-related guidance for peacekeeping activities, no member-state went as far as to endorse an idea that had been the subject of media speculation in advance of the debate: Would the United Nations mandate a "Green Helmets" peacekeeping force to respond to climate change disasters?[11]

Among the countries skeptical of or opposing a Security Council role on climate change, several alluded to the hypocrisy inherent in a situation where the P5—which emit the largest amounts of greenhouse gases—are telling other countries to take action. Not surprisingly, they focused attention on the need for action by the major emitters. Costa Rica's statement was representative:

The permanent members of the Security Council—all major emitters and, with their right of veto, endowed with exceptional powers within this organ—should in particular make a clear political commitment to reducing greenhouse gases. That would be the best and largest contribution they could make to ensuring that climate change does not become an even greater threat to international peace and security.

Nigeria underscored this point, while also stressing the need for adaptation assistance:

Seated around this table are those who could encourage developed countries to implement their commitments to reducing emissions and supporting developing countries with the requisite technological and financial assistance to address climate change effectively. Nigeria therefore calls for enhanced efforts for the equitable distribution of adaptation funds and capacity-building programming, as well as promotion of the Global Environment Facility programme steered by the United Nations Development Programme.

The Climate Security Council?
A Presidential Statement, Unanswered Questions

In total, sixty-two member-states spoke in the day-long debate, making this one of the largest meetings in the Council's sixty-five-year history. In the end, it did prove possible to agree on a cautious Presidential Statement that declared the Council's concern, reiterated the primacy of the UNFCCC on the issue, and called on the secretary-general to provide climate-related "contextual information" in his reporting to the Council on conflict situations around the world.[12]

Amid the controversy over the Security Council's proper role, there remain a number of unanswered questions concerning the security implications of climate change. Some of these were well articulated by Portugal:

How do we deal with populations that need to be resettled? Where do they go? How do they get there? How does one manage and defuse the tensions that resettlement entails? How do we address the legal consequences of the loss of territory, such as the definition of borders, economic zones and continental shelf rights? Our failure to deal collectively with such questions may lead not only to humanitarian disaster but also to a surge of serious tensions in a vast region, threatening peace.

Neither the Security Council, nor the UN system as a whole, has yet provided clear answers to these questions.

NOTES

1. There was a third Security Council debate on climate change in February 2013, jointly organized by Pakistan and the United Kingdom as an informal or "Arria formula" meeting of interested Council members. See Security Council Report, "What's in Blue: Arria Formula Meeting on Climate Change" (2013); available at http://www.whatsinblue.org/2013/02/arria-formula-meeting-on-climate-change.php.

2. Parts of this introductory section are adapted from J. Thwaites, "Pakistan's Shifting Discourse on Climate Change at the United Nations Security Council," *Journal of International Service* 23, no. 1 (Spring 2014).

3. Charter of the United Nations (1945), Chapter V, Article 24.

4. Charter of the United Nations (1945), Chapter VII, Article 39.

5. UN Security Council, *The Security Council Working Methods Handbook* (New York: United Nations, 2012).

6. For a full transcript of the 2007 debate, see UN Security Council (2007), 5663rd meeting, Security Council Open Debate: Energy, Security and Climate, Provisional Record (S/PV.5663 and S/PV.5663 Resumption 1).

7. P. Adriázola, A. Carius, L. Ruthner, D. Tänzler, J. Thwaites, and S. Wolters, *Climate Diplomacy: New Approaches for Foreign Policy* (Berlin: Adelphi/German Federal Foreign Office, 2013), p.18; available at http://www.adelphi.de/en/publications/dok/43509.php?pid=1795.

8. UN Security Council, Annex to the Letter Dated 1 July 2011 from the Permanent Representative of Germany to the United Nations Addressed to the Secretary-General: Maintenance of International Peace and Security: The Impact of Climate Change: Concept Note (S/2011/408).

9. This and all subsequent quoted statements are excerpted from the transcript of the 2011 debate. See UN Security Council (2011), 6587th meeting, Security Council Open Debate: Maintenance of International Peace and Security: The Impact of Climate Change. Provisional Record (S/PV.6587 and S/PV.6587 Resumption 1).

10. This is a reference to a 2009 report of the UN secretary-general to the General Assembly; see United Nations General Assembly (2009), Climate Change and Its Possible Security Implications: Report of the Secretary-General (A/64/350).

11. S. Goldenberg, "UN Security Council to Consider Climate Change Peacekeeping," *The Guardian,* July 20, 2011; available at http://www.theguardian.com/environment/2011/jul/20/un-climate-change-peacekeeping.

12. UN Security Council (2011), Statement by the President of the Security Council (S/PRST/2011/15).

PART SIX

ECOLOGICAL JUSTICE

SOME OF THE MAIN CONTROVERSIES SURROUNDING THE PARADIGMS OF SUSTAINABLE development and environmental security involve questions of justice. Critics have raised concerns that these paradigms can blur issues of fairness, power, and distribution. Worse, environmental arguments might be used to justify measures that deepen social inequality, promote authoritarian measures, or otherwise concentrate power in the hands of elites. Thus, questions of justice are raised not only by the socially unequal effects of pollution and ecosystem destruction but also by the socially unequal effects of environmental policy responses.

Concerns about the relationship between environmental protection and social equity have been voiced since the Stockholm conference first placed the environment on the international agenda in 1972.[1] As the pace of environmental degradation has accelerated and policy responses to environmental problems have grown more complex and ambitious, the question of how various forms of environmental change affect different social groups has become increasingly central to environmental debates. Today, the link between ecology and justice is articulated by a diverse array of voices: people of color in cities throughout the United States are challenging the "environmental racism" of concentrating toxic facilities in minority communities; rural women in India and elsewhere are protesting the impacts of deforestation and large-dam construction on their lives and communities; green activists in Europe are framing climate change as a matter of injustice against poor people, vulnerable communities, and future generations; indigenous peoples are organizing to reclaim their lands and their traditions as an alternative to the ecological onslaught of modernity.[2]

Given this diversity of causes and concerns, is it possible to identify a single paradigm of ecological justice based on a common set of core arguments? While there are many different visions of an ecologically just world, a number of common themes lie at the heart of the ecological justice paradigm: first, the close linkage between violence against nature and violence against human beings; second, the linkage between the power to control nature and the power to control people; third, the observation that not all people or groups are affected equally by environmental problems or by the responses to those problems; fourth, the pursuit of solutions that are both ecologically sound and socially just, because neither can endure in the absence of the other; and fifth, the need for a fundamental transformation of politics, economics, and society.

The eco-justice paradigm can be used to analyze questions of ecology and justice at many different social levels. The question of justice among nations, with a particular focus on North-South inequality, was a central dispute at the Stockholm

313

conference (see the selection by Castro in Part One). Twenty years later at the Rio Earth Summit the question had not been resolved. According to Mahathir Mohamad, at that time Malaysia's prime minister, addressing the Rio conference:

> We know that the 25 per cent of the world population who are rich consume 85 per cent of its wealth and produce 90 per cent of its waste. Mathematically speaking, if the rich reduce their wasteful consumption by 25 per cent, worldwide pollution will be reduced by 22.5 per cent. But if the poor 75 per cent reduce consumption totally and disappear from this earth altogether, the reduction in pollution will only be by 10 per cent.
>
> It is what the rich do that counts, not what the poor do, however much they do it. . . . The rich will not accept a progressive and meaningful cutback in their emissions of carbon dioxide and other greenhouse gases because it will be a cost to them and retard their progress. Yet they expect the poor people of the developing countries to stifle even their minute growth as if it will cost them nothing. . . . Malaysia will do what can reasonably be expected of it for the environment.[3]

Despite the optimistic view at the 1992 Earth Summit that "sustainable development" had merged the conflicting concerns of the North and the South with regard to environment and development, distributional issues have remained central to the North-South environmental debate. The question of justice applies not only to who should pay the costs of environmental protection but also to who holds decision-making power and who bears historical responsibility for the planet's predicament.

One of the most important themes of the eco-justice paradigm, however, is the idea that global environmental justice is not simply a question of equity among nation-states. Power and risk are distributed unequally not only among nations but also within them, in social divisions based on race, class, gender, ethnicity, and region. Inequality of access, power, and voice are issues not only in interstate negotiations but also within societies, in the workings of intergovernmental organizations, and even in dealings among environmentalists and other nonstate actors.

Certainly, environmental threats such as climate change raise dramatic concerns about how both the effects of change and the costs of adjusting to change are distributed in society. We begin this section with an excerpt from a report by the office of the UN High Commissioner for Human Rights, which examines links between climate change and human rights. Historically, the relationship between human rights and the environment has been complex and, at times, uneasy. Many human rights activists have been uncomfortable expanding the definition of *human rights* to include "socioeconomic" rights such as environmental quality alongside more traditional concepts of political rights and civil liberties; at the same time, many eco-justice advocates have viewed a human right to clean water or breathable air as simply a minimum standard for human existence, rather than in terms of the more ambitious aim of social equality. Nonetheless, as demonstrated in the report's many substantive connections between climate change and rights at risk, the rights framework can be a powerful device for linking justice and sustainability.

The inequality that goes with environmental harm is not limited to income level. When the devastating tsunami that slammed into Southeast Asia in December 2004 receded, a troubling pattern emerged: the floodwaters had brought death and injury disproportionately to women and girls. A report by the grassroots development organization Oxfam International documented gender disparities in the tsunami's consequences in several villages in India, Sri Lanka, and Indonesia, and offered this explanation:

> Some of the causes of these patterns are similar across the region: many women died because they stayed behind to look for their children and other relatives; men more often than women can swim; men more often than women can climb trees. But differences too are important: women in Aceh, for example, traditionally have a high level of participation in the labor force, but the wave struck on a Sunday morning when they were at home and the men were out on errands away from the seafront. Women in India play a major role in fishing and were waiting on the shore for the fishermen to bring in the catch, which they would then process and sell in the local market. In Sri Lanka in Batticoloa District, the tsunami hit at the hour women on the east coast usually took their baths in the sea.[4]

If, as many climate scientists fear, climate change brings with it an increase in the frequency and intensity of extreme weather events such as droughts and storms, then programs that promote climate adaptation, social resilience, and disaster risk reduction become essential. Such programs will have to grapple centrally with the reality that different social groups are impacted differently. We include in Chapter 29 a short training manual, put together by Oxfam, on how to ensure that the organization's disaster risk reduction work is gender-sensitive.

The possibility that such policy responses will not be sensitive to the needs of particularly vulnerable social groups raises another important theme of ecological justice: that the "solutions" to environmental problems also can be unjust, both locally and globally, in which case they may not be solutions at all. This idea is evident in indigenous peoples' rejection of dialogues between developers and environmental organizations that exclude them (see Chapter 7 in Part One). The essay by Nancy Lee Peluso (Chapter 30) raises the same concerns in an even more provocative fashion. Writing at the time of the 1992 Rio Earth Summit, Peluso argued that international environmental organizations, detached from the reality of local resource struggles, sometimes participated in environmental preservation efforts that demonized local people and bolstered oppressive, authoritarian regimes. Using wildlife conservation efforts in Kenya as an example, Peluso argued that the result—"coercing conservation"—was to pit the environment against social justice considerations, precluding an outcome that is both socially and ecologically sustainable.

While some conservation organizations have taken such lessons on board, questions remain about the commitment of the conservation community as a whole to involving local communities in efforts to protect nature.[5] Questions arise when "solutions" involve dramatic changes for local patterns of land use, land tenure, property rights, and access to nature. Here we include two contemporary examples: the impact of supposedly "sustainable" fuel production for the European market on land rights and poverty in West Africa, and the controversies surrounding efforts to sequester carbon by reducing deforestation and desertification. On biofuels, the Liberian environmental activist Silas Kpanan'Ayoung Siakor points out (in Chapter 31) that the cost of expanding production of the agricultural inputs for so-called green biofuels has been to push poor farmers off the land. Siakor's critique is hardly an antienvironmental rant: in 2006 he received the prestigious Goldman Environmental Prize for his courageous work in documenting the links among timber cutting, illicit revenues, the arms trade, and Liberia's devastating civil war. He argues that we should challenge the "sustainability" of a renewable-energy global commodity chain that relies on "land grabs," social displacement, and deepening poverty to feed the world's consumption machine with nominally green fuels.

Our second example of the need to evaluate the distributive consequences of nominally "green" solutions is seen in the controversies surrounding REDD+, which stands for Reducing Emissions from Deforestation and Forest Degradation. Deforestation plays a nontrivial role in greenhouse-gas emissions (perhaps as much as 20 percent). As the world's effort to negotiate limits on the use of fossil fuels has stalled, some have argued that land-use mechanisms are an increasingly important avenue for climate-change mitigation efforts. The concept of REDD+ is intended to create financial incentives for such land protections, either through development assistance or by allowing polluters to meet regulatory requirements by investing in ecosystem-protection schemes far from the site of their polluting activities. Such payment-for-ecosystem schemes remain controversial, despite their obvious potential for carbon sequestration. They shift the locus of climate responses from the climate problem's origin in the world's industrialized urban centers to rural areas in developing countries, and they threaten (once again) to impose "solutions" without the voice of people who will primarily pay the cost of adjustment. We include in Chapter 32 a short briefing paper on these issues from REDD-Monitor, an activist blog that "aims to facilitate discussion about the concept of reducing deforestation and forest degradation as a way of addressing climate change" and which has raised substantial skepticism about trading in carbon credits as a way to address global warming.[6]

We conclude this section with a short essay by the economist and Nobel laureate Joseph Stiglitz, who points to yet another element of the environment-justice link: the need for a fair society as a platform from which to pursue the sometimes difficult challenges of sustainability. Stiglitz argues that a certain degree of perceived fairness in society is likely to be a prerequisite for willingness to participate in the project of building a sustainable future. If society pursues policies (environmental or otherwise) that erode social solidarity, then the capacity to make the kinds of collective adjustments that are needed is one more casualty of growing inequality. If Stiglitz is correct, then environmental policies that worsen inequalities rather than addressing them may be moving us further from sustainability, even if they succeed in imposing short-term environmental gains.

If there is a unifying theme across the voices in this section, it is to reject the notion that effective environmental protection requires increasingly authoritarian governance. On the contrary, these authors argue that genuine sustainability and meaningful environmental security will require responses to environmental problems that are not only ecologically effective but also socially just in their impacts and participatory in the ways they are conceived and executed.

Thinking Critically

1. After reading the essays in this section, are you persuaded that the environment is a social justice issue? Must there be social justice for there to be environmental protection? Are there difficult trade-offs to be made between these two values?

2. Do you accept the suggestion that some types of global environmental protection impose an unfair burden on the global South? Does this mean that the resistance of many governments of the South to particular forms of international environmental protection has the effect of promoting social justice? What might the Coordinating Body for the Indigenous Peoples' Organizations of the Amazon Basin (COICA) (Chapter 8 in Part One) have to say to the head of state of a developing country who claimed that primary responsibility rested with the global North, as Mahathir Mohamad of Malaysia stated at the 1992 Earth Summit? How might the latter respond?

3. Are the views of globalization in this section consistent with that of the Working Group on Development and Environment in the Americas (discussed in Part Two)? How are they similar or different?

4. Contrast the picture of international environmental NGOs drawn by Peluso with the essay by Jethro Pettit in Part Two. Are Pettit's concerns about the challenges of solidarity within the environmental movement being borne out in this case? What sorts of adjustments in social movement coalitions are required to address these concerns?

5. Governments focused on the problem of climate change have spent most of their time bargaining over which countries must cut their greenhouse-gas emissions and by how much. Does a human rights analysis of the climate change problem suggest a different or expanded agenda for international negotiations? What additional responsibilities of nations, individually and collectively, should be identified?

NOTES

1. For a discussion of some of these issues prior to the Stockholm conference, see United Nations, *Development and Environment: Report and Working Papers of a Panel of Experts Convened by the Secretary General of the U.N. Conference on the Human Environment,* Founex, Switzerland, June 4–12, 1971.

2. For a discussion of the links between ecology and social justice, see Nicholas Low and Brendan Gleeson, *Justice, Society, and Nature* (New York: Routledge, 1998).

3. Mahathir Mohamad, "Statement to the U.N. Conference on Environment and Development," *Environmental Policy and Law* 22, no. 4 (1992): 232.

4. Oxfam International, "The Tsunami's Impact on Women," *Oxfam Briefing Note,* March 2005.

5. Mac Chapin, "A Challenge to Conservationists," *World Watch* 17, no. 6 (November/December 2004): 17–31.

6. The text of this briefing paper is available at http://www.redd-monitor.org/.

28

THE RELATIONSHIP BETWEEN CLIMATE CHANGE AND HUMAN RIGHTS

OFFICE OF THE UNITED NATIONS
HIGH COMMISSIONER FOR HUMAN RIGHTS*

Climate change, environmental harm and human rights

16. An increase in global average temperatures of approximately 2° C will have major, and predominantly negative, effects on ecosystems across the globe, on the goods and services they provide. Already today, climate change is among the most important drivers of ecosystem changes, along with overexploitation of resources and pollution.[15] Moreover, global warming will exacerbate the harmful effects of environmental pollution, including higher levels of ground-level ozone in urban areas. In view of such effects, which have implications for a wide range of human rights, it is relevant to discuss the relationship between human rights and the environment.

17. Principle 1 of the 1972 Declaration of the United Nations Conference on the Human Environment (the Stockholm Declaration) states that there is "a fundamental right to freedom, equality and adequate conditions of life, in an environment of a quality that permits a life of dignity and well-being." The Stockholm

Declaration reflects a general recognition of the interdependence and interrelatedness of human rights and the environment.[16]

18. While the universal human rights treaties do not refer to a specific right to a safe and healthy environment, the United Nations human rights treaty bodies all recognize the intrinsic link between the environment and the realization of a range of human rights, such as the right to life, to health, to food, to water, and to housing.[17] The Convention on the Rights of the Child provides that States parties shall take appropriate measures to combat disease and malnutrition "through the provision of adequate nutritious foods and clean drinking water, taking into consideration the dangers and risks of environmental pollution."[18]

19. Equally, the Committee on Economic, Social and Cultural Rights (CESCR) has clarified that the right to adequate food requires the adoption of "appropriate economic, environmental and social policies" and that the right to health extends to its underlying determinants, including a healthy environment.[19]

Effects on specific rights

20. Whereas global warming will potentially have implications for the full range of human rights, the following subsections provide examples of rights which seem to relate most directly to climate change–related impacts identified by IPCC [Intergovernmental Panel on Climate Change].

1. The right to life

21. The right to life is explicitly protected under the International Covenant on Civil and Political Rights and the Convention on the Rights of the Child.[20] The Human Rights Committee has described the right to life as the "supreme right," "basic to all human rights," and it is a right from which no derogation is permitted even in time of public emergency.[21] Moreover, the Committee has clarified that the right to life imposes an obligation on States to take positive measures for its protection, including taking measures to reduce infant mortality, malnutrition and epidemics.[22] The Convention on the Rights of the Child explicitly links the right to life to the obligation of States "to ensure to the maximum extent possible the survival and development of the child."[23] According to the Committee on the Rights of the Child, the right to survival and development must be implemented in a holistic manner, "through the enforcement of all the other provisions of the Convention, including rights to health, adequate nutrition, social security, an adequate standard of living, a healthy and safe environment. . . ."[24]

22. A number of observed and projected effects of climate change will pose direct and indirect threats to human lives. IPCC AR4 projects with high confidence an increase in people suffering from death, disease and injury from heat waves,

floods, storms, fires and droughts. Equally, climate change will affect the right to life through an increase in hunger and malnutrition and related disorders impacting on child growth and development, cardio-respiratory morbidity and mortality related to ground-level ozone.[25]

23. Climate change will exacerbate weather-related disasters which already have devastating effects on people and their enjoyment of the right to life, particularly in the developing world. For example, an estimated 262 million people were affected by climate disasters annually from 2000 to 2004, of whom over 98 percent live in developing countries.[26] Tropical cyclone hazards, affecting approximately 120 million people annually, killed an estimated 250,000 people from 1980 to 2000.[27]

24. Protection of the right to life, generally and in the context of climate change, is closely related to measures for the fulfillment of other rights, such as those related to food, water, health and housing. With regard to weather-related natural disasters, this close interconnectedness of rights is reflected in the Inter-Agency Standing Committee (IASC) operational guidelines on human rights and natural disasters.[28]

2. The right to adequate food

25. The right to food is explicitly mentioned under the International Covenant on Economic, Social and Cultural Rights, the Convention on the Rights of the Child and the Convention on the Rights of Persons with Disabilities and implied in general provisions on an adequate standard of living of the Convention on the Elimination of All Forms of Discrimination against Women and the International Convention on the Elimination of All Forms of Racial Discrimination.[29] In addition to a right to adequate food, the International Covenant on Economic, Social and Cultural Rights also enshrines "the fundamental right of everyone to be free from hunger."[30] Elements of the right to food include the availability of adequate food (including through the possibility of feeding oneself from natural resources) and accessible to all individuals under the jurisdiction of a State. Equally, States must ensure freedom from hunger and take necessary action to alleviate hunger, even in times of natural or other disasters.[31]

26. As a consequence of climate change, the potential for food production is projected initially to increase at mid to high latitudes with an increase in global average temperature in the range of 1–3°C. However, at lower latitudes crop productivity is projected to decrease, increasing the risk of hunger and food insecurity in the poorer regions of the world.[32] According to one estimate, an additional 600 million people will face malnutrition due to climate change,[33] with a particularly negative effect on sub-Saharan Africa.[34] Poor people living in developing countries are particularly vulnerable given their disproportionate dependency on climate-sensitive resources for their food and livelihoods.[35]

27. The Special Rapporteur on the right to food has documented how extreme climate events are increasingly threatening livelihoods and food security.[36] In

responding to this threat, the realization of the right to adequate food requires that special attention be given to vulnerable and disadvantaged groups, including people living in disaster-prone areas and indigenous peoples whose livelihood may be threatened.[37]

3. The right to water

28. CESCR has defined the right to water as the right of everyone to sufficient, safe, acceptable, physically accessible and affordable water for personal and domestic uses, such as drinking, food preparation and personal and household hygiene.[38] The Convention on the Elimination of All Forms of Discrimination against Women and the Convention on the Rights of Persons with Disabilities explicitly refer to access to water services in provisions on an adequate standard of living, while the Convention on the Rights of the Child refers to the provision of "clean drinking water" as part of the measures States shall take to combat disease and malnutrition.[39]

29. Loss of glaciers and reductions in snow cover are projected to increase and to negatively affect water availability for more than one-sixth of the world's population supplied by meltwater from mountain ranges. Weather extremes, such as drought and flooding, will also impact on water supplies.[40] Climate change will thus exacerbate existing stresses on water resources and compound the problem of access to safe drinking water, currently denied to an estimated 1.1 billion people globally and a major cause of morbidity and disease.[41] In this regard, climate change interacts with a range of other causes of water stress, such as population growth, environmental degradation, poor water management, poverty and inequality.[42]

30. As various studies document, the negative effects of climate change on water supply and on the effective enjoyment of the right to water can be mitigated through the adoption of appropriate measures and policies.[43]

4. The right to health

31. The right to the highest attainable standard of physical and mental health (the right to health) is most comprehensively addressed in article 12 of the International Covenant on Economic, Social and Cultural Rights and referred to in five other core international human rights treaties.[44] This right implies the enjoyment of, and equal access to, appropriate health care and, more broadly, to goods, services and conditions which enable a person to live a healthy life. Underlying determinants of health include adequate food and nutrition, housing, safe drinking water and adequate sanitation, and a healthy environment.[45] Other key elements

are the availability, accessibility (both physically and economically) and quality of health and health-care facilities, goods and services.[46]

32. Climate change is projected to affect the health status of millions of people, including through increases in malnutrition, increased diseases and injury due to extreme weather events, and an increased burden of diarrheal, cardio-respiratory and infectious diseases.[47] Global warming may also affect the spread of malaria and other vector-borne diseases in some parts of the world.[48] Overall, the negative health effects will disproportionately be felt in sub-Saharan Africa, South Asia and the Middle East. Poor health and malnutrition increase vulnerability and reduce the capacity of individuals and groups to adapt to climate change.

33. Climate change constitutes a severe additional stress to health systems worldwide, prompting the Special Rapporteur on the right to health to warn that a failure of the international community to confront the health threats posed by global warming will endanger the lives of millions of people.[49] Most at risk are those individuals and communities with a low adaptive capacity. Conversely, addressing poor health is one central aspect of reducing vulnerability to the effects of climate change.

34. Non-climate-related factors, such as education, health care, [and] public health initiatives, are critical in determining how global warming will affect the health of populations.[50] Protecting the right to health in the face of climate change will require comprehensive measures, including mitigating the adverse impacts of global warming on underlying determinants of health and giving priority to protecting vulnerable individuals and communities.

5. The right to adequate housing

35. The right to adequate housing is enshrined in several core international human rights instruments and most comprehensively under the International Covenant on Economic, Social and Cultural Rights as an element of the right to an adequate standard of living.[51] The right to adequate housing has been defined as "the right to live somewhere in security, peace and dignity."[52] Core elements of this right include security of tenure, protection against forced evictions,[53] availability of services, materials, facilities and infrastructure, affordability, habitability, accessibility, location and cultural adequacy.[54]

36. Observed and projected climate change will affect the right to adequate housing in several ways. Sea level rise and storm surges will have a direct impact on many coastal settlements.[55] In the Arctic region and in low-lying island States such impacts have already led to the relocation of peoples and communities.[56] Settlements in low-lying mega-deltas are also particularly at risk, as evidenced by the millions of people and homes affected by flooding in recent years.

37. The erosion of livelihoods, partly caused by climate change, is a main "push" factor for increasing rural to urban migration. Many will move to urban slums and informal settlements where they are often forced to build shelters in hazardous areas.[57] Already today, an estimated 1 billion people live in urban slums on fragile hillsides or flood-prone riverbanks and face acute vulnerability to extreme climate events.[58]

38. Human rights guarantees in the context of climate change include: (a) adequate protection of housing from weather hazards (habitability of housing); (b) access to housing away from hazardous zones; (c) access to shelter and disaster preparedness in cases of displacement caused by extreme weather events; (d) protection of communities that are relocated away from hazardous zones, including protection against forced evictions without appropriate forms of legal or other protection, including adequate consultation with affected persons.[59]

6. The right to self-determination

39. The right to self-determination is a fundamental principle of international law. Common article 1, paragraph 1, of the International Covenant on Economic, Social and Cultural Rights and the International Covenant on Civil and Political Rights establishes that "all peoples have the right of self-determination," by virtue of which "they freely determine their political status and freely pursue their economic, social and cultural development."[60] Important aspects of the right to self-determination include the right of a people not to be deprived of its own means of subsistence and the obligation of a State party to promote the realization of the right to self-determination, including for people living outside its territory.[61] While the right to self-determination is a collective right held by peoples rather than individuals, its realization is an essential condition for the effective enjoyment of individual human rights.

40. Sea level rise and extreme weather events related to climate change are threatening the habitability and, in the longer term, the territorial existence of a number of low-lying island States. Equally, changes in the climate threaten to deprive indigenous peoples of their traditional territories and sources of livelihood. Either of these impacts would have implications for the right to self-determination.

41. The inundation and disappearance of small island States would have implications for the right to self-determination, as well as for the full range of human rights for which individuals depend on the State for their protection. The disappearance of a State for climate change–related reasons would give rise to a range of legal questions, including concerning the status of people inhabiting such disappearing territories and the protection afforded to them under international law (discussed further below). While there is no clear precedence to follow, it is clear that insofar as climate change poses a threat to the right of peoples to self-determination, States have a duty to take positive action, individually and jointly, to address and avert this

threat. Equally, States have an obligation to take action to avert climate change impacts which threaten the cultural and social identity of indigenous peoples.

Effects on specific groups

42. The effects of climate change will be felt most acutely by those segments of the population who are already in vulnerable situations due to factors such as poverty, gender, age, minority status and disability.[62] Under international human rights law, States are legally bound to address such vulnerabilities in accordance with the principle of equality and nondiscrimination.

43. Vulnerability and impact assessments in the context of climate change largely focus on impacts on economic sectors, such as health and water, rather than on the vulnerabilities of specific segments of the population.[63] Submissions to this report and other studies indicate awareness of the need for more detailed assessments at the country level and point to some of the factors which affect individuals and communities.

44. The present section focuses on factors determining vulnerability to climate change for women, children and indigenous peoples.

1. Women

45. Women are especially exposed to climate change–related risks due to existing gender discrimination, inequality and inhibiting gender roles. It is established that women, particularly elderly women and girls, are affected more severely and are more at risk during all phases of weather-related disasters: risk preparedness, warning communication and response, social and economic impacts, recovery and reconstruction.[64] The death rate of women is markedly higher than that of men during natural disasters (often linked to reasons such as: women are more likely to be looking after children, to be wearing clothes which inhibit movement and are less likely to be able to swim). This is particularly the case in disaster-affected societies in which the socioeconomic status of women is low.[65] Women are susceptible to gender-based violence during natural disasters and during migration, and girls are more likely to drop out of school when households come under additional stress. Rural women are particularly affected by effects on agriculture and deteriorating living conditions in rural areas. Vulnerability is exacerbated by factors such as unequal rights to property, exclusion from decision-making and difficulties in accessing information and financial services.[66]

46. Studies document how crucial for successful climate change adaptation the knowledge and capacities of women are. For example, there are numerous examples of how measures to empower women and to address discriminatory practices have increased the capacity of communities to cope with extreme weather events.[67]

47. International human rights standards and principles underline the need to adequately assess and address the gender-differentiated impacts of climate change. In the context of negotiations on the United Nations Framework Convention on Climate Change, States have highlighted gender-specific vulnerability assessments as important elements in determining adaptation options.[68] Yet, there is a general lack of accurate data disaggregated by gender in this area.

2. Children

48. Studies show that climate change will exacerbate existing health risks and undermine support structures that protect children from harm.[69] Overall, the health burden of climate change will primarily be borne by children in the developing world.[70] For example, extreme weather events and increased water stress already constitute leading causes of malnutrition and infant and child mortality and morbidity. Likewise, increased stress on livelihoods will make it more difficult for children to attend school. Girls will be particularly affected as traditional household chores, such as collecting firewood and water, require more time and energy when supplies are scarce. Moreover, like women, children have a higher mortality rate as a result of weather-related disasters.

49. As today's children and young persons will shape the world of tomorrow, children are central actors in promoting behavior change required to mitigate the effects of global warming. Children's knowledge and awareness of climate change also influence wider households and community actions.[71] Education on environmental matters among children is crucial and various initiatives at national and international levels seek to engage children and young people as actors in the climate change agenda.[72]

50. The Convention on the Rights of the Child, which enjoys near universal ratification, obliges States to take action to ensure the realization of all rights in the Convention for all children in their jurisdiction, including measures to safeguard children's right to life, survival and development through, inter alia, addressing problems of environmental pollution and degradation. Importantly, children must be recognized as active participants and stewards of natural resources in the promotion and protection of a safe and healthy environment.[73]

3. Indigenous peoples

51. Climate change, together with pollution and environmental degradation, poses a serious threat to indigenous peoples, who often live in marginal lands and fragile ecosystems which are particularly sensitive to alterations in the physical environment.[74] Climate change–related impacts have already led to the relocation of Inuit communities in polar regions and affected their traditional livelihoods. Indigenous

peoples inhabiting low-lying island States face similar pressures, threatening their cultural identity, which is closely linked to their traditional lands and livelihoods.[75]

52. Indigenous peoples have been voicing their concern about the impacts of climate change on their collective human rights and their rights as distinct peoples.[76] In particular, indigenous peoples have stressed the importance of giving them a voice in policymaking on climate change at both national and international levels and of taking into account and building upon their traditional knowledge.[77] As a study cited by the IPCC in its Fourth Assessment Report observes, "Incorporating indigenous knowledge into climate change policies can lead to the development of effective adaptation strategies that are cost-effective, participatory and sustainable."[78]

53. The United Nations Declaration on the Rights of Indigenous Peoples sets out several rights and principles of relevance to threats posed by climate change.[79] Core international human rights treaties also provide for protection of indigenous peoples, in particular with regard to the right to self-determination and rights related to culture.[80] The rights of indigenous peoples are also enshrined in [International Labour Organization] Convention No. 169 (1989) concerning Indigenous and Tribal Peoples in Independent Countries.

54. Indigenous peoples have brought several cases before national courts and regional and international human rights bodies claiming violations of human rights related to environmental issues. In 2005, a group of Inuit in the Canadian and Alaskan Arctic presented a case before the Inter-American Commission on Human Rights seeking compensation for alleged violations of their human rights resulting from climate change caused by greenhouse gas emissions from the United States of America.81 While the Inter-American Commission deemed the case inadmissible, it drew international attention to the threats posed by climate change to indigenous peoples. . . .

Conclusions

92. Climate change–related impacts, as set out in the assessment reports of the Intergovernmental Panel on Climate Change, have a range of implications for the effective enjoyment of human rights. The effects on human rights can be of a direct nature, such as the threat extreme weather events may pose to the right to life, but will often have an indirect and gradual effect on human rights, such as increasing stress on health systems and vulnerabilities related to climate change–induced migration.

93. The effects of climate change are already being felt by individuals and communities around the world. Particularly vulnerable are those living on the "front line" of climate change, in places where even small climatic changes can have catastrophic consequences for lives and livelihoods. Vulnerability due to geography is often compounded by a low capacity to adapt, rendering many of the

poorest countries and communities particularly vulnerable to the effects of climate change.

94. Within countries, existing vulnerabilities are exacerbated by the effects of climate change. Groups such as children, women, the elderly and persons with disabilities are often particularly vulnerable to the adverse effects of climate change on the enjoyment of their human rights. The application of a human rights approach in preventing and responding to the effects of climate change serves to empower individuals and groups, who should be perceived as active agents of change and not as passive victims.

95. Often the effects of climate change on human rights are determined by non-climatic factors, including discrimination and unequal power relationships. This underlines the importance of addressing human rights threats posed by climate change through adequate policies and measures which are coherent with overall human rights objectives. Human rights standards and principles should inform and strengthen policy measures in the area of climate change.

96. The physical impacts of global warming cannot easily be classified as human rights violations, not least because climate change–related harm often cannot clearly be attributed to acts or omissions of specific States. Yet, addressing that harm remains a critical human rights concern and obligation under international law. Hence, legal protection remains relevant as a safeguard against climate change–related risks and infringements of human rights resulting from policies and measures taken at the national level to address climate change.

97. There is a need for more detailed studies and data collection at [the] country level in order to assess the human rights impact of climate change–related phenomena and of policies and measures adopted to address climate change. In this regard, States could usefully provide information on measures to assess and address vulnerabilities and impacts related to climate change as they affect individuals and groups, in reporting to the United Nations human rights treaty monitoring bodies and the United Nations Framework Convention on Climate Change.

98. Further study is also needed of protection mechanisms for persons who may be considered to have been displaced within or across national borders due to climate change–related events and for those populations which may be permanently displaced as a consequence of inundation of low-lying areas and island States.

99. Global warming can only be dealt with through cooperation by all members of the international community. Equally, international assistance is required to ensure sustainable development pathways in developing countries and enable them to adapt to now unavoidable climate change. International human rights law complements the United Nations Framework Convention on Climate Change by underlining that international cooperation is not only expedient but also a human rights obligation and that its central objective is the realization of human rights.

NOTES

15. See Millennium Ecosystems Assessment 2005, *Ecosystems and Human Well-being,* Synthesis, pp. 67 and 79.

16. A joint seminar on human rights and the environment organized by OHCHR and UNEP in 2002 also documented a growing recognition of the connection between human rights, environmental protection, and sustainable development (see E/CN.4/2002/WP.7).

17. ILO Convention No. 169 (1989) concerning Indigenous and Tribal Peoples in Independent Countries provides for special protection of the environment of the areas which indigenous peoples occupy or otherwise use. At the regional level, the African Charter on Human and Peoples' Rights and the San Salvador Protocol to the American Convention on Human Rights recognize the right to live in a healthy or satisfactory environment. Moreover, many national constitutions refer to a right to an environment of a certain quality.

18. Convention on the Rights of the Child (CRC), art. 24, para. 2 (c).

19. Committee on Economic, Social and Cultural Rights (CESCR), general comments No. 12 (1999) on the right to adequate food (art. 11), para. 4, and No. 14 (2000) on the right to the highest attainable standard of health (art. 12), para. 4.

20. International Covenant on Civil and Political Rights (ICCPR), art. 6; CRC, art. 6.

21. Human Rights Committee, general comments No. 6 (1982) on art. 6 (Right to life), para. 1, and No. 14 (1984) on art. 6 (Right to life), para. 1.

22. Human Rights Committee, general comment No. 6, para. 5. Likewise, the Committee has asked States to provide data on pregnancy- and childbirth-related deaths and gender-disaggregated data on infant mortality rates when reporting on the status of implementation of the right to life (general comment No. 28 (2000) on art. 3 (The equality of rights between men and women), para. 10.

23. CRC, art. 6, para. 2.

24. Committee on the Rights of the Child, general comment No. 7 (2006) on implementing rights in early childhood, para. 10.

25. IPCC AR4 Working Group II (WGII) Report, p. 393.

26. United Nations Development Programme (UNDP), Human Development Report 2007/2008, *Fighting climate change: Human solidarity in a divided world,* p. 8.

27. IPCC AR4 Working Group II Report, p. 317.

28. Inter-Agency Standing Committee, *Protecting Persons Affected by Natural Disasters— IASC Operational Guidelines on Human Rights and Natural Disasters,* Brooking-Bern Project on Internal Displacement, 2006.

29. International Covenant on Economic, Social and Cultural Rights (ICESCR), art. 11; CRC, art. 24 (c); Convention on the Rights of Persons with Disabilities (CRPD), art. 25 (f) and art. 28, para. 1; Convention on the Elimination of All Forms of Discrimination against Women (CEDAW), art. 14, para. 2 (h); International Convention on the Elimination of All Forms of Racial Discrimination (ICERD), art. 5 (e).

30. ICESCR, art. 11, para. 2.

31. CESCR general comment No. 12 (1999) on the right to adequate food (art. 11), para. 6.

32. IPCC AR4 Synthesis Report, p. 48.

33. UNDP Human Development Report 2006, *Beyond scarcity: Power, poverty and the global water crisis.*

34. IPCC AR4 WGII Report, p. 275.

35. IPCC AR4 WGII, p. 359. United Nations Millennium Project 2005, *Halving Hunger: It Can Be Done,* Task Force on Hunger, p. 66. Furthermore, according to the Human Rights Council Special Rapporteur on the right to food, "half of the world's hungry people . . . depend for their survival on lands which are inherently poor and which may be becoming less fertile and less productive as a result of the impacts of repeated droughts, climate change and unsustainable land use" (A/HRC/7/5, para. 51).

36. See e.g. A/HRC/7/5, para. 51; A/HRC/7/5/Add.2, paras. 11 and 15.

37. See e.g. CESCR general comment No. 12 (1999) on the right to adequate food (art. 11), para. 28.

38. CESCR general comment No. 15 (2002) on the right to water (arts. 11 and 12), para. 2. While not explicitly mentioned in ICESCR, the right is seen to be implicit in arts. 11 (adequate standard of living) and 12 (health). General comment No. 15 provides further guidance on the normative contents of the right to water and related obligations of States.

39. See CEDAW, art. 14, para. 2 (h); CRPD, art. 28, para. 2 (a); CRC, art. 24, para. 2 (c).

40. IPCC AR4 Synthesis Report, pp. 48–49.

41. Millennium Ecosystems Assessment 2005, *Ecosystems and Human Well-being,* Synthesis, p. 52.

42. According to the UNDP Human Development Report 2006, the root causes of the current water crisis lie in poor water management, poverty, and inequality, rather than in an absolute shortage of physical supply.

43. IPCC AR4 WGII Report, p. 191. UNDP Human Development Report 2006.

44. CEDAW, arts. 12 and 14, para. 2 (b); ICERD, art. 5 (e) (iv); CRC, art. 24; CRPD, arts. 16, para. 4, 22, para. 2, and 25; International Convention on the Protection of the Rights of All Migrant Workers and Members of Their Families (ICRMW), arts. 43, para. 1 (e), 45, para. 1 (c), and 70. See also ICESCR arts. 7 (b) and 10.

45. CESCR general comment No. 12, para. 8.

46. See CESCR general comment No. 12, CEDAW general recommendation No. 24 (1999) on art. 12 of the Convention (women and health); CRC general comment No. 4 (2003) on adolescent health and development in the context of the Convention on the Rights of the Child.

47. IPCC AR4 Synthesis, p. 48.

48. Uncertainty remains about the potential impact of climate change on malaria at local and global scales because of a lack of data and the interplay of other contributing nonclimatic factors such as socioeconomic development, immunity, and drug resistance (see IPCC WGII Report, p. 404).

49. A/62/214, para. 102.

50. IPCC AR4 WGII Report, p. 12.

51. ICESCR, art. 11. See also Universal Declaration of Human Rights, art. 25, para. 1; ICERD, art. 5 (e) (iii); CEDAW, art. 14, para. 2; CRC, art. 27, para. 3; ICRMW, art. 43, para. 1 (d); CRPD, arts. 9, para. 1 (a), and 28, paras. 1 and 2 (d).

52. CESCR general comment No. 12, para. 6.

53. See CESCR general comment No. 7 (1997) on the right to adequate housing (art. 11 (1) of the Covenant): Forced evictions.

54. CESCR general comment No. 12, para. 8.

55. IPCC AR4 WGII Report, p. 333.

56. IPCC AR4 WGII Report, p. 672.

57. A/63/275, paras. 31–38.

58. UNDP Human Development Report 2007/2008, *Fighting climate change: Human solidarity in a divided world,* p. 9.

59. In this regard the Guiding Principles on Internal Displacement (E/CN.4/1998/53/Add.2, annex) provide that "at the minimum, regardless of the circumstances, and without discrimination, competent authorities shall provide internally displaced persons with and ensure safe access to: . . . basic shelter and housing" (principle 18).

60. The right to self-determination is enshrined in Articles 1 and 55 of the Charter of the United Nations and also contained in the Declaration on the Right to Development, art. 1, para. 2, and the United Nations Declaration on the Rights of Indigenous Peoples, arts. 3 and 4.

61. Human Rights Committee, general comment No. 12 (1984) on art. 1 (Right to self-determination), para. 6. See also Committee on the Elimination of Racial Discrimination (CERD), general recommendation 21 (1996) on the right to self-determination.

62. See e.g. IPCC AR4 WGII Report, p. 374.

63. National communications, submitted according to arts. 4 and 12 of UNFCCC, make frequent references to the human impacts of climate change, but generally do so in an aggregate and general manner, mentioning, for example, that people living in poverty are particularly vulnerable.

64. IPCC AR4 WGII, p. 398. See also submission by the United Nations Development Fund for Women available at: http://www2.ohchr.org/english/issues/climatechange/index .htm.

65. E. Neumayer and T. Plümper, *The Gendered Nature of Natural Disasters: The Impact of Catastrophic Events on the Gender Gap in Life Expectancy, 1981–2002,* available at http://ssrn.com/abstract=874965. As the authors conclude, based on the study of disasters in 141 countries, "[a] systematic effect on the gender gap in life expectancy is only plausible if natural disasters exacerbate previously existing patterns of discrimination that render females more vulnerable to the fatal impact of disasters" (p. 27).

66. Y. Lambrou and R. Laub, "Gender perspectives on the conventions on biodiversity, climate change and desertification," *Food and Agriculture Organization of the United Nations (FAO), Gender and Population Division,* pp. 7–8.

67. See e.g. IPCC AR4 WGII Report, p. 398; International Strategy for Disaster Reduction, *Gender Perspectives: Integrating Disaster Risk Reduction into Climate Change Adaptation. Good Practices and Lessons Learned,* UN/ISDR 2008.

68. UNFCCC, *Climate Change: Impacts, Vulnerabilities and Adaptation in Developing Countries,* 2007, p. 16.

69. UNICEF Innocenti Research Centre, *Climate Change and Children: A Human Security Challenge,* New York and Florence, 2008; UNICEF UK, *Our Climate, Our Children, Our Responsibility: The Implications of Climate Change for the World's Children,* London, 2008.

70. World Bank, *Global Monitoring Report 2008-MDGs and the Environment: Agenda for Inclusive and Sustainable Development,* p. 211.

71. UNICEF UK (see footnote 69 above), p. 29.

72. For example, UNEP and UNICEF have developed an environmental resource pack for child-friendly schools designed to empower children (see footnote 69 above, UNICEF Innocenti Research Centre, p. 28).

73. See e.g. CRC, general comment No. 4 (2003) on adolescent health and development in the context of the Convention on the Rights of the Child.

74. M. Macchi and others, *Indigenous and Traditional Peoples and Climate Change,* International Union for Conservation of Nature, 2008.

75. See e.g. report of the Special Rapporteur on the situation of human rights and fundamental freedoms of indigenous peoples, A/HRC/4/32, para. 49.

76. In April 2008, the Permanent Forum for Indigenous Issues stated that climate change "is an urgent and immediate threat to human rights" (E/C.19/2008/13, para. 23).

77. E/C.19/2008/13, para. 4. The Permanent Forum also recommended that a mechanism be put in place for the participation of indigenous peoples in climate change negotiations under UNFCCC (ibid., para. 30).

78. IPCC AR4 WGII Report, p. 865 (citing Robinson and Herbert, 2001).

79. Key provisions include the right to effective mechanisms for prevention of, and redress for, actions which have the aim or effect of dispossessing them of their lands, territories or resources (art. 8); the principle of free, prior and informed consent (art. 19), the right to the conservation and protection of the environment and indigenous lands and territories (art. 29), the right to maintain, control, protect and develop their cultural heritage and traditional knowledge and cultural expressions (art. 31).

80. See the provisions on cultural rights in ICCPR, art. 27, and ICESCR, art. 15.

81. Available at: http://inuitcircumpolar.com/files/uploads/icc-files/FINALPetitionICC .pdf.

29

GENDER, DISASTER RISK REDUCTION, AND CLIMATE CHANGE ADAPTATION: A LEARNING COMPANION

OXFAM*

1 About This Learning Companion

This Learning Companion aims to provide Oxfam program staff with the basis for incorporating gender analysis and women's rights into Disaster Risk Reduction (DRR) and Climate Change Adaptation (CCA) programming. Climate Change Adaptation and Disaster Risk Reduction are priorities for Oxfam GB, as are strengthening women's rights and gender equality.

This Companion is one of a series that covers key topics for program staff. You should read the Learning Companions "An Introduction to Disaster Risk Reduction" and "An Introduction to Climate Change Adaptation" first for definitions of DRR and CCA and other key terminology, as well as Oxfam's "Disaster Risk Reduction Program Policy" and "Climate Change Adaptation Program Policy Guidelines." This Companion assumes that you already have an understanding of Adaptation and Risk Reduction and of Oxfam's approach to project cycle management, and that you

*The material from "Gender, Disaster Risk Reduction, and Climate Change Adaptation: A Learning Companion" http://policy-practice.oxfam.org.uk/publications/gender-disaster-risk-reduction-and-climate-change-adaptation-a-learning-compani-218230 is reproduced with the permission of Oxfam GB, Oxfam House, John Smith Drive, Cowley, Oxford OX4 2JY, UK www.oxfam.org.uk. Oxfam GB does not necessarily endorse any text or activities that accompany the materials.

understand the basic concepts of gender and poverty analysis. For more information, please see the "further reading" section at the end of this document.

Learning objectives

After reading this Companion, you should

- have a theoretical overview of how poverty and inequality shape the experiences of women and men during disasters, and as a result of climate change;
- understand Oxfam's approach to strengthening gender equality and women's rights through gender mainstreaming, and how this is applied to adaptation and risk reduction work in practice;
- understand what gender equality, women's rights, and women's empowerment mean in terms of changes in the lives of women and men who are vulnerable to the impacts of climate change and at risk of disaster; and
- know where to go to learn more.

2 Why is gender important to Oxfam's adaptation and risk reduction work?

The poverty experienced by millions of women and men is shaped by inequalities that discriminate against and marginalize certain social groups by denying them their right of access to resources, opportunities, and power. The most pervasive of these inequalities, and the one which affects all communities, is gender inequality. Oxfam believes that gender inequality is a fundamental abuse of women's human rights, as well as a major barrier to sustainable development. Across the world, women tend to hold less power and to have control over fewer resources than men, at every institutional level. Women's disadvantage—their unequal access to resources, legal protection, decision making and power, their reproductive burden,[1] and their vulnerability to violence—consistently render them more vulnerable than men to the impacts of climate change and disasters. Understanding how gender relations shape women's and men's lives is therefore critical to effective Climate Change Adaptation and Disaster Risk Reduction.

. . .

The impacts of climate change and disasters magnify existing inequalities between men and women. Women tend to be more vulnerable to the effects of climate change and are affected in their multiple roles as food producers and providers, as guardians of health, as care-givers, and as economic actors.[2] Drought, saline intrusion into water sources, and erratic rainfall all cause women to work harder to secure resources such as food, water, and fuel. They mean that women have less time to earn an income, to access education or training, or to participate in decision-making processes. This, in addition to the fact that women make up the majority of the world's poor, means that climate change and disaster are likely to have disproportionately negative effects on them, potentially increasing their poverty and unequal status.

Some examples of this are:

- Women are more likely than men to be killed or injured as a direct result of climate-related disasters.
- Women depend most directly on natural resources to provide for their families. They are usually the main collectors of water and fuel, and most women farmers depend on rain-fed agriculture.
- Female-headed households are often among the poorest and the most vulnerable to disaster and climate change, as they may have little choice other than to live in precarious locations such as flood-prone lands, or on steep slopes.
- Women tend to have fewer assets to rely on than men. In economic terms, they are less likely to own their own land, or have access to credit, agricultural extension services, and transportation.
- Violence against women, both from intimate partners and unknown men, is known to rise after disasters. The risk of this may be increased by a lack of privacy and safety in camps or shelters; coercion to provide sex for goods or services; and a backlash against women who have taken on new leadership roles.

. . .

Women are not just victims of climate change and disasters, however. They demonstrate extraordinary powers of resilience during disasters and they can also be powerful agents of change. Women have repeatedly led initiatives to adapt to the impacts of climate change, and their knowledge and responsibilities related to natural resource management have proven critical to community survival.[3] They have shown themselves essential in mobilizing communities to prepare for and to respond to disaster. The skills, experiences, and capacities of women need to be harnessed alongside those of men by those implementing Adaptation and Risk Reduction programs. Understanding how gender relations shape a community's response to disaster and climate change is therefore critical to ensuring effective program planning, as well as to ensure that women are empowered by the process, rather than further disadvantaged.

3 Oxfam's approach to gender mainstreaming in adaptation and risk reduction

Oxfam's work on gender is driven by the belief that achieving gender equality is both a question of **justice** and of **basic rights,** and a means of **addressing poverty**

and suffering more effectively. Oxfam aims to "put women's rights at the heart of all its work" through gender mainstreaming.

Oxfam understands **gender mainstreaming** as a process of ensuring that all of its work, and the way it is carried out, contributes to gender equality by transforming the balance of power between women and men. The aim is to ensure that programs benefit women and men equally, do not harm or exclude women, and help to redress existing gender imbalances. Gender mainstreaming addresses the concerns of both men and women and the relations between them. However, since women bear the greater burden of poverty and suffering across the world due to systematic discrimination against them at all institutional levels, gender mainstreaming is largely about supporting women's empowerment. Critical to the success of this work is actively engaging with men to acknowledge the role they play in either reinforcing or alleviating women's subordination, and securing their support to ensure that adaptation and risk reduction initiatives uphold women's rights and strengthen gender equality.

In its Adaption and Risk Reduction (ARR) work, Oxfam is committed to taking action to meet women's specific practical needs, such as those relating to their perceived responsibilities in the home, as well as addressing their longer-term strategic needs, i.e. redressing the balance of power between women and men. Oxfam's **aims in terms of gender equality** are to support women in their efforts to challenge stereotyped gender roles, to reduce their reproductive burden, and to achieve the following:

- greater access to and control over resources;
- stronger participation and leadership in decision-making processes;
- protection from gender-based violence; and
- an increasing sense of empowerment.

In practice, this means ensuring that the different concerns and priorities of both women and men **fundamentally shape the whole program management cycle,** and that the following steps are taken in the design and implementation of all programs:

- Ensure that risk assessments are informed by a gender analysis (gender analysis should be included in the terms of reference for all assessments and research);
- Build objectives on gender equality and women's empowerment into the plans and budgets of program, policy, and campaign work;
- Assess the different implications of planned program interventions for women and men;
- Proactively seek out and engage with appropriate women's rights organizations and female community leaders when selecting partners;

- Ensure that women participate equally and actively alongside men and are enabled to take up leadership positions throughout the program management cycle;
- Monitor and evaluate changes in gender relations using gender-sensitive indicators; and
- Ensure that the institutional arrangements of implementing organizations (Oxfam and partners) support gender equality.

Gender mainstreaming is as important to **advocacy work** on ARR as it is for program work. Institutional frameworks, policies, and legislation at local, national, and global levels need to uphold women's rights and to contribute to gender equality. The organizations, institutions, and governments responsible for ARR work need to demonstrate accountability to women; and specific funds need to be allocated to support these processes. As an example, increasing the active participation of women in the United Nations Framework Convention on Climate Change (UN-FCCC) bodies and annual climate change meetings is essential if climate change policies are to promote rather than hamper gender equality. In supporting such processes, Oxfam needs to engage with global women's rights alliances working on gender and climate change.

It is also important that gender is mainstreamed into the work of agencies at the national level that are responsible for implementing the commitments of the Hyogo Framework for Action (2005–2015). This sets out concrete measures to make communities and nations more resilient to disasters and includes an agreement between the 168 signing nations that: "a gender perspective should be integrated into all disaster risk management policies, plans and decision-making processes, including those related to risk assessment, early warning, information management, and education and training."

4 Project cycle management: adaptation and risk reduction from a gender perspective

4.1 Program identification: gender analysis

The first step in the process of mainstreaming gender throughout the project cycle is to carry out a gender analysis. This is an exploration of power relationships between women and men in a particular program context. It allows us to understand how poverty affects men, women, boys, and girls differently, and to identify their specific different needs, concerns and priorities. It leads to the identification of program objectives and strategies which aim to promote gender equality.

A gender analysis should identify the following issues:

- differences in the lives of poor women and men in the target community;
- the status of women and their ability to exercise their human rights;
- the different skills, capacities, and aspirations of women and men;
- the division of labor between women and men;
- the different access to and control over resources enjoyed by women and men;
- the different levels of participation and leadership enjoyed by women and men;
- indications of the number of women experiencing gender-based violence; and
- the barriers that unequal gender relations present to women's development in this particular community.

. . .

One tool that can be used for analyzing risk and for planning interventions is Participatory Capacity and Vulnerability Analysis (PCVA). This is a participatory learning and action planning process which facilitates an understanding of the hazards faced by a population and the factors which make them vulnerable to these hazards, as well as identifying the capacities they have to respond to disasters. For more information on this, see Oxfam's resources on PCVA listed in the "further reading" section; and UNISDR[,] *Making Disaster Risk Reduction Gender Sensitive: Policy and Practice Guidelines* (2009).

For further tools and resources on gender analysis, see Oxfam's *Rough Guide to Gender Analysis* (2005).

4.2 Planning and design

Program and policy objectives
The outcomes of any gender analysis carried out during risk, vulnerability, and capacity analysis must be built into the identification of community programming and policy objectives. This should be approached in two ways:

- Ensure that all objectives acknowledge and address gender differences. For example, rather than "improve *people's* access to early warning information," a gender-sensitive objective would be "to ensure that *women and men* have better and more equal access to early warning information, and that the communications system is *tailored to the different behavior patterns of men and women*."

- Identify specific objectives to strengthen women's empowerment and gender equality, for example reducing their household workload.

Program design
The following list should guide the design of gender-sensitive programming:

- Actively promote women's dignity and empowerment;
- Support women to carry out their responsibilities in their traditional areas of authority, such as providing food and water for the family and managing the family's health.
- But also support and encourage women and men to take on non-traditional gender roles so that women are able to take on more strategic and empowering roles, while men take on a share of reproductive work (reducing women's overall workload).
- Support women's right to ownership and control of strategic assets such as housing and land. Where appropriate, create "collective asset bases" for women (e.g. a shared boat or land), as these are more sustainable than other assets, and it is easier for women to retain control over them;
- Protect women and girls from the likelihood of increased violence during and following disasters;
- Challenge attitudes and beliefs that discriminate against women;
- Work with men to secure their support for program activities that uphold women's rights and empowerment;
- Be aware of the vulnerabilities and concerns of different groups of women, such as widows, girl children, and women with disabilities;
- Ensure accountability by establishing mechanisms that enable both female and male beneficiaries to give feedback on programs. It is important that this includes feedback on program activities that particularly relate to gender issues;
- Influence local and national-level policy making on ARR to ensure that gender equality and women's rights issues are addressed, and that women actively participate and lead in decision-making processes alongside men.

4.3 Implementation and management:
gender mainstreaming in practice

This section contains examples of activities to increase gender equality and empower women in Adaptation and Risk Reduction programs.

Gender-sensitive climate change adaptation

TABLE 29.1 Gender-sensitive climate change adaptation

Change	Impact	Gendered program activity examples
Temperature increase on land and water	Heat stress on crops	Ensure that women farmers as well as men have access to heat-tolerant crops and varieties, and that their cultivation and/or processing does not place an additional burden on women
	Increased water demand for crops	As above, for drought-tolerant and fast-maturing crops and varieties
		Include women in training sessions on how to increase soil's organic content
		Include women in training sessions on water-conserving crop-management practices and ensure that the practices promoted do not place an extra physical burden on women
		Promote water capture and storage, ensuring that women are consulted on appropriate systems
	Heat stress on livestock	Tree planting (for shade and fodder) done in consultation with women and men so that it is done in appropriate areas, and women are included and treated equally in planting activities
Sea-level rise	Saline intrusion	Provision of water for households and productive use, ensuring that women are involved in designing systems that meet their requirements
Changed seasonality	Farmers uncertain about when to cultivate, sow and harvest	Ensure that both men and women farmers have access to appropriate, accessible and reliable weather forecasts and know how to use this information
		Promote crop diversification and crop mixing, ensuring that their cultivation and/or processing does not place an additional burden on women
	Crops damaged by dry spells within growing season	Ensure that both men and women farmers have access to appropriate, accessible and reliable weather forecasts and know how to use this information
		Promote crop diversification and crop mixing, ensuring that their cultivation and/or processing does not place an additional burden on women
		Water capture and storage; access to fast maturing/drought tolerant varieties; soil and crop management to conserve water
	Crops damaged by unseasonal heavy downpours	Ensure that both men and women farmers have access to appropriate, accessible and reliable weather forecasts and know how to use this information
		Ensure that women farmers as well as men have access to flood-tolerant crops and varieties, and that their cultivation and/or processing does not place an additional burden on women
		Promote crop diversification and crop mixing, ensuring that their cultivation and/or processing does not place an additional burden on women

Source: Oxfam

Gender-sensitive disaster risk reduction

Make DRR a priority at all levels, with a strong institutional basis for implementation:

- Ensure that the priorities of grassroots women's organizations are represented in co-ordination mechanisms for DRR, such as national platforms;
- Ensure that analysis and planning for DRR capacity development is prioritized equitably for men and women;
- Ensure that budget allocation for DRR implementation in all sectors and levels is prioritized for action that benefits women;
- Promote the involvement of women in participatory community planning processes for DRR through the adoption of specific policies; in the creation of networks; and when determining roles and responsibilities, authority over, and management of available resources.

Identify and monitor risks, and enhance early warning:

- Involve both women and men equally in the development of risk and hazard maps and data, and identify gender-specific aspects of risk and vulnerability;
- Support research, analysis, and reporting on long-term and emerging issues that might increase the risks faced by women;
- Encourage the participation of women where possible in early-warning systems and ensure they are appropriate and accessible to both women and men. This means that communication alerts, media, and technology need to be tailored to the preferences and behavior patterns of women and men.

Build understanding and a culture of safety and resilience at all levels:

- Ensure that women's as well as men's knowledge is promoted to build a culture of safety;
- Ensure that activities and events to build understanding of risk target women as key change agents, and that the means of communication are appropriate for women;
- Promote the targeting of children, especially girls, with risk knowledge through formal and informal channels;
- Ensure equal access to DRR training and educational opportunities for women.

Reduce underlying risk factors:

- Ensure that critical safety facilities and infrastructure (e.g. evacuation shelters and emergency housing, water, sanitation, and health systems) are resilient to hazards, accessible to both women and men, and that women have adequate privacy and security;

- Promote the importance of support to women and groups involved in sustainable ecosystems and natural resource management, including planning land-use to reduce risk;
- Promote diverse livelihoods options for women to reduce their vulnerability to hazards, and ensure that risks faced by women are not increased by inappropriate development policy and practice;
- Ensure that the development of financial risk-sharing mechanisms prioritizes the involvement of women, and that they are accessible and appropriate to the needs of women at risk of disaster;
- Raise awareness among both women and men about a woman's right to live free from violence at home and in the public domain.

Strengthen preparedness to respond effectively at all levels:

- Disaster preparedness and response plans should take into account gender-differentiated vulnerabilities and capacities, be disseminated to both women and men in languages both can understand, and prioritize actions to reduce the risks faced;
- The importance of women as key change agents should be promoted and women fully involved in community disaster management committees, disaster response drills, etc.

Policy and advocacy

Oxfam aspires to use advocacy on women's rights and gender equality in the following ways in its ARR work.

Internally: Oxfam should ensure that its own strategies for ARR promote gender equality and women's rights.

Locally: Oxfam can help to ensure that gender analysis is incorporated into data collection on the impacts of climate change and local adaptation responses, and can influence policy at the local level by raising awareness of best practice on gender in ARR responses.

Nationally: Oxfam should aspire to lead advocacy on specific aspects of gender equality and the protection of women's rights in processes such as national coordination and advocacy forums, e.g. the national platforms responsible for taking forward the commitments of the Hyogo Framework, or coalitions working on national climate change adaptation policy. Oxfam should also hold governments to account for the development and funding of adaptation policies for vulnerable communities, and advocate on issues of specific identified risk, such as environmental protection. The focus should be on ensuring: that ARR interventions respond to the needs of both women and men; that specific measures are taken to protect women's rights and support their empowerment; and that it is accepted that women's active participation and leadership in the relevant decision-making processes is essential, in order to achieve such policy change.

Internationally: Oxfam advocates a major transfer of international funds towards ARR, including the demand that such work is implemented in an equitable, pro-poor, and gender-sensitive manner. It should also advocate increasing the active participation of women in international bodies such as the UNFCCC, as well as other relevant institutions and mechanisms, and in annual climate change meetings.

At all levels: Oxfam needs to form alliances with women's rights networks which are working to ensure that climate change and DRR policy making are gender-responsive.

. . .

4.4 Monitoring and evaluation

There are several sources of guidance which can be used as a starting point for developing a monitoring and evaluation framework. For instance, the Companion in this series on "Measuring the Impact of DRR" gives detailed guidance on measuring program impact, developing indicators, collecting data to measure effectiveness, and using it to inform program design. You can also refer to Oxfam's set of minimum standards for rapid onset emergencies, and John Twigg's "Characteristics of a disaster-resilient community."

In this Companion, our concern is to ensure that indicators are gender-sensitive, and that specific indicators are developed to measure changes in gender relations over time. The key questions to ask are:

- How did the project or policy work benefit women and men differently?
- To what extent were the different vulnerabilities and capacities of women and men taken into account?
- Did the project or policy work enhance gender equality and women's empowerment, or work against it? In what ways?
- Is the project having positive or negative effects on gender relations?

Gender-sensitive indicators should be identified at the start of the project, ideally through a participatory research process with women and men. Data collected at the start of the project will give a "baseline analysis" of gender relations and the status of women. If this data is collected at several points during the life cycle of the project, it will give a picture of how gender relations are changing. We can then make judgments as to whether or not it is the influence of the project itself that is causing those changes.

Output or *process* **indicators** should explore issues such as:

- Was gender-disaggregated data produced in risk and vulnerability assessments and used to inform program objectives?
- Were measures taken to ensure that women and men participated actively on an equal basis in assessments and project decision making?

Outcome or *impact* **indicators** which are gender-sensitive can be developed by first defining broad areas of change which lead toward more equal gender relations. These can generally be defined for most contexts as follows:

- Women and men participate in decision making in public and private domains on a more equal basis;
- Women have more equal access to, and control over, economic and natural resources and basic social services;
- Fewer women suffer gender-based violence, and women have increased control over their own bodies;
- Gender stereotypes and discriminatory attitudes towards women and girls are challenged and begin to change;
- Women are empowered, i.e. they have increased power to think and act freely, exercise choice, and fulfill their potential as full and equal members of society. This includes increased capacity to organize, and to become active agents of change.

Further examples can be found in Oxfam's training pack on "Gender, Disaster Risk Reduction and Climate Change Adaptation" (2010).

5 Summary of key learning

- Oxfam believes that strengthening women's rights and gender equality are prerequisites for addressing poverty and suffering, and are also a question of justice and basic rights.
- Poverty and inequality shape women's and men's vulnerability to disaster and the impacts of climate change, and their capacity to cope and recover in the post-disaster period.
- Since women and men are affected differently by disaster and climate change, their different vulnerabilities and capacities must be analyzed, and their gender-specific concerns and priorities addressed.
- Women must be recognized for their resilience in the face of disaster, and for the roles they play as active agents of change in helping communities to recover and adapt, rather than just as victims.

- Mainstreaming gender in ARR programs means ensuring that the different concerns and priorities of women and men fundamentally shape the whole project management cycle. The aim is that all programs and policy work contribute to gender equality by transforming the balance of power between women and men.
- Ensuring women's equal participation, dignity, empowerment, and freedom from violence are key principles in program design and implementation.
- Monitoring and evaluation using gender-sensitive indicators is important to assess whether changes in gendered power relations are occurring as a result of program interventions.

6 Further reading

Oxfam resources

C. March, I. Smyth, and M. Mukhopadhyay (1999) *A Guide to Gender-Analysis Frameworks*, Oxford: Oxfam GB. Available from http://developmentbookshop.com

C. Pincha (2008) 'Gender-sensitive Disaster Management: A Toolkit for Practitioners', Oxfam America and the NANBAN Trust, Mumbai: Earthworm Books. Available to download from http://www.reliefweb.int/rw/lib.nsf

Oxfam GB (2009) 'Introduction to Climate Change Adaptation: A Learning Companion', and 'Introduction to Disaster Risk Reduction: A Learning Companion', internal documents, Oxford: Oxfam GB.

Oxfam GB (2009) 'A Framework for Gender Equality Programming in Humanitarian Settings', internal document, Oxford: Oxfam GB

Oxfam GB (2010) 'Gender, Disaster Risk Reduction and Climate Change Adaptation: a training pack for development and humanitarian programs', Oxford: Oxfam GB.

Oxfam GB (2009) 'Participatory Capacity and Vulnerability Analysis Training Pack', Oxford: Oxfam GB.

Oxfam GB (2008)'Sisters on the Planet', DVD and booklet, see http://www.oxfam.org.uk/get_involved/campaign/climate change/sisters/index.html

Oxfam GB (undated) 'Policy on Gender Equality', http://www.oxfam.org.uk/resources/issues/gender/policy.html

Oxfam GB (2005) 'Rough Guide to Gender Analysis', internal document, Oxford: Oxfam GB.

Other resources

Terry, G. (2007) *Women's Rights*, London: Pluto Press.

Terry, G. (2009) *Climate change and gender justice*, Working in Gender and Development series, Rugby: Practical Action Publications.

Twigg, J. (2007) 'Characteristics of a Disaster-resilient Community: A Guidance Note,' DFID Disaster Reduction Interagency Group, available at http://www.provention consortium.org/?pageid=90

UNISDR (2009) *Making Disaster Risk Reduction Gender Sensitive: Policy and Practice Guidelines,* UNISDR,

UNDP and IUCN, http://www.preventionweb.net/english/professional/publications /v.php?id=9922

UNISDR (2008) *Gender Perspectives: Integrating Disaster Risk Reduction into Climate Change Adaptation: Good Practices and Lessons Learned,* UNISDR, http://www.preventionweb.net /english/professional/publications/v.php?id=3391

IUCN and UNDP (2009) *Training Manual on Gender and Climate Change,* IUCN and UNDP as part of the Global Gender and Climate Alliance, http://www.iucn.org

NOTES

1. Reproductive burden or workload refers to the care and maintenance of the household and its members, such as cooking, washing, caring, bearing children, and building and maintaining the home. This work is generally unpaid, undervalued, and mostly done by women.

2. WEDO (2007) 'Changing the climate: Why women's perspectives matter', WEDO: New York.

3. A. Araujo et al., (2008) 'Gender Equality and Adaptation', IUCN, http://www.wedo .org/wp-content/uploads/genderequaladaptation.pdf.

30

COERCING CONSERVATION

Nancy Lee Peluso*

The flurry of ecological awareness and action in the late 1980s has led to a proliferation of international environmental agreements among nation-states. . . . Such agreements assume that each nation-state, including those which have only recently emerged from colonialism, has the capacity, the internal legitimacy, and the will to manage all resources falling within its territorial boundaries. The implication is that the nation-state should be able to control the behavior of all users of all resources located within the state's (self) declared jurisdiction, whatever the origin of the state's claim, whatever the nature of competition for those resources, and whatever the nature or origins of resistance to the state's resource control.[1]

These strategies have elicited the formal commitment of many Third World officials and policymakers who, not surprisingly, stand to benefit from their involvement in such initiatives. Some states or state interests, however, appropriate the conservation concerns of international environmental groups as a means of eliciting support for their own control over productive natural resources. Indeed, some tropical developing states use conservation ideology to justify coercion in the name of conservation, often by using violence. The state's mandate to defend threatened resources and its monopolization of legitimate violence combine to facilitate state apparatus-building and social control. "Legitimate" violence in the name of resource control also helps states control people, especially recalcitrant regional groups, marginal groups, or minority groups who challenge the state's authority.

The environmental community, perhaps inadvertently, justifies coercive-protective actions on the basis of moral high grounds which are difficult to dispute,

*Reprinted from *Global Environmental Change*, 3/2, Nancy Lee Peluso, Coercing Conservation?: The politics of state resource control, 199–217, Copyright (1993), with permission from Elsevier.

such as the preservation of the world's biological heritage or our common security. Indeed, the recognition of the "urgent need" to defend at any cost endangered species, endangered habitats, or whole ecosystems is becoming a more frequent part of the discourse of conservation.[2] Those who abhor state violence against its people are in some cases willing to turn a blind eye to the practice of violence or the threat of violence when conservation for (global) common security is being protected.[3] . . . Nevertheless, when a state must resort to violent means of protecting its own or the global community's claims to natural resources, it is an indicator of a failed, incomplete, or nonexistent legitimacy to govern society. Moreover, the states in question may (and often do) apply the tools and equipment they use to establish their resource sovereignty beyond the conservation endpoints envisioned by international facilitators of conservation, and appropriate the moral ideology of global conservation to justify state systems of resource extraction and production. . . .

Clashes between Central States and Local Resource Users

It is in developing countries, many of which are still struggling to redress the legacies of colonialism and the difficulties of maintaining multiethnic nation-states, that the most difficult circumstances for conservation are found. The origins of their territorial integration lie in colonialism, and were enforced by colonial armies and arms. Though international colonial pressures may have largely died down in the wake of worldwide independence movements, world market linkages continue to influence the decisions of former colonies by increasing the returns of market activities to the national elites who control the trading links.[4] Despite their contempt for the colonial regimes that preceded them, many contemporary developing states have adopted colonial policies for land and resource control, sometimes making them even more coercive.[5] Moreover, to enforce control where state hegemony is tenuous—because of deep-seated rifts between social groups, regional disparities in resource distribution, or competing concepts of appropriate or rightful use of resources—in many Third World countries, state leaders are increasingly members of, controlled by, or strongly allied with the military.[6]

Power struggles between the state and society are played out constantly in the process of allocation, control, and accessing of resources. Both internal and external pressures on states cause them to manage resources using particular tactics to achieve conservation or (sustainable) production management objectives. A state or a faction of the state may coerce conservation under one or all of three circumstances: when the resources are extremely valuable, when the state's legitimate control of the resource is questioned or challenged by other resource users, and when coercion is considered either the last resort or the easiest means of establishing control over people and territory. . . .

The conservation agenda, which is generally depicted as being in the common interest of the entire global community, is seen by some as a justification for external intervention in what were previously the sole affairs of states.[7] From a local perspective, however, both states and international conservation groups may be seen as illegitimate controllers of local resources. . . .

International intervention or support does not guarantee the realization of environmental goals or state legitimacy, however. Replacing or strengthening power holders in order to control resources may encourage increasing local resistance or rebellion against state or international controls on local resources. State concerns with the economic value of resources may influence conservation groups to use economic terms to justify their protection and preservation strategies. Whether for intensive production or for preservation, valuation strategies for resource territories frequently disenfranchise local people who had long histories of local resource use and may have played significant, though unrecognized, roles in creating "wild" habitats. Not only does this often have the effect of undermining conservation; it also changes the way resources are perceived, defined, valued, allocated, and used. When these management strategies change who has access to and control over local resources, the use of violence becomes an expedient means of exerting state control, in the name of "conservation" or "legitimate domain."

In sum, externally based resource claimants (including the state itself) frequently redefine resources, the means by which they will be conserved or harvested, and the distribution of benefits from their protection. Such redefinitions often override, ignore, or collide with local or customary forms of resource management. When competition between external and local legitimation mechanisms is played out in the environmental arena, the result is social and political conflict, which causes environmental degradation and ultimately fails to achieve the goals of international conservation interests.

Nevertheless, the state may not "lose." Even if conservation goals are not achieved, the state may succeed in strengthening its capacity to govern via the use of force.[8] No one monitors this type of aggression or this outcome of international conservation strategy. The means of violence and the ideologies of state stewardship of global resources, obtained directly or indirectly from the international conservation community, may facilitate the state's imposition and enforcement of its right to govern. . . .

Kenya

The resources discussed in this section are the lands set aside for national parks and wildlife reserves and resources within those lands (wildlife, pasture, and water). The traditional users of these lands, the Maasai, Somalis, and pastoralists of other ethnic groups, have been excluded from access to these lands to various degrees over the past century. State claims to nearly two-thirds of traditional Maasai lands were first made by the British colonial state at the turn of the twentieth century. In 1904 the Maasai, who used to occupy all the land from Mt. Kenya in the north to the border with (and into) what is today Tanzania, were resettled in two reserves. Several years later, those in the northern reserve were resettled again in an extension of the southern reserve. By 1912, they were confined to an area of approximately 38,000 square kilometers.[9] The British allocated some of the Maasai's traditional lands to European planters whose activities were believed by colonial officials to be "more productive."[10] Early on, however, the British did not subscribe to the theory that the Maasai could not coexist with wildlife. Thus, in 1906 they created the Southern Game Reserve—a wildlife reserve within the Maasai reserve because the Maasai were not believed to threaten wildlife, having coexisted with the region's wild game for thousands of years.[11]

It was not until the 1940s and 1950s that the colonial government gave in to pressures from game hunters and some conservation groups to set aside rangeland exclusively for wild game. At that same time, the state wanted to settle the Maasai in fixed places, which meant changing their traditional migratory cattle-raising practices. The Amboseli Basin, occupying some 3,200 km of both the Maasai Reserve and the Southern Game Reserve, was an important source of water during the dry season for the region's wildlife as well as the Maasai and their cattle. Dams and boreholes to provide water outside the Amboseli Basin were constructed to benefit the Maasai. As the number of Maasai cattle increased, as they continued to migrate to areas where wild game also sought drinking water, and as hunters threatened wildlife in a different manner, conservationist interests grew more concerned that the wildlife dependent on the Basin waters were being threatened. Along with big game hunters, they pressured the colonial government to create reserves where human use would be more restricted. The Southern Game Reserve was abolished in 1952 and four smaller reserves were created, including a new one outside the area of the old Southern Game Reserve, called Maasai Mara. In the 1950s, hunting was first outlawed within these reserves, although the government issued permits for hunting outside the reserves. In the early 1960s livestock grazing was also forbidden in an 80 km^2 area of the Amboseli reserve, which was a direct threat to Maasai lifestyles and livelihoods.[12]

The Maasai did not so easily give up their traditional patterns of migration to seasonal water supplies; nor were water development efforts sufficient to permit them to do so. When their principal means of livelihood was restricted by reserve authorities, the Maasai responded by killing rhinoceroses and elephants. A decade later, some allegedly began collaborating with ivory poachers. They also resisted further appropriation of their access rights by increasing their use of the area surrounding the livestock-free zone, and later demanded tenure rights to all these lands.[13]

Meanwhile, another development increased the state's direct interest in the protection of wild game and the reservation of parklands: the increase in wildlife-oriented tourism beginning in the 1960s. Some tourism revenues, including hunting fees, were given to various Maasai district councils as an incentive to win their acceptance of the reserves.[14] Fees and revenues grew through the 1960s and early 1970s, after Kenyan independence. Not all district councils, however, truly represented the interests of the people in the immediate vicinity of the reserves and parks. In Amboseli, for example, the Kajiado Council receiving park revenues was 150 km from the park boundaries. Thus some Maasai were benefitting from the Park's existence, but not necessarily those who had the most to lose from the Park's creation.

The value of wildlife tourism soon became clear to the central government. In 1974, the government designated 488 km² of the Amboseli Basin as a national park, while still negotiating with the Maasai. In 1977 this area was reduced to 390 km², which was gazetted as a park and would remain free of livestock. A de facto buffer zone was to be established around the core area of the park, and group ranches—a brand-new form of social organization for these Maasai—were established to further the government's intentions of sedentarizing the Maasai. In addition, the Maasai were expected to allow wildlife to graze on these ranches in exchange for a "wildlife utilization fee," which was supposed to compensate them for losses of water and grazing area to their own livestock.[15]

By 1989, tourism in Kenya was contributing about 20 percent of the nation's total foreign exchange.[16] By 1991, tourists were spending some 50 million dollars a year to view elephants and other wildlife.[17] In this way, as Knowles and Collett have pointed out, the creation of national parks to protect wildlife has not only separated the Maasai from their livestock production base and created a mythical nature devoid of humans for tourist consumption but also provided the government with the financial means to "develop" and "modernize" them.[18] Moreover, "National Parks and Game Reserves are never justified solely in terms of the economics of tourism: both the conservationists and national governments support the creation and maintenance of these areas with *moral arguments* based on the need to conserve wildlife and the intangible benefits that conservation confers on humanity."[19]

The plans for development of the Maasai in Amboseli have not worked as well as they have in Mara. Some blame the failure on the basic conflict in the lifestyles of the Maasai and their unwillingness to allow outsiders to make decisions about their lives and their uses of resources. Collett, for example, claims that the main reason the provision of water supplies outside the park has not achieved the government's development goals is the preference of the Maasai for a migratory, pastoralist lifestyle.[20] However, a recent report by the World Bank indicates that there were also significant technical problems:

> [The conflicts] may be attributed . . . to failure to implement the agreements, to the lack of an official written agreement outlining the management responsibilities of the different parties and policy changes. The water pumping system, financed by the New York Zoological Society and the World Bank, worked well for a few years and then

began to fail due to technical and administrative problems which were not corrected by the central Government which had built it. An inadequate water supply left the Maasai little option but to return to find water inside the Park. The problems were aggravated by a drought in 1984, in which the Maasai lost a substantial part of their livestock and received no assistance from the Park authorities. The wildlife utilization fees were paid regularly until about 1981, then the payments became sporadic without explanation to the Maasai. The agreement for group ranches to retain a portion of Park entry fees fell through, perhaps due to administrative changes. . . . Anticipated income from tourism did not increase as quickly as expected. . . . Construction of new lodges and viewpoint circuits on group ranch lands did not materialize as expected. Finally, the 1977 hunting ban eliminated anticipated income from safari hunting license fees.[21]

In the past few years, the basic conflicts over land and resource fights in Kenyan national parks and reserves have been reconstructed in terms of a government mandate to stop the poaching of wildlife, especially of elephants and rhinoceroses. Major international environmental organizations, including the Worldwide Fund for Nature, the African Wildlife Foundation, World Conservation International (WCI), the International Union for the Conservation of Nature (IUCN), Conservation International, and the National Geographic Society, have publicized the poaching issue and its threat to global and African biodiversity. The efforts of these and other environmental groups led to the creation of the Convention on International Trade in Endangered Species (CITES). By 1991, 105 world nations had signed the CITES declaration to ban the raw ivory trade in their effort to protect elephants in Asia and Africa.[22]

A great deal, however, has been left out of the international discussion of the poaching issue, and neither the origins nor the implications of the proposed solutions to the poaching problem have received the critical analysis they merit. Two gaps in the conservation community's discussion are particularly glaring. The first is the lack of historical perspective on the political and ecological contexts within which parks were created to protect wildlife, and the resulting dismissal of local people in creating particular environments. The other is the failure to consider the political-economic implications of the provision of arms and other equipment intended (at least ostensibly) to protect wildlife.

In April 1989, Richard Leakey became the director of Kenya's Wildlife Service. Since then Leakey has made his mark by firing administrative and field staff believed to be involved in the illegal ivory or rhino horn trade, by giving raises to underpaid and overworked park rangers, and by arming these rangers with automatic rifles and helicopter gunships in order to wage war more effectively on the poachers invading Kenya's national parks. Wage war they have: within two years of his taking over, more than a hundred poachers had been killed, many of them with no chance for discussion or trial; the rangers are licensed, like military in a state of emergency, to shoot to kill.[23] The Wildlife Service has also reclaimed direct control over the Maasai Mara Reserve, where the combination of wildlife management with local participation and benefits had reportedly been more successful. The government claimed that the reserve had been inadequately maintained and was deteriorating, denying earlier reports that elephants and rhinoceros populations within this park had been increasing while antipoaching costs were virtually negligible.[24]

. . . In their campaigns to save animals, international conservation groups never specify who the poachers are, although some fingers are pointed and accusations made. A letter to members from the WWF, for example, says, "Some poachers, tribesmen displaced from traditional occupations by drought or civil war, use primitive methods to kill elephants and transport tusks. But most use high-powered weapons and even airplanes and various sorts of poisons."[25]

What tribe these "tribesmen" are from is not clarified, whether they are Maasai, or Kikuyu, or one of the smaller ethnic minorities within the country. Later in the letter, however, "Somali tribesmen" are directly implicated, as well as people from an apparently different social group, i.e., "Somali officials." In reference to ivory tusks sold or stockpiled within Somalia, the letter says, "These tusks were not legally confiscated. Instead, they probably were poached from Kenya's nearby Tsavo National Park by well-equipped Somali tribesmen, then smuggled out of Kenya with the complicity of Somali officials."[26] The Somali president himself also apparently wrote a letter guaranteeing his government's purchase of ivory tusks from neighboring countries.[27]

The WWF does not specifically accuse the Maasai of killing wildlife for ivory, but implies that their increasing populations are a major threat to the survival of the elephants and other wildlife. Nowhere in the letter to WWF members is it mentioned that the Maasai and other pastoral and hunter-gatherer groups coexisted with elephants and other savannah wildlife over thousands of years; or that people—as well as the elephants—play an important role in creating and maintaining the contemporary savannah habitat that supports them both. Rather, they imply that the presence of the Maasai is a new phenomenon to which elephants must adapt: "One broad cause of the decrease in elephant numbers is surely the advance of human populations into *their* habitat. . . . To some extent, elephants are able to adapt to the growing presence of pastoralists such as Kenya's Maasai."[28]

Chadwick, writing for *National Geographic,* reflects a more explicit "people versus wildlife" view, with only conservation researchers and supporters exempt:

Tusks became a sort of underground currency, like drugs, spreading webs of corruption from remote villages to urban centers throughout the world. . . . The seventies saw the price of ivory skyrocket. Suddenly, to a herder or subsistence farmer, this was no longer an animal, but a walking fortune, worth more than a dozen years of honest toil. . . . Ivory was running above a hundred dollars a pound, and officials from poorly paid park rangers to high ranking wildlife ministers had joined the poaching network. . . . Poaching gangs, including bush-wise bandits called shifta from Somalia, armed with AK-47 assault rifles, were increasingly turning their guns on tourists. This has all but shut down Meru National Park in the north.[29]

What is wrong with this description is its "snapshot" of a contemporary situation, with the camera angled in such a way as to keep the background out of focus. Everyone in the picture is considered equally guilty, regardless of the roots of their involvement, their power to prevent its happening, their public stance, or the historical basis of their claims to being where they are in relation to the wildlife and the lands. Both the average reader and the writer of the article are unfamiliar with the social history of these "wildlife habitats" and this gap in understanding is neither missed nor deemed necessary. The story, after all, is about people against nature. The people for nature, the heroes, are not the local people who lived alongside wildlife for thousands of years before their lands were appropriated by colonial and contemporary state agencies and carved into parks. The implicit heroes are Western wildlife scientists, environmental activists, and the conservation armies who rout the poachers. The indigenous people are implicated because of their proximity to the parks and the logistics of outside poachers gaining access, although it is unlikely that any "peasant farmer" sees one hundred dollars for any pound of ivory he has had a hand in obtaining. Peasants in this view are also guilty of "encroachment" on the elephants' habitat—the areas from which they were excluded not many decades ago: "Ultimately, though, people, not poachers, and growth, not guns, pose the most serious long-term threat to the elephant's survival."[30]

Ironically, Chadwick hints at another motive underlying the involvement of certain state and would-be state actors in this conservation drama: "To currency-strapped governments and revolutionaries alike [ivory poaching] was a way to pay for more firearms and supplies. In the eighties Africa had nearly ten times the weapons present a decade earlier, which encouraged more poaching than ever."[31]

Hence the "need" for increasing the power of the "good" government officials, particularly those working in the parks. As the WWF letter explained, "Anti-poaching forces have been traditionally paid poorly, had insufficient training and equipment, and were understaffed. Moreover, they rarely enlisted the aid of nearby villagers by offering them economic incentives."[32]

As a result, WWF and its partners (IUCN, TRAFFIC, and WCI) began providing "emergency assistance to key African wildlife departments," improving ranger incentives and providing antipoaching equipment and training. They claim that "the only long-term security for elephants in Africa lies in strengthening national capabilities in wildlife conservation and management." Moreover, to its credit, WWF and other groups are "working to ensure that protected areas benefit from the income generated through access fees."[33] Leakey also asked the African Wildlife Foundation for assistance, which AWF has provided, including airplanes and vehicles for antipoaching patrols in Tsavo National Park. Though it is a relatively small operation, AWF occasionally takes a more direct role in coercive wildlife protection by "mounting extra patrols when an emergency arises."[34]

That these aircraft, radios, vehicles, night-goggles, and other antipoaching equipment might serve another purpose besides conservation has been a secondary consideration in view of the emergency status of the quest to protect these wildlife. And yet, in an article appearing in January 1989, three months before Leakey's takeover and the subsequent high-powered, highly publicized crackdown on poaching, reports from Kenya showed how the government was already using its mandate to protect and manage resources to assert its authority where local people had resisted state controls on their activities since the colonial period.[35]

Ostensibly to settle a dispute over grazing rights between Somali and Borana groups residing in the north, the government sent in police, army helicopters, military aircraft, and the paramilitary General Service Unit. Over 600 people were detained and "large numbers" were killed in the course of the current incident. The conflict is not a new one: a 1984 clash left 2,169 people dead, and in 1987 some 200–300 Home Guards, none of them Somali, were armed "to assist in policing grazing rights and local disputes."[36]

Many of these disputes date from the time that the Kora National Reserve was created, when Somali pastoralists were excluded from access to parklands for grazing. Whole communities of Somalis were resettled onto arid lands in Borana districts. In the course of their resettlement, they were deprived of pasture and water for their livestock. Seeking these resources in the vicinity of the reserve, they are harassed by the Kenyan security forces in the same manner as illegal Somalis engaged in the smuggling trade. The present government's harassment of both the settled and nomadic Somali in the region is couched in conservation rhetoric, but dates back to the region's efforts to secede from independent Kenya in 1967. The colonial government also had difficulty establishing its authority previously. In the course of the recent clash near the Kora reserve, it was reported that "under the state of emergency, security forces have powers to act without warrant and detain without specific reason . . . clean-up operations are commonplace."[37] Moreover, the officials involved in the political security operations now form an integral part of the antipoaching operations.

The political implications of this trend in conserving Kenyan wildlife are clear. Though equipment and funds may be allocated to protect nature, they can directly or indirectly be used by the state to serve its own political ends. In this way, the commitment to preservation of wildlife for tourism and research serves both the economic and political interests of the Kenyan government, while its actual effectiveness in doing so is questionable. . . .

Conclusion

The environmental community's tacit or explicit support of coercive conservation tactics has far-reaching consequences. First, local resistance to what are perceived as illegitimate state claims and controls over local resources is likely to heighten, and may lead to violent response, sabotage of resources, and degradation.[38] Second, and most important, the outside environmental community may be weakening local resource claimants who possess less firepower than the state. While some conservationists are also "arming" local nongovernment organizations with symbolic and financial support, their ultimate goal is as much or more to influence state policy as to empower local resource users. The ethics underlying the spread of Western conservation ideologies, without considering their inevitable transformation when accepted or appropriated by developing states, require close reexamination. . . .

[A] growing body of evidence show[s] that wherever the state directly claims, controls, or manages land-based resources, state organizations and individual state actors have strong vested interests in the commercial exploitation of resources. Their control over the territories within which the resources occur, and over the people living within them, is a major aspect of their strategic territorial control. Militaries, paramilitary organizations, and state agencies often create or exacerbate resource-based conflicts by their participation in protective activities, their involvement as actors, or their coercive tactics. . . . Just as some military leaders can be co-opted to work for the sake of conservation agendas, conservation groups' resources and ideologies can be co-opted for separate military agendas. Once coercive conservation tactics are accepted, such co-optation is nearly impossible to prevent.

Failing to venture beyond the concept of thinking globally and acting locally, the writers of international conservation initiatives often brush aside or simply ignore the political implications of empowering states to coercively control access to natural resources. The militarization of resource control—whether for protection or production—leads to damaging relations with the environment, not benign ones. Whatever their approach on the ground, these conservation groups seek ultimately to change state policy and practice. Unfortunately, coercive conservation also strengthens or extends the state's military capacity—not only with the weapons of enforcement but also with new "moral" justifications to legitimate coercion in enforcing a narrowly defined "global community's" environmental will.

NOTES

1. Piers Blaikie, *The Political Economy of Soil Erosion in Developing Countries* (London: Longman, 1985); Nancy Lee Peluso, *Rich Forests, Poor People: Resource Control and Resistance in Java* (Berkeley, CA: University of California Press, 1992).

2. Daniel Deudney, "Case Against Linking Environmental Degradation and National Security," *Millennium: Journal of International Studies* 19, no. 3 (1990):461–476; Jeffrey A. McNeeley, Kenton R. Miller, Walter V. Reid, Russell A. Mittermeier, and Timothy B. Wemer, *Conserving the World's Biodiversity* (Washington, DC: Worldwide Fund For Nature, 1988).

3. Deudney, "Case Against Linking."

4. Eric Wolf, *Europe and the People Without History* (Berkeley, CA: University of California Press, 1982).

5. Michael Watts, *Silent Violence: Food, Famine, and Peasantry in Northern Algeria* (Berkeley, CA: University of California Press, 1983); Ramachandra Guha, *The Unquiet Woods: Ecological History and Peasant Resistance in the Indian Himalaya* (Berkeley, CA: University of California Press, 1990); Peluso, *Rich Forests, Poor People.*

6. Charles Tilly, "War-Making and State-Making as Organized Crime," in Peter B. Evans, Dietrich Rueschemeyer, and Theda Skocpol, eds., *Bringing the State Back In* (Cambridge: Cambridge University Press, 1985).

7. World Commission on Environment and Development, *Our Common Future* (New York: Oxford University Press, 1987); Lester Brown et al., *State of the World 1990* (New York: W. W. Norton, 1990).

8. Tilly, "War-Making and State-Making"; [Joel] Migdal, *Strong Societies [and Weak States* (Princeton, NJ: Princeton University Press, 1988].

9. W. K. Lindsay, "Integrating Parks and Pastoralists: Some Lessons from Amboseli," in David Anderson and Richard Grove, eds., *Conservation in Africa: People, Policies, and Practice* (Cambridge: Cambridge University Press, 1987), pp. 152–155.

10. David Collett, "Pastoralists and Wildlife: Image and Reality in Kenya Maasailand," in Anderson and Grove, *Conservation in Africa*, p. 138.

11. Ibid.

12. Lindsay, "Integrating Parks," pp. 153–155.

13. David Western, "Amboseli National Park: Enlisting Landowners to Conserve," *Ambio* 11, no. 5:304; Lindsay, "Integrating Parks," p. 155.

14. Western, "Amboseli National Park," p. 305; Lindsay, "Integrating Parks," p. 154.

15. Lindsay, "Integrating Parks," pp. 156–157; Agnes Kiss, *Wildlife Conservation in Kenya* (Washington, DC: World Bank, 1990), p. 72.

16. Joan N. Knowles and D. P. Collett, "Nature as Myth, Symbol, and Action: Notes Towards an Historical Understanding of Development and Conservation in Kenyan Maasailand," *Africa* 59, no. 4 (1989):452.

17. Douglas H. Chadwick, "Elephants—Out of Time, Out of Space," *National Geographic* 179, no. 5 (1991):11, 17.

18. Knowles and Collett, "Nature as Myth," p. 452.

19. Collett, "Pastoralists and Wildlife," p. 129; emphasis added.

20. Ibid., p. 144.

21. Kiss, *Wildlife Conservation*, p. 72.

22. Chadwick, "Elephants," p. 14.

23. Ibid., pp. 26–31.

24. Kiss, *Wildlife Conservation*, pp. 71, 74.

25. World Wildlife Fund, "A Program to Save the African Elephant," *World Wildlife Fund Letter*, no. 2, 1989, p. 6.

26. Ibid., pp. 8–9.

27. Ibid., p. 9.

28. Ibid., pp. 4–5; emphasis added.

29. Chadwick, "Elephants," p. 24.

30. Ibid., p. 14.

31. Ibid., p. 24.

32. World Wildlife Fund, "A Program to Save the African Elephant," *World Wildlife Fund Letter,* no. 2, 1989, p. 7.

33. Ibid., p. 10.

34. African Wildlife Foundation, "1989 Was a Very Good Year: Annual Report," *Wildlife News* 25, no. 2:3–5.33.

35. "Kenya: Crackdown on Somalis," *Africa Confidential* 30, no. 1 (1989):6–7.

36. Ibid.

37. Ibid.

38. Blaikie, *The Political Economy of Soil Erosion*; Susanna Hecht and Alexander Cockburn, *The Fate of the Forest: Developers, Destroyers, and Defenders of the Rainforest* (New York: Verso, 1989); Guha, *Unquiet Woods*; Peluso, *Rich Forests, Poor People.*

31

THE REAL PRICE OF EUROPE
GOING GREEN

SILAS KPANAN'AYOUNG SIAKOR*

Silas Kpanan'Ayoung Siakor, Liberian, is a social justice and community rights campaigner. He works for the Sustainable Development Institute and focuses on community rights in the natural resource sector especially on forestry, land and agriculture expansion. In 2002, he was awarded the Whitley Awards for Environment and Human Rights (www.whitleyaward.org), in 2006 the Goldman Environmental Prize for outstanding environmental achievements in Africa (http://www.goldmanprize.org), and in 2012 the Award for Outstanding Environmental and Human Rights Activism (http://www.alexandersorosfoundation.org).

Introduction

As Europe, the US and the emerging economies of Brazil, Russia, India, China and South Africa (BRICS) continue to promote development models that rely on economic growth, which is often driven by over-consumption, questions are now being raised about how much longer the human society can continue on this path. Understandably, these concerns are driving innovations for example in the energy sector. But, while politicians and big businesses promote renewable energy technologies as a breakthrough that should be harnessed, the social and environmental costs associated with the raw materials they feed on [have] cast doubts about their "sustainability." The "green" credentials of some renewable energy technologies are under fire as evidence of environmental degradation and

*Originally published on the web site of AfricAvenir International e.V., www.africavenir.org. Copyright © 2013 AfricAvenir e.V. Reprinted with permission.

human rights abuses, associated with the raw materials that fuel them, continue to multiply.

There is evidence that with increasing tension and competition for natural resources, the poor and marginalized will be pushed further into poverty. To expect a more equal, just and peaceful world in this context would be an illusion as wealthy nations fight to keep their places at the top of the economic ladder. This paper, drawn on experiences from Liberia, highlights the environmental and human costs renewable energy supplies in Europe pose to the poor in southern countries.

Behind the Renewable Energy Myth

Crude palm oil and biomass are two raw materials some renewable energy technologies rely on. To produce these two commodities in large quantities, multinational corporations secure agricultural lands to establish large-scale plantations. Studies show that rising demand for these biofuels is driving land grabs, displacement and increasing poverty in Africa. The World Bank estimates that of the 56 million hectares of farmland leased in 2009 alone, more than 70% of the demand was for land in Africa.[1] That most of the land was leased in countries with weak governance, and where the extraction of natural resources [is] linked to poverty and human rights abuses, should be of concern. The Commission on Legal Empowerment of the Poor warns that in countries with weak governance "the plight of the poor is often rooted in political systems in which citizens are denied a voice; government institutions have no obligation to answer to the people, and special interests exploit resources without fear of scrutiny."[2]

In the context of European countries including Sweden and Germany, the Liberian experience is particularly relevant. The biomass producer Buchanan Renewables entered into an agreement with the Government of Liberia to build and power an electricity plant using wood chips from unproductive rubber trees.[3] The company's claim that unproductive rubber trees would be the primary raw material needed was a major selling point of the agreement. But, more than four years after the signing of this agreement, only the billboards proudly claiming "Lighting Up Liberia" have materialized.

Instead of delivering the project, Buchanan Renewables entered into an agreement with the Swedish energy giant Vattenfall to supply wood chips to their plants in Europe. On June 16, 2010 Vattenfall announced that together with Swedfund they had acquired a 30% share in Buchanan Renewables.[4] The justification was standard; "using biomass is an important key to reducing Vattenfall's emission of fossil carbon dioxide."[5] The company went on to explain that the move would help them transition from burning coal to burning wood and that given limited supply of biomass in Europe the move was necessary to meet the increasing demands.

Unbeknown to their customers[,] who would proudly claim that their energy supply is from renewable sources, were the human rights abuses and environmental pollution linked to the "unproductive rubber trees" they would be paying for indirectly. Firestone Liberia, the largest supplier of rubber trees to Buchanan Renewables, was one of several plantation companies named in a United Nations and Government of Liberia report for appalling human rights abuses on their plantations.[6] This situation is however not unique to Firestone.

The Potential New Suppliers

Sime Darby Plantation Liberia (SDPL) and Golden Veroleum Liberia (GVL) both acquired large quantities of lands in Liberia to grow oil palm and rubber. The Government of Liberia awarded 311,187 hectares of land to SDPL in 2009 and in 2010 awarded another 350,000 hectares to GVL. The crude palm oil both companies produce is a major ingredient for biofuel, which is also promoted as renewable energy. Both companies are members of the Round Table on Sustainable Palm Oil (RSPO), the international body that certifies crude palm oil as sustainable.[7] As members of the scheme[,] both companies claim that their crude palm oil is produced in an environmentally friendly and socially responsible manner.

But, the realities are far from this picture. First, all the land allocated to them were taken from the customary owners without due process. They were neither consulted nor did they give consent for their land to be allocated. Both companies have been at the centre of controversies since they started operations. At the start of its operations in Liberia SDPL destroyed farms and planted palm on farmlands that provide livelihoods and food for the local communities, leaving very few alternative livelihood options available to those not incorporated into the company workforce. As a result, in 2011 communities in Garwula, Grand Cape Mount County filed a complaint with the RSPO claiming that SDPL was violating their rights, including polluting their water sources and taking their land for which they had not consented. The company had also cleared forests used for various cultural practices to plant oil palm.[8] In October 2012 a separate complaint was filed to the RSPO against GVL because the company had allegedly failed to follow RSPO procedures[,] including failure to secure consent from land owners before clearance.[9]

In addition to the issues raised in these complaints, the contracts negotiated with the government of Liberia have also come under criticism. The terms of both agreements allow the companies to take community lands and to displace or resettle communities without compensation or due process.[10] In spite of these problematic terms of their agreements[,] both companies have forged ahead with implementation of those contracts.

Conclusions

As communities suffered the social and environmental impacts of Firestone Liberia plantations[,] their unproductive rubber trees sold well to Buchanan Renewables, who then resold them as wood chips to Vattenfall. The electricity or heating generated from their use then branded as renewable and sustainable energy was sold to European consumers. While politicians and big businesses promote renewable energy technologies as a breakthrough that should be harnessed, the social and environmental costs associated with the raw materials they need is often ignored. It is therefore understandable that environmentalists and human rights defenders question the "green" credentials of renewable energy technologies.

Additionally, the crude palm oil that SDPL and GVL will produce in the coming years will be branded as environmentally friendly and socially responsible commodities to European consumers. While it may be true that the technology used to turn the crude palm oil into biofuel relies on renewable raw material, the manner in which these raw materials are produced should raise some ethical questions for the European consumer. European consumers cannot feign lack of awareness on these issues[,] because [the authors of] various studies have [expressed alarm] at the trend in large scale land deals—especially in Africa. For example, the World Bank reported that approximately 56 million hectares of farmland, with more than 70% in Africa, was leased in 2009 alone. Most of the countries that leased land have weak governance . . . where the extraction of natural resources is strongly linked to poverty, human rights abuses, and environmental degradation. To therefore present energy produced from raw material accessed in this context as sustainable is misleading. . . .

NOTES

1. The World Bank (2011) *Rising Global Interest in Farmland: Can It Yield Equitable and Sustainable Benefits?*

2. The Commission on Legal Empowerment of the Poor: *Making the Law Work for the Poor, Vol. 1, 2008,* p. 46.

3. The Power Purchase Agreement Between the Liberia Electricity Corporation and Buchanan Renewables (Monrovia) Power Inc., Dated 16th January 2009.

4. Vattenfall Press Statement, June 16, 2010 [online]. Available from: www.businesswire.com/news/home/20100616005697/en/Vattenfall-Acquires-Share-Buchanan-Renewables-Fuel-Liberia [Accessed: January 30, 2013].

5. Ibid.

6. Joint Government of Liberia and United Nations Mission in Liberia Rubber Plantations Task Force, Report, 2006.

7. See the RSPO website online: http://www.rspo.org/en/who_is_rspo.

8. Silas Kpanan'Ayoung Siakor, Uncertain Futures, 2012 [online]. Available from: www.fern.org/publications/recommended-reading/uncertain-futures-impacts-sime-darby-communities-liberia.

9. Complaint available from: http://www.rspo.org/en/status_of_complaint&cpid=24.

10. Tom Lomax, Human rights-based analysis of the agricultural concession agreements between Sime Darby and Golden Veroleum and the Government of Liberia, 2012 [online]. Available from: www.forestpeoples.org/sites/fpp/files/publication/2012/12/liberiacontractanalysisfinaldec2012_0.pdf [Accessed: January 30, 2012].

32

REDD: AN INTRODUCTION

REDD-Monitor[*]

REDD, or reduced emissions from deforestation and forest degradation, is one of the most controversial issues in the climate change debate. The basic concept is simple: governments, companies or forest owners in the South should be rewarded for keeping their forests instead of cutting them down. The devil, as always, is in the details.

The first detail is that the payments are not for keeping forests, but for reducing emissions from deforestation and forest degradation. This might seem like splitting hairs, but it is important, because it opens up the possibility, for example, of logging an area of forest but compensating for the emissions by planting industrial tree plantations somewhere else.

The idea of making payments to discourage deforestation and forest degradation was discussed in the negotiations leading to the Kyoto Protocol, but it was ultimately rejected because of four fundamental problems: leakage, additionality, permanence and measurement.

- **Leakage** refers to the fact that while deforestation might be avoided in one place, the forest destroyers might move to another area of forest or to a different country.
- **Additionality** refers to the near-impossibility of predicting what might have happened in the absence of the REDD project.
- **Permanence** refers to the fact that carbon stored in trees is only temporarily stored. All trees eventually die and release the carbon back to the atmosphere.

---

[*]Originally published on the web site of REDD-Monitor, *http://www.redd-monitor.org*, February 2011. Reprinted with permission.

- **Measurement** refers to the fact that accurately measuring the amount of carbon stored in forests and forest soils is extremely complex—and prone to large errors.

Although much has been written about addressing these problems, they remain serious problems in implementing REDD, both nationally and at project level.

REDD developed from a proposal in 2005 by a group of countries led by Papua New Guinea calling themselves the Coalition for Rainforest Nations. Two years later, the proposal was taken up at the Conference of the Parties to the UNFCCC [UN Framework Convention on Climate Change] in Bali (COP-13). In December 2010, at COP-16, REDD formed part of the Cancun Agreements, in the Outcome of the Ad Hoc Working Group on Long-term Cooperative Action [AWG/LCA] under the Convention.

REDD is described in paragraph 70 of the AWG/LCA outcome:

Encourages developing country Parties to contribute to mitigation actions in the forest sector by undertaking the following activities, as deemed appropriate by each Party and in accordance with their respective capabilities and national circumstances:
  (a) Reducing emissions from deforestation;
  (b) Reducing emissions from forest degradation;
  (c) Conservation of forest carbon stocks;
  (d) Sustainable management of forest;
  (e) Enhancement of forest carbon stocks.

This is REDD-plus (although it is not referred to as such in the AWG/LCA text). Points (a) and (b) refers to REDD. Points (c), (d) and (e) are the "plus" part. [Editors' note: On this distinction between "REDD" and "REDD+" see also the web site of the UN-REDD Programme, available at www.un-redd.org/.] But each of these "plus points" has potential drawbacks:

- **Conservation** sounds good, but the history of the establishment of national parks includes large scale evictions and loss of rights for indigenous peoples and local communities. Almost nowhere in the tropics has strict "conservation" proven to be sustainable. The words "**of forest carbon stocks**" were added in Cancun. The concern is that forests are viewed simply as stores of carbon rather than [as] ecosystems.
- **Sustainable management of forests** could include subsidies to industrial-scale commercial logging operations in old-growth forests, [in] indigenous peoples' territory or in villagers' community forests.
- **Enhancement of forest carbon stocks** could result in conversion of land (including forests) to industrial tree plantations, with serious implications for biodiversity, forests and local communities.

There are some safeguards annexed to the AWG/LCA text that may help avoid some of the worst abuses. But the safeguards are weak and are only to be "promoted and supported." The text only notes that the United Nations "has adopted" the UN Declaration on the Rights of Indigenous Peoples. The text refers to indigenous peoples' rights, but it does not protect them.

But perhaps the most controversial aspect of REDD is omitted from the REDD text agreed in Cancun. There is no mention in the text about how REDD is to be funded—the decision is postponed until COP-17 that will take place in Durban in December 2011. [Editors' note: For up-to-date information on REDD funding initiatives, see Climate Funds Update, a joint initiative of the Heinrich Böll Foundation and the Overseas Development Institute, available at http://www .climatefundsupdate.org/. Climate Funds Update seeks to increase the transparency of funding for climate-related activities.]

There are two basic mechanisms for funding REDD: either from government funds (such as the Norwegian government's International Forests and Climate Initiative) or from private sources, which would involve treating REDD as a carbon mitigation "offset," and getting polluters to pay [so as to] have their continued emissions offset elsewhere through a REDD project. There are many variants and hybrids of these two basic mechanisms, such as generating government-government funds through a "tax" on the sale of carbon credits or other financial transactions.

Trading the carbon stored in forests is particularly controversial for several reasons:

- Carbon trading does not reduce emissions because for every carbon credit sold, there is a buyer. Trading the carbon stored in tropical forests would allow pollution in rich countries to continue, meaning that global warming would continue.
- Carbon trading is likely to create a new bubble of carbon derivatives. There are already extremely complicated carbon derivatives on the market. Adding forest carbon credits to this mix would be disastrous, particularly given the difficulties in measuring the amount of carbon stored in forests.
- Creating a market in REDD carbon credits opens the door to carbon cowboys, or would-be carbon traders with little or no experience in forest conservation, who are exploiting local communities and indigenous peoples by persuading them to sign away the rights to the carbon stored in their forests.

Yet many REDD proponents continue to argue that carbon markets are needed to make REDD work. Environmental Defense Fund, for example, on its web site states that,

Reducing emissions from deforestation and forest degradation (REDD), which EDF helped pioneer, is based on establishing economic incentives for people who care for the forest so forests are worth money standing, not just cleared and burned for timber and charcoal. The best way to do this is to allow forest communities and tropical forest nations to sell carbon credits when they can prove they have lowered deforestation below a baseline.

While there has not yet been any agreement on how REDD is to be financed, a look at some of the main actors involved suggests that there is a serious danger that it will be financed through carbon trading. The role of the World Bank is of particular concern, given its fondness for carbon trading.

The World Bank's main mechanism for promoting REDD is a new scheme, launched in Bali in 2007: the Forest Carbon Partnership Facility (FCPF). The FCPF was set up with the explicit aim of creating markets for forest carbon, as the Bank announced in a press release on 11 December 2007: "The facility's ultimate goal is to jump-start a forest carbon market that tips the economic balance in favor of conserving forests, says Benoit Bosquet, a World Bank senior natural resources management specialist who has led the development of the facility."

Carbon markets are not included in the Cancun REDD text. Yet in December 2010, the World Bank's Special Envoy for Climate Change, Andrew Steer, wrote that one outcome of Cancun was that "Forests [are] firmly established as a key for addressing climate change, and to be included in a future carbon trading system."

There is a serious risk of REDD leading to increased corruption, if large sums of money start to flow—particularly for unregulated trade in REDD carbon credits in poorly governed countries. Forestry departments are among the most corrupt departments in some of the most corrupt countries in the world. The complexity of carbon markets combined with poor regulation leads to the increased risk of fraud and corruption in the rich countries. Billions of dollars have already been lost from carbon markets in Europe through fraud.

Peter Younger at Interpol is already concerned. "Alarm bells are ringing. It is simply too big to monitor," he said in October 2009, adding that "Organized crime syndicates are eyeing the nascent forest carbon market."

"Fraud could include claiming credits for forests that do not exist or were not protected or by land grabs. It starts with bribery or intimidation of officials, then there's threats and violence against those people. There's forged documents too. Carbon trading transcends borders. I do not see any input from any law enforcement agency in planning REDD."

Without monitorable and enforceable safeguards, and strict controls and regulation, REDD may deepen the woes of developing countries—providing a vast pool of unaccountable money which corrupt interests will prey upon and political elites will use to extend and deepen their power, becoming progressively less accountable to their people. In the same way that revenues from oil, gold, diamond and other mineral reserves have fuelled pervasive corruption and bad governance in many tropical countries, REDD could prove to be another "resources curse." Ultimately, this will make protection of forests less likely to be achieved and will do nothing to ameliorate carbon emissions.

33

INEQUALITY AND
ENVIRONMENTAL POLICY

Joseph E. Stiglitz[*]

Environmental degradation is everyone's problem, but it's especially a problem for the poor, and for obvious reasons. Their position is more precarious, so when things go wrong, whether it's pollution in a neighborhood or rising sea levels swallowing a country, they are less able to respond effectively. In this sense, inequality ought to be a fundamental consideration when fashioning environmental policies. Let me give two examples.

The first is in a global context, focusing on global warming, which has enormous distributional consequences. Pollution originates disproportionately from advanced industrial countries. Though more recently we've been in a race between the United States and China in which China has finally pulled ahead (in aggregate, but not per capita terms), the United States has contributed more than a quarter of the cumulative carbon emissions since 1750. Yet it is the poorest countries making the least contribution to carbon emissions that are going to be the most adversely affected, and the reason is quite obvious.

The most deleterious effects of global warming are felt in the tropics. Of course, even in the far North, there are big environmental costs. But from the point of view of people in the tropics, adverse consequences are overwhelming—for instance, for agriculture and diseases.

Some dramatic examples: Bangladesh is likely to suffer widespread flooding as a result of global warming. For some drought-stricken countries in the Sahel of Africa, even their political problems have been vastly exacerbated by climate

---

[*]By Joseph E. Stiglitz, University Professor at Columbia University. This is an edited version of Professor Stiglitz's lecture delivered for Resources for the Future's "Resources 2020" event in October 2012.

change–related famine and land shortages. And small island nations risk being completely submerged by rising seas. Wealthy countries may not have intended to do them any harm, but it's hard to think even a war against them would have done more destruction than what we are doing through global warming. Over and over, throughout the world, the theme is clear: Those with the least capacity to respond to environmental crisis are poised to receive the most direct and punishing blows, and these are the countries that have contributed the least to global warming.

Let me give another kind of example from the United States. Here as well, those with fewer means pay the highest price. My colleague Janet Currie has provided compelling evidence that children born to less educated minority mothers are more likely to be exposed to pollution before they're born. She shows that this exposure affects birth weight, with consequences that are life-long and reflected in lifetime earnings. And even more, the effects continue across generations; children of people who have been harmed by environmental pollutants, their children are also of lower birth weight, with lower lifetime prospects.

America has the least equality of opportunity and the least social mobility of the developed countries. Probably the most important of the reasons has to do with lack of equal access to good education. But clearly these environmental impacts are also an important aspect of the intergenerational transmission mechanism that perpetuates inequality.

There is a two-way relationship between environment and inequality. So while environmental degradation contributes to inequality, inequality can also contribute to environmental degradation. The mechanism here, very basically, is a political one. When you're poor, your focus is not on the complex issues of the environment and how the environment affects your economic future. Those seem too esoteric. You're focused on survival. You're focused on income and economic growth.

The result is that in democracies, the desperately poor tend to have less of an interest in pursuing policies designed to protect the environment, because their most important concern is doing whatever's necessary to get out of the current situation. So societies with more inequality will get less support for good environmental policies.

Partha Dasgupta, whom I've worked with a great deal, has emphasized the environment-inequality nexus in the context of development. It is the destitute who turn to the forest for their energy, but in doing so, they destroy their own future well-being. This behavior is individually rational, perhaps, but collectively irrational. The interesting thing is that in societies with a reasonable degree of social cohesion, social-control mechanisms may, and often do, actually work. But inequality tends to undermine social cohesion.

The importance of social cohesion was evident in a recent visit to Bhutan, the Himalayan country that has made its national objective Gross National Happiness (GNH), rather than the more traditional GDP [Gross Domestic Product]. At the start, everybody was allowed to cut down three trees a year. I asked, "How do you enforce this?" The Bhutanese answered, "Nobody would disobey." A few years later, the limit was reduced to two trees, and the Bhutanese people adapted to that.

The point is that in societies with a high degree of social cohesion, people can work together and solve some of these problems better than they can in societies with less social cohesion and more inequality. When the tide of inequality becomes too great, what economists call "social capital" tends to break down.

Let me make a few observations about this. First, it turns out that small interventions can have very big effects. That's important for those of us who are involved in policy because, quite often, we can't solve the big problems. We can't persuade our government to adopt a carbon price, but we can make a big difference even with some small interventions. An example on a national scale that is relevant in many developing countries is the adoption of more efficient cook stoves. These are cook stoves that use less energy, so that the people who use them have to cut down fewer forests. It also means they are exposed to less indoor air pollution, which is a major source of health problems in developing countries, for lungs and eyes.

Interestingly, more efficient cook stoves also help alleviate inequality because the people who bear the cost of gathering the wood and spend a very large fraction of their time doing so are women. When you have a little innovation like this, it changes the well-being of one part of society that in many developing countries is very oppressed. You might not think of distributing efficient cook stoves as gender policy or even an inequality policy. But a good environmental policy like this one can have very big effects on inequality.

The second general observation I want to make is the fact that these two-way relationships mean that there can exist multiple societal equilibria. You get an equilibrium in which you have a lot of inequality, and that leads to weaker environmental policies, and those weak environmental policies lead to a lot of inequality, and the problem perpetuates itself. But a much better equilibrium can be obtained, where you have low levels of inequality. With a low level of inequality, you have high demand for good environmental policies, and those good environmental policies then lead to less inequality. This feedback mechanism is really important in understanding that one cannot just assume the market by itself will lead to an efficient outcome. Government intervention can nudge the economy to a better equilibrium.

Another issue involves the longstanding literature on the tragedy of the commons. According to the classic thinking behind the tragedy of the commons, the real problem with overutilization of common resources is that we haven't privatized land. But the privatization agenda often leads to high levels of inequality. So while private property is one mechanism for regulation, there are other ways of regulating asset usage. Nobel Laureate Elinor Ostrom pointed out that in some communities, people were able to get together and have social-control mechanisms without private property.

One of the arguments for the enclosure movement in the 15th, 16th, and 17th centuries in Britain and Scotland was that it prevented overgrazing. But in the process of limiting access to pastures, the movement created a lot of wealth at the top and a lot of misery at the bottom. So the enclosure movement had enormous distributional consequences. It was not, I think, the best way of solving the problem of the commons.

One of the discussion points that economists debate forever is the virtues of price versus quantity regulation in dealing with environmental issues. But we typically ignore that these different mechanisms can have very different distributional effects and that we typically cannot—or in any case do not—offset the distributional effects. From a practical point of view, one of the things we ought to be thinking about very carefully as we discuss the merits of one or another way of protecting the environment is who benefits and who loses.

What I hope has been evident from these brief remarks is that inequality is not just a moral issue—it's an efficiency issue. We pay a high price for inequality in terms of how our economy performs. If young people at the bottom don't get the education that allows them to live up to their potential, we are wasting our most valuable resource. If children of low-income parents are exposed to toxic environmental effects that undermine their potential to be fully productive, we bear a high cost as a society.

Distributional concerns need to move front and center in environmental and resource economics, especially given America's high inequality—both of outcome and of opportunity. Doing so will provide new perspectives on old policy debates and make what we say of greater relevance in the policy discourse.

INDEX